1989

# Contradictions

The modern era has been uniquely productive of theory. Some theory claimed uniformity despite human differences or unilinear progress in the face of catastrophic changes. Other theory was informed more deeply by the complexities of history and recognition of cultural specificity. This series publishes books that explore the problems of theorizing the modern in its manifold and sometimes contradictory forms and that examine the specific locations of theory within the modern.

Edited by Craig Calhoun
*Social Science Research Council*

# 1989

## Revolutionary Ideas and Ideals

## Krishan Kumar

Contradictions, Volume 12

University of Minnesota Press
Minneapolis
London

Published by the University of Minnesota Press
111 Third Avenue South, Suite 290
Minneapolis, MN  55401-2520
http://www.upress.umn.edu

Printed in the United States of America on acid-free paper

Library of Congress Cataloging-in-Publication Data

Kumar, Krishan, 1942–
    1989 : revolutionary ideas and ideals / Krishan Kumar.
        p.    cm. — (Contradictions ; 12)
    ISBN 0-8166-3452-1 (HC) — ISBN 0-8166-3453-X (PB)
    1. Europe, Eastern—Politics and government—1989–  2. Europe,
Central—Politics and government—1989–  3. Revolutions.  4. Socialism.
5. Democracy.  I. Title: 1989: Revolutionary ideas and ideals.  II. Title.
III. Series.
    DJK51 .K85 2001
    943'.009'045—dc21
                                                                00-012820

The University of Minnesota is an equal-opportunity educator and employer.

12 11 10 09 08 07 06 05 04 03 02 01     10 9 8 7 6 5 4 3 2 1

*To the students, staff, and faculty
of the sociology department of the
Central European University, Prague (1991–95)*

# Contents

# Preface

The 1989 revolutions—and their sequel in 1991—that brought about the fall of communism in Central and Eastern Europe were undoubtedly among the most important events of this century. In some respects they can be said to be among the most important events of the past two centuries, bringing to a close, at least provisionally, a conflict of ideas and ideals that began with the French Revolution of 1789. No doubt it is mere coincidence that these revolutions occurred in the precise year of the bicentennial of the "Great French Revolution," but it is impossible not to see some symbolic significance in this.

This book does not aim to give a narrative account of the 1989 revolutions; there are many such accounts to which the reader can be referred. Rather, it is concerned with the ideas and ideals that surrounded these revolutions. Everyone is aware that the 1989 revolutions were about much more than the fate of certain regimes in East Central Europe. They opened up questions about a vast range of issues that concerned Europe, the West, and the wider world. The aspiration of East Central European societies to "return to Europe" raised the questions, What is Europe, and what is its future shape? Their actions in throwing off communism and launching new political experiments reopened inquiry into concepts and practices that had long been neglected or taken for granted in the West: democracy, civil society, nationalism, revolution itself. They offered instances of societies' "recovering," "restarting," or reinventing their histories—and in the process forcing Western societies to reflect on their own uses of history in constructing collective identities. The 1989 revolutions even provoked declarations that history, understood in a particular sense, was at an end, and so launched a vigorous debate on the future of political ideologies and the possible alternatives, if any, to what seemed the worldwide triumph of capitalism and liberal democracy.

In short, the 1989 revolutions were about the West as much as the East, about "us" as much as "them." They touched off a remarkably fertile and still-continuing debate about some of the central questions facing all modern societies today. In that sense they have not become dated, or become "mere history" (is there, indeed, any historical event that should be so disparaged?). If anything, with the passage of time—and what is ten years in the life of a revolution?—their significance has grown rather than diminished.

This book is about those general questions occasioned by the 1989 revolutions. It is meant primarily as a contribution to social and political thought. But it would be wrong to deny that there are any historical associations. Some of the chapters were originally presented as papers or lectures at conferences and universities in Central and Eastern Europe, especially in the first half of the 1990s. Many of them were also given as talks or lectures to the students and faculty of the Central European University in Prague during the period (1991–95) when I was a visiting professor in the sociology department. They were conceived and delivered, that is, during the time when the most intense debates were taking place about the meaning and significance of the 1989 revolutions. This gives them not just, as I hope, a thematic unity, but also perhaps a certain unity of mood. They were contributions to the discussions taking place, and they share to some extent in the mood of uncertainty and exhilaration that marked the aftermath of the revolutions. To me, at least, they are redolent of the excited atmosphere I experienced in Sophia and Veliko Turnovo, Budapest and Bucharest, Prague and Krakow, Kyiv and Moscow.

In the case of the essays that were previously published (chapters 2–6 and 8) I have made a number of small changes, but otherwise left them in their original form. It has seemed to me right to do this to preserve their original spirit. However, in all cases except for that of the most recently published (chapter 8), I have added a "Further Note" that seeks to review developments and debates since the time of original publication. Part of the purpose of this note is also to bring bibliographical references up to date. This has not been necessary in the case of those chapters (1, 7, and 9) published for the first time here, since these have been extensively revised. Chapters 1 and 9 have indeed specifically been written or rewritten for this volume, the first to provide context and suggest historical continuity, the second to highlight the theoretical implications of the 1989 revolutions. I have also added a select bibliography of works that relate in the broadest way to the background, history, and theoretical understanding of the revolutions.

It remains to thank those individuals and institutions who helped in one way or another to bring these essays into being. The British Academy, the British Council, and the University of Kent were generous with travel grants that enabled me to attend conferences and give lectures in various parts of Central and Eastern Europe. Much of the thinking of these essays came from those visits and from conversations with people encountered there. It is impossible to thank all the individuals I met whose thoughts stimulated my own, but I should particularly like to mention Sorin Antohi, András Bozóki, Lena Danilova, Zsusza Ferge, Mária Heller, Ferenc Miszlivetz, Ani Mitrea, Edmund Mokrzycki, Lyuben Nikolov, Brandusa Palade, Alex Sogomonov, Emanuela Todeva, Arpad Szakoczai, Aviezer Tucker, Ivan Vejvoda, Veljko Vujacic, and Edmund Wnuk-Lipinski. A special thanks is owed to Piotr Sztompka for his encouragement and the stimulus of his own work, and, for sparkling conversation, to Oleg Kharkhordin and Vadim Volkov. In Britain and America I should like to thank Jeffrey Alexander, Zygmunt Bauman, Chris Brown, Phil Brown, Christopher Bryant, Craig Calhoun, Richard Crampton, John Hall, Chris Hann, Martin Jay, Steven Lukes, William Outhwaite, Frank Parkin, Katy Pickvance, Larry Ray, Richard Sakwa, Adam Seligman, and Jeff Weintraub. Warm thanks also to Katya Makarova for her support and her constructive criticism of these ideas over many years.

But the place and people with which these essays are most associated in my mind are the Central European University (CEU) in Prague and its students, staff, and faculty. The sociology department there, where I taught for several years, afforded a wonderful opportunity to try out ideas on the many bright students from the region who came to study there. In class discussions and informal conversations with those students I was forced to defend and rethink my views. It was an enjoyable and instructive experience; I am most grateful to them for it. The CEU was also a magnet for many eminent scholars—Dahrendorf, Habermas, Offe, Popper—from both East and West, who came to lecture on themes relevant to the great changes taking place in the region; I learned much from these visits. Moreover, the late Ernest Gellner, whose wit and intelligence I sadly miss, had established his Centre for the Study of Nationalism there; this, too, was the host to visitors such as John Hall, Miroslav Hroch, Michael Mann, and Tom Nairn, and provided a forum for much profitable discussion. All in all, one could not have wished for a better vantage point from which to consider the significance of the 1989 revolutions. So I should like to thank the people who made it possible for me to share in this immensely stimulating venture: Jirí Musil, the rector of the Prague College of the CEU; Ray Pahl, the first director of the sociology department; Claire Wallace, the director of studies in sociology and later the head of the department; the able and agreeable tutors Charles Bonner, Mark Griffin, and Sukumar Periwal; Jaroslava Stastna, the academic supervisor who arranged my visits; and Vlasta Hirtova, the department's highly efficient and helpful secretary. I am glad to consider them friends as well as coworkers in the great endeavor to understand the 1989 revolutions and their consequences.

Finally, I should like to thank Craig Calhoun, the general editor of the series in which this volume appears, for his advice, support, and encouragement throughout, and Carrie Mullen and Robin A. Moir of the University of Minnesota Press for their guidance and their unfailing helpfulness in seeing the manuscript through the press. Thanks also to Marilyn Martin for her splendid work with the copyediting.

Charlottesville, Virginia
January 2000

# One

# The Relevance of the Past: Understanding Central and Eastern Europe in Time

*If you are a small nation . . . you do not make history. You are always the object of history.*

Milan Kundera

*Every Central European family has its own stormy history in which family catastrophes and national catastrophes are mingled. History is more than erudition here, it is the inner meaning of actions, a validating tradition, a largely unconscious norm and parameter for conduct today.*

György Konrád

## "The Lands In-Between"

Nothing more vividly illustrates the predicament of the countries of East Central Europe than the difficulty of defining who they are, where they belong. Western Europe is an imprecise term, but its members, for solid historical reasons, have had little difficulty in situating themselves within a particular tradition and a particular civilization (roughly coincident with the borders of the empire of Charlemagne). Eastern Europe, too, is a slippery term, encompassing as it often has all the Slavonic peoples of Europe. But it has a firm anchor in Russia: Eastern Europe without Russia is unthinkable, and therefore even if at times it includes more than Russia, it nearly always relates to Russian concerns and the Russian sphere of influence.

But "Central Europe"—or, as it is often referred to today in scholarly discussions, "East Central Europe"—where or what is that?[1] At times the term is used to include all the lands in a broad belt from the Baltic to the Aegean Sea. That is, it includes Finland and Estonia as well as Greece and Bulgaria. But the editors of the University of Washington Press's well-regarded series *A History of East Central Europe* follow much common practice in excluding the Baltic and certain more eastern peoples—Finns, Estonians, Latvians, Lithuanians, Belorussians and Ukrainians—from their purview, though, as they say with an air of resignation, "they appear repeatedly in these books." For them the limits of "East Central Europe" are "the eastern linguistic frontier of German and Italian-speaking peoples on the west, and the political borders of Russia or the former Union of Soviet Socialist Republics on the east." This means that East Central Europeans are mainly Poles, Czechs, Slovaks, Hungarians, Romanians, the peoples of the former Yugoslavia, Albanians, Bulgarians, and Greeks—a list that conforms reasonably well to both popular perception and standard academic treatment, though everyone acknowledges its inadequacy.[2]

The difficulties of determining the limits of Central or East Central Europe are compounded by a widespread recognition of major "fault lines" within the region. Again, these are partly geographical: a northern zone comprising the great unbroken plain of the North European Lowlands and including such countries as the former East Germany, Poland, and Lithuania; a middle zone dominated in the west by the Austrian Alps and in the east by the Carpathian Mountains and including such countries as the former Czechoslovakia, Austria, Hungary, Romania, and Slovenia; and a Balkan zone south of the Sava and Danube rivers including such countries as Bulgaria, Albania, and Greece as well as the countries of the former Yugoslavia. Overlaying these divisions and to some extent accentuating them are religious and cultural fault lines that reflect the different historical experiences of the countries of the region. Primarily these consist of the religious divisions within Christianity—Orthodox, Catholic, and Protestant; the differing legacies stemming from differential incorporation in the great multinational dynastic empires that dominated this region for so long—the Habsburg, Hohenzollern, Romanov, and Ottoman Empires, the legacy in the last case encompassing substantial Islamic components; and economic divisions that reflect varying degrees of "backwardness" as compared with the economically advanced West. Gale

Stokes, employing a broad concept of "Eastern Europe" to define the region, summarizes these divisions as follows:

> Eastern Europe constitutes a specific arena of European historical development defined by three long-standing and fundamental fault lines and strongly influenced by nationalism and ethnic diversity. A religious fault line separates Orthodox Christianity from Catholicism and its Protestant heirs. Russia and the Orthodox East pursued a very different historical trajectory than did the Catholic countries. Crosscutting this more or less north-south line is the roughly east-west line separating the Ottoman Empire and the European empires, particularly the Habsburgs. Whereas Greeks, Serbs, Bulgarians, and Romanians looked south and east [toward Constantinople / Istanbul] for cultural and political models for hundreds of years, central Europeans looked toward Rome, Vienna, and Berlin. The third fault line, the economic one, ran southeast along the Elbe River and then south to Trieste, but lay several hundred miles to the west of the Orthodox-Catholic line. It separated the commercial and developing West from the agricultural East.[3]

So if East Central Europe is a unity, it is one marked by deep fractures and fissures. This suggests a diversity of experience that may indeed be the hallmark of the region. But it is not the diversity of independent agents able to vary their behavior according to need and circumstances. It is, to a good extent, an enforced diversity. It is the result of the fact that the peoples of the region have for centuries not been masters of their own fates. They have lived under a variety of rulers who have had ideologies and interests that often made them regard the wishes of the people of the region as of secondary importance. The unity of East Central Europe—a unity in diversity—is the result of the common experience of dependence.

It is not simply that the rulers of the region were often "foreign"—Russian, German, Turkish. These terms meant less than they mean today, and in any case "foreign" rule was the norm throughout Europe (think of England's German monarchy, right up to the present day). Indeed, in many cases the peoples of the region were given a generous share in the imperial administrations that controlled their societies. Poles, Hungarians, and Italians were to be found alongside Germans throughout the Habsburg Empire; Balts achieved high office in the Russian Empire; Greeks were powerfully implanted in the administration of the Ottoman Empire.

The more important thing was that for a period stretching over some four to five hundred years the peoples of East Central Europe were pawns in a game of dynastic power politics. However well (or badly) they were treated, however enlightened their rulers, they did not develop that autonomy that allowed reasonably compact groups of Western European peoples to develop according to their own will and principles. It is this, rather than some condescendingly "orientalist" approach toward "the other Europe," that has allowed scholars to treat the region as some sort of unity.[4] There are unsurprising similarities of structure and outlook that reflect a common history of subordination to great powers, as well as, in many cases, memories of past greatness. It was for similar reasons that for much of the recent period scholars could talk of a "third world" of formerly colonial societies that shared the decisive experience of dependence on European colonial powers. With time, that "third world" has been breaking up as these societies have rediscovered aspects of their own past traditions or struck out in new and different directions. We might expect the same thing to happen in East Central Europe now that, as for a brief period after 1918, the countries of the region have been set free to retrieve their pasts and to make their own futures. But, in understanding the sort of societies that made the 1989 revolutions, we are right to stress commonalities. These are societies that for most of their modern history have undergone a remarkably similar experience of subjection and subordination.

The Czech writer Milan Kundera once pointed out to an English interviewer that the Czech national anthem begins with a question, "Where is my homeland?" For Czechs and other East Central Europeans, he said, "the homeland is understood as a question. As an eternal uncertainty." He compared the Czech and Polish national anthems with those of Britain and Russia. The latter make claims to power, glory, and immortality inconceivable in the case of the former. The English and Russians had no doubt about the continued existence of their nations. "You may question England's politics, but not its existence. . . . You never ask yourselves what will happen when England does not exist any more. But it is a question that is constantly being asked in these small countries [of East Central Europe]."[5] Poland once existed, the greatest power in sixteenth-century Europe; then it disappeared off the map altogether for over a century following the partitions of the late eighteenth century; after 1918 it was resurrected and had a brief independent existence; in 1939 it was partitioned again, between Nazi

Germany and the Soviet Union; and in 1945 it was swallowed up in the Soviet Empire. Such a history haunts all the peoples of East Central Europe. Merely to survive, let alone thrive, seems a major triumph.

An evocative and poignant phrase to describe the region is "the lands in-between."[6] This phrase aptly catches the predicament of the region's peoples for much of their history. Caught between the growing powers of Germany to the west, Russia to the east, and the Ottoman Empire in the south, East Central Europe became the battleground of competing claims. Its peoples found themselves in one empire, one "sphere of influence," after another. Parts of the region were exchanged like so many pawns on a chessboard. The city of Vilnius might find itself one day in Lithuania; another day—as Wilno—in Poland; yet again in Lithuania, but this time—as Vilna—as part of a Tzarist Russian province; then once more as Vilnius, but this time as part of the Soviet Union. Slovakia—not necessarily so called—might be part of Hungary, as it was for hundreds of years, then part of the new post-1918 state of Czechoslovakia, then the Nazi puppet state of Slovakia during World War II, then once more part of Czechoslovakia—but this time within the Soviet imperial orbit, then—for the first time in its history—after 1993 an independent state (but, it might wonder, for how long?). Practically all parts of the "lands in-between" can record such histories. Such gyrations not surprisingly have conferred a certain spectral quality on the region and have given rise to the well-known Central European attitudes of irony, satire, cynicism, and fatalism or pessimism.[7] Jacques Rupnik quoted one "Josef K., Prague, 1980" as writing: "From the standpoint of history, Europe can be divided into three blocks: the historicity of the West, the absurd history of Central Europe, the ahistoricity of the East."[8] It is a good summary of much Central European feeling, compounded of a sense of powerlessness, loss, and desire.

## "Backwardness" and East Central European Society

How best can one consider the main features of the societies of East Central Europe? A common—and convenient—way is to see them as partaking of the characteristics of both East and West, both the social type typified by Russia and that typified by the countries of Western Europe. A celebrated exercise of this kind was carried out by the Hungarian historian Jenő Szücs in *The Three Historical Regions of Europe*.[9] Szücs's main focus is on the West, on its distinctiveness as compared both with Eastern Europe (Russia) and southern Europe, the area of Byzantine and then Ottoman rule. Western development after the fall of the western Roman Empire was marked by a decisive separation of state and society. This was the result of the competition between papacy and empire in the Middle Ages, leading to the separation of sacred and secular spheres; the special nature of the feudal tie in the West, which encompassed a strong contractual element that later became the basis of liberal and even revolutionary claims to freedom on the part of "society"; the fragmented political sovereignty that resulted from the failure of Charlemagne and other emperors of the Holy Roman Empire to reconstitute the Roman Empire; and the rise of the towns as dynamic economic and relatively autonomous political units in the interstices of feudal society, a condition made possible by the competing sovereignties of church and state, kings and barons. What István Bibó called "the plurality of small spheres of freedom" is seen as the key to western development. Sociologically one important consequence was the growth of a strong middle class, centered on the towns, which was able to balance the power of the aristocracy and, though formerly a tool of the crown, eventually turn on monarchical power itself.

In the East and the southeast one sees, by contrast, the growth of the "caesaro-papist" power of czars, kings, and emperors in the lands of Christian Orthodoxy (later Ottoman conquests detached the southeast altogether from "Europe"). The church was tied to and subordinate to the state. Towns were politically weak and economically undeveloped, existing mainly to garrison troops or as administrative centers for the crown. The nobility was a state or service nobility, almost entirely dependent on the ruler and relying on state power to prevent the peasants from fleeing from their estates. Peasants, especially after the "second serfdom" of the sixteenth century—a controversial concept—were bound to the soil and unfree in a way that ceased to be the case among the peasantries of western Europe after the Black Death.

East Central Europe, according to Szücs, hovered uneasily between these two poles. Fundamentally it was on "the Eastern margin of Western Europe" in the sense that by virtue of its mainly Latin Christianity and the relative strength of its aristocracy it echoed much Western development and deviated from the caesaro-papist, statist model of the East. But Eastern elements were also strong in East Central Europe. Its towns tended to follow the Eastern pattern, in being undeveloped economically and largely dependent on royal patronage. Its peasantry in many areas remained in a state of serfdom, especially after the sixteenth century, when the economy of the region became almost entirely geared to agricultural production for the fast-developing West. The economy came to be dominated by the large estates of the nobility, worked by the forced labor of peasants who were tied to the estates. Consequently the commercial middle class was weak, and no match for an aristocracy that disdained it socially and politically and developed a contempt for "trade."

The main difference between East Central Europe—especially in Poland, Hungary, and the Czech lands—and the East—as represented by Russia—lay in the position of the nobility. The nobility remained strong throughout the region and did not become a state nobility on the Russian pattern. This allowed for important developments in the political sphere; the Polish nobility can justly claim to have led the way toward liberal politics, as revealed in the radical constitution of 1791. But that constitution was also the final throe of a nobility that had overreached itself and fatally weakened the Polish state (abetted, of course, by the ambitions of powerful neighbors). The Czech nobility, too, was more or less eliminated as an independent force after its defeat by the emperor's forces at the battle of the White Mountain (1620). The Hungarian nobility remained vigorous, but its members' hostility to trade and commerce, their dependence on the state to keep the peasantry in check, and their attachment to state service as the way to power and prosperity led to the phenomenon of the overgrown nobility and worship of bureaucracy that afflicted the region as a whole. "The Hungarian Middle Ages," says Szücs, "bequeathed to Modern Times a mass nobility comprising 4–5 percent of the population (and in Poland's case 7–8 percent), as compared with an average of 1 percent in the West."[10] A boorish, uneducated nobleman—"the most noxious phenomenon in the development of modern Hungary," according to Bibo—was preferred to a middle-class professional or commercial townsman, especially as the latter was frequently a "foreigner," a German, or a Jew.

Szücs's account, though by no means the first of its kind, has been remarkably influential in "placing" the countries of East Central Europe on the European map and in characterizing their main features of social and political development.[11] Students of the region have varied mainly in terms of whether they accentuated the "Western" or the

"Eastern" elements of its mixed heritage. For Piotr Wandycz, East Central Europe—at least the "core" areas of Hungary, Poland, and the Czech lands—is undeniably Western. Christianity had come to its peoples predominantly in its Western, Roman, form, and "the Western impact was the dominant and the lasting one." Although in the early stages of their history Byzantine influences were important, and later the Ottomans made their impact, their culture and politics were decisively shaped by Western developments:

> They were shaped by and experienced all the great historical currents [of the West]: Renaissance, Reformation, Enlightenment, the French and Industrial Revolutions. They differed drastically from the East, as embodied by Muscovy-Russia, or the Ottoman Empire that ruled the Balkans for several centuries. . . . Muscovite autocracy and the subordination of the church to the state was alien to the Western tradition. So too was the Ottoman system based on Islam. No wonder that historic Hungary and Poland, bordering on Muscovy and the Ottoman lands, regarded themselves, and were regarded by others, as the bulwark of Christendom *(antemurale christianitatis)*. Their eastern frontiers marked the frontiers of Europe.[12]

But from another point of view, reflecting a sense of the incompleteness of East Central Europe's incorporation of Western traits, East Central Europe is the "failed West." Yes, says George Schöpflin, its societies "shared in aspects of feudalism, medieval Christian universalism, the Renaissance, the Reformation and Counter-Reformation, and the Enlightenment. Yet each one of these was shared slightly differently, less intensively, less fully, with the result that East [Central] European participation in the European experience was only partial."[13] As a result, compared with the West, the tendencies of East Central Europe to autocracy and bureaucracy were stronger, the nobility clung closer to the state, the intelligentsia was less moderate (being alternately ultraconformist or ultrarevolutionary), towns and the bourgeois class were weaker, hostility to entrepreneurial values was greater, the peasantry was more conservative and less free, and the working class was smaller and politically less influential. This is the legacy that the region brought into the twentieth century. Communism added its own peculiar ingredients, but these in many ways took the region even further away from the West, above all in the stifling of a nascent "civil society."

Schöpflin touches on the general theme of "backwardness" that has been one of the dominant notes of the debate about East Central

Europe for over a century. The problem for the region, in this understanding, is that it is a backward, underdeveloped part of the West. Its task is to catch up with the West, seen as the model of modernity. This is how the great Hungarian leader Count István Széchenyi saw it in the early nineteenth century when he lamented the laziness and backwardness—"Eastern traits," he called them—that he found in his countrymen, and he urged them to learn from their more progressive Western neighbors.[14] It is another Hungarian, the sociologist Elemer Hankiss, who speaks of the "neurosis of backwardness" that still afflicts the people of the region today.[15]

The argument is that the societies and economies of East Central Europe were part of the periphery or "semiperiphery" of the advanced societies of the West. Developments in the region—at least after Western expansion and economic acceleration beginning in the sixteenth century—were therefore not autonomous, but were reactions to the needs and requirements of the "core" capitalist countries in the West. Hence such features as the concentration on agriculture, the big landed estates, the "second serfdom," the low level of urbanization, and the enhanced role of the state in modernization. Nor is "backwardness" to be conceived entirely or even mainly in economic terms. The alignment with the West, the desire to remain connected to it and to catch up with it while doing so from a position of weakness and dependence, had reverberations throughout East Central European society. What Andrew Janos says about Hungary can, in the eyes of those who accept the thesis of backwardness, be applied generally in the region. Hungary, says Janos, in reacting to developments in the core countries of the West, reversed its historical experiences:

> This is to say that the modern state took shape before the modern economy; it came into being not as a product, but as a potential instrument of social change. This reversal of the historical "sequences" of development then had important secondary and tertiary consequences, but overall was responsible for the ascendancy of the state over all aspects of social life. For, having been established in a backward society, the state gradually preempted the public in politics, subverted the market by slowing down the commercialization of land and labor, two of the basic commodities of a capitalist economy, and became responsible for a particular pattern of social mobility by diverting talent from entrepreneurship into professional politics. Thus instead of gradual democratization we encountered a progressive narrowing of political regimes; instead of the development of a capitalist

economy we could only witness a gradual increase in etatism; and in the place of "bourgeois" society we would find a society of pariah entrepreneurs, and of political classes competing for the spoils of the state.[16]

What has emerged from this social formation, it is further argued, is a set of attitudes characteristic of the region: conservatism, suspicion of change, and a tendency to look to communal and corporatist institutions for identity and security rather than looking to individual enterprise and achievement. *Gemeinschaft* rather than Western-style *Gesellschaft* patterns predominate. Equally significant has been the "international demonstration effect." Images and expectations of material progress, deriving from the West, have encountered the more recalcitrant realities of East Central European society, leading to deep-seated resentments and frustrations in the population at large that have resurfaced time and again in outbursts of violent protest. For their part elites, however wealthy, have felt the status envy that comes from exercising power in societies that are themselves relatively impotent on the world stage. Extreme nationalism and authoritarianism, shading over into fascism, have been a natural recourse; so too, depending on circumstances, have been populism and communism. The common feature has been a "politics of resentment" that aims to break with Western models.[17]

"The original paradox of Central European politics," says Jacques Rupnik, "is the incongruity between its endorsement of Western civilization, political ideas and institutions, and the reality of the area's social and economic development. . . ." He gives as an example the case of the celebrated Polish Constitution of May 3, 1791, the "first coherent statement in Central Europe of the principles of constitutional democracy."[18] The constitution stated that "in society, everything is derived from the will of the nation." But in the Polish case "the nation" comprised only the nobility, the *szlachta*—admittedly a whacking 10 percent of the population, but still only a small minority. This was an embarrassingly slender basis on which to put into effect the ringing egalitarian principles of the French Revolution, from which the Polish Constitution derived. The Polish Constitution can hardly be blamed, as it sometimes still is, for the extinction of Poland after the Third Partition of 1795—a clear case of the fallacy of *post hoc propter hoc*, but it undoubtedly illustrates vividly the troubling relation between aspiration and actuality in East Central Europe.

The Polish example, like many others that can be drawn from the modern history of the region, indicates the great persuasiveness of the thesis of "backwardness." Evidently it does capture an essential aspect of the character of East Central European society and of its historical development. But one can have too much of a good thing. That is equally clearly the problem with the "backwardness" approach. Hailing as it does from a largely Marxist direction, it suffers from the usual deficiencies of economic determinism. It tends to paint the region in one color—in this case, an unrelieved gray. All social, cultural, and political developments are poured into the mold of economic backwardness. Little respect is paid to the specificity of the region as an area with its own traditions and ways of doing things. Most writers of the backwardness school accept the distinctiveness of Bohemia and Moravia as an area that not only equaled, but in some respects surpassed, Western nations in economic development.[19] But they are loath to see any other basic variations in the "other Europe."[20] Dependence undoubtedly produces certain uniformities, as can be seen also in the case of Latin America. But dependence can take many forms, as the many countries of Latin America surely indicate, and as, to an even greater degree, do those countries of Africa and Asia that were also drawn in as "peripheral" regions of the Western-dominated world economy. Moreover, dependence can be of different kinds, with different effects. In the case of East Central Europe there is not just Western Europe to consider, but, more immediately and in many ways more palpably, there are the great empires that divided the region between them. These, too, gave to the region a characteristic coloring—but one somewhat different from that supplied by its incorporation in the Western economy. However much one might view the Habsburg, Romanov, and Ottoman Empires as struggling to maintain their power in a fast-industrializing world, it would never do to reduce their lives to ones of simply trying to ape the West. They had their own principles and traditions, differing sharply from each other as well as from the West. The societies that were subject to them bore, and arguably still bear, the marks of those differences.

We shall return to this discussion in a moment. But first we need to consider one of the other aspects of the region that is often taken as contributing to the "unbearable burden of history" in East Central Europe.

## Nationalism and Ethnicity

It is a commonplace of commentators on East Central Europe that the region is exceptionally, almost pathologically, prone to national and ethnic conflicts. Eastern Europe, says Gale Stokes, "has been one of the most important laboratories of the quintessentially modern political ideology, nationalism, a fact made especially salient by the region's extremely confused ethnic situation. Eastern Europe is a shatterzone whose ethnic map in 1900, if indeed one could be drawn, would resemble the cracked bottom of a dried mud puddle."[21] Students of nationalism have even invented a special category, "Eastern nationalism," to describe the peculiarly intense nature of nationalism in the region. In a contrast made influential by Hans Kohn, Western nationalism of the French or American kind is individualistic, liberal, and politically defined; Eastern nationalism, taking its lead from Herder and the German Romantics, is ethnic, cultural, and *völkisch*. Backwardness once more enters the stage. In the West, national consciousness arose within already existing, territorially defined, historic states; in Central and Eastern Europe, "because of the backward state of social and political development," nationalism arose among peoples who lacked states and who had therefore to create them forcibly against the opposition of "alien" rulers. The result was a cultural nationalism, forged by alienated intellectuals, that was frequently mystical, irrational, and authoritarian. According to Kohn, "It lent itself more easily to the embroideries of imagination and the excitations of emotion. Its roots seemed to reach into the dark soil of primitive times and to have grown through thousands of hidden channels of unconscious development, not in the bright light of rational political ends, but in the mysterious womb of the people, deemed to be so much nearer to the forces of nature."[22]

There is certainly no difficulty in painting a picture of a region full of ethnic rivalries and ripe for ethnic explosion. Ethnic groups were scattered and intertwined with each other in kaleidoscopic variety. There were Hungarians in what were to become Slovakia, Serbia, and Romania (and, contrariwise, Slovaks, Serbs, Croats, Romanians, Germans, and Jews in pre-1918 Hungary); Serbs and Croats in Croatia; and Serbs, Croats, and "Muslims" (converted Serbs and Croats treated as an ethnic group, "Bosnjaks") in Bosnia. There were Czechs, Slovaks, and Germans in Czechoslovakia, leading to the eventual expulsion of some and separation of others. There were Muslim Albanians in Serbia (Kosovo) and Muslim Turks and Pomaks (Slav Muslims) in Bulgaria. After World War I, Poles made up less than 70 percent of the population of the new Poland, the rest being made up of Ukrainians, Belorussians, Jews, and Germans. Jews and Germans, indeed, along with Greeks and Gypsies, were at one time dispersed throughout the region, the former concentrated mainly in cities (Jews made up a third of the population of Warsaw and a quarter of the population of Budapest before World War I; in cities in Belorussia, Ukraine, and Lithuania, they often made up more than 50 percent of the population). Nothing, it might be thought, better symbolizes the region's ethnic complexity than Macedonia, with its Macedonians, Albanians, Bulgarians, Greeks, Vlachs, Jews, Gypsies, and Turks—a volatile mixture that has given the French and Italians their words for fruit cocktail.[23]

The passage of time has "clarified" this ethnic heterogeneity. War, the Holocaust, "ethnic cleansing," forced migrations, and mass expulsions largely removed Jews, Germans, Gypsies, and Armenians from the region and in general tidied up the ethnic map. The abrupt movement of borders, such as those of Poland after World War II, and the breakup of multiethnic states such as Czechoslovakia and Yugoslavia in the 1990s, brought a further correspondence between ethnicity and state boundaries. But considerable ethnic variety remains, enough to fuel discontents and provide ready-made scapegoats. To many commentators East Central Europe remains an ethnic tinderbox. Its legacy of folk nationalism, antiurban and antimodern, lies ready to ignite once more the sparks of ethnic conflict after a period in which the Soviet presence kept it largely under control. As Jerzy Jedlicki asks, "Will not 20 or so nationalities and ethnic groups, having broken the chains of enforced communist uniformity, rush at one another with their centuries-old grievances?"[24]

There have been conflicts enough since 1989 to give some substance to this perception. Yugoslavia alone, with its bloody and continuing ethnic wars, might appear sufficient to confirm this picture of a region beset by ethnic dilemmas. And nationalists have sounded the drum loudly in Hungary, Slovakia, Ukraine, and several of the Baltic states. But have they not also done so in Scotland, Quebec, Catalonia, Brittany, and Belgium (with its Flemings and Walloons)—not to mention India (with its Hindus, Sikhs, Kashmiris, and so on), Indonesia, East Timor, and vast sections of Africa? Is nationalism, or "neonationalism," not a current sweeping the entire world at the end of the twentieth century, for reasons that still perplex and confound the experts? Admittedly nothing in the West matches the horrors of the former Yugoslavia; but the conflicts in Rwanda, Somalia, Sudan, East Timor, India, and elsewhere in Asia and Africa show that ethnic and national conflict is no prerogative of East Central Europe today. One might indeed be surprised, given the stereotype of the region, that, with the exception of Yugoslavia, there has been so little ethnic conflict. The Czechs and Slovaks quietly disengaged; Hungarian nationalism so far shows no signs of becoming expansionist; the Baltic republics have softened the initially hostile attitudes to the many Russians in their midst; Poland has not sought to exploit the ethnic feeling of the million or so Poles in Belarus, Ukraine, and Lithuania; Turks in Bulgaria, following initial repression under the former communist government, have come to play an active part in the new postcommunist Bulgaria.[25]

Nor, going back into the history of the region, do ethnic conflicts loom particularly large. Again, what might strike the unprejudiced student is the extraordinary stability, if not unqualified success, of ethnic relations in the area. Jews and Germans, with their special technical and commercial skills, were specifically invited by the rulers of medieval Poland, Bohemia-Moravia, and Hungary to settle within their borders. They spread throughout the area; by the late nineteenth century Germans had come to constitute a quarter of the population of the Czech lands and a tenth of the population of Hungary. Jews were numerous not just in Poland (10 percent of the population), Lithuania (8 percent), Ukraine, and Belarus, but also in Hungary (5 percent) and Romania (5 percent). They were also encouraged by the Ottomans to settle in their domains; by 1900 they made up more than 50 percent of the city of Salonika in Macedonia and 30 percent of the population of Bucharest; they were also numerous in Istanbul (5 percent). Greeks and Armenians also spread through the European part of the Ottoman Empire, playing an important commercial and administrative role not just in Istanbul, but in Bulgaria and the Romanian principalities.[26]

We are too inclined to read back into the history of the region the tragic twentieth-century outcomes of the relations between these ethnic groups, notably Germans, Jews, Gypsies, Poles, Ukrainians, Turks, Greeks, and Armenians. Ethnic relations are rarely harmonious; the differences are readily observable, evidenced by food, dress, religion, language. Conflicts can flare up over relatively small matters; they can

also quiet down equally quickly. No one would want to say that ethnic relations in East Central Europe were always easy. But by the standards of later times, not just in that region but throughout the world,
what is more remarkable is the long period, lasting several centuries,
during which ethnic groups of widely differing kinds came to live in
some sort of equilibrium in this area of Europe. True, this was not so
much due to mingling as to each group's finding its "ecological niche."
But within the economies and polities of the empires that dominated
the region each group found a place to pursue its particular bent and
way of life, and the groups did so by living with a reasonable degree
of tolerance and respect for each other. Moreover, there was a considerable degree of interpenetration and assimilation. Croats, Serbs,
and Muslims in Bosnia lived in the same towns and villages and inter-
married among themselves. Greeks, Bulgarians, and Armenians converted to Islam and rose high in the Ottoman administration. The
success of Jews in commercial, professional, and intellectual occupations led many of them to identify closely with the countries in which
and peoples with whom they lived. By 1910, 92 percent of the Jews
living in Galicia professed to be Poles; 75 percent of the Jews living
in Hungary professed themselves to be Hungarian. Jews joined the
Hungarian gentry's struggle against Austria and the struggle of the
Polish nobility against Russia.[27]

In the late nineteenth century the empires that dominated East
Central Europe experienced severe economic and political crises, largely owing to the increasing power and pressure of the West, but also because of their own rivalries. One response was to tighten political control over their territories and to go in for increasingly nationalistic
policies. Germans and Hungarians in the Austro-Hungarian Empire asserted their predominance over other nationalities ever more strongly;
Turks in the Ottoman Empire began to take the initiative in reform and
to fashion a newfound sense of national identity; the czarist government
launched a series of measures aimed at "Russification" of the Empire.
None of these moves saved their respective empires—indeed, quite the
contrary—but they had the effect of producing drastic changes in the
otherwise relatively loose texture and tolerant character of ethnic relations in the area. The Jews, the historic enemies of Christians, were the
prime casualties of the changed atmosphere, with horrific consequences
at a later date. But Poles, Balts, Czechs, Slovaks, Slovenes, Croats,
Serbs, Romanians, Bulgarians, Armenians, and numerous other ethnic

groups also found themselves increasingly oppressed by the more dominant groups in the region. They, in response, turned to an increasingly strident nationalism—even the Jews, who initiated Zionism. The stage was set for the bitter enmities and bloody conflicts that marked this region for much of the first half of the twentieth century, until they were at least temporarily halted by the stern hand of the communist state.

So it is right to see ethnicity and nationalism as enduring features of the region. But it is wrong to see them as in some sense intrinsic to it, the effects of some pathological virus that sets this region apart from others in Europe. The ethnic conflicts of this region have been sharp and at times brutal, but no more so than in several other parts of Europe, not to mention other parts of the world. They partly reflect the increased salience of ethnicity and nationalism throughout Europe since the late nineteenth century. But, more important, they are, in many cases, the effects of great power rivalry in the area. The great powers—in this region Russia, Germany, Austria-Hungary, and the Ottomans—have been only too ready to set ethnic groups at each other's throats, in pursuit of specific goals and on time-honored principles of divide and rule. Nazi policies continued, admittedly to an unprecedented extent, principles already practiced by the imperial powers before 1914, such as in the Jewish pogroms in Russia and the Bulgarian and Armenian massacres in the Ottoman Empire. Certainly these have left a heritage of bitterness and suspicion; but to accuse the peoples of East Central Europe of a peculiar proclivity to ethnic conflict is surely to blame the victims rather than the perpetrators of this condition.

## Legacies of Empire

East Central European societies have been marked by the legacy of two kinds of empire: the old dynastic empires and the newer Soviet empire that oversaw many of the post-1945 developments in the region. In some respects the effects have been similar in the two cases; in others they have differed sharply.

The most obvious common effect has been the legacy of dependence. For three hundred years or so the peoples of this region lived under a succession of autocratic dynastic rulers whose imperial interests often meant the sacrifice of the aspirations of the communities they ruled. In some cases, as with the Czechs, the native aristocracy was annihilated; in the more extreme case of Poland the whole country disappeared for a time. An alien ruling class—German, Russian,

Hungarian, Ottoman—dominated the whole society, separated from the other classes often by language and religion as well as by general culture. Dynastic interests and ambitions—the *drang nach osten*; the clash between Catholic, Orthodox, and Islamic cultures; the struggle for control of the Black Sea; the rivalry for the allegiance of the Slavs under Ottoman rule—constantly involved the peoples of the region in conflicts, conquests, and partitions in which they had no say and often no interest.

In 1918 the empires that had dominated this region—Romanov, Habsburg, Hohenzollern, Ottoman—came crashing down. Under the beneficent hand of President Woodrow Wilson and the victorious allies at Versailles new states were established and old ones resurrected: Poland, Czechoslovakia, Yugoslavia, the Baltic States. For twenty brief years the states of this region experienced an unprecedented freedom, though the uses to which this was put did not on the whole please the powers that had set them up. Then in the later 1930s the region reverted to its customary condition of dependence. First the Nazis, then the Soviet Communists, swept over the area, turning the formerly independent nations into colonies, clients, or satellites. A social revolution took place in the region; but it was a revolution that took place under Nazi and Soviet auspices. Once more East Central Europe entered a phase of development over which its control was relatively slight. To the West it was "the other Europe"; but to a good extent it was so in relation to itself as well, in the sense that it was others who directed its destiny.

The first legacy of empire, then, and the overriding one, is this fact of a common dependence. It gives rise to a certain psychology, familiar in those who have not had, or been allowed to have, autonomy and a corresponding responsibility. In the old empires it produces a social structure heavily skewed in the direction of an imperial system, with an especially important status attached to the bureaucracy and military; an urban middle class, often of "alien" origin, developed to serve the interests of the court and nobility; and a peasantry alternately regarded as a source of cheap labor for the estates of the aristocracy and as cannon fodder for the wars of the imperial state. Politically its main effect is statism. The state is worshiped as the source of all power and status. All ambitions are channeled into state careers, military or bureaucratic. As compared with the West, the church occupies a much lower position, both in terms of status and of power. The state directs and regulates economic development in strictly mercantilist terms, as a matter of the enhancement of state power and the increase of state revenues. All this is to a good extent consonant with absolutist systems in Europe as a whole; the difference is that in East Central Europe features of the absolutist system persisted until the twentieth century.[28]

What is more, the communist regimes of the period after World War II perpetuated many of these features of the old imperial systems to a remarkable degree. Above all there was the statism, carried to an even higher degree. Shorn of the symbolism of monarchy and empire, but expressing instead the equally potent divinity of the party, the bureaucracy together with the party hierarchy assumed the dominant role, much as before. State power was glorified as never before. All good things flowed from and to it. Careers were made within it: there were virtually no worthwhile ones to be found anywhere else. Intellectuals and artists depended on state patronage, though they might with some care and creativity manage to develop a modestly critical stance toward the political establishment. Former peasants, mostly turned urban workers, remained as before material for the implementation of state policies, even though—unlike as in the past—those policies were carried out strictly in their name.

There was continuity, then, between old and new empire. But even this account suggests some important differences. We can, if we use the word with care, describe the communist societies as totalitarian and the former imperial societies as (merely) autocratic. Ideology marked the principal divide. Communism regarded all parts of society as essentially related to each other and as aspects of an integrated whole. The state, therefore, conceived it as its right and duty to intervene in every sphere of life, personal as well as social, economic as well as political, artistic as well as educational, religious, and recreational. Autocratic society certainly regarded the state as the highest embodiment of society. But it never conceived the state as omnicompetent. It respected property rights, on the whole; it made room for private commerce and industry; it encouraged the growth of independent professional and cultural institutions; it accepted that the church had its own sphere of influence. In all these respects it rarely went so far as societies in the West, especially after the eighteenth century. But it shared with the West an acceptance of the fundamental autonomy of society.

It is here that the communist experience might turn out to have left its deepest legacy. For communism, following Marx, abrogates the distinction between state and society. It leaves no room for the independent development of social practices separate from the state. It is profoundly hostile, that is, to "civil society," understood as the social sphere that is public but not state.[29] Insofar as communism took root in the societies of East Central Europe, it brought in the "Eastern" model of Russia and other societies that were influenced by the Byzantine system.

There are, of course, a number of questions about this. Communist practice rarely followed communist principles, neither in the heartland of communism, the Soviet Union, nor in the Soviet satellites in East Central Europe. Hence, the extent to which civil society was suppressed or disappeared entirely is a moot point. Moreover, there was great variation in communist control. In Poland a considerable amount of property in the countryside remained in private hands; the church, too, enjoyed relative freedom. Hungary after 1956 followed a policy of cautious reform, allowing for a fair degree of economic freedom. Czechoslovakia until 1968 also had relatively large spaces in which independent developments could take place, culminating in the "Prague Spring" of 1968. Yugoslavia did it differently, experimenting with workers' "self-management" and opening itself up to the West on a considerable scale. In none of these countries or elsewhere in the communist bloc was private life completely suppressed, nor is it possible to imagine (except in Orwellian terms) how it could be. None of this discussion is meant to minimize the loss of freedom, personal or social, in the communist world. It merely raises a question about the precise legacy of the communist period, the different experiences of communism, the extent to which civil society disappeared, and the varying possibilities, therefore, in the postcommunist world. Gale Stokes has said that "the entire history of Eastern Europe from 1945 to 1989 . . . can be considered one spasmodic imposition of Stalinism followed by forty years of adjusting, accommodating, opposing, reinterpreting, and rejecting."[30] This clearly allowed for a great variety of responses, which were bound to affect future developments in the different states.[31]

Moreover, there is the bigger question: How far could forty or forty-five years of communist rule override the deeper legacies of the region? We have seen that there are some continuities between the old and new empires in this area. Dependence and loss of autonomy continued to be the main fact of life for its peoples. But we have also seen that there were differences between the kinds of dependency experienced under autocratic and totalitarian imperialism and that there were great variations within the order imposed by victorious communism. Even greater variation is to be found in the experiences of the different societies of East Central Europe in the period of old imperial rule—a period lasting in most cases for about three hundred years, from the early seventeenth century to the early twentieth century. How do these experiences compare with the later experiences of independence—the twenty years or so between the two world wars— and the forty or so years of communism? What are the legacies of the *longue durée* compared with those of these much shorter periods?

It would be remarkable if anyone were able to give a clear or satisfying answer to this question. We do not have the tools to gauge such things. The mere number of years tells us very little. It is perfectly possible that the forty years of communist rule—though less likely in the case of the interwar period—were so overwhelming in their impact that they have all but wiped out the traces of the former periods.[32] Certainly modern technology, and the techniques of modern totalitarianism, give contemporary rulers a far greater degree of potential control over their societies than was ever available to any earlier autocrat, be he ever so despotic.[33] But that fact does not by itself answer the question, either. There are many factors that affect the use of such machinery, not least an assessment of the limits of popular tolerance, the point at which forcible imposition might be excessively costly and inefficient. Different communist leaders at different times have read this point differently, with differing consequences for the development of postcommunist societies. There were also radical divergences, ranging from Hungary's Kadar to Romania's Ceausescu, in the ways in which leaders interpreted communism, as a goal and as the appropriate means toward the goal. These divergences, too, gave rise to societies with varying patterns of social and political life. We have many individual accounts of the experience of communist rule, such as Czesław Miłosz's *The Captive Mind* (1953); it is impossible to sum these into any comprehensive assessment of the impact of communism as a whole, in the region generally or in the different societies that compose it.

So it may not be mere nostalgia that has led some commentators, both within the region and outside, to speculate on the likely effects of earlier traditions of imperial rule in the countries concerned.[34] These go beyond vague hankerings after "old Austria-Hungary," and dreams of its resurrection, to a more hard-headed appraisal of how the legacies of an earlier history might affect the current efforts to create liberal and democratic societies. In so speculating, the fact of difference stands out immediately.

We return to the earlier "fault lines" and the finer discriminations within them. We shall consider first the lands that fell mostly and for much of the time within the realm of the Habsburg Monarchy (after 1804 the Habsburg Empire, after 1867 Austria-Hungary). These are the lands that, by common consent, came closest to the "Western" pattern and therefore are the likeliest candidates for the successful transition to liberal market societies. They included southeastern Poland (Galicia), the Czech lands, Hungary (including contemporary Slovakia and Romanian Transylvania), Slovenia, and Croatia. For the most part there was reasonable commercial and urban development in the area, some important cities (Cracow, Prague, Budapest), a strong representation of Germans and Jews (always a progressive sign), and, above all, traditions of aristocratic rule and resistance that allowed for the growth of certain "protoparliamentary" institutions, such as the noble diets. This latter feature was by no means uniform, and it was subject to some violent vicissitudes. Therefore, the Czechs lost their aristocracy after the battle of the White Mountain in 1620; the Polish aristocracy lost their country after the late eighteenth-century partitions of Poland and had to continue the struggle in exile; central parts of Hungary were for nearly two hundred years (after the battle of Mohács in 1526) under Ottoman rule, though with a considerable degree of autonomy. But the memories of aristocratic independence were always there, and to a good extent the practice, too, though it took the Czechs two centuries to recover from the crushing defeats of the sixteenth and seventeenth centuries. Generally, also, it was the lands within the Habsburg Empire that shared most in the movements of the Renaissance, the Reformation, the Scientific Revolution, and the Enlightenment. Nor can a region that contributed Jan Hus, Jan Comenius, and Nicholas Copernicus be thought of as simply marginal to these cultural developments.

The other empire that penetrated deep into East Central Europe was the "Eastern" empire of Russia, the Romanov Empire. At various times this incorporated large parts of Poland, Lithuania, Latvia, Estonia, Ukraine, and Belarus; it also exercised indirect control over the Danubian principalities of Moldavia and Walachia (modern Romania) throughout the nineteenth century. The lands of the Austrian Empire were mostly Catholic, and so shared their religion with the imperial regime. In Russia's European empire Orthodoxy and Catholicism clashed, leading to a strong sense of cultural divide and to what at times amounted to a veritable *kulturkampf*. This was particularly marked during czarist "Russification" policies in the second half of the nineteenth century, when indigenous languages as well as religion came under attack. As an autocratic power of even stronger hue than the Habsburgs—Eastern "caesaro-papism" allowed no room for an independent church or clergy—Russia's impact on Eastern Europe was correspondingly more violent. It allowed few representative institutions to develop; town life was less vigorous and more strictly controlled; the landed estates with their serfs followed the Russian pattern; opinion and intellectual life were closely scrutinized and vetted by the authorities; and resistance was vigorously repressed. Where opposition could develop, it took a characteristically violent and conspiratorial form— again modeled on the opposition in Russia itself. All of this was carried over into the social and political life of the independent states that were formed in the area, the more so as the later Soviet period to a good extent repeated the pattern of czarist rule.

In the south and southeast yet another empire held sway, the Ottoman Empire. With varying degrees of control, especially as the nineteenth century progressed, the Ottoman possessions included Bulgaria, Moldavia and Walachia, Greece, Serbia, Bosnia, and Albania. Large parts of Hungary, too, came under Ottoman rule for a considerable period. The Ottoman legacy is peculiarly complex. With its Islamic religion, its Turkic language, and its Asiatic origin, the Ottoman Empire was the least "Western" of the empires that competed in this region. Indeed, both Western and Eastern Europe, both the Habsburgs and the Romanovs, saw the Turkish advance as the greatest threat to Christian civilization. "Europe" was to a large extent created out of resistance to the Ottomans. The Ottoman Empire came, in the European mind, to be synonymous with "oriental despotism" in its cruelest and most alien form.[35]

Ottoman rule was undeniably autocratic, and opposition was often stringently put down, though generally no more cruelly than in the other empires. But at the same time Ottoman rule was in many ways the most "enlightened" of that of all the three empires. The Ottoman rulers were anxious to learn from Europe. They adopted much of the administration of the Byzantine Empire that they superseded in the region, and they allowed many of the peoples of the area, notably the Greeks, to share in the administration of the empire. Jews, Italians, and Armenians were welcomed as merchants, bankers, and other skilled professionals. The *millet* system allowed for a remarkable degree of toleration and self-rule, with the Orthodox Church and Orthodox clergy playing a particularly important role. Bosnia under the Ottomans, with its mixture of Muslims, Orthodox, Catholics, and Jews; its pattern of coexistence and frequent interaction between these groups; and its general air of lively tolerance, is as good an example as any of the character of Balkan life under the Ottomans.[36]

One should not idealize Ottoman rule, as perhaps this account tends to. The Bulgarian and Armenian massacres are infamous examples of what such rule could mean. And as Ottoman power waned in Europe and Turkish nationalism waxed within the empire, pitting itself against the equally strong nationalisms of the subject nations, the rough side of the Ottoman Empire became increasingly apparent. But one should remember that the Ottoman legacy in the Balkans is not as unrelievedly grim and gloomy as Balkan peoples today, especially the Bulgarians and Serbs, like to pretend it is. For much of the time Ottoman rule was as liberal and enlightened as that to be found in any of the absolutist states of the West. It may be that memories of this have not yet been entirely effaced in the Balkans; this should give some hope in a region that has become a byword, not the least at the present time, for intolerance and fanaticism.

The Ottoman case well illustrates the difficulty of disentangling the complex heritage of empire in East Central Europe. There are so many contradictory currents. So many influences cross and crisscross. There are repeated borrowings and overlaps. Since whole countries passed from one empire to another, they were subjected to violently contrasting policies and styles of rule. Areas that were later put together, usually by external powers, as independent states had sometimes been incorporated simultaneously in two or three empires. Poland, shared between Prussia, Russia, and Austria, is the most famous case; but Hungary, too, for two centuries was divided between the Ottomans and Habsburgs, whereas Czechoslovakia was made up of lands that, though all fell within the Habsburg Empire, had had relatively separate histories as parts on the one hand of Austria (Bohemia, Moravia, and Silesia) and on the other of Hungary (Slovakia and Carpathian Rus').

Romania was composed of the two Danubian principalities, Moldavia and Walachia, that had been under Ottoman rule; later, after World War I, it acquired Transylvania, a region that had been a historic part of Hungary for a thousand years. Most bizarre, perhaps, was the history of Yugoslavia, made up of six or so peoples, about half of whom had lived under the Habsburgs and the rest under the Ottomans. The fact that it held together for so long, and for a time seemed to be emerging as one of the most successful creations in the region, is eloquent testimony to the civilizing effects of both empires, Habsburg and Ottoman, and the fact that the mixing of traditions was not necessarily dangerous or destructive. But its final disintegration, and the many fissures that seem to follow the fault line between the Orthodox/Ottoman and Catholic/Habsburg cultures, gives plenty of ammunition to those who think that the old empires represented civilizations that do not readily combine.[37] The mixed heritages of most of the countries of East Central Europe make it doubly difficult to assess legacies and predict outcomes.

What finally of the system of 1919–39, on the ruins of which the Soviet system was constructed? What is the legacy of the period in which many of the East Central European peoples finally realized their aspiration toward independence? Much is usually made, by Czechs and others, of the interwar experience of democracy in Czechoslovakia and the strong basis this offers for the renewed effort at democracy after 1989.[38] But, quite apart from the brevity of the experience when set against centuries of autocratic rule, it was a democracy that proved stubbornly unable or unwilling to accommodate the claims of the minority groups—Germans, Slovaks, Hungarians, Rusyns, Gypsies, and others—that between them made up nearly half of the population of the new state.[39] Nor is the expulsion of three million Sudeten Germans after World War II a reassuring precedent for a state that makes liberal claims, as many Czechs themselves acknowledge today, although the secession of Slovakia in 1993 may be seen as the logical culmination of an unhappy historical experience.[40]

Elsewhere in the region the legacy of interwar independence is bleaker by far. Virtually without exception, the countries lapsed into authoritarian and dictatorial rule. Marshal Pilsudski in Poland, Admiral Horthy in Hungary, King Carol's "guided democracy" in Romania, King Boris's "disciplined democracy" in Bulgaria, King Alexander's "constitutional dictatorship" in Yugoslavia, King Zog's self-proclaimed "royal dictatorship" in Albania, right-wing authoritarian regimes throughout the new Baltic states of Lithuania, Latvia, and Estonia: it would be hard to imagine a more comprehensive dashing of the great liberal and democratic hopes that accompanied the establishment of these new states after the World War I.[41] It is true that other states at this time, Italy and Germany notably, were also falling into right-wing dictatorships, often of a more virulent kind, but this fact does little to offset the crushing rebuttal of the aspirations of those, like Czechoslovakia under its first president, Tomas Masaryk, who dreamed of the construction of a free and democratic Central Europe of small nations standing between the great powers of Germany and Russia.

The legacy of the interwar period, therefore, added little new, except perhaps in the case of Czechoslovakia, to previous legacies. Authoritarianism and corporatism, in politics and economics, continued to be the norm.[42] Nationalism, antisemitism, and ethnic conflicts—the pattern of the late nineteenth century—flourished and received added impetus from the poisonous new fascist ideologies arising in Europe. Intellectuals were attracted to extremist ideologies as of old. As before, the peoples of the region remained dependent on the great powers to their east and west. It is the great powers that set them up as independent states in 1919; it was the great powers, in the form of Hitler's Germany and Stalin's Soviet Union, that extinguished that independence in World War II. Germany, in particular, one of the region's historic enemies, established a reign of terror. It was not surprising that after the war many people turned to the communists as offering a new, untried way—even if one of the consequences might be that they would fall into the arms of the other historic enemy, Russia.[43]

The tracing of legacies in the life of a nation is not a science. One can only assume that nations exist in time, and that the patterns of their history will continue to exert an influence; with what force, and for how long, it is impossible to calculate. In the case of East Central Europe we have briefly discussed three layers of its past: that of the old dynastic empires, that of the period of interwar independence, and that of communist rule. The first, lasting over three centuries in most cases, was the longest by a great deal; the other two lasted no more than twenty and forty years, respectively. But length of time is no necessary guarantee of force or persistence. The downfall of the old empires in war and revolution in 1914–18; the searing experience of the Great Depression and the ruthless depredations of powerful neighbors in the 1930s; the even more cataclysmic experience of war, occupation, and imposed social revolution during World War II; forty years of one-party, quasitotalitarian rule thereafter: it would be a brave person who asserted that these counted for little against the weight of the older legacy. The traditions of all three legacies have intertwined and overlapped each other in infinitely complex ways. To separate them, to weigh their respective contributions, would be like separating and weighing the currents that make up the sea. All we can be reasonably sure about is that these traditions live on in the minds and souls of the peoples of the region, and are bound to have an effect on their endeavors as they now enter another phase of their history.

What is even more difficult to gauge is the effect of even deeper myths and memories. Lacking, as they see it, a usable past from the relatively modern period, intellectuals and politicians in the postcommunist states of the present have been tempted to appeal to older traditions and memories of glory and greatness. Bulgarians remember the time of the First Bulgarian Empire of the ninth century, when under Khan Krum and Khan Boris they routed the great Byzantine Empire and established a vast territory that equaled that of the Franks and Byzantines. They also claim (wrongly, it appears) the monks Cyril and Methodius, the ninth-century founders of the Slavonic alphabet and Slavonic literature, as their own.[44] To indicate the resurgent qualities of Bulgaria, they can also point to the Second Empire, established after a successful revolt against Byzantium by the Asen brothers, Ivan and Peter, in the twelfth century.

Other countries in the region can boast equally proud achievements and bask in equally glorious memories. The Serbs remember their powerful medieval kingdom, which was overthrown by defeat in the battle of Kosovo (1389) at the hands of the Turks. The Croats, too, established a strong medieval state. Hungary under King Stephen and his successors grew into an extensive kingdom stretching from the Carpathians to the Adriatic. The Czechs have on occasion referred to the Greater Moravian Empire of the ninth century, which united Czechs, Slovaks, and Rusyns and could be seen as a forerunner of twentieth-century Czechoslovakia. Later there was the strong state of Bohemia, founded by the Premyslids, the great cultural efflorescence under Charles IV in the fourteenth century, and the religious reformation led by Jan Hus in the fifteenth century. As for the Poles and Lithuanians, there has always been the memory of the great Polish-Lithuanian Commonwealth of the sixteenth century, the dominant state in Europe of its time, and, as one historian has put it, "the largest and most ambitious experiment with a republican form of government that the world had seen since the days of the Romans."[45]

Much of this is, of course, the material of myth and "constructed" memory.[46] No matter. This is the stuff of nation building. No more than in the case of the later historical legacies is it possible to discount the possible effect of these memories, especially if they can be shown to have some contemporary relevance. The obvious recent example is the meaning of Kosovo for the Serbs. But the Czechs can still call on Jan Hus and the Hussites for inspiration, as can the Hungarians on their great fifteenth-century king Matthias Corvinus, who was not only responsible for the "gathering in" of the Hungarian lands, but was the founder of a vibrant Renaissance court society. All societies live on historical memories of this sort; the English, for instance, at their time of greatest peril during World War II were urged to imitate the fortitude and courage shown at the battle of Agincourt (1415), as presented by Shakespeare. But the societies of East Central Europe, with their history of long-lasting dependence, perhaps have greater reason to revive these ancient memories.[47]

## East Central European Traditions and the 1989 Revolutions

Though unexpected, and indeed a matter of great surprise to many, including the participants, the 1989 revolutions did not come out of nowhere. As with so many fateful episodes in the past of the region, the major determining force once more was external—in this case, the political strategy of the hegemonic power, the Soviet Union. The Soviet Union let East Central Europe go. After forty years in most cases, longer in others (e.g., Ukraine and Belarus), East Central Europe was left at least formally free to determine its future.

What the region has to fall back on is inevitably the legacy discussed earlier in this chapter. The questions that arose in the course of the revolutions and immediately afterward nearly all had to do with picking up old traditions and resuming interrupted strivings. That was what was meant by the oft-repeated slogan "the rebirth of history." What was the region's relation to Europe, especially Western Europe, and how could it achieve "a return to Europe"? What was the state of its "civil society," and how could it be regenerated? What was its experience of democracy, and how could democratic institutions be established or reestablished? To what extent had traditions of market society existed, and what might be necessary to revive them? What was the region's legacy of socialism, and how far did it create obstacles to the creation of liberal market societies? To what extent, indeed, could or should the past dictate outcomes?[48] The different levels of the past—dynastic empire, national independence, and communist rule—all had their contribution, positive or negative, to make in answering these questions. And even where the answer was a blank—that is, there might be no tradition or relevant experience available to draw on—that, too, was significant.

One obvious feature of the change brought about by the 1989 revolutions was the breakup of the entity "Eastern Europe," seen as an artificial creation of the Soviet Empire that yoked together Russia and the adjoining countries to its west. But what, then, was the "Central Europe" or East Central Europe thereby set free? Intellectuals in the region, such as Milan Kundera, Václav Havel, György Konrád, Adam Michnik, and Czesław Miłosz, had argued in the 1980s that there was a distinctive Central European identity and culture that had been suppressed by Soviet and communist rule. It was a culture that partook of the elements of both East and West. It accepted the individual, but not at the expense of the group or community. It recognized the claims of nationality and ethnicity, but also acknowledged the irreducible mixture of ethnicities and the large number of minorities that existed in every area, and the need to preserve this diversity as a matter of strength, not weakness. It tempered the imperatives of technology and economic growth, whether capitalist or socialist, with a recognition of the claims of nature and the need to preserve a certain way of life. There was no denying the fact of dependence and subordination to great powers; that was the great unifying force of Central European history. But out of such dependence—out of the compromises, the complexity, the absence of chauvinism and dogmatism—had come the writings of Hašek, Capek, Kafka, and Musil; the music of Mahler, Janacek, and Bartok; the thought of Husserl and Freud.[49]

But if "Eastern Europe" has dissolved, might that not also be true of "Central Europe"? Once the unifying fact of dependency, and the enforced culture and complexity it creates, has disappeared, what prevents the nations of the region from flying apart? The recovery of their history, as they see it, also seems to mean a recovery of their differences. They once had very separate histories, ranging from the national power of Bulgaria and Poland to an existence as no more than a province of a larger state, as in the case of Slovakia. Then, for a long time, they fell under the sway of a few large empires, including the communist empire. Now that they are once more free, in some cases for the first time ever, will they not wish to emphasize their separateness, their distinctiveness as national cultures? There is not simply their heritage of different imperial experiences; there is also their fervent wish to determine their own future destinis. The nations of the region want to distinguish themselves not just from their common past, but from each other.[50]

Already, since 1989, it has been noticeable how intellectuals—some turned statesmen, such as Havel—have been playing down a Central European identity and stressing instead the impeccably Western credentials of their nations. The states of the region have broken ranks and are vying with each other for membership in NATO and the European Union.[51] The winning tactic in this contest is to show qualities, real or putative, that might make one country seem a more suitable partner than its rivals to the Western states that control these organizations. One way of doing this might be to give a heavily selective reading of the country's history, emphasizing relevant traditions, as Romanians for instance do in claiming descent from the Dacians of Roman times, and Slovenes and Croats do in pointing to their Habsburg inheritance. The trick is to appear more "Western" than neighboring countries. Inevitably this distorts the real history of the region, and its many common experiences, not the least the experience of communism. But the urge of each country to put the immediate past behind it, and to advertise instead those traditions that set that country apart from others that are otherwise embarrassingly close, is bound to increase the fragmentation of the region. This can be viewed as a "return to diversity" so long as we are aware that this tells only half of the story of the region's history.[52]

The 1989 revolutions have an interest in and for themselves. They marked a radical departure in the history of the postwar world. Arguably they represent an even greater rupture. They seem, for the moment at least, to have put an end to two centuries of competition and conflict between the warring ideologies of capitalism and socialism. They have also renewed the idea of revolution, although in a rather special way. In all these ways they belong, like the American and French Revolutions two hundred years ago, to the whole world and not just to any particular countries.[53]

But they also belong, of course, to the peoples of East Central Europe. They came out of their history, and were shaped by it. Much of their language and many of their aspirations may have come from the Western revolutionary tradition, though we should not forget that East Central Europe, from the Hussites and Taborites of the fifteenth century to the 1848 revolutions of the nineteenth, played its part in forming that tradition. But the way those aspirations were conceived, the forms of action, and the chances of realizing the goals that were set were inevitably constrained by the circumstances of the societies in which the revolutions took place. If what took place was the "revenge of history," as Alex Callinicos has called it,[54] it was a many-sided affair. On the one hand, the societies of East Central Europe protested against their historic state of dependence and sought to free themselves to make their own history. On the other hand, they found that history of dependence and interdependence meeting them at every turn. The outcome of this encounter is still to be seen.

## Two

# The Revolutions of 1989:
# Socialism, Capitalism, and Democracy

*Many journalists and scholars will look for the correlation of that chain of spectacular transformations that changed, as if at one blow, the fates of tens of millions of individuals and the hitherto firm bipolar picture of the modern world. . . . Today, many people are talking and writing about the role of the intellectuals, students, and the theatre, or the influence of the Soviets' perestroika, and economic difficulties. They're right. I myself as a playwright would also add the influence of humour and honesty, and perhaps even something beyond us, something maybe even unearthly.*

Václav Havel

## 1989 and the Sense of an Ending

Everyone in the West was clear about two things concerning the events of 1989 in Central and Eastern Europe. One was that there had been a revolution (or revolutions). The other was that 1989 spelled the end of several major projects in modern European history. No one seemed capable of escaping an eschatological solemnity.

About revolutions we shall speak in a moment. But what were these things that were ending? First, and most obvious, was socialism; Right, Left, and Center, whatever conclusions they derived from the fact, were agreed on that. "Less than seventy-five years after it officially began," affirmed Robert Heilbroner, "the contest between capitalism and socialism is over: capitalism has won."[1] "Socialism is dead," agreed Ralf Dahrendorf, echoing a hundred pronouncements of a like kind; and, just in case an alternative terminology might be brought in to dispute the point, he added for good measure: "Communism is gone, never to return."[2]

There were, indeed, those who seemed self-consciously restrictive in their claims, though agreeing on the main point. "This was the year communism in Eastern Europe died," said Timothy Garton Ash, probably the best-known commentator in the English-speaking world on the events of 1989.[3] But most commentators, although recognizing the varieties of socialism, were disinclined to let this modify their verdicts. One might indeed separate (Western) "democratic" socialism from (Eastern) "state" socialism or communism, but, argued William Rees-Mogg, "Both types of socialist systems have failed."[4]

It is not surprising to hear these assessments from the conservative Right and the liberal Center of the political spectrum. The events of 1989 were evidently a greater challenge to the Left. All the more remarkable, then, that they, too, accepted the general verdict, and often in terms strikingly similar to those used by the Right and the Center. What we were seeing, said the left-wing historian and long-standing Communist Party member Eric Hobsbawm, was not just the crisis of communism, but "its end. Those of us who believed that the October Revolution was the gate to the future of world history have been shown to be wrong."[5] All over Western Europe erstwhile communist parties, following the example of their counterparts in Eastern Europe and elsewhere, have hurried to throw off the "communism" of their titles. Sometimes, as in the case of the Italian Communist Party, they have not even been able to swallow "socialism" as a substitute: the Italian CP, after agonizing months during which it was simply referred to as "*la cosa*" ("the thing"), settled tentatively for "the Democratic Party of the Left" *(Partito Democratico della Sinistra)*.[6]

Even where the old names remain, there have been some extraordinary turnabouts and transformations of policy. Introducing the *Manifesto for New Times* to the Forty-first Congress of the Communist Party of Great Britain, Martin Jacques, editor of the party's theoretical journal *Marxism Today,* was comprehensive in his dismissal of traditional aims: "It is the end of the road for the communist system. Stalinism is dead and Leninism has had its day. We are witnessing the defeat of socialism."[7] *Marxism Today* itself, under Jacques's editorship, presided over a far-reaching revision of traditional Marxist thought. It proclaimed "New Times," an era of post-industrial, "post-Fordist" capitalism in which almost all of Marx's original diagnoses and prognoses had to be discarded. In its place were such concepts as "socialist individualism" and talk of "a new socialist morality of enterprise, individual responsibility and initiative."[8] The *Manifesto for New Times* embodied the new thinking; it was adopted as official party policy in 1989. The word *socialism* evidently remained; but what of the thing? What content did it still have, and how did that relate to socialist philosophy in any of its traditional senses?

With the presumed death of socialism has been coupled the death of another of the great projects of modernity: the quest for utopia. Utopia was always a figurative thing. No one, or almost no one, expected to realize in practice More's *Utopia* or Bacon's *New Atlantis,* let alone copy the ways of the noble Houyhnhnms of Swift's *Gulliver's Travels.* But the utopian ideal represented a striving for perfection that found its ways into countless schemes for the reorganization and regeneration of society in the eighteenth and nineteenth centuries. Among these schemes was socialism. Despite the energetic attempts by Marx and Engels to repudiate the utopian label, it has been clear to most thinkers that socialism embodied one of the grandest utopias of modern times. Socialism has been, indeed, according to Zygmunt Bauman, "*the* utopia of the modern epoch."[9] All other utopias have either been marginalized or absorbed by it.

If in our time utopia has been socialism, then the death of socialism must also spell the death of utopia. "With the fall of communist regimes in so many countries of Eastern Europe," says Wolf Lepenies, "the utopia of socialism has died as well."[10] "The catastrophe of historical communism," says Norberto Bobbio, signifies that "in a seemingly irreversible way, the greatest political utopia in history . . . has been completely upturned into its exact opposite."[11] But the death of utopia goes beyond the fate of any particular social philosophy. It has been seen as the final repudiation of all secular creeds, all modern ideologies that put their faith in history and the historical process. "The 1980s," says Gareth Stedman Jones, "have brought to an end . . . all lingering beliefs in the historical promise of secular utopias." The collapse of communism, "the most concentrated expression of that faith," has also undermined "the props upon which that faith relied, the secular scientific inquiry into Man."[12] The chain of causation has expanded relentlessly: the death of socialism has led to the demise of utopia, which, in turn, has dissolved the belief in science and secularism.

Tying socialism to utopia, considering socialism as a utopia, is all the more important for the vehement rejection of utopia and utopian politics by many of the leading spokesmen of the new order in Central and Eastern Europe. For many years this has been one of the principal themes of Alexander Solzhenitsyn's utterances, especially since his exile to the West in 1974. In the new climate of *glasnost* and *perestroika*, Solzhenitsyn has seen fit to renew his charges against the Soviet Union and its reigning ideology. In a tract entitled "How We Are to Rebuild Russia"—published not in the West, but in the Moscow daily *Komsomolskaya Pravda*, the organ of the Communist Youth League, with a circulation of 22 million—he urged a return to the days and ways of Russia before 1917, to the values of the old rural society and to some of its political institutions, such as the *zemstva*. What must be decisively abandoned, he said, was the hubris of utopian politics: "For 70 years . . . we have been hitched to the Marxist-Leninist utopia, which was blind and evil at birth."[13]

Solzhenitsyn may have sounded extreme. He had, in the eyes of some commentators, come to appear almost a throwback to the "Old Believers," a Slavophile preaching the revival of the peasant community under the stern guidance of a purified Orthodoxy (he has often expressed his contempt for the Russian Orthodox Church under communism, "a church ruled by atheists"). But not only were his views not so very different from much of what was being said in Russia after the revolutions, we find gentler echoes of them in the writings of many prominent East European intellectuals, formerly in opposition or exile and now, in several cases, in charge of the destinies of their countries. Especially strong are the echoes of Solzhenitsyn's antiutopianism.

Václav Havel, in an address of 1984, saluted "the author of *The Gulag Archipelago*" not just for the courage of his stand against the Soviet authorities, but also for the terms in which it was made. Solzhenitsyn opposed "personal experience and the natural world" to impersonal, "objective" bureaucratic power, and so unmasked its guilt. Havel, too, inveighed against the tyranny of the scientific or positivistic worldview, and mourned the "tens of thousand of lives . . . sacrificed on the altar of a scientific Utopia about brighter tomorrows."[14]

Elsewhere Havel has shown that he is aware of the appeal, even the necessity, of utopia. He has said that "visions of a better world and dreams about it" supply that "transcendence of the given" without which human life loses all meaning and dignity. But utopia is only too prone to degeneration and petrifaction. The living idea becomes a set of techniques that do violence to life. Utopia is easily hijacked by what Havel calls "the fanatic of the abstract project, the practising Utopian"—the Marats, Robespierres, Lenins, Pol Pots ("I would not include Hitler and Stalin in this category; if I did, it would have to include every criminal").[15]

Havel lamented his country's "postwar lapse into Utopianism" of the Leninist-Stalinist variety. His country had paid a cruel price for it. But, as an antidote to the utopian poison, he was glad to be able to invoke "a distinctive central European scepticism" formed out of the bruising historical experience of that region of Europe. Czechoslovakia's experience of utopianism, he said, has resulted in "a new and far-reaching reinforcement of our central European scepticism about Utopianism of all colors and shadings, about the slightest suggestion of Utopianism." The central European mind—"sceptical, sober, anti-Utopian"—offers the resources of hope. It can become the basis for the construction of an "anti-political politics," a "politics outside politics." This Havel presented as a counter to the systematizers, the fanatics, the technicians of power—in a word, the utopians. It was offered as a political philosophy for the emerging post-communist states of Central and Eastern Europe.[16]

I shall return to this "anti-political politics." It is, it seems to me, of considerable importance in understanding the political predicament of East European societies today. But first there is one further apocalyptic pronouncement, perhaps the most arresting, to consider. It is that with the revolutions of 1989 we witnessed "the end of history," no less.

This was the title of an article published in 1989 by Francis Fukuyama, by his own account "a relatively junior official" of the U.S. State Department. To his evident surprise, not only was the article widely noted, but it aroused considerable controversy in America and Europe. Everyone, from William F. Buckley, Margaret Thatcher, and *Encounter* on the Right to *The Nation, Marxism Today,* and Mikhail Gorbachev on the Left, rushed to ridicule the idea that "history had ended." As Fukuyama wryly noted, he had come to think that his true accomplishment was to achieve "a uniquely universal consensus, not on the current status of liberalism"—the subject of the article—"but on the fact that I was wrong."[17]

The reason behind both the interest and the outrage that greeted Fukuyama's article is not hard to find. Fukuyama was saying what many people were thinking, and were indeed themselves uttering in their different ways; but he used a tone and a set of concepts that many found unsettling and in some ways offensive. It is not common to find a State Department official deploying Hegelian concepts and arguments. That is what Fukuyama did.

Fukuyama drew upon Alexandre Kojève's interpretation of Hegel's *Phenomenology of Mind* to argue that Hegel's view of mankind's history had been proved essentially correct. The events of 1989 demonstrated more effectively than ever before that history, understood as the history of thought, of contending ideas about the fundamental principles of government and society, had indeed come to an end. Hegel had been right to think that Napoleon's defeat of the Prussian monarchy at the Battle of Jena in 1806 marked the end of history, because it symbolized the victory of the ideals of the French Revolution and their embodiment in the "universal homogenous state" (*sic* Fukuyama), the state based on liberty and equality. Much remained, of course, to be done in the further diffusion of these ideals and their actual implementation in the institutions of different states over the face of the earth. That had been the achievement of the subsequent two centuries, accompanied by the frightful stresses of social revolution, two world wars, and the ultimately unsuccessful challenges of fascism and communism.

But now, at the end of the twentieth century, there can be no doubt about the truth of Hegel's insight. What we are witnessing, said Fukuyama, is not simply the end of the Cold War or of a particular period of postwar history, but "the end of history as such: that is, the end point of mankind's ideological evolution and the universalization of Western liberal democracy as the final form of human government." The detours and regressions of the last two centuries have finally proved to be just that: not real alternatives, but the growing pains of world liberal society, the society inaugurated by the American and French Revolutions. As Fukuyama said, "The century that began full of self-confidence in the ultimate triumph of Western liberal democracy seems at its close to be returning full circle to where it started: not to an "end of ideology" or a convergence between capitalism and socialism, as earlier predicted, but to an unabashed victory of economic and political liberalism."[18]

It is unnecessary to speak of the misunderstandings and simplifications to be found in most of Fukuyama's critics. He did not say that there would be an end of conflict, nor of what most people understand as history, history as events. There is room enough in his account of the future for severe struggles, even wars, springing from nationalism, racism, and ethnic rivalries. He was aware of the scale of environmental destruction and the enormous problems this poses for the whole world. What he insisted was that none of these involve massive ideological conflicts—history as the clash of ideas—of the kind that have marked past epochs. "To refute my hypothesis," he wrote in reply to his critics, "it is not sufficient to suggest that the future holds in store large and momentous events. One would have to show that these events were driven by a systematic idea of political and social justice that claimed to supersede liberalism."[19]

It has to be said that very few of Fukuyama's many critics have so far met the challenge. Indeed, despite a frequently arrogant and sneering tone,[20] what is more striking is the degree of coincidence between their views and his. We have seen this already in the many expressions of "the death of socialism," which are usually accompanied, explicitly or implicitly, by an acknowledgment of the victory of capitalism, or of the market, or of liberalism. Ralf Dahrendorf's argument that 1989 represented the triumph of the "open society" seems no different in kind, despite his attempt to distinguish the open society from the social system of capitalism, as well as all other "systems."[21] In theory it may be possible to construct an abstract model of an open society unrelated to historic capitalism; in actual fact, all "open societies"—Dahrendorf's examples include Britain, France, postwar Germany, and the United States—have evolved along with the evolution of liberal capitalist systems. Dahrendorf caviled at Hayek's—and Fukuyama's—equation of the open society with market society. Economic liberalism, it is true, is not the same thing as political liberalism, nor need it entail such liberalism. But there seems to be no example of a society that is politically liberal that is not at the same time characterized by economic liberalism. A degree of reciprocity, if not of dependence, seems clear. Capitalism without liberal democracy is not uncommon (if not very efficient). Liberal democracy without capitalism is so rare that no case springs to mind.[22]

It may also be true to say, as did Gareth Stedman Jones, that "the present global triumph of liberal capitalism" will not necessarily be permanent or even long-lasting, and that "it says more about the weakness and exhaustion of the historical alternatives offered than about the intrinsic strength of liberal capitalism itself."[23] There are certainly some serious objections to be made to Fukuyama's thesis on the score of the apparently irreversible victory of liberal capitalism (though not, as is sometimes done, on the grounds of his apparent blindness to the moral and spiritual shortcomings of liberal individualism).[24] The real problem, though, as Fukuyama noted, is precisely "the weakness and exhaustion of the historical alternatives" with what are offered as real ideological rivals to liberal capitalism today. Here there seems to have been a marked reluctance or inability on the part of his critics to come up with anything. Dahrendorf, for instance, in searching for the intellectual antecedents of the open society, fell back upon the very eighteenth-century thinkers—Hume, Locke, Kant, Burke, the American authors of the *Federalist Papers*—who are invoked by the devotees of liberal capitalism, such as Hayek.[25] Eric Hobsbawm mocked Fukuyama for his shortsightedness in expecting that "henceforth all would be plain liberal, free-market sailing." But he, too, admitted that "for the time being there is no part of the world that credibly represents an alternative system to capitalism."[26] Fukuyama has clearly provoked irritation and anger; but it is equally clear that his critics have found it extremely hard to avoid mimicking him, whatever the difference of terms.

Jürgen Habermas remarked about a "peculiar characteristic" of the 1989 revolution, "namely its total lack of ideas that are either innovative or orientated towards the future."[27] François Furet, too, said that "with all the fuss and noise, not a single new idea has come out of Eastern Europe in 1989." He further observed that, for the first time in 150 years, no alternative total view of society was on offer in the intellectual and political battles of the world.[28] For Eric Hobsbawm, too, this was the predicament posed by the events of 1989. He argued that many of the gains in Western capitalist democracies—the welfare state, a secure place for labor organizations, Keynesian policies to combat unemployment—were "the result of fear": that is, they were the consequence of the ruling elites' fear of the appeal of the alternative presented, in however corrupt a form, in Eastern Europe. "Whatever Stalin did to the Russians," Hobsbawm noted, "he was good for the common people of the West." With the loss of that alternative, the rich and powerful need no longer concern themselves with the common people. They can allow welfare to erode and the protection of those who need it to atrophy. "This is the chief effect of the disappearance of even a very bad socialist region from the globe," according to Hobsbawm.[29]

There was evidently something strange about the revolution of 1989. It seems to have been peculiarly uncreative, unfertile in ideas. Rather than—as in 1776, 1789, 1848, and 1917—confronting the world with a grand alternative, a new set of values and practices to live by, it seems to have regarded as its main task the suppression of alternatives. If it paid tribute to any new ideas, it was to the postmodernist perception of the end of "metanarratives," the impossibility now of conceptualizing our reality according to any comprehensive scheme of history and society, such as Marxism or positivism (or, for that matter, liberalism in its more normative varieties).[30]

Is this then our condition—or our predicament? The breakup of the competing models of society that have been the dynamic of world history in the last two centuries? The end of the "global civil war"? Not "Three Worlds," but only One World?[31] A sort of global entropy of ideas, a final end of all ideologies (for an ideology without opposition is no ideology)? There may not be much to celebrate in this, for, in Hegel's famous expression, "when philosophy paints its grey in grey, then has a shape of life grown old."[32] But before we assess these and other apocalyptic utterances, we need to look a little more closely at the events of 1989 themselves.

## The Revolution of 1989

Almost everyone, observers as much as participants, seems inclined to call the events of 1989 a revolution, and this is not the place to quibble about that.[33] Definitions of revolution are notoriously controversial, but there is at least a reasonable degree of agreement on the idea of varieties of revolution. Let us, then, accept for now (time has a way of altering these contemporary verdicts) that 1989 was a variety of revolution.[34] What kind of revolution was it? How are we best to understand it?

One way of understanding is by analogy. All revolutions since the French have in part looked back, seeking to connect their own revolutionary moment with those of past revolutions. They have invited comparisons with past revolutions both in terms of continuities and of declared departures from them. Lenin was fond of claiming the kinship between the French and Russian Revolutions, even though the whole point of the Russian Revolution was to go beyond the bourgeois achievements of the French. Revolutionaries are the most tradition-minded of political actors, even as they announce their aim of renewing the world.

The revolution of 1989 has, as we have noted, so far been unusually cautious in its claims. The "pathos of novelty" that Hannah Arendt saw as the hallmark of modern revolution has been conspicuously absent. Far from it, the revolution of 1989 has displayed something like nostalgia for the achievements of past revolutions. It did not wish to go forward; it wished to go back. Not back to 1917, of course, that was, in its eyes, the great error, the beginning of the great catastrophe,[35] but back to 1848, back to 1789 and 1776 (invocations of 1688, the British "Glorious Revolution," have so far not been heard, but there is still time, and, what with talk of monarchical restoration in some places, such as Romania, may not appear so absurd).

Habermas referred to the events of 1989 in Central and Eastern Europe—leaving out the Soviet Union as a different case—as a "rectifying revolution." He said that the revolution of 1989 "presents itself as a revolution that is to some degree flowing backwards, one that clears the ground in order to catch up with developments previously missed out." Poland, Hungary, Czechoslovakia, East Germany, Romania, and Bulgaria—the countries that, unlike Russia, had socialism imposed on them by military force from outside—all showed the desire to return to old symbols of nationhood and to restore, where possible, the political traditions and party organization of the interwar years. The idea of "rectification" also works at a deeper and more fundamental level, stretching further back into the historical past. It is in these countries that one sees the clearest signs of the wish, as Habermas put it, "to connect up constitutionally with the inheritance of the bourgeois revolutions, and socially and politically with the styles of commerce and life associated with developed capitalism, particularly that of the European Community."[36]

The revolution of 1789, the classic "bourgeois revolution," is therefore one obvious point of reference for the 1989 revolution. This is so, first, in terms of its aims, taken in the broadest sense as encompassing many of the radical demands of the eighteenth-century Enlightenment.

Locke and Shaftesbury, Hume and Smith, Kant and Montesquieu, the American Declaration of Independence and the American Constitution, liberty and equality, the Rights of Man and of the Citizen, constitutionalism and popular sovereignty: these names and themes would seem to express as compellingly in 1989 as in 1789 the aspirations of the revolutionaries.

The "return of 1789" has been hailed as one of the more extraordinary consequences of the revolution of 1989 in Eastern Europe. The revolution of 1989 has in particular reflected sternly on the claims of the revolution of 1917 that it was the real revolution, the universal revolution going beyond the "bourgeois" limits of the revolution of 1789. The reverse, declares François Furet, now seems to be the case:

> The universal character of the principles of 1789 seems truer than ever before. . . . The Bolsheviks thought that with 1917 they had buried 1789. Here, at the end of our century, we see that the opposite is happening. It is 1917 that is being buried in the name of 1789. This extraordinary reversal, unpredictable and unforeseen, imbues the famous principles of 1789 with a certain freshness and with renewed universality. As we begin to close the long and tragic digression that was the Communist illusion, we find ourselves more than ever confronted by the great dilemmas of democracy as they appeared at the end of the 18th century, expressed by ideas and by the course of the French Revolution.[37]

1789 also seems relevant in terms of the manner of revolution, how it begins and how it proceeds. Here the most significant thing is the role of the people. The mass movement of Solidarity, the scenes of mass protest in Budapest, Prague, Leipzig, and Timisoara—all these readily bring to mind the classic explosions of popular protest and action in the early phases of the French Revolution: the storming of the Bastille, the march on Versailles, the invasion of the Tuilleries.

For those such as Habermas who see 1989 in terms of "spontaneous mass action," the parallel with 1789 is practically irresistible. Habermas has employed Lenin's famous formulation: in 1989 as in 1789, revolution broke out because those below were no longer willing, and those above were no longer able, to go on in the old way: "The presence of large masses gathering in squares and mobilizing on the streets managed, astoundingly, to disempower a regime that was armed to the teeth."[38] These were techniques, Habermas further points out, that, like the goals, were of the most traditional kind: "The recent rectifying revolutions took their methods and standards entirely from the familiar repertoire of the modern age." It is this that makes untenable "postmodernist" interpretations of the revolution of 1989, which would see it as a revolution that aimed to go "beyond reason," to the release of "self-empowering subjectivity." 1989, on the contrary, showed itself as belonging squarely to the age of modernity launched by the Enlightenment and the eighteenth-century revolution.[39] It spoke the language of 1789 and employed many of its methods. Since these were the elements that in the nineteenth century came to constitute the classic model of the liberal-democratic revolution, 1989 has to be seen as continuing rather than surpassing the modern revolutionary tradition.

So much can be granted while not stilling doubts about the appropriateness of the parallel with 1789. The drawbacks are fairly obvious. The men and women of 1989 were liberals and democrats, but they were also—or saw themselves as—victims of ideological politics. The French Revolution was conceived in liberty but, as almost everyone from Edmund Burke onward was at pains to point out, it gave birth to despotism. Under "the tyranny of the idea" it moved inexorably to the Terror, war, and dictatorship. Havel, we may remember, instanced Marat and Robespierre as the very type of the "practising Utopians" that had to be fought against. However much 1989 may owe to 1789—and the legacy is undeniable—the violence of the course of the French Revolution and the methods it used to overcome its opponents are bound to make that revolution suspect in the eyes of 1989 liberals.

There is a further problem with seeing the revolution of 1789 as parallel to that of 1989. If that view is meant to suggest that the revolution used as its model a revolution of popular mass insurrection, it is seriously misleading as to the causes of the revolution (or revolutions) of 1989. It is, of course, also true that the old view of the French Revolution, as a mass rising of an oppressed populace, is no longer held by most contemporary historians. Tocqueville's "revisionist" analysis, stressing the role of a reforming monarchy and an "enlightened" nobility, has become the starting point for practically all historians of the Revolution.[40] But there is no doubt that, from the point of view of popular perceptions and even of its general place in the revolutionary tradition, 1789 has become associated with mass movements and popular uprising. The iconography of that Revolution—the poetry of

Wordsworth and Shelley, the paintings of David, the prints of the great revolutionary festivals—has mythologized indelibly the heroic portrait of the *sansculottes,* the common people who, singing the *Marseillaise,* swept away almost miraculously the reactionary armies of kings and emperors.[41] It was from the French Revolution, with its myth of *le peuple* as the sovereign force, that Trotsky derived his defining principle of revolution: "The most indubitable feature of a revolution is the direct interference of the masses in historic events."[42]

There is no reason to doubt the importance of popular pressure in 1989 any more than in 1789. The problem of how to view the revolution of 1989 has to do not with the popular desire for change nor with the eagerness with which opportunities were seized when they were offered, but with the astonishingly rapid success of the revolution. The regimes of Central and Eastern Europe crumbled faster than anyone had imagined—or dared hope. Commentators found themselves rewriting their books before the ink was dry on the copy for the first edition. What brought about, in the space of a few months, so spectacular a collapse of anciens régimes?

There has always been a problem with Lenin's formulation—often repeated, as by Habermas—that revolutions break out when the lower classes will not, and the upper classes cannot, continue the old order. Apart from the suspicion of tautology, which is rife in any case in most etiologies of revolution, there is too symmetrical a balance between the "will not" of the lower classes and the "cannot" of the upper classes as reciprocal but independent variables. Is it not the case, rather, that it is only when the upper classes cannot maintain the old order that we find clear evidence of the determination of the lower classes to end it? Does this not suggest that causal priority has to be assigned to the problems of the existing power structure and the existing power holders in society—that is, to the distemper at the top rather than at the bottom of society? Discontent, latent or manifest, among the lower classes can be taken as more or less given with regard to most stratified social orders. Regimes can be peppered with popular rebellions without succumbing to them, despite these expressions of manifest disaffection on the part of the people. This was the case with the majority of the agrarian empires of the preindustrial world.

It is only when the ruling structures of society are in a clear state of decay or dissolution that popular discontent can express itself in a

confident way. Then we usually find spokesmen from the upper classes urging on popular feeling against the regime. Revolutionaries, often
released from prison or returned from exile abroad, busy themselves
with organizing the mass discontent. After the success of the revolution the idea of a popular uprising against a hated tyranny becomes
the official myth of the new regime. This conceals the fact that the old
regime died, often by its own hand, rather than been overthrown in a
popular outburst of indignation. When E. H. Carr wrote of the October
1917 revolution that "Bolshevism succeeded to a vacant throne," he
was pointing to the "negligible" contribution of Lenin and the Bolsheviks to the overthrow of czarism. But he could just as easily have
been referring to what Auguste Blanqui called the "happy surprise" of
revolutionaries everywhere at finding that the main work of destruction had already been done by some of the most distinguished and
powerful representatives of the ancien régime.[43]

In book 8 of *The Republic* Plato observed that "in any form of
government revolution always starts from the outbreak of internal
dissension in the ruling class. The constitution cannot be upset so long
as that class is of one mind, however small it may be."[44] This statement may need some qualification, but its essential truth stands up
remarkably well. Was that not shown, as well as anywhere, in the
revolutions of 1989? No one has doubted the widespread feeling of
discontent, even despair, among the populations of East European societies for many decades. The evidence has been plain to see, not the
least in the revolts or urgent attempts at reform in East Germany in
1953, in Hungary and Poland in 1956, in Czechoslovakia in 1968, and
in Poland again in 1980. All were suppressed, sometimes brutally.
After the suppression of Solidarity in 1981, many observers predicted a
long period of resentful quiescence in the countries of the Soviet bloc.

They were wrong. In the second half of the 1980s first Poland,
then with gathering speed other communist societies, began to reform.
Reform turned, in the space of a few breathless months in 1989, into
revolution. How was that possible? Popular rebellions had repeatedly
failed. Liberal attempts at reform had been crushed. The dissident intelligentsia was largely impotent. Why did change finally occur at that
time—and change on a scale scarcely dreamed of by even the most
hopeful reformer?

The answer, in a word, is as banal as it is inevitable: Gorbachev.
Gorbachev was replaying Khrushchev with a vengeance. Just as the lat-

ter's denunciation of Stalin at the Twentieth Congress of the Communist Party of the Soviet Union in 1956 sparked the Hungarian and Polish uprisings of that year, so the former's unleashing of the forces of *glasnost* and *perestroika* sparked the revolutions of 1989.

"Gorbachev," of course, stood for many things. He was the leader of the reform movement launched by Yuri Andropov in the early 1980s. He expressed the Soviet Union's urgent recognition that it was slipping desperately behind the West in its industrial progress. He was part of that widespread liberalization of opinion in the Soviet Union that acknowledged that, although a command economy may work well enough for the early stages of industrialization, it is ill equipped to deal with the later, more sophisticated stages. He accepted, equally, the view of most educated people in the Soviet Union that pluralism in the economy must go hand in hand with pluralism in the polity, that a market economy, even a "social market" economy, requires a liberal state. He was also, it appears, a sincere man, genuinely committed to reform in the interests of the Soviet people and nation, knowing that it would take time but also that time was what he did not have. He was, or represented, no doubt, much more. To show all of that, one would have to examine in detail the developments in the Soviet Union at the time of Gorbachev. This is not the place to attempt such a thing.[45]

In any event, Gorbachev stood for the Soviet Union in the age of the global economy and the information society. National autarky is no longer feasible; in the satellite age populations cannot be insulated and cordoned off from images and ideas that flood the world. The Soviet Union had to change; and in changing it brought about the downfall of the regimes of its client states all over Central and Eastern Europe. This is where Gorbachev supplied the necessary condition for revolution as specified by Plato. The Soviet Union had been at the apex of the power structure of the East European states. So long as its party and army supported the rulers of those states, they were safe from popular uprisings and able to handle the radicals within their own ranks. Once that support was withdrawn, the ruling elites were deprived of that legitimacy and, more critically, that ability to use force that had been the mainstay of their power. Their regimes collapsed like a house of cards.

Nothing demonstrates the truth of this more clearly than the fate of the revolution in Romania. Why was this the country where the change was accompanied by the greatest bloodshed? Surely because this was the one country where the ruling party did not depend on Soviet troops for its power.[46] The policies of Gheorghe Gheorghiu-Dej and Nicolae Ceausescu had led to Romania's growing independence of the Soviet Union and its increasingly friendly relations with China and the West. No Warsaw Pact troops had been allowed on Romanian soil since 1962. Ceausescu condemned the Warsaw Pact intervention in Czechoslovakia in 1968 and refused to participate in it.[47] Therefore, when protest erupted in Timisoara and Bucharest there was not—as in other East European countries—a restraining Soviet hand laid on the military and the police. Hence the bloodiness of the ensuing conflict between the people and the Securitate.

Even in the case of Romania, though, we must be careful not to see the revolution too exclusively in terms of a people's uprising. There is evidence of a coup against Ceausescu long planned from within the Romanian Communist Party. The plot involved top-ranking Party officials, army units, many generals, and a section of the Securitate secret police. When the army swung to the side of the people during the uprising, this was not, as has been generally put about in Romania and the West, a spontaneous conversion under popular stimulus, but the result of the plotters' work within the army.[48] The Romanian revolution, therefore, like all revolutions, had as much the character of the classic *fronde* as of a people's revolution.[49]

In the remainder of Eastern Europe *fronde*-like features, such as a divided and weakened ruling class, were so obvious that they scarcely need to be documented. By confining Soviet troops to their barracks and proclaiming an attitude of "benevolent neutrality," Gorbachev effectively disarmed the rulers of the East European states. There was to be no repeat of 1956, 1968, and 1981. In December 1956, when the leaders of the workers' councils told János Kádár that they had the Hungarian people behind them, he replied that he had the Soviet tanks behind him. In 1989 that was no longer true for the majority of the leaders in Eastern Europe.

Neither the Soviet government nor the reformers, it is true, expected the complete collapse of one-party communist rule. The Soviet leadership, largely through the agency of the KGB, was active in promoting opposition to the East European conservatives.[50] But it did not aim to undermine the power of the communist parties; it merely aimed to reform them. The institution of "socialism with a human face" was the limited intent, as in the Soviet Union itself. However, once started, events were difficult to stop. The reform movement, fueled by popular feeling, developed into a revolutionary torrent that swept away the one-party state.

The Soviet government acquiesced. It would do nothing to save the ruling parties. In 1989 the Soviet Union made it clear that it had decisively abandoned the Brezhnev doctrine of the priority of "proletarian internationalism" over the particular interests and wishes of individual socialist states. Already in 1987 Gorbachev had announced, "The time of the Communist International . . . is over. . . . All parties are completely and irreversibly independent." In May 1989 Foreign Minister Eduard Shevardnadze said he could imagine no occasion on which Soviet troops might intervene in a Warsaw Pact country. At the Warsaw Pact meeting in Bucharest in July 1989 Ceausescu, supported by Erich Honecker, reversed his stance in 1968 and called for armed intervention against the Solidarity government in Poland. The Soviet Union's opposition was decisive. As if to set the seal on this rejection of the past, the Warsaw Pact meeting in December 1989 unequivocally denounced the suppression of the Prague Spring of 1968, a resolution endorsed by the Supreme Soviet in the same month.[51] The Brezhnev doctrine was buried. In its place Gorbachev proclaimed what his spokesman Gennadi Gerasimov called "the Sinatra doctrine": let every nation do it in its own way.

The revolution of 1989, then, for all the homage it may have paid to that of 1789, departed from the perceived model of that revolution in several important ways. It was not a revolution that can be considered primarily in terms of the interaction of internal forces.[52] It was not a case of an isolated revolutionary bastion standing embattled against an array of enemies (Russia in 1917 is a better parallel with France in 1789 in that respect). It was not an ideological revolution—not, at least, in the sense of a revolution that aimed to transform the world in accordance with the logic of a new, dominating, idea. Ideas are important, but those that spurred 1989 are old ideas. 1989 did not want to invent anything new. It had had enough of novelties. Indeed, it attempted to recover an older, pre-1789, meaning of revolution: the seventeenth-century understanding of revolution as restoration, as when Clarendon termed the restoration of Charles II in 1660 a "revolution" or Locke saw the 1688 revolution as the restitution of rights usurped by James II.[53]

If 1989 was not parallel to 1789 or 1917, was it parallel to 1848?

For several observers, 1848, "the springtime of nations," offers a better vantage point from which to consider the events of 1989.[54] For one thing, looking forward from 1848 allows us to speak of revolutions, rather than simply revolution, and to acknowledge the distinctiveness of the changes in the different countries of Central and Eastern Europe. At the same time, in both 1848 and 1989 there was the same phenomenon of the "chain reaction" of revolutions, a revolutionary contagion spreading across the whole region. In both cases, too, a key role was played by the flanking superpowers—in Russia's case, the same superpower—in the sequence of events.

Then there is the fact that 1989, like 1848, erupted after nearly forty years of peace and prosperity (though there were growing signs of economic distress). In both cases, too, the revolutions were remarkably peaceful, at least in the early stages (Romania was the obvious exception). In 1848 as in 1989, rulers ceded their thrones almost without a shot's being fired. In both cases they lost their nerve, along with their belief in their right to rule.

More significantly, 1989 was, like 1848, a "revolution of the intellectuals," though not necessarily of the ideologues. It was led by poets, playwrights, musicians, philosophers, journalists, and university professors.[55] "Truth shall prevail" was the motto of 1989. But this was not an ideological slogan, not one that proclaimed that truth had been discovered and only needed to be applied. The revolutions of 1989 and 1848 alike were led by liberals who were fearful of the "democratic despotism" that had befallen the 1789 revolution. Ideology, they were acutely aware, could compromise liberty. For similar reasons, both in 1989 and 1848 there was a fear that the "social question"—the consequences of rapid economic change—could derail the political settlement that was the prime aim of the revolution.

There are further illuminating parallels between the two revolutions. 1848 threw up questions of nationality and of class that returned to haunt the victors of 1989. In 1848, the ethnic melting pot that was the Habsburg Empire exploded under the pressure of nationalism. Germans against Poles, Magyars against Czechs, Czechs against Slovaks: the number of actual and potential ethnic and national conflicts ran into double figures. Many of the same conflicts were being replayed in 1989, with the added complication of state boundaries mostly established in 1918. The case of the Hungarians alone, with large minorities in Transylvania (Romania), Slovakia (Czechoslovakia), and Vojvodina (Yugoslavia), indicates the scale of the national problem.[56] Not its least intransigeant expression was the national question within the Soviet Union itself, inspired both by the internal reform movement and by the example of the East European revolutions beyond Soviet boundaries. The nationalist demands of the Baltic republics and of Georgia, Moldavia, Ukraine, and even Russia, show how possible it might have been for the Soviet Union to go the way of the Habsburg Empire in 1848 and again in 1918.[57]

1848 opened up not just nationalism, but the class struggle. Both Tocqueville and Marx, in their different ways, wrote eloquently about that. What the class struggle—otherwise known as "the social question"—revealed was the possible contradiction between political and economic justice. In 1989 and since, the echoes of this have been strong throughout Eastern Europe, including the Soviet Union. The workers may not have had much love for the old regimes, but they have been accustomed to a certain, quite considerable, degree of economic and social security. The move from a command economy to a market economy, which was necessary for political as much as economic reasons as the social basis of liberalism, was bound to upset that security.[58]

Writing of the 1848 revolution in France, Marx said that "the February Revolution was the beautiful revolution, the revolution of universal sympathy." The June Revolution was, by contrast, "the ugly revolution, the repulsive revolution." It was the point at which the social conflicts hidden beneath the harmony of the February revolution broke through and set Frenchman against Frenchman on the barricades.[59] However, analogies should not be pushed to their extremes. A "June Days" revolution, in that form, is unlikely in Eastern Europe. But the dangers remain. Certainly once the honeymoon period of Civic Forum, New Forum, Democratic Forum, and all the other opposition movements of citizens was over, the underlying economic conflicts were bound to surface.

1848 was the year of the "failed bourgeois revolutions." Liberalism and constitutionalism suffered severe defeats, and the result was a different direction for such societies as Germany and Italy. What greater chance of success had the bourgeois revolutions of 1989, if they were to pick up the legacy of those earlier revolutions? The societies of Eastern Europe were attempting the transition both to a pluralist democracy and to a market economy. In the conditions in which they find themselves, with traditions that are shaky on both counts, this is clearly a formidable challenge. What resources are there to meet the challenge? What are the alternatives in Eastern Europe?

## Capitalism, Socialism, and Democracy

After the revolutions of 1989 it was clear that the international context was likely to be of major importance in determining the future of Eastern Europe. Whether the former communist countries would join the European Economic Community; whether a new and larger federal Europe—from the Atlantic to the Urals?—could be designed to include its eastern and western halves; whether the West would invest on a large scale in Eastern Europe: all these would clearly have a profound, though indeterminate, impact on the economies and societies of the new states.

At a different level, and with even less predictable consequences, was the issue of the end of the Cold War. At the Paris meeting of the Conference on Security and Cooperation in Europe in November 1990, President Gorbachev spoke in ringing tones of "the chance of building a hitherto unknown world order." The Soviet Union, he said, was becoming a state "anchored in the rule of law and political pluralism." Nothing then fundamentally prevented a "united democratic and prosperous Europe" from becoming an "irreversible reality in the coming century." But he warned, too, of the possibilities of the "Balkanization"—or, even worse, "Lebanonization"—of entire regions of the continent.[60]

Because the international arena is the least stable environment—witness the Gulf War—within which to make predictions and projections, I shall say no more here about these hopes and fears. Nor, too, shall I make any attempt to compare "the transition to democracy" in Central and Eastern Europe with what are often said to be similar transitions in southern Europe, South America, and Southeast Asia (not to mention the "denazification" of several Western European states in the postwar period). The parallels are certainly there, and they can be instructive. To consider Spain and Portugal, say, or Chile and Argentina, or South Korea and the Philippines, along with Poland and Hungary, is to be made aware of similar traditions of authoritarianism and militarism that may pose similar problems in the attempts to achieve democracy. And there have also been certain uniformities in the mode of opposition, and in the role of religion in that opposition, in many of these countries.[61]

At the same time, the different historical experiences of these countries and continents limit the usefulness of the comparison. It is, indeed, difficult enough to generalize about Eastern Europe on its own without adding the complication of further comparisons. Moreover, as Ralf Dahrendorf has pointed out, there is one important respect in which Eastern Europe differs fundamentally from these other countries. In none of these others was there the same near-total monopoly of a party over state, economy, and society, making the three "almost indistinguishable" in the communist world. Elsewhere there was authoritarian dictatorship with more or less thriving "unsocial market economies." This affects the scale of the change achieved by the different revolutions. As Dahrendorf has said, "The Portuguese 'revolution of carnations' may sound as appealing as the Czechoslovak 'velvet revolution,' but in fact the notion of revolution is much more applicable to Eastern Europe, where the all-encompassing claims of the ruling *nomenklatura* had to be broken."[62]

The future of Eastern Europe will turn to a good extent on its own internal resources, on the traditions and practices of the various countries now seeking an independent path forward. East Germany is already committed to sharing the destiny of West Germany, with whatever painful experiences, along with the benefits, will accompany the merger. Elsewhere the answers to two sets of questions might throw some light on future outcomes. First, what are the conceptions of politics that are dominant in the outlook of the leaders of the new regimes? With what resources of experience and ideas do they come to their tasks? Second, how completely have the East European states converted to the idea of the market, or of capitalism? Can their future simply be described as the more or less wholesale absorption of capitalist values and practices? What, if anything, is left of socialism?

It has been impossible to ignore, in the writings by and about the East European opposition, the revival of the language of "civil society" and "citizenship." This is for Eastern Europe, says Dahrendorf, "the hour of the citizen." "1989," says Garton Ash, "was the springtime of societies aspiring to be civil. . . . The language of citizenship was important in all these revolutions."[63] By "civil society" in this context is meant not so much—as in the usual Marxist use of the term—the sphere of the private, nonpolitical life of citizens, but rather their associational life in their professional, civic, and other voluntary organizations. Use of the term "civil society" in this sense—Hegelian and

Gramscian—is an attempt to define an alternative realm of the political, a realm that is neither of the party nor of the state, nor, at the same time, is it confined to the concerns of the private life of individuals. It is in the active, educative life of these associations, mediating between the state and the individual, that the politics of citizenship will be sought.[64]

A conception of this sort, with variations, has of course long been the theoretical underpinning of some prominent views of pluralist democracy in the West. It goes back to Montesquieu and Madison, to Burke and Tocqueville and Durkheim, and has been popular with many American and British social scientists.[65] Its fruitfulness in the case of Western societies is not the issue here, nor even its notorious vagueness. What is more problematic is how far it can be realistically applied to the conditions of East European societies. For one of the things repeatedly stressed in the accounts of those societies under communist rule was the more or less total destruction of civil society. In what Václav Havel calls the "post-totalitarian" states of the communist world, society had been atomized, individuals cowed and driven back into private life. The prevailing attitudes toward politics were despair, cynicism, apathy, indifference, and resignation: hardly the qualities to sustain a thriving civic culture.[66] "Voluntary" associations, civic and cultural, were mostly shams, fronts for party control of areas of life where a policy of indirect rule might be preferred to one of direct rule.

It is true that what Adam Michnik calls the strategy of "social self-organization" or "social self-defense" for the reconstitution of civil society has scored some notable successes. Poland is the best example, with the birth of the Workers' Defense Committee (KOR) in 1976 and Solidarity in 1980.[67] But Charter 77 in Czechoslovakia, the "democratic opposition" in Hungary (also launched in 1977), and the numerous citizens' forums created everywhere in the opposition movement leading up to 1989 have shown many of the same characteristics as their Polish counterparts: wide-ranging activities including *samizdat* publishing, trade union organization, and ceaseless political discussion in the workplace, in schools and universities, and anywhere else where the party could be evaded or, increasingly, ignored.

But what has been the fate of these agencies of "social self-organization"? Solidarity, the most spectacular example, was badly split. The civic forums elsewhere also dissolved with the onset of power, or have been pushed aside by other forces. In the 1990 elections the East German New Forum received only 2.9 percent of the vote. In Hungary the Democratic Opposition, which organized the main liberal opposition to Kadarism, was defeated by its more conservative rivals, the Democrative Forum, in the elections of March 1990. In both cases previously loose alliances of opposition groups crystalized into formal political parties. In Czechoslovakia, the Civic Forum indeed swept all before it in the elections of 1990. But in the face of mounting instability and constitutional crisis the harmony of the opposition movement has been shattered. Vaclav Klaus, the finance minister and chairman of Civic Forum, declared that the future of the Civic Forum must be as a "rightwing political party." President Václav Havel, the outstanding symbol of the new politics of nonparty civic opposition, somewhat reluctantly endorsed this view. "The idea of an overwhelming public movement is over," he said.[68]

Everywhere civic associations have been prominent in the period of opposition in the struggle to overthrow the party state. They have been virtual models of democratic, peaceful protest. But, once successful in achieving the immediate goal—the removal of Communist Party rule—they have largely disintegrated. They have been phenomena of extraordinary revolutionary politics; with the onset of ordinary politics they have shown that they lack the capacity to sustain themselves.

This is no shame. It is surely what we should expect. Given the history of *gleichschaltung* in these countries in the last forty years, it is quite extraordinary what they have managed to achieve. Clearly there were spaces, after all, in the totalitarian society. But this is a far different matter from developing the habits and practices that constitute the politics of civil society. Leaving aside the five centuries or so that Norbert Elias allots to the "civilizing process" in Western Europe, we can note that even in T. H. Marshall's more restricted concept of citizenship in Britain the acceptance of the idea, and its imperfect realization, took about three centuries.[69] The United States had rather less time, though the institutions of the colonial period provided a good starting point. In any case, as Dahrendorf points out, the strength of pluralist democracy in America comes not so much from its age as from the fact that "civil society was there first, and the state came later, by the grace of civil society, as it were."[70] In the case of Eastern Europe what has to be contemplated is, in effect, the creation of civil society by the state. In the absence of the necessary intermediate structures, the new regimes will deliberately have to institute autonomous centers of power that will act as a check on their own power. This is a formidable task. Few new states have been successful in it.

It has to be said that the task will not, on the whole, be helped by the political ideas that are being brought to it by many of the new leaders of Eastern Europe. The absence of a functioning civil society, of an independent sphere of public opinion, has produced, as its intellectual counterpart, a conception of politics that deliberately and defiantly turns its back on practical politics. This is the "anti-political politics" that we have already noted in the writings of Václav Havel. György Konrád, another influential advocate of this philosophy, states its basic position in the clearest terms:

> Antipolitics and government work in two different dimensions, two separate spheres. Antipolitics neither supports nor opposes governments; it is something different. . . . A society does not become politically conscious when it shares some political philosophy, but rather when it refuses to be fooled by any one of them. . . . Because politics has flooded nearly every nook and cranny of our lives, I would like to see the flood recede. We ought to depoliticize our lives, free them from politics as from some contagious infection. . . . Official premises belong to the state, homes to "society." Home and free time: these are the spatial and temporal dimensions of civic independence. . . . We are not trying primarily to conquer institutions and shape them in our image but to expand the bounds of private existence.[71]

Konrád may stress the privateness of antipolitics more than other East European intellectuals. But he is at one with them in seeing antipolitics as a separate sphere from ordinary politics. Politics is the Machiavellian sphere of power; antipolitics is the sphere of the mind and spirit. It is the quintessential realm of the intellectuals—the intellectuals who made the revolutions of 1989. The intellectuals are the universal class, the bearers of internationalism and world culture. To the power of the state they oppose the "authority of the spirit." They do not seek political power, nor do they foment strikes and revolutions. They exercise influence indirectly, "by changing a society's customary thinking patterns and tacit compacts."[72]

Václav Havel's powerful account of what he takes to be the only worthwhile kind of politics echoes this conception. For him, antipolitics is "politics as practical morality, as service to the truth, as essentially human . . . care for our fellow humans." It is the politics of the powerless, a politics that opposes truth and morality, even when uttered only by a single voice, to an oppressive system that cannot be challenged by any other means. This might make it sound a politics of last resort, a politics of despair. This is not, at least, Havel's view of it. Out of the Czech people's predicament, out of the whole historical experience of Central Europe, there has emerged a more fundamental understanding of politics than is available to those living in traditional democracies or traditional dictatorships. The experience of "post-totalitarian" systems has forced people to go back to the roots of politics to understand its existential basis. This is a politics beyond parties and movements, beyond even those courageous movements of opposition that arose in Eastern Europe. It is a "living within the truth," within the natural realm of "the existential and the pre-political," whose elemental forces of truth and morality are the weapons to use against the "automatism" and ideology of the political system—any political system. "Living within the truth" confronts "living within a lie" and so exposes the system at its core.[73]

Looking to the future, Havel says:

> People who live in the post-totalitarian system know only too well that the question of whether one or several political parties are in power, and how these parties define and label themselves, is of far less importance than the question of whether or not it is possible to live like a human being. . . . A genuine, profound and lasting change for the better . . . can no longer result from the victory . . . of any particular traditional conception, which can ultimately be only external, that is, a structural or systemic conception. More than ever before, such a change will have to derive from human existence, from the fundamental reconstitution of the position of people in the world, their relationships to themselves and to each other, and to the universe. If a better economic and political model is to be created, then perhaps more than ever before it must derive from profound existential and moral changes in society.[74]

It is true that this was written more than ten years before the 1989 revolution. But there are many more recent similar expressions, by Havel as well as others.[75] If there was a political philosophy to the 1989 revolution in Eastern Europe, it seems to have been made up of elements of this antipolitical politics. As a political philosophy, of the kind discussed in academic seminars, it is perhaps not very original, but it is expressed with depth and feeling. As a testament of the dissident intellectuals of Eastern Europe, it is profoundly moving. More than that, its categories pose a challenge to all existing political systems, Western as well as Eastern.

That is perhaps its greatest problem. One has to ask not how true or attractive its terms are, but how adequate they are to the task facing the new rulers. A political philosophy that is a blanket rejection of all existing forms of politics is all very well for a revolutionary theorist or academic philosopher, but it does not very well equip politicians with an urgent job of reconstruction in front of them. They need to dirty themselves with the business of winning support, building alliances, conciliating old enemies, holding together societies that threaten to split apart under the pressure of class, ethnicity, and nationalism.

The experience of the new rulers has largely been of dissident politics: a politics carried out through *samizdat* publications, covert meetings in private apartments, letters and articles smuggled out of prison and published abroad, quasi-conspiratorial organization. It is the politics of intellectuals who, like the men of 1848, now find themselves, to their own surprise, in power. Like the revolutionaries of 1848, they are threatened on all sides by more seasoned political forces.

There are atavistic nationalists, authoritarian populists, cynical and resentful old-guard conservatives. All of these have large constituencies, based on long-standing traditions and practices, in the mass of the population. The liberals will in most cases have to forge new constituencies, among populations with little experience of, and perhaps not much taste for, liberal democracy.[76]

The politics of truth and authenticity can be a great inspiration. Without it politics can degenerate into mere power seeking and manipulation. But its very sublimity disables it as a guide to the practical problems of the day. Currently what East European politics needs is less of Rousseau and the moral or existential revolution and more of Jeremy Bentham and the politics of practical reconstruction.

There is a final point to be made, one that brings us back to the "death of socialism" and the many other alleged fatalities connected with it. Probably the surest way to stifle liberal democracy in Eastern Europe at birth is the rapid wholesale introduction of market capitalism. Poland may already be an early casualty, with the workers turning to Lech Walesa as the strong leader to save them from some of the consequences of the Balcerowicz plan inspired by the International Monetary Fund (despite Walesa's own clear complicity in the development of the plan). The truth is that, despite the rhetoric of some of the new office holders, there is little evidence that the populations of Eastern Europe have turned their backs on all types and every type of socialism.

The unexpected electoral victory in Hungary of the Democratic Forum over the Alliance of Free Democrats has been plausibly attributed to the Free Democrats' "almost messianic commitment to radical free-market policies" compared with the more cautious approach of their rivals.[77] In the June 1990 elections in Czechoslovakia, the only country in postrevolutionary Eastern Europe where the Communist Party has defiantly refused to "dilute" its name, the Communist Party of Czechoslovakia remarkably received a consistent 13 percent of the vote in almost every region in the country, beating the well-fancied Christian Democrats into third place. It is also clear that the Civic Forum is badly split between those, such as Václav Klaus and Pavel Bratinka, who want a quick transition to a market economy and those, such as Václav Havel and Petr Uhl, who are opposed to "unadorned capitalism" and who have protested against those members of the government who, in Havel's words, are "more Friedmanite than Friedman."[78] In Romania and Bulgaria, rearguard communists, though renouncing their former name, continue to battle for public support; and their success in the 1990 elections in their two countries has generally been accepted as genuine, reflecting either actual support for their policies or at least a disinclination to trust the free-market promises of their liberal opponents. The East Germans have opted for the capitalist paradise of union with West Germany; but the devastating effect of the market on the East German economy and society has already made some former dissidents—not to mention many ordinary workers—look back with nostalgia to at least certain aspects of the old German Democratic Republic.[79]

In the wake of forty years of communist domination and political stagnation, it is hardly surprising if *communism* and even *socialism* are now dirty words in the vocabulary of most parts of Eastern Europe. This may not turn out to be permanent. The dislocations inevitably involved in the conversion to a capitalist economy—assuming that this is the goal—are bound to stimulate the rise of political groupings of the kind we traditionally associate with social democracy in Western Europe. Misha Glenny's assessment seems more accurate than the many pronouncements of radical free marketeers in both East and West: "Conservatives in both West and East have . . . been dancing on what they believe to be the graves of socialism in Warsaw, Berlin,

Prague, Budapest, Bucharest, Sofia and Belgrade. This makes for excellent theatre, but the left's demise is an illusion. As large parts of the population are being adversely affected by the introduction of new economic conditions, they will have to find ways to defend their interests and improve their situation, which is in many cases quite pitiful."[80]

What, in any case, is meant by the phrase *the transition to the free market* in Eastern Europe? What kind of free market? Is it the kind that obtains in the majority of contemporary capitalist societies, including the most successful economically, such as Germany and Japan? Because, if so, as John Kenneth Galbraith is fond of pointing out, this is a "free market" only in name. Capitalism has survived only because it has undergone massive transformation. Crucially, it has come to accept, indeed to promote, a powerful structure of regulation and, in the interests of social peace, a large measure of social welfare. Capitalism in the West and in Japan—and, one might add, the dynamic industrializing states of Southeast Asia—is state-regulated capitalism. It would be a cruel irony if, in their bid to imitate successful Western models, East Europeans allowed themselves to be trapped by the "simplistic ideology" of early industrial capitalism despite its continuing celebration by its more devout theologians in the West. As Galbraith says: "Those who speak, as so many do so glibly, even mindlessly, of a return to the Smithian free market are wrong to the point of a mental vacuity of clinical proportions. It is something in the West we do not have, would not tolerate, could not survive. Ours is a mellow, government-protected life; for Eastern Europeans pure and rigorous capitalism would be no more welcome than it would be for us."[81]

"We say there is no third way. There is no credible alternative between western capitalism and Eastern socialism." So declared a leading member of Hungary's Free Democrats to Timothy Garton Ash.[82] This may be, in a general sense, a fair way of putting it; but it may also be too general, too abstract a formulation. It fails to suggest the variety of the social forms of capitalism. There is a capitalist economic system, now more or less global in its operations, and there are different kinds of capitalist societies. Sweden is capitalist, no doubt, but its welfare system and its policies of redistribution put it at some distance from the capitalist society of the United States. Even if, as seems clear, East Europeans—or at least their leaders—are bent on establishing or restoring some form of capitalist market economy, the manner, timing, and eventual goal of their efforts allow considerable room for choice and debate. Not only must East Europeans, as Adam Michnik has warned, beware of replacing a "utopian socialism" with a "utopian capitalism," a free-market utopia;[83] they must also see that the alternatives in Eastern Europe, however dominated by Western models, can be cast far wider than they currently appear to imagine.

This is not necessarily to smuggle the "third way" in again through the back door. Despite the hopes of certain intellectuals, often those involved in the "new social movements" of East and West, most East European societies (the countries of the former Soviet Union apart) seem to have set themselves firmly on a course toward capitalism.[84] If the third way is regarded as a full-blooded alternative to both "socialism" and "capitalism"—if it is conceived, that is, as a different kind of social system—not only do we lack a coherent account of what it is, but—and perhaps partly for that reason—it is doubtful if it would presently receive any substantial political support from the populations of the East European societies. Time may change this; but for the moment the third way, as a political project, is a pipe dream.

This talk of a third way, the third way as an alternative system, in any case obscures a more important and more relevant consideration. If capitalism is our future for the time being, how are we to think about that capitalism? How are we to live with it, criticize it, challenge its terms, and monitor its progress? Capitalism, to repeat, is not one thing, but many. It has changed greatly over the past two hundred years, and will go on changing. It has coexisted with many social and political forms, some brutal and repressive, some tolerant and democratic. It has spawned, as a "counterculture," some of the most energetic and creative social and cultural movements of the modern period. Whether or not they aimed to overthrow it, they have succeeded in modifying it and redirecting its energies in countless ways. There may be no teleological terminus to capitalism; or, at least, if there is one, it may not be the right thing to be concerned about at the moment. But there is plenty to do in the meantime by way of the constant struggle to civilize capitalism.

Capitalism can, as the many courageous efforts in the past have demonstrated, be made to be more compassionate, more democratic, more responsive to the spiritual and moral needs of individuals. It can be forced to see the necessity of working with rather than against nature. If the attempts to regulate it in this way ultimately kill it off, so be it. By that time we may have come up with something more acceptable to replace it. It may even be called socialism. But that is for a future now some way off. This is the time to be alerted to the problems and possibilities within "actually existing capitalism,'" the system that, now more clearly than ever before, encircles the globe. "Socialism with a human face" may not now have many followers; it is even more important, in the period of capitalism's unrivaled dominance, to make sure that we give capitalism a human face.

This is why one aspect of the 1989 revolutions can seem particularly dispiriting. The victory of the West, of Western political ideals and economic institutions, has had as one of its effects the obliteration of all sense of the differences and divisions that lie within and between societies of the Western type. It is a familiar experience in the history of wars and revolutions. So appalled are people at the monstrosities of one system that, in the relief of being rid of it, they can see the alternative system only in its most resplendent guise. They perceive the gross or general features, the system as type or genus, and are blind or indifferent to the differentiating details that constitute the variety or species. They ignore or look benignly upon the defects of the system as the pardonable faults of an otherwise satisfactory and in any case infinitely preferable social existence. They become, in its defense, *plus royaliste que le roi,* scornful or incredulous of criticisms. Both revolutionaries and counter-revolutionaries have throughout the ages appealed to so natural a feeling at times of social crisis and heightened emotion.

It is natural, but can be baleful. In embracing the Western model so wholeheartedly, the revolutionaries of 1989 have not only caused a certain amount of disquiet—to put it no more strongly—among radicals in the West. More important, they have aroused a chorus of Western triumphalism that threatens to drown all criticism, all sense of alternatives, within the prevailing capitalist mode. "It is striking," as Fred Halliday has remarked, "how, amidst the triumph of consumer capitalism and the collapse of 'communism,' the possibility of aberrations is now being submerged in the name of a new international political and cultural conformity: all aspire to, and supposedly endorse, a composite transnational utopia, distilled from, and defined by, the lifestyles of California, Rheinland-Westfalen and Surrey. That this new utopia contains profound structures of inequality, defined on class, sex, race and regional bases, is evident, but repressed in most prevailing public discourses."[85]

Socialism is dead, chorus the pundits. To which one might fairly reply that, though Stalinist communism may have had its day (though any such prediction is foolhardy), socialism has yet to see its day. But that is, by the way, the sort of remark that many find evasive or frivolous (as with analogous remarks about Christianity). The more important point has to do with socialism not as an alternative to capitalism, but as its most formidable and searching antagonist. Zygmunt Bauman has pointed to socialism's function as the "active utopia" of modern times. It has been the "counterculture of capitalism," the philosophy and political movement that throughout has reminded capitalism of the universalism of its promise and has kept up a relentless critique of its practices.[86] That function continues, and must continue, unabated, the more so now that "actually existing socialism" has ceased to be able to perform it. This suggests a continuing role not just for socialism, but also for utopia.[87]

And was 1989 "the end of history"? Several commentators have pointed out that, whatever the verdict may be for the West or the world as a whole, so far as Eastern Europe is concerned the revolutions of 1989 signify not the end, but "the rebirth of history." Eastern Europe is returning to its past, to the point where its evolution was frozen some forty years ago, in order to resume "its proper history."[88] This claim has to be treated with some caution: what or when was Eastern Europe's "proper history"? But the point has force nevertheless. It reminds us once again of the variety of choices facing the societies of Eastern Europe. The artificial uniformity imposed by membership of the Soviet-dominated "Eastern bloc" has ended. The generic "people's democracies" are rediscovering their own independent histories. They will make their own futures—insofar as any country can in an increasingly interlinked world—according to whatever values and traditions they choose to recover from their past.

In doing so, they may also kick-start the stalled engine of history in the West. Most East Europeans have seen the recovery of their history as a "return to Europe," to quote the Civic Forum's election manifesto issued in June 1990. Again, the vexed questions arise: What is Europe, Which Europe? But there is also another point, forcibly put by Václav Havel on several occasions. To return to Europe does not mean to return to Europe's past or even to its present. Neither of these alternatives, in truth, has much to offer Central and Eastern Europe. To return to Europe must therefore mean to play a part in building a new

Europe. It must mean joining in the creation of a common future. As Havel says, "To ponder our return means for us to ponder a whole Europe, to ponder the Europe of the future."[89]

Does this not also suggest that the impact of the 1989 revolutions will not be restricted to Eastern Europe but will have profound consequences for the politics of the West as well? Edward Thompson has referred to "the spaces of opportunity" opened up by developments in Eastern Europe. He regrets the failure so far of "the Western peace movement and progressive forces" to "hasten on reciprocal process in the West to match the decomposition of Cold War ideological controls in the East."[90] But it is not only radical politics that may be affected by the momentous events in the East. The whole structure of politics, the whole cast of thought, in the West (as in the East) has for the past forty years—perhaps even the past seventy years—been conditioned by Cold War fear and rivalry. The West and its ways may have won that war; but take away the fear and rivalry, and will history be content to slumber, as after a task already done?

## A Further Note

This chapter presents the most general discussion in this book of the 1989 revolutions. Many of its themes—the end of socialism and of history, the idea of revolution and of civil society, the "return to Europe," and the uses of history—are treated in more detail in later chapters. Additional comments are therefore best left in the main to those chapters. But a few points are in order here.

### Events

Since this chapter was first written (though not since it was first published), the Soviet Union has disappeared (in December 1991) and Mikhail Gorbachev, too, has been blown away by the winds of change. Thus was confirmed one of the oldest perceptions of revolutions, that "like Saturn, it devours its children." Gorbachev—having, like the nobility of France in 1789, started the revolution—was himself swept away by the torrent. The failed August 1991 coup against him indirectly prepared his end by immeasurably strengthening the hand of his bitter enemy Yeltsin. It was Gorbachev and the Soviet Union that made the revolutions of 1989 possible; both were among the first victims of those revolutions.

Yugoslavia, too, has all but disappeared. First came the secession of Slovenia, Croatia, Bosnia-Hercegovina, and Macedonia. Then came a bitter and bloody war in Bosnia that ended with a Bosnia more or less partitioned between Serbs, Croats, and Bosnian "Muslims" (religion being in this case the only way this third group could be distinguished from the other two). In 1999 came a further bloody civil war, this time in Serbia, which ended with the formerly autonomous and overwhelmingly Albanian province of Kosovo being created a United Nations-protected territory within the state of Serbia. The prospects of an independent Kosovo (or a Kosovo united to Albania) looked likely, as did the further breakup of what was left of Yugoslavia by the secession of Montenegro from the rump Yugoslav Federation. That would leave Serbia carrying the Yugoslav torch on its own.

Elsewhere in the region of former communist rule there have been other striking, though less brutally conducted, changes. Czechoslovakia is no more. The Czechs and Slovaks have peaceably separated; the Czechoslovak "velvet revolution" was followed fairly swiftly by a "velvet divorce," though this was more a divorce between politicians than between people. East Germany—the former German Democratic Republic—has rejoined West Germany, though the unification has produced great political and economic stresses on both sides. Poland, Hungary, and the Czech Republic have been admitted to NATO, and other countries in the region—such as the newly independent Baltic states of Estonia, Latvia, and Lithuania—are also anxious to join the alliance. There is an even stronger wish to join the European Union. So far no new members from the former communist bloc have been admitted to the "West European club"; who, if any, will get in and when are likely to be major items on the European agenda in the first years of the coming century.

Many of these events are briefly surveyed in new editions of a number of works mentioned in my text. See Joseph Rothschild, *Return to Diversity: A Political History of East Central Europe since World War Two*, second edition (New York: Oxford University Press, 1993); Misha Glenny, *The Rebirth of History: Eastern Europe in the Age of Democracy*, new edition (London: Penguin Books, 1993); Keith Sword, ed., *The Times Guide to Eastern Europe*, second edition (London: Times Books, 1991); Stephen White, Alex Pravda, and Zvi Gitelman, eds., *Russian and Post-Soviet Politics*, third edition (London: Macmillan, 1994). In addition, for general treatments of post-1991 developments, see Stephen White, Judy Blatt, and Paul G. Lewis, eds.,

*Developments in East European Politics* (London: Macmillan, 1993); Leslie Holmes, *Post-Communism: An Introduction* (Durham, N.C.: Duke University Press, 1997); R. J. Crampton, *Eastern Europe in the Twentieth Century—and After* (New York: Routledge, 1997), 391–458.

On Gorbachev, Yeltsin, and the breakup of the Soviet Union, see Andrei Grachev, *Final Days: The Inside Story of the Collapse of the Soviet Union* (Boulder, Colo.: Westview Press, 1995); Jonathan Steele, *Eternal Russia: Yeltsin, Gorbachev and the Mirage of Democracy* (Boston: Faber and Faber, 1995); Jerry F. Hough, *Democratization and Revolution in the USSR, 1985–1991* (Washington: The Brookings Institution Press, 1997). On the background to the changes, see also Moshe Lewin, *The Gorbachev Phenomenon: A Historical Interpretation* (London: Hutchinson Radius, 1989); David Lane, *Soviet Society under Perestroika* (Boston: Unwin Hyman, 1990); Geoffrey Hosking, *The Awakening of the Soviet Union* (London: Mandarin, 1991); Stephen White, *Gorbachev and After* (Cambridge: Cambridge University Press, 1991); Rachel Walker, *Six Years that Shook the World: Perestroika—the Impossible Project* (Manchester and New York: Manchester University Press, 1993).

On the breakup of Yugoslavia, see Bogdan Denitch, *Ethnic Nationalism: The Tragic Death of Yugoslavia,* revised edition (Minneapolis: University of Minnesota Press, 1996); Branka Magas, *The Destruction of Yugoslavia: Tracing the Break-Up, 1980–1992* (London: Verso, 1992); Misha Glenny, *The Fall of Yugoslavia: The Third Balkan War* (London: Penguin, 1992). On the breakup of Czechoslovakia, see Paul Wilson, "The End of the Velvet Revolution," *New York Review of Books* (August 13, 1992): 57–63, and "Czechoslovakia: The Pain of Divorce," *New York Review of Books* (December 17, 1992), 69–75; Jiri Musil, ed., *The End of Czechoslovakia* (Budapest: Central European University Press, 1995); Carol Skalnik Leff, *The Czech and Slovak Republics* (Boulder, Colo.: Westview Press, 1996); John F. N. Bradley, *Post-Communist Czechoslovakia* (New York: Columbia University Press, 1997). On German reunification, see Timothy Garton Ash, *In Europe's Name: Germany and the Divided Continent* (New York: Vintage Books, 1994); Harold James and Maria Stone, *When the Wall Came Down: Reactions to German Unification* (New York: Routledge, 1993); Pekka Kalevi Hamalainen, *Uniting Germany: Actions and Reactions* (Boulder, Colo.: Westview Press, 1994). See also the works discussed by Gordon Craig, "United We Fall," *New York Review of Books* (January 13, 1994): 36–40.

## The 1989 Revolutions

I need to add new or omitted contributions to the literature. For additional general accounts, see Alex Callinicos, *The Revenge of History: Marxism and the Eastern European Revolutions* (Cambridge: Polity Press, 1991); Judy Blatt, *East Central Europe from Reform to Transformation* (London: Pinter, 1991); Vladimir Tismaneanu, *Reinventing Politics: Eastern Europe from Stalin to Havel* (New York: The Free Press, 1992); Ken Jowitt, *New World Disorder: The Leninist Extinction* (Berkeley: University of California Press, 1992); Bruce Ackerman, *The Future of Liberal Revolution* (New Haven: Yale University Press, 1992); Gale Stokes, *The Walls Came Tumbling Down: The Collapse of Communism in Eastern Europe* (New York: Oxford University Press, 1993); Mark Frankland, *The Patriots' Revolution: How Eastern Europe Toppled Communism and Won Its Freedom* (Chicago: Ivan R. Dee, 1993); Leslie Holmes, *The End of Communist Power: Anti-Corruption Campaigns and Legitimation Crisis* (Cambridge: Polity Press, 1993); Michael Waller, *The End of the Communist Power Monopoly* (New York: Manchester University Press, 1993). See also David S. Mason, *Revolution and Transition in East-Central Europe,* second edition (Boulder, Colo.: Westview Press, 1996); Milton F. Goldman, *Revolution and Change in Central and Eastern Europe* (Armonk, N.Y.: M. E. Sharpe, 1996); Daniel Chirot, ed., *The Crisis of Leninism and the Decline of the Left: The Revolutions of 1989* (Seattle: University of Washington Press, 1991); Ivo Banac, ed., *Eastern Europe in Revolution* (Ithaca, N.Y.: Cornell University Press, 1992); J. Adam, ed., *Why Did the Socialist System Collapse in Central and Eastern European Countries?* (London: Macmillan, 1996); John Elster, ed., *The Roundtable Talks and the Breakdown of Communism* (Chicago: Chicago University Press, 1996); Valerie Bunce, *Subversive Institutions: The Design and Destruction of Socialism and the State* (Cambridge: Cambridge University Press, 1999); Vladimir Tismaneanu, ed., *The Revolutions of 1989* (New York: Routledge, 1999); Sorin Antohi and Vladimir Tismaneanu, eds., *Between Past and Future: The Revolutions of 1989 and Their Aftermath* (Budapest: Central European Press, 1999).

See also the special issue of *East European Politics and Societies* 13, no. 2 (1999): "The Revolutions of 1989: Lessons of the First Post-Communist Decade."; and the new edition, with a new postscript "Ten Years After," of Timothy Garton Ash, *The Magic Lantern: The Revolution of '89 Witnessed in Warsaw, Budapest, Berlin and Prague* (New York: Random House, 1999).

In addition, there are the following book chapters and articles: Daniel Chirot, "What Happened in Eastern Europe in 1989?" in Chirot, ed., *The Crisis of Leninism and the Decline of the Left,* 3–32; Ferenc Miszlivetz, "The Unfinished Revolutions of 1989: The Decline of the Nation-State?" *Social Research* 58, no. 4 (winter 1991): 781–804; Sasha Weitman, "Thinking the Revolutions of 1989," *British Journal of Sociology* 43, no. 1 (1992): 11–24; S. N. Eisenstadt, "The Breakdown of Communist Regimes and the Vicissitudes of Modernity," *Daedalus* 121, no. 2 (spring 1992): 21–41; Barbara A. Misztal, "Understanding Political Change in Eastern Europe: A Sociological Perspective," *Sociology* 27, no. 3 (1993): 451–70; George Schöpflin, "The End of Communism in Central and Eastern Europe," in George Schöpflin, *Politics in Eastern Europe* (Oxford: Blackwell, 1993), 224–55; Ivan Szelenyi and Balazs Szelenyi, "Why Socialism Failed: Toward a Theory of System Breakdown—Causes of Disintegration of East European State Socialism," *Theory and Society* 23, no. 2 (1994): 211–31; Andrew G. Walder, "The Decline of Communist Power: Elements of a Theory of Institutional Change," *Theory and Society* 23, no. 2 (1994): 297–323; Jeffrey C. Isaac, "The Meanings of 1989," *Social Research* 63, no. 2 (1996): 291–344; Larry Ray, "The Rectifying Revolutions?" in Larry Ray, *Social Theory and the Crisis of State Socialism* (Cheltenham, U.K.: Edward Elgar, 1996), 167–99; Gale Stokes, "Modes of Opposition Leading to Revolution in Eastern Europe," in Gale Stokes, *Three Eras of Political Change in Eastern Europe* (New York and Oxford: Oxford University Press, 1997), 161–80.

On the revolutions in particular countries, see Jadwiga Staniszkis, *The Dynamics of the Breakthrough in Eastern Europe: The Polish Experience* (Berkeley: University of California Press, 1990); David Ost, *Solidarity and the Politics of Anti-Politics: Opposition and Reform in Poland since 1968* (Philadelphia: Temple University Press, 1990); Roman Laba, *The Roots of Solidarity* (Princeton: Princeton University Press, 1991); Lawrence Goodwyn, *Breaking the Barrier: The Rise of Solidarity in Poland* (New York: Oxford University Press,

1991); George Sanford, ed., *Democratization in Poland 1988-90* (London: Macmillan, 1992); Janine P. Holc, "Solidarity and the Polish State: Competing Discursive Strategies on the Road to Power," *East European Politics and Societies* 6, no. 2 (1992): 121–40; Andrzej W. Tymowski, "Poland's Unwanted Social Revolution," *East European Politics and Societies* 7, no. 2 (1993): 169–202; Jan Kubik, *The Power of Symbols against the Symbols of Power: The Rise of Solidarity and the Fall of State Socialism in Poland* (University Park, Pa.: Pennsylvania State University Press, 1994). See also György Csepeli and Antal Örkény, eds., *Ideology and Political Beliefs in Hungary: The Twilight of State Socialism* (London: Pinter, 1992); Nigel Swain, *Hungary: The Rise and Fall of Feasible Socialism* (London: Verso, 1992); László Bruszt, "1989: The Negotiated Revolution in Hungary," in A. Bozóki, A. Körösényi, and G. Schöpflin, eds., *Post-Communist Transition: Emerging Pluralism in Hungary* (London: Pinter, 1992), 45–59; Agnes Horváth and Arpád Szakolczai, *The Dissolution of Communist Power: The Case of Hungary* (New York: Routledge, 1992); Rudolf L. Tökes, *Hungary's Negotiated Revolution: Economic Reform, Social Change and Political Succession* (Cambridge: Cambridge University Press, 1996); Bernard Wheaton and Zdenek Kavan, *The Velvet Revolution: Czechoslovakia, 1988–1991* (Boulder, Colo.: Westview Press, 1992); Ladislav Holy, "The End of Socialism in Czechoslovakia," in C. M. Hann, ed., *Socialism: Ideals, Ideologies, and Local Practice* (London: Routledge, 1993), 204–17. See also Theodor Draper, "A New History of the Velvet Revolution," *New York Review of Books* (January 14, 1993), 14–20, and "The End of Czechoslovakia," *New York Review of Books* (January 28, 1993): 20–26; "Special Section on the Former Czechoslovakia," *Telos* 94 (winter 1992–93); Melvin J. Lasky, *Voices in a Revolution: The Collapse of East German Communism* (New York: Transaction Publishers, 1992); Christian Joppke, "Why Leipzig? 'Exit' and 'Voice' in the East German Revolution," *German Politics* 2, no. 3 (1993): 393–414, *East German Dissidents and the Revolution of 1989* (London: Macmillan, 1994), and "Intellectuals, Nationalism, and the Exit from Communism: The Case of East Germany," *Comparative Studies in Society and History* 37, no. 2 (1995): 213–41; Lawrence H. McFalls, *Communism's Collapse, Democracy's Demise? The Cultural Context and Consequences of the East German Revolution* (London: Macmillan, 1994); Charles S. Maier, *Dissolution: The Crisis of*

*Communism and the End of East Germany* (Princeton: Princeton University Press, 1997).

Romania's 1989 revolution has continued to generate more controversy than most of the others. For an account that more or less takes a position similar to mine, see John Sislin, "Revolution Betrayed? Romania and the National Salvation Front," *Studies in Comparative Communism* 24, no. 4 (1991): 395–411. See also Istvan Deak, "Survivors," *New York Review of Books* (March 5, 1992), 43–51. Deak raises the question of "whether [Ceausescu] was brought down by a spontaneous popular rising or by a Communist clique that cleverly exploited a popular uprising, or whether the popular uprising itself had been stimulated by a group of Communists intent on seizing power." Ibid., 45. Though he says that the events of those days and months are "still shrouded in mystery," he thinks it "much more likely that it was popular revolution and not the conspirators which was responsible for overthrowing the dictators." This is his response to two correspondents, George Ross and Radu J. Bogdan, who both put forth the opposing view. See the exchange in the *New York Review of Books* (May 28, 1992), 56–57, and the *New York Review of Books* (July 16, 1992): 53–54. Although Deak does not provide any new evidence for his view and developments after 1989 largely confirmed the argument of a "palace revolution," there is clearly much more to be learned about what took place. For a good narrative account that sees the revolution "snatched" out of the hands of the people by the anti-Ceausescu communist conspirators, see Nestor Ratesh, *Romania: The Entangled Revolution* (New York: Praeger, 1991); see also Matei Calinescu and Vladimir Tismaneanu, "The 1989 Revolution and Romania's Future," *Problems of Communism* 40, no. 1 (1991): 42–59. For a strong statement, based on new evidence, of the view that the "revolution" was fomented by Iliescu and the anti-Ceausescu faction backed by the Soviets, see John Simpson, "Ten Days That Fooled the World," *The Independent* (December 16, 1994), p. 14. A restatement of the view of the revolution as "democratic" and popular, together with a critique of the "conspiracy" theory, is Richard Andrew Hall, "The Uses of Absurdity: The Staged War Theory and the Romanian Revolution of December 1989," *East European Politics and Societies* 13, no. 3 (1999): 501–42.

Finally, I should mention a number of books that provide valuable primary material—writings and speeches by some of the principal

participants, eyewitness accounts, historical documents—for think-
ing about the meaning of the revolutions of 1989. See William M.
Brinton and Alan Rinzler, eds., *Without Force or Lies: Voices from the
Revolution of Central Europe in 1989–90* (San Francisco: Mercury
House, 1990); Dirk Philipsen, *We Were the People: Voices from East
Germany's Revolutionary Autumn of 1989* (Durham, N.C.: Duke
University Press, 1992); Lyman H. Letgers, ed., *Eastern Europe:
Transformation and Revolution, 1945–1991* (Lexington, Mass.: D. C.
Heath, 1992); Tim D. Whipple, ed., *After the Velvet Revolution:
Václav Havel and the New Leaders of Czechoslovakia Speak Out*
(New York: Freedom House, 1991). For brief historical treatments of
the whole period since 1945, see also Patrick Brogan, *The Captive
Nations: Eastern Europe, 1945–1990* (New York: Avon Books, 1990);
Geoffrey Swain and Nigel Swain, *Eastern Europe since 1945* (London:
Macmillan, 1993); Paul Lewis, *Central Europe since 1945* (London:
Longman, 1993). There is also much useful historical material in
Z. A. B. Zeman, *The Making and Breaking of Communist Europe*
(Oxford: Blackwell, 1991). And, for the important role of religion in
the 1989 revolutions, see Niels Nielsen, *Revolutions in Eastern Europe:
The Religious Roots* (Maryknoll, N.Y.: Orbis Books, 1991); George
Weigel, *The Final Revolution: The Resistance Church and the Col-
lapse of Communism* (New York: Oxford University Press, 1992);
William H. Swatos, Jr., ed., *Politics and Religion in Central and East-
ern Europe* (New York: Praeger, 1994).

## Ideas, Ideologies, and Ideals

These are mostly taken up in later chapters, so additional discussion is
reserved for them. I can note here, though, that one of the principal
contributions, Francis Fukuyama's article "The End of History?" has
been converted into a full-length book: Francis Fukuyama, *The End of
History and the Last Man* (London: Penguin Books, 1992). Some of
the other contributions, by Habermas, Hobsbawm, and others on the
left, have been anthologized in Robin Blackburn, ed., *After the Fall: The
Failure of Communism and the Future of Socialism* (New York: Verso,
1991). For some stimulating discussions, see also the special issue of
*Daedalus*: "The Exit from Communism," *Daedalus*, 121, no. 2 (spring
1992); the review symposium "The Great Transformations? Social
Change in Eastern Europe," *Contemporary Sociology* 21 (May 1992),
and the special issue of *Theology and Society*: "Theoretical Implications

of the Demise of State Socialism," *Theory and Society* 23, no. 2 (1994). I should also mention here an earlier book that remains invaluable for the breadth of its coverage and the perceptiveness of its judgments: Jacques Rupnik, *The Other Europe: The Rise and Fall of Communism in East-Central Europe* (New York: Pantheon Books, 1989).

*Three*

# The 1989 Revolutions and the Idea of Europe

*For a thousand years, Czechoslovakia was part of the West. Today, it is part of the empire to the east. I would feel a great deal more uprooted in Prague than in Paris.*

Milan Kundera

*It is in the West's own interest to seek the integration of Eastern and Central Europe into the family of European democracy because otherwise it risks creating a zone of hopelessness, instability and chaos, which would threaten Western Europe every bit as much as the Warsaw Pact tank divisions of old.*

Václav Havel

## The 1989 Revolutions As an International Phenomenon

Revolutions have always, since the seventeenth century at least, been international. They have embodied ideas—the rule of law, tolerance, justice, freedom, equality—which, whatever their particular form and provenance, have crossed frontiers to become the property of a host of nations. Increasingly they have become the inheritance of the whole world. Even where, as in the case of the English Civil War and the American War of Independence, the participants may have genuinely thought they were arguing particular cases appropriate to their particular countries alone, it proved impossible to contain the forces of example and emulation. The ideas of the English Civil War survived the Restoration to inspire the men of 1776 across the Atlantic; the Americans' struggle against the British, in turn, provided the example and the rallying cry to the French in their own conflicts in 1789.

It was the French who generalized their revolution to make its principles the principles of the whole world. Since the time of the French Revolution it has indeed been possible, and plausible, to argue that revolution in the modern world partakes of the character of an international civil war.[1] Revolutionaries have appealed to like-minded people in other countries as potential allies; counter-revolutionaries have done the same. The armies of many nations have marched back and forth across national frontiers in pursuit of various revolutionary or counter-revolutionary aims. Often a country could, without direct intervention but merely by a show of support or displeasure, influence the outcome of a revolution. Such was the case with both Britain and Russia throughout the nineteenth century. In the twentieth century the United States and the Soviet Union have played similar roles. Communist revolutions, the principal revolutions of our century, are indeed more or less by definition international, irrespective of the will or intention of the revolutionaries. In this sense the Russian Revolution of 1917 set the seal on the international character of modern revolutions.[2]

So there is nothing strange, in principle, in considering the 1989 revolutions in Central and Eastern Europe from the point of view of their international significance. Neither participants nor observers, in fact, seemed capable of thinking about them in any other way. The 1989 revolutions were accompanied by a series of apocalyptic utterances that purported to see in the revolutions not merely a transnational significance, but an almost metaphysical symbolism. The 1989 revolutions, it was said, spelled the end of communism, or of socialism. They were the decisive repudiation of all utopian experiments. They represented no less than "the end of history," the final and irreversible victory of modern liberal ideas over all competitors. The very form of the revolutions, as a chain reaction spreading rapidly across the middle of the continent, suggested a force and a purpose that transcended the concerns of individual countries.[3]

Even with the less grandiose claims there was a distinct sense of an objective movement sweeping across a whole continent. The 1989 revolutions, many said, represented the "return to Europe" of Central and Eastern Europe after a lengthy period of exile. They were also, so some claimed, the assertion or reassertion of a distinctively Central European identity, a culture and a set of values that had their own unique contribution to make to the totality of European society. They were the recovery of earlier traditions and earlier histories whose principles and artificially arrested development the revolutions had set free. In this view the 1989 revolutions spelled not so much the end of history as its rebirth.[4]

All these claims serve to underline the extent to which the 1989 revolutions were an international phenomenon right from the start. In this they continued the general pattern of twentieth-century revolutions. But they appeared to go beyond it in the unusual degree to which they were marked by this feature. In the events of 1989 one has the sense that many of the participants seemed to be observing themselves and their actions from the outside, as it were. They were the spectators of happenings whose origins seemed to lie beyond their world, and over whose outcome they had only limited control. This is perhaps what Václav Havel had in mind when he referred to that "something beyond us, something maybe even unearthly," that played a part in the 1989 revolutions.[5] Certainly *externality* seems the hallmark of the 1989 revolutions, to a greater extent than with any other revolution this century. The causes of the revolutions, and the conditions of their success, were largely external (changes in Soviet policy); the ideas were mainly derived from external sources (Western liberal ideas going back to the Enlightenment and the French Revolution); the models of the revolution were also derivative (from the revolutions of 1789 and 1848, mostly); and the fate of the revolutions in the individual countries is, by general consent, dependent to a large degree on the reactions and intentions of the international community toward the new regimes.[6]

There is a further sense in which the international character of the 1989 revolutions reveals itself. Everyone is convinced that, except in the unlikely event of a return to the pre-1989 order in Eastern Europe, the 1989 revolutions initiated a new phase in international history. The prospect opens up of a decisive realignment of blocs and regions in Europe. The "end of the Cold War"—if such indeed proves to be the case—of course suggests a far more profound realignment in the world as a whole. The determining influence of superpower rivalry and struggle for hegemony may be at an end; the "three worlds" of conventional analysis may turn out, more clearly than ever before, to be only one. The Gulf War has already provided a spectacular instance of the new things that may be in store in a changed world order in which one of the erstwhile superpowers is effectively disabled.

To speculate further on this would take me and, I suspect, most people beyond the range of sufficient competence. In this chapter I want mainly to examine the 1989 revolutions in their specifically European context. What sort of Europe did they aspire to? What does it mean to speak of their "return to Europe"? To what extent is there a "Central European way," and what part might it play in a future Europe? How much realism and how much fantasy reside in these ideas? To discuss these questions is of course not simply to talk about the countries that experienced the 1989 revolutions. It is to talk about the European experience as a whole, its past and its possible future. Here is yet another way in which the astonishing events of 1989—predicted by virtually no one—disclose their extraordinary fruitfulness.

## The Idea of Central Europe

The "rediscovery of Central Europe" was one of the great themes of 1989.[7] The revolutions did not, of course, begin the process of rediscovery. Rather, one might say they symbolized it. More than that, they aimed to realize its aspirations. An idea that, like the idea of Poland in the last century, had been partly elaborated in exile—in Paris and New York, partly in "internal exile" in Prague and Budapest—now arrived at its moment of truth. What could it offer, and with what hope of realization?

The idea of Central Europe is primarily a "contrast concept." Its structure and content are determined to a good extent by what it opposes, or what opposes it, what it excludes, and what seeks to exclude it. "Central Europe" as a concept is not necessarily marginal, but it is to a good extent residual. It is what remains after you have taken away "Western" and "Eastern" Europe.

There is, it is true, the germ of an independent content in a previously existing form. The idea of Central Europe is, properly speaking, a twentieth-century idea. But it harks back irresistibly to a past stretching back three centuries or more, the period of the Habsburg Empire and its later incarnation, the Austro-Hungarian Empire.

The lands of what later came to be called Central Europe did not all belong to the Austro-Hungarian Empire (much of Poland, for example, was ruled by Russia, and parts of Hungary were ruled by the

Ottoman Turks); but most of them did. After the Empire was dissolved in 1918 and the independent nations of Central Europe were hurled into the vortex first of fascism and then of communism, it was only natural that some intellectuals should look back nostalgically to the empire and to wonder if it had not, after all, offered some kind of home to the many nationalities of Central Europe. And not only a political haven. It is not only Central Europeans who have pondered deeply the extraordinary outburst of creative energy in the cities of the empire in the last years of the nineteenth century and the early years of this fading century. A culture that could give rise to Kafka, Musil, Kokoschka, Mahler, Schönberg, Kraus, Freud, Wittgenstein—was this not something to feel intense pride in? And might it not offer something of a model for a future Central Europe?

We know how partial this picture is. We know that it speaks mainly of the life of a few of the cities—Vienna, Budapest, Prague—and a few of the peoples—Germans, Magyars, Jews—of the many that made up the Habsburg Empire. We know, too, that the Vienna that produced Freud and Wittgenstein also bred Lueger and Schönerer, who taught Hitler his politics and persuaded a reluctant Herzl that Zionism was the only solution to the Jewish question.[8] Nevertheless, there remains an undeniable seductiveness in the idea of the empire. Who can resist the appeal of the self-description of Odon von Horvath, the author of *Tales from the Vienna Woods* (1930): "If you ask me what is my native country, I answer: I was born in Fiume, I grew up in Belgrade, Budapest, Pressburg, Vienna and Munich, and I have a Hungarian passport; but I have no fatherland. I am a very typical mix of old Austria-Hungary: at once Magyar, Croatian, German and Czech; my country is Hungary, my mother tongue is German."[9]

Insofar as a concept of Central Europe was developed during the time of the Austro-Hungarian Empire, it was couched in this spirit of cosmopolitanism and cultural pluralism. Its aspirations were universalistic and supranational, disdaining what Bismarck once contemptuously referred to as the "tribal claims" of Central Europe. "The idea of the Austrian Empire," wrote Franz Werfel, "required from the men who composed it their own transformation. . . . It implied that they were not just Germans, Czechs, Poles but men with a higher, universal, identity."[10] This Rousseauan or Hegelian transformation of self was unfortunately only too rarely achieved by the men who ran the empire. Germans and Hungarians, aided by Jews, only too clearly ruled

the roost. Hence the typical expression of the Central European concept increasingly took on a mocking or satirical air. The best-known
of these is undoubtedly Robert Musil's bitingly ironic account, in *The
Man without Qualities* (1930–32), of "Kakania": a contradictory,
confused realm of "*kaiserlich und königlich*" rule, and also, the name
implies, "Shitland."[11]

It was, however, only during World War I and its aftermath—that
is, after the breakup of the Habsburg Empire—that the idea of Central
Europe properly developed. In the years since, it has become obvious
to most serious commentators that Austria-Hungary cannot serve as a
model for a regenerated Central Europe. It is possible to mourn the
downfall of the empire as a tragic lost opportunity, even to regard its
existence, as Milan Kundera does, as "irreplaceable."[12] But the idea of
reviving Austria-Hungary, in any real sense, is an empty dream. There
are many reasons for this, but one of the most important has to do
with the disappearance of the structural diversity that, it is generally
agreed, gave the empire its vitality and creativity (as well as its
headaches).

Austria-Hungary was not simply a congeries of various nations
under the aegis of the Habsburg emperor. More significantly, it was a
group of territories in which different ethnic groups occupied the same
space. Budapest, for instance, was a city in which Magyars, Germans,
and Jews interacted in a complex, unequal division of labor. Most
other cities and regions were similarly mixed. What has happened
since 1918 has been a progressive homogenization of the various territories that once made up the empire. The Holocaust removed most of
the Jews from Central Europe. Forced "repatriation" and expulsion
after World War II removed most of the Germans from Poland and
Czechoslovakia. These two groups, which had played a critical commercial and cultural role in the life of the region, were the largest minority groups in the lands between Vienna and Moscow. Policies of
population exchange and enforced resettlement were applied to other
groups after 1945, further "clarifying" the ethnic composition of the
Central European states. As Jacques Rupnik has said: "The complex
Central European ethnic puzzle was simplified through murder, migration, and forced assimilation. What was left in 1945 was a series
of ethnically 'pure' states incorporated into the Soviet Empire. The
great dream of rightwing nationalists finally came through under the
Communists."[13]

It hardly needs saying that ethnic problems in Central Europe remain acute and the source of unending conflict (for instance, the position of the Hungarians in Transylvania and Slovakia and of the Slovaks in Czechoslovakia—not to mention that of the Gypsies everywhere in the region). The point, however, is one of the relative significance of the ethnic mix in this area. As Tony Judt says, "On the whole the furious arguments around these questions which characterized the history of East-Central Europe from 1848 to 1939 are . . . largely in the past. . . . When compared to the patchwork of 1938, for example, not to mention 1914, the problem of ethnic, religious and national minorities in Central and Eastern Europe is much diminished."[14] That *terrible simplification* that has had, from a political point of view, a pacifying effect, has had, from a cultural point of view, a narcotizing effect. Certainly if part of the appeal of Central Europe is the memory of past cultural glories, the grim "rationalization" of the national question in the region makes the revival of such glories less likely.

It is likely that no positive concept of Central Europe can do without some remembrance of the Austro-Hungarian Empire. The historical resonances are too powerful (the ubiquity of the baroque, for one thing), the cultural achievements too rich, not to be pressed into service of the idea. But what have mainly competed for attention in the twentieth century are ideas of Central Europe that acknowledge the historical and political realities of the region. Here the perception of Central Europe as something residual, as "the lands in-between," has dominated the debate.[15]

We can pass quickly over the idea of *Mitteleuropa* announced by Friedrich Naumann and other German publicists in the midst of World War I. This proposal of an economically autarkic and politically federal superstate *(Oberstaat)*, driven by the spirit of a new Germany *(Neudeutsches Wesen)*, was a scarcely disguised cover for German imperialism in the area. The same concept, tied now also to the notion of *lebensraum,* served the Nazis equally well in their designs on Central and Eastern Europe.[16]

It is interesting that the man who apparently was the first to coin the term *Central Europe* at the turn of the century, the British geographer Sir Halford Mackinder, had in mind the creation of a strong buffer zone between Germany and Russia. This was the proposal for Central Europe that he urged upon the Peace Conference at Versailles in his book *Democratic Ideas and Reality* (1919). Mackinder argued that the Wilsonian ideal of national self-determination was a dangerous delusion in the conditions of Central Europe. Applied there, it would create an unstable and vulnerable region of small states. The need was for a strong, unified power that was able to stand up to both Germany and Russia, and so prevent the domination of Eastern Europe—and, Mackinder believed, the world—by one or the other of these two states.[17]

There is a certain continuity between this hard-headed, realpolitik version of Central Europe and the more liberal concept espoused by Czech President Tomas Masaryk in the interwar period. Masaryk accepted, indeed proclaimed, the need for democracy and national self-determination in Central Europe (or what he preferred to call—to distinguish it from the German *Mitteleuropa* concept—East Central Europe). The peoples of this area had, for far too much of their history, been subjected to alien and despotic rule. They needed to discover, or rediscover, their own principles of development. But, like Mackinder, Masaryk was well aware of the threat posed to this project by the historic "superpowers" in the region: Germany to the west and Russia to the east. Unlike Mackinder, he was unwilling to accept the idea of a supranational state in Central Europe. This was too strongly reminiscent of the old Habsburg monarchy. Masaryk put his faith in the power of the democratic and liberal spirit of Central Europe to create an autonomous zone, a "third force," between Germany and Russia.[18]

What might appear, with hindsight, utopian in the conditions of the 1920s and 1930s did not seem quite so to the intellectuals of the 1970s and 1980s, who once again took up the Central European idea. Masaryk's vision lived again, but now in a radically different historical and political context. Where once Central Europe was primarily defined against the threat from Germany, it has, since 1945, been defined by Russian domination. The rediscovery of Central Europe is a movement associated with the "long revolution against Yalta."[19] "Central Europe," in this phase of its history, is a concept opposed to "Eastern Europe." Its countries seek to recover their independent identity after forty years of forced—and, as they see it, artificial—absorption into Eastern Europe. And "Eastern Europe"—that is, the Soviet Union— has, since Gorbachev, seen fit to loosen its hold on Central Europe to the point where most of the nations in the region are now formally free to pursue their own paths ("the Sinatra doctrine"). Moreover, the existence of a strong and relatively unified Western Europe not only acts as a pole of attraction to Central Europeans; it offers some sort of guarantee that their newly found freedom will not be as precarious as it was in the interwar period.

## Central Europe: A Middle Way? A Third Way? A Western Way?

There is no reason, in principle, why this revived interest in Europe should not also keep alive the idea of Central Europe as a "third force," or a "third way." This has always been part of its traditional appeal: Central Europe as a buffer zone, as a cultural and political zone of transition between East and West. Such a conception emphasizes the historical uniqueness and the distinctive mission of Central Europe. Central Europe, says Agnes Heller, provides a "middle way" between Western individualism and Eastern collectivism. This puts the stress on ideology and values, on what Central Europe has to offer the world.[20] Others, such as István Bibó and Mihaly Vajda, stress more the distinctive historical and sociological character of Central Europe as a region lacking—or, what perhaps comes to the same thing, possessing—both the autonomous "civil society" of the West and the state absolutism of the East.[21]

But the difficulties—or perhaps, rather, the ambiguities—of this position are well illustrated in the thinking of the Hungarian intellectual György Konrád. Konrád says firmly: "On no account are we West Europeans but we are not East Europeans either."[22] His book *Antipolitics* is subtitled *Mitteleuropäische Meditationen*. Konrád speaks of "the consciousness of Central Europe," of a "Central European strategy." Central Europe is marked out as the region of "antipolitics." It is a place where civil society has to turn its back on the state and replace it with its own values and structures. Poland's Solidarity—"a reference to society's spontaneous cohesion, independent of the state"—is "the true Central European type of movement, different from Western and Eastern models." It puts the emphasis on "communal self-governance," and "the demand for self-government is the organizing focus of the new Central European ideology."[23]

Central Europeans reject the privatized, consumerist, individualist ideology of Western capitalism as much as they reject the totalitarianism of the East. Friendship and sociability—rather than the private life of the nuclear family—remain core Central European values. Central

Europe, says Konrád, still, unlike the West, preserves something of the European past. "We have not yet destroyed the old, green Europe," he says. "Here we can still have a great deal of what has perished in the developed West (where life is bleaker for its loss)." Central Europe today may be only a dream, but it is a dream based on historical reality. In any case, it is a necessary dream, a "cultural counterhypothesis" that must be kept alive as the goal of current aspirations. Central Europe has "the allure of nostalgia and utopia." It is the function of the intellectuals to nourish this dream; for, more than anywhere else in Europe, they are the bearers of spiritual and cultural authority in the face of an amoral and Machiavellian politics.[24]

But in the same book Konrád can also write: "It is East Central Europe's historical misfortune that it was unable to become independent after the collapse of Eastern, Tartar-Turkish hegemony and later the German-Austrian hegemony of the West, and that it once again came under Eastern hegemony, this time of the Soviet-Russian type. This is what prevents our area from exercising the Western option taken out a thousand years ago, even though that represents our profoundest historical inclinations."[25]

This appears to subsume the Central European identity in some larger, but nevertheless distinctly West European, tradition. The impression is reinforced by Konrád's appeal to a continental "European utopia" that offers the prospect of an escape from "the tutelage of the two nuclear world powers." This utopia, "rooted in our past and present," consists of "a wealth of nuance, the art of fine compromise, an apprehension of our environment as art, a wry independence of personality toward the fetishes of state and money, and a sense of man's superiority to his works."[26] Konrád also refers to "liberalism" as the most acceptable political philosophy and practice for Central Europe. This principle, which is seen as a general European legacy, is also linked to democracy: and "democracy is the highroad of European history."[27]

There is a clear sense here that Central Europe is not really so different, so independent, after all. It is actually a lost or broken-off part of Western Europe, struggling to regain its proper home. This is what is meant by the "return to Europe." "Europe" in this usage is not a geographical concept, but what Mihaly Vajda calls "a specific value system, a way of thinking," and even, in the context of Central Europe, "a political concept." This is why Vajda, who accepts the sociological distinctiveness of Central Europe, does not speak of a special Central European identity, but instead speaks of the "de-Europeanization" of the region. Like Konrád, he believes that Central Europe has lost or been deprived of its previously existing Western bearings. Central Europe is "not-yet-Europe" or "not-any-more-Europe."[28]

But the important thing, says Vajda, is that Central Europe has never lost sight of its original western orientation: "The outstanding characteristic of the East-Central European area is the fact that it did set out along the same route as the Western model. . . . It is not only in their basic attitudes and behaviour that the peoples of East-Central Europe are 'Europeans.' Not only do they have certain ideas against which they are constantly measuring their reality; these ideals do, in fact, closely resemble those of Western Europe."[29]

The slide here is obvious. "Central Europe" is "Europe" (but perhaps temporarily "de-Europeanized"), and "Europe" is really Western Europe. In the recoil from "Eastern Europe," the most eloquent and enthusiastic partisans of the Central European idea have come to insist ever more strongly that Central Europe is essentially a part of Western Europe. Its incorporation in Eastern Europe as "western Asia" (Joseph Brodsky) has been a grotesque and tragic error. Properly viewed, it is at the eastern edge of Western Europe. As such, its true role is as the defender of Western culture against the barbarism of the East.[30] Once again the memory of Austria is invoked. *Oesterreich* means "the Eastern Empire." Its original name, restored for his own purposes by Hitler, was *Ostmark*, the Eastern March. It was the eastern outpost of Western civilization. It was there, at the gates of Vienna in 1683, that the westward march of the Turks was finally halted. For contemporary Central Europeans, the Russians have replaced the Turks. Russian communism has succeeded Ottoman militarism in inheriting the mantle of anti-Western "oriental despotism."

Even so subtle a thinker as Václav Havel seems to find it impossible, in the end, to avoid the Western embrace. Havel, as a dissident writer, was one of the most persuasive exponents of the Central European idea. He often attacked the commercialism and consumerism of the West. The soulless "automatism" of Soviet-type societies, he claimed, was "merely an extreme version of the global automatism of technological civilization," the civilization invented by the West. It was the West, too, in the theory and practice of Jacobinism, that had invented politics as a technology of terror. Eastern communism merely perfected the techniques. To this politics, and to technological civilization in general, Western democracy, "that is, democracy of the traditional parliamentary type," was no more of a solution than Eastern collectivism. Here Havel explicitly endorsed Solzhenitsyn's withering critique of the Western society he encountered in his exile.[31]

What might be the alternative, the Central European, way? Havel made no great claims. Central Europe had rarely had the chance to develop its own way. Its history had largely been one of a struggle for elemental survival. Still, out of that bitter experience had come a philosophy and an attitude of mind that had something real to offer against the confident dogmatisms of both East and West. As Havel said: "I believe that a distinctive central European scepticism is inescapably a part of the spiritual, cultural, and intellectual phenomenon that is central Europe as it has been formed and is being formed by certain specific historical experiences, including those which today seem to lie dormant in our collective unconscious."[32]

This Central European skepticism has, according to Havel, "little in common with, say, English scepticism." It is darker and more tragic, as is consonant with a different kind of history. It is tinged with irony and "black humour," with a deep sense of the ridiculous, often directed against itself. These are all characteristics strongly present in Central European writers such as Musil, Kafka, and Hašek. They breed an attitude of reserve that arms Central Europeans with a justifiable suspicion of all utopias, whether offered by Western peaceniks or Soviet Marxists. The "central European mind"—"a sceptical, sober, anti-Utopian, understated mind"—has seen through the superficiality of conventional politics, of all politics that does not take as its starting point the existential, moral condition of mankind. It is impatient with old-fashioned polarities of Left and Right, capitalism and socialism. It knows only the polarity of right and wrong. Like Konrád, Havel advocates an "anti-political politics," a "politics outside politics," "a politics outside the sphere of power." He wrote: "I favour politics as practical morality, as service to the truth, as essentially human and humanly measured care for our fellow humans."[33]

And yet a few years later, when this same Havel, as president of the Czechoslovak Republic, announced that he was determined to lead Czechoslovakia "back to Europe," he made it clear that by "Europe" he meant the West. It is not only that, in a period of reconstruction, the West is seen as an indispensable source of political and economic support; the West is also the source of many of the vital elements of that reconstruction itself: constitutionalism, democracy, a tradition of tolerance of dissent and of acceptance of diversity. Havel proclaimed the need to join "the family of European democracy," whose members somewhat surprisingly include not just the European Community, but also NATO (which Havel once advocated scrapping altogether). Even more poignant is the admission that it is Western, not Central European, critics who are most aware of "a certain loss of purpose in life" and who are the most vocal about the social and environmental problems afflicting the world today. This is to cede the moral high ground that was formerly seen as the special preserve of the Central European consciousness. As Havel said, "Here it is not very popular to mention these crises elements. Paradoxically, it is often the highest representatives of Western democracies who point out these problems to me. If they made their opinions public in this country they might be accused of being leftists."[34]

It is almost as if, when faced with the practical task of state building, the idea of a separate Central European identity proves too ghostly, too insubstantial, to provide the essential building blocks. The things they need in Central Europe, moral as well as material, seem only too clearly marked with a West European tag (and they are honest enough to say so). This is perhaps even true of capitalism, or at least the market economy. Gorbachev has said that "the market came with the dawn of civilisation and it is not an invention of capitalism," and that in Russia "the market functioned for a thousand years until the revolution."[35] This may be true in a strictly technical sense. But Central Europeans know that a fully developed market economy came late to Russia and did not have time to establish itself before the revolution. They also know that in most of the Central European countries it remained thin and undernourished for much of their history.[36] If going back to Europe also means restoring capitalism or the market, this must mean largely copying Western forms and learning from Western experience.

It is quite true that, just as "Europe" has been elevated to stand for "a value system and a way of thinking," so in these uses of "the West" there is a similarly conscious and deliberate idealization. The West is conceived in terms of what are seen as its central values: tolerance, democracy, diversity, respect for individual rights. No one is blind to the West's repeated lapses from these high ideals. But, so the argument goes, it is the West, and the West alone, that has elaborated these values and tried to live up to them. Such values may already, as some claim, be embodied in the Central European tradition; or there may be a need to disinter them, or even to import them wholesale. Whichever way—to endorse or to espouse these values—is, once more, to return to the Western homeland.

## What Is Europe?

Timothy Garton Ash has discerned, in the "new Central Europeanism," a "mythopoeic tendency—the inclination to attribute to the Central European past what you hope will characterize the Central European future, the confusion of what should be with what was." As he wrote, "We are to understand that what was *truly* Central European was always Western, rational, humanistic, democratic, sceptical and tolerant. The rest was East European, Russian or possibly German. Central Europe takes all the *Dichter und Denker,* Eastern Europe is left with the *Richter und Henker.*"[37]

The most powerful recent statement of this view of Central Europe has undoubtedly come from the Czech writer Milan Kundera. For Kundera, it is axiomatic that Central Europe is part of Europe, and that "Europe" means Western Europe: "What does Europe mean to a Hungarian, a Czech, a Pole? For a thousand years their nations have belonged to the part of Europe rooted in Roman Christianity. They have participated in every period of its history. For them, the word 'Europe' does not represent a phenomenon of geography but a spiritual notion synonymous with the word 'West.' The moment Hungary is no longer European—that is, no longer Western—it is driven from its own destiny, beyond its own history: it loses the essence of its identity."[38]

Kundera appeals to one of the oldest notions of Western European historiography, that an iron wall separates the historical development of Western Europe from that of its Eastern half: "'Geographic Europe' (extending from the Atlantic to the Ural mountains) was always divided into two halves which evolved separately: one tied to ancient Rome and the Catholic Church, the other anchored in Byzantium and the Orthodox Church. After 1945, the border between the two Europes shifted several hundred kilometers to the west, and several nations that had always considered themselves to be Western woke up to discover they were now in the East."[39]

The predicament of Central Europe, then, is that it is a part of the

West that has been "kidnapped" by the East. It is "culturally in the West and politically in the East."[40] The kidnapper is Russia. Russia, for all the contribution of its artists and writers to "the common European cultural legacy," remains the carrier of "anti-Western obsessions." It is "on the eastern border of the West"—that is, in Central Europe—that Russia is seen, more clearly than anywhere else, "not just as one more European power but as a singular civilization, an *other* civilization." Western Europeans, removed from direct contact with Russia, are often fascinated and attracted by its civilization. They can afford to be so. But to Central Europeans Russia has time and again revealed "its terrifying foreignness." As Kundera wrote: "Russia knows another (greater) dimension of disaster, another image of space (a space so immense entire nations are swallowed up in it), another sense of time (slow and patient), another way of laughing, living, and dying."[41]

It is against this alien force that Central European countries have, since 1945, struggled to preserve their identity—"or, to put it another way, their Westernness." And in doing this they have had to contend not just with Soviet armed power, but also with Western indifference to the plight of Central Europe. Cold War politics obliterated the existence of a Central Europe with an independent identity. There were only West and East. This, says Kundera, has been the tragedy of Central Europe—to be at once oppressed by its historic enemy and to be abandoned by its historic family.

It is important to realize that, despite the achievement of political independence from the Soviet bloc, many intellectuals and politicians in Central Europe continue to harbor these thoughts about "East" and "West." The turn to the West, in particular, and the flight from Russia and all that it stands for, is especially marked.[42] It may be that these attitudes are even more relevant now, after the revolutions, than they were before. For now the countries of Central Europe have the opportunity they have always sought, to realize their own destinies and make their own histories. What they think their past is, where they draw their inspiration from, to whom they look for models, will be an important determinant of their future development.

All the more necessary, then, to question the equation of "Europe" and "the West" and the identification of Central Europe with this putative entity. Equally there is the need to question the idea of the West's uniquely comprehensive contribution to European civilization.

If Europe is not just the West, if there are other traditions that go into its making, Central Europe may not feel so constrained to follow the single and rather narrow path of "Westernization"; it can acknowledge the various strands and influences that make up the European mosaic.

Among these strands are not just the contributions of the lands of Eastern Europe, but the different traditions of the different Central European countries themselves. Some of these point more to the West, some more to the East; some indeed may perhaps be distinctively "Central European." In any case, there is no need for Poland, Hungary, Czechoslovakia, or any of the other countries that may count themselves Central European, to feel that they must pursue a common path or that they inescapably share a common destiny. That surely would be simply to be locked into the pattern of the past. The Central European countries are in the process of emerging from a condition in which they were uniformly subjected to the rule of the great power to the east and had a uniform system of state socialism imposed on their separate identities. It would be a pity if, having broken out of this involuntary and unwelcome common condition, they were to continue to be dominated by the sense of a common fate. That would be to make themselves the prisoners of their own past. They would show themselves to be like long-term prisoners who are incapable of using their newly gained freedom and once more seek the security of prison. If the countries of Central Europe seek to liberate themselves by rediscovering their own histories, they cannot do so as long as they remain enthralled to the sense of a collective identity imposed by their recent past. Central Europe as a part of "Eastern Europe" was an artificial creation; a Central Europe desperately seeking an exclusively Western European identity would be equally artificial.

As Sir James Eberle has said, 'What is Europe?' is no longer an academic question for historians. It is a political question for policy-makers."[43] It is doubtful whether the question has ever been free from politics, certainly if politics is part of ideology. The influential equation of European civilization with distinctively Western values or "the Western tradition" was first suggested by the great liberal historians of the nineteenth century—Ranke, Acton, Bryce. It was powerfully asserted in the interwar period by historians and publicists such as Christopher Dawson and Charles Morgan. In the post-World War II era it hardened into a dogma and an article of faith. East was East and

West was West, and ne'er the twain should meet—except, perhaps, in the nuclear apocalypse.[44]

"Those who call European civilization Western," said the Polish historian Oskar Halecki, "are inclined to decide in advance one of the most difficult and controversial questions of European history."[45] Let us leave aside, as too big for our present purposes, the mind-stretching perspectives of the Chinese, Indian, Persian, Arab, and African contributions to European civilization. Such contributions are undoubted, and they are undoubted to such a degree that for many thinkers they shatter the whole idea of defining an exclusively European culture or community.[46] We are concerned here with the more limited interpretation of the questions "What is Europe," "Where is Europe?"—namely, with the limits and divisions of the European continent itself.

The idea of an "East-West" divide in Europe comes down fundamentally, in the first place, to religion. Russia, the inheritor of Byzantine Christianity and caesaro-papism, is excluded from "Europe" because it did not share the beliefs and institutions of Roman Christianity. The fact that for more than a millennium Christendom was defined primarily by its exclusion of and struggle against infidels—mainly the Muslims— paradoxically did little to save the lands of Orthodox Christianity for the Christian cause, at least in the eyes of the West. Once Constantinople rejected the supremacy of Rome in the eleventh century, once the Mongols and the Tartars overran Russia and the Ottoman Turks overran the Balkan Slavs and Constantinople itself, Orthodox Christians were regarded for all practical purposes as existing on the other side of the line separating true Christians from infidels and barbarians. As Hugh Seton-Watson has written, "Christendom became coextensive with Catholic Europe west of the Tartar and Ottoman borders."[47]

The consequence of this basic divide, it is argued, excluded Russia from all the well-known formative experiences of European civilization: medieval universalism and pluralism, Renaissance and Reformation, the Scientific Revolution and the Enlightenment. Political differences appear especially important: the disappearance of the "free cities" in the Russian case, and the separation of secular and religious power in the Western case (as George Schöpflin has said, "It is inconceivable that the Tsar of Russia or any Asiatic ruler would ever have subjected himself to hair-shirt and rope as Henry IV did before Gregory VII [at Canossa]").[48]

But of course things can look very different from the other side of
the divide. According to Hugh Seton-Watson:

In the Orthodox view, the Catholics were schismatics who had se-
ceded from the true faith—and of course the Protestants after the
Reformation were schismatics from schismatics. Once Muscovy had
shaken off the Tartar yoke, its ruler—Great Prince, later Czar (a
Slavicization of the word Caesar)—was the only independent
Orthodox ruler in the world, which meant the only truly Christian
ruler. Christendom, the land ruled by a Christian monarch, *was*
Muscovy: nothing else was. Muscovy faced to the west and north
the schismatics whose vanguards were the Romanist Poles and the
Protestant Swedes; and in the east and south the infidels—Tartars
and Ottomans.[49]

Geoffrey Barraclough has enlarged on this view by pointing out
that, if Roman culture and civilization are regarded as a primary inspiration of European civilization, "the direct heir of Rome was not
the West but Byzantium, where Roman civilization and the very
structure of the Roman state continued . . . down to the fall of
Constantinople in 1453." If, on the other hand, the emphasis is put
on the contribution of the Latin fathers and the Latin Church to
Christianity, as the "heirs of the western tradition" and "the reposito-
ry of the 'old Roman culture,'" we should remember that Christianity
in important respects sought to break with the Roman world. As
Barraclough has written: "The early church—as represented (for example) by Tertullian and Jerome, by St. Ambrose and St. Augustine—
[was] filled with antipathy to Roman traditions, which it regarded as
the work of anti-Christ. The places that really mattered in the early
Christian centuries were not in Europe at all, but were cities like
Alexandria and Carthage in Africa, or Nicaea and Cappadocia in Asia
Minor; and even as late as the seventh and eighth centuries half the
popes in Rome were Greeks or Syrians by birth."[50]

If, finally, we want to make Christianity as well as the classical inheritance central to our understanding of European civilization, it is
Russia—as the heir of Byzantium, rather than the West—that has the
better claim to be both the standard-bearer of Christianity and the principal carrier of the Roman imperial tradition. Barraclough explains:

It was Byzantium which—unlike the western empire—was both the
linear descendant of Rome and (in Sir Maurice Powicke's words) for
eight hundred years "the chief Christian state in the world." And this is

a fact of the greatest historical significance; for when Constantinople, the "second Rome," fell to the Turks in 1453, it was to Russia that the imperial and Christian tradition of Byzantium passed. After 1453 Russia emerged as heir to the Byzantine inheritance. The Russian ruler was hailed as the "new Constantine," legitimate successor to the "Roman emperor and czar who ruled the whole world," and Moscow established the proud claim to be the "third Rome." "Two Romes have fallen," proclaimed the monk, Philotheus of Pskov, "but the third is standing; and there shall be no fourth." In this way the imperial mission of Rome was transmitted through the Orthodox church from Byzantium to Holy Russia.[51]

The emphasis on the profoundly Christian character of Russian civilization can be double edged from the point of view of those who wish to deny Russia's Europeanness. For if it was religion that initially divided the West from Russia, it was the absence of religion that later confirmed the divide. So long as the unifying idea of Europe was Christendom, it was problematic to exclude Russia, whatever might be thought of Orthodox Christianity and caesaro-papism. The secularization of Western Europe in the seventeenth and eighteenth centuries raised a new wall. Europe was now increasingly defined in terms of secular values and institutions: science, the nation-state, the democratic and rationalist ideals of the French Revolution, the technology and economic dynamism of the Industrial Revolution. These, the emblems of modernity, were now the hallmarks of Europe; and by these tokens Russia was even more decisively excluded than it had been in the age of faith. Russia was backward, barbaric, unmodern. Its traditions of authority and autocracy kept its people submissive and superstitious. Its idea of its Christian mission in the world made it an archaic and dangerous force. When, after 1815, Russia aspired to ascendancy in Europe and Alexander I advocated the unification of Europe on the basis of Christian principles, his proposal was regarded by most educated Europeans as both quaint and reactionary: a clear indication of Russia's backwardness and of its distance from the European mainstream.

The Bolshevik Revolution of 1917, according to this view, did almost nothing to alter this picture. It merely substituted an atheistic absolutism for a religious one. Russian traditions of autocracy and authoritarianism continued; caesaro-papism lived on, not least in its imperial aspirations, in a new guise. There might have been some catching up with the West in science and technology, but in politics and culture, after a brief period of experimentation, Russia stood outside all modern developments. Communism perpetuated Russia's non-European face, the face of Asiatic despotism. The transfer of the Russian capital from St. Petersburg to Moscow was symbolic. As Hugh Seton-Watson says, "Bolshevism turned its back on Europe."[52]

But is not Marxism the most Western of ideologies? Is it not, as many have held, "a triumph of western rationalism and technique," the logical complement of Enlightenment thought?[53] And does not its adoption in Russia represent a continuation of the dramatic modernization of the country begun by Peter the Great? From the time of Peter, Russia has been part of the European state system; since that time it has been impossible to consider continental European politics without considering Russia. Internally, the new city of St. Petersburg, Russia's "window on the West," symbolized Russia's determination to emulate and surpass the ways and achievements of Western Europe. Peter set Russia on a course of Westernization that, fused to its Christian inheritance, made it ever more firmly a part of Europe.[54]

"The age of St. Petersburg," it has been said, "from 1702 to 1918, was the age of Russian membership of Europe."[55] During this period the Russian upper class and intelligentsia were thoroughly "Europeanized," in the sense of succumbing to secular European culture and the French language. From Pushkin to Blok and beyond, Russian letters dazzled Europe. Nor did the celebrated controversy between "Westernizers" and "Slavophiles" imply a repudiation of the European inheritance. Was it not the famous Slavophile, Feodor Dostoyevsky, who said that "Europe is our mother, to whom we owe much and shall owe more"? The Slavophile "revolt against Europe" was a revolt not against Europe *tout court,* but against the encroaching rationalism and materialism of modern bourgeois Europe.[56] It was, in other words, a revolt of one part of Europe against another, a protest against certain recent developments from the viewpoint of other, often older, European traditions, especially Christian ones. In this the Slavophiles joined many of the best minds, from John Stuart Mill to Nietzsche, in Western Europe, even if the sources of their criticisms were sometimes very different.

The conflict between "capitalism" and "communism" in the twentieth century has been of the same kind. It has been a conflict between values and practices that are all squarely within the European tradition. Russian membership in Europe did not cease in 1918. "Russian communism" opposes "Western capitalism" on the grounds of the latter's inhumanity and inefficiency; Western capitalism opposes Russian communism on much the same grounds. Both sides to the conflict use different terms and concepts—"individualism," "competition," "freedom" on the one side, "exploitation," "alienation," "collectivism" on the other. They are borrowings from the same common European store.

This discussion underlines the main point in the debate about "Russia and Europe": European civilization is not of one piece. More than is the case with other civilizations, its strength and vitality come from the diversity of strands that make up its fabric. Russian culture has, for more than a thousand years, contributed one of those strands. It has been a powerful and creative element in European life—never more so, perhaps, than in the twentieth century, when it confronted the West with a counterimage of the West's own making.[57]

## Central Europe

To emphasize Russia's Europeanness is neither to deny Central Europe's claims of its essentially "Western" character nor to dismiss its search for its own distinctive identity. Rather, it is to indicate to Central Europeans—and perhaps to others—that the choice is not between one thing or the other, "East" or "West." Europe includes both "East" and "West," and individual European countries, especially those in the "lands in-between," are likely to find elements of both in their make-up. And if this is so, if Europe's whole history has been an amalgam of diverse and often contradictory tendencies, there is nothing to prevent Central Europeans from attempting to *make* their own identity. That is, whether or not such a thing existed in the past, there is no reason why Central Europeans should not seek to create one for the future.[58]

It is striking how many Central European writers—even those who believe in an existing, if suppressed, Central European identity—stress the largely symbolic quality of the claims of a distinctive Central European way. In their eyes, Central Europe is as much an aspiration as a fact, a hope as much as a reality. "What is revolutionary about the idea of Central Europe," says György Konrád, "is precisely the fact that today it is only a dream. Visions have a chance of realization. . . . By contrast with the political reality of Eastern Europe and Western Europe, Central Europe exists only as a cultural counterhypothesis. . . . Being a Central European does not mean having a nationality, but rather an outlook on the world."[59]

Milan Kundera says that "Central Europe is not a state; it is a culture or a fate. Its borders are imaginary and must be drawn and redrawn with each new historical situation."[60] Czesław Miłosz believes that Central Europe can be known not in any purely geographical sense, but rather through a distinctive "tone and sensibility" in its writers, and in the "ways of feeling and thinking" of its inhabitants. He goes further: "Central Europe is an act of faith, a project, let us say, even a utopia."[61] This is also Egon Schwarz's view, though less confidently put: "Since there is no definable Central Europe, we are free to postulate a utopian one. . . . Let us admit, then, that this Central Europe, weak in the past, elusive in the present, and more than uncertain in the future, is a symbol for what is not but should be, a spiritual attitude, an ethos."[62]

This attitude can coexist with a robust belief that these hopes are realistically grounded in a distinctive history and culture. "The 'separateness' of the area remains a stubborn reality," says Ferenc Fehér.[63] Despite shifting frontiers and slippery definitions, says Csaba Kiss, "I have no doubt that there exists a particular cultural-historical region at the centre of Europe."[64] Miłosz is no less sure. He believes that the countries of Central Europe are not "pure-bred Western." Not only have they absorbed Russian and other non-Western influences, but they have mixed these and other experiences in their own characteristic way: "Ideas from abroad penetrating these lands, diluted and transformed, acquired a specific quality, local habits were persistent, institutions took forms unheard of in the Western part of Europe. . . . A hygienic reason behind our choosing the term Central Europe is that it authorizes us to look for the specificity of its culture and protects us from the temptation of misleading analogies."[65]

There is nothing to suggest that this is a self-defeating or self-deceiving task. The lack of precision in the concept of Central Europe may make taxonomists (and tidy-minded positivists) weep, but that is their problem. One of Kundera's points—often ignored in the controversy over his thesis of "a kidnapped West"—is that Europe *needs* the concept of Central Europe to remind it of some of its most important values and some of its most creative episodes. The real tragedy for Central Europe, in the end, was not so much Russian domination as Europe's forgetfulness and its indifference to the region's existence as a cultural entity. And this was because "in Europe itself Europe was no longer experienced as a value."[66]

If this is so, Central Europeans cannot simply look to the past, real or imagined, or to their current confused relationship to Europe. The elements of the Central European identity may need to be discovered and forged anew. If Europe has lost confidence in its ability to define itself, to see where its true nature and real promise lie, Central Europe may need to make a bolder departure than it has so far attempted. To harp constantly on its Europeanness, to seek to find its identity in some past membership in Western civilization, is to court the danger of imitativeness and superficiality. Marx once wrote that "the social revolution . . . cannot draw its poetry from the past, but only from the future."[67] The same may be true of the idea of Central Europe. The Polish writer Witold Gombrowicz warned his fellow Central Europeans against seeing themselves too much in the image of the West or settling for some pallid notion of the lands "in-between." They had to seek an authentic identity of their own. This would require, in the first place, an act of rupture with Europe:

> "We cannot become a truly European nation," he said, "until we separate ourselves from Europe, since our Europeanness does not mean submergence, but that we may become a part of it, indeed a very particular part not interchangeable with any other. Consequently, only by opposing the Europe that created us can we ultimately . . . create a life of our own. . . . If . . . we have the sense simply to accept ourselves as we are, we are certain to discover hitherto unknown and unexplored possibilities in ourselves—we shall certainly be capable of assuming a beauty fundamentally different from what we have had until now."[68]

## A Further Note

In January 1990, shortly after he had been inaugurated as the first president of the newly reconstituted Czechoslovak Republic, Václav Havel made a stirring appeal to the idea of Central Europe in an address to the Polish Parliament:

> There is before us the real historic chance to fill with something meaningful the great political vacuum that appeared in Central Europe after the break-up of the Habsburg Empire. We have the chance to transfer Central Europe from a phenomenon that has so far been historical and spiritual into a political phenomenon. We have the chance to take a string of European countries that until recently were colonised by the Soviets and that today are attempting the kind of friendship with the nations of the Soviet Union which would be founded on equal rights, and transform them into a definite special

body, which would approach Western Europe not as a poor dissident or a helpless, searching amnestied prisoner, but as someone who has something to offer.[69]

Here Havel spoke as a former dissident, addressing other former dissidents in language that he felt sure would find a resonance. The idea of Central Europe, the sense that there was something distinctive about the region that separated it from both Eastern and Western Europe, the feeling that it had something valuable to contribute to Europe and the world: these were views, as we have seen, common among many of the intellectuals that were laying the ideological ground for the revolutions of 1989. These intellectuals—many of them, at any rate—were now in power. Their problem was to give this idea institutional form, to promote it as a political project.

There have been a few half-hearted moves in that direction in the years since 1989. Most visibly, there has been the formation of the "Visegrad Group," named after the meeting of Hungarian, Polish, and Czechoslovak heads of state at Visegrad (Hungary) in February 1991. The three countries—four after Czechoslovakia divided—agreed to set up schemes of mutual cooperation in the region. The firstfruits of this group's labors was the Central European Free Trade Agreement of December 1992 (formally inaugurated in March 1993), open in principle to other countries in the region, though so far only Slovenia has joined (in 1996). There has also been the Central European Initiative, a much broader economic group including Austria and Italy and building on the Danube-Adria Group established in 1989.[70]

The general consensus is that so far these developments have yielded little of real substance. Indeed, their main function seems to have been to try to persuade Western European countries that the former communist countries were capable of taking the initiative and were not simply passively waiting for the West to help them out. But the economic realities of the region have prevented these moves from being much more than symbolic. For instance, intraregional trade is only a modest fraction of total trade for most Central European countries—less than 5 percent for Hungary and Poland, and less than 10 percent for the Czech Republic and Slovakia.[71] Economically, at least, the region looks outward, not inward toward the consolidation of its own identity.

Nor has there been much evidence of cultural consolidation.

There is a Central European University, formerly in Prague, now with headquarters in Budapest and branches in Warsaw and elsewhere. But that was set up by an American philanthropist, George Soros, and much of its faculty and administration comes from the West. It has indeed been the source of much resentment among native intellectuals in the region, who see in it a form of cultural imperialism. Much the same suspicion hangs over the many other universities, research institutes, and cultural foundations that have been set up in the region since 1989, most with Western money and generally under Western auspices. These have in many cases bypassed or marginalized the existing and in many instances long-standing cultural institutions in the region, thereby creating even greater frustration and resentment.[72]

All this points to what has seemed to most observers the most obvious tendency in the region since the 1989 revolutions: a decisive turning toward the West. Far from cultivating an identity as members of a common Central European culture, as Havel urged, the countries of the former communist bloc seem to have been falling over each other in an unseemly scramble to catch the Western eye and to gain admission to several rather exclusive Western clubs. Chief among these are NATO and the European Union. All over the region one has the impression of countries' breaking ranks and seeking to promote their own cases at the expense, if need be, of their Central European neighbors. "Me first" seems to sum up the general mood.

For some the strategy has paid off, at least in part. In March 1999, on the fiftieth anniversary of NATO's founding, Poland, Hungary, and the Czech Republic were formally admitted to membership in NATO. Central European leaders were unanimous in their view that this marked a momentous turn in their history. The burden of their remarks was a reprise of the highly charged slogan of 1989, "the return to Europe." Bronislaw Geremek, a medieval historian and former Solidarity intellectual, now Polish foreign minister, compared accession to NATO with Poland's conversion to Christianity nearly a thousand years ago. Polish President Aleksander Kwasniewski saw the move as healing the historic division of Europe, and declared: "This is the most important moment in our history." For the Czech President Václav Havel, who once advocated scrapping NATO as a threat to the peace of Europe, Czech membership now meant that "we will have a solid security anchoring for the first time in our history, and an anchoring in the democratic world, in the world of protection of democratic values."[73]

Havel's remark brings out the subtext of what was generally pro-claimed by the assembled foreign secretaries of the three Central Euro-pean nations, at a ceremony in Independence, Missouri, that was held to mark the occasion: that joining NATO meant not just a return to Europe, but a return to the West. The spiritual homecoming was not just to Europe, but to Europe understood as a part of a distinctively Western civilization with traditions and values that set it off from "the East" (Russia and generally the lands of Orthodoxy). This was there-fore a Europe that included America and other offshoots of Western Europe. The coded words would have been understood by all, even if they had not been underscored by heavily accented cultural and histor-ical references. As Geremek stated, "Poland forever returns where she has always belonged: the free world." Geremek laced his statement with a humorous reference to the poster of the film *High Noon* that had accompanied Solidarity's electoral campaign against the commu-nists in 1989. Gary Cooper's lone, heroic stand against evil and injus-tice paralleled that of the Polish opposition to the communist state. "For the people of Poland," Geremek said, "high noon comes today." The Czech Foreign Minister, Jan Kavan, noted that the very existence of Czechoslovakia was the result of the ideals and striving of an American president, Woodrow Wilson. Kavan, exiled in London from 1968 to 1989 after the Russian tanks finished off the "Prague Spring," declared that "accession to NATO is a guarantee that we will never again become powerless victims of any foreign aggression." The threat remained the Russian bear, the historic enemy of Western Enlighten-ment and liberalism. The Hungarian foreign minister, Janos Martonyi, was clearest of all. Hungary, he said, had long dreamed of belonging to "the community of Western democracies" and was now returning to "her natural habitat." He continued: "It has been our manifest des-tiny to rejoin those with whom we share the same values, interests and goals. . . . Hungary has come home. We are back in the family."[74]

Of course only a few of the Central European countries have so far been allowed back in the Western family. But others in the region press their case for joining NATO by insisting on their European cre-dentials, as good as those of the "core" Central European nations that have been favored—and better by far, they pointedly insist, than those of Turkey, a member of NATO since 1952. The peoples of Baltic States—Estonia, Latvia, and Lithuania—remind us that it was among them (in Riga, to be precise ) that Johann Gottfried Herder first formulated his theory of the "national soul," as a result of finding it so impressively inscribed in Baltic folklore, and that they have carried a distinctive northern European identity, predominantly Protestant, through two hundred years of "alien" Slavic rule.[75] Slovakia, Slovenia, and Croatia stress their centuries-old membership in the Habsburg Empire and their contribution to the mainstream of European culture. Romania proclaims its inheritance from the Roman Empire and points to the Latin basis of its language as a mark distinguishing it from all its Slav neighbors (the majority of which, including Hungary, Poland, and the Czech Republic, did not share the benefits of Roman rule). As for Bulgaria, the eminent poetess and former vice president of Bulgaria, Blaga Dimitrova, faced with cynics who say that Bulgaria wishes to be adopted, like an orphan, into the family of European nations, retorts that like other nations in the region, Bulgaria has "always been in Europe. We were separated from our home by force. And now we are longing to go back there. But let the old lady Europe receive us not out of charity, like orphans; let her remember that we are her children in mind and body though we had been abandoned far away for many years."[76]

Dimitrova, however, does not see the European inheritance as purely Western. She recognizes a distinctive contribution made by the lands of Orthodoxy—Russia, Bulgaria, Serbia, and others. Nor would she want to rule out the significance of the Turkish elements incorporated in several of those cultures as the result of five hundred years of Ottoman rule; just as few could deny the importance of the Arab contribution to the evolving culture of the European Middle Ages. This remains an important perspective in East Central Europe. Not everyone shares the views of the Central European politicians who steered their countries into NATO and are trying to assert a largely Western identity. As the moment for actual entry into NATO loomed, polls showed a marked decline in enthusiasm among the populations of the countries affected: from a high of 80 percent in 1998 down to 60 percent by the spring of 1999 for the Poles and Hungarians, and from 55 percent to 50 percent for the Czechs.[77]

There have been similar fluctuations, in a downward direction, in popular support for that even more fervently embraced project of Central European leaders: entry into the European Union (EU). For many Central European politicians and publicists this seems to have taken on the quality of a panacea; their critics complain that they have turned it into a utopia or a phantasmagoria. Perhaps it is the very difficulty of entry that has created these extreme responses. Entry into NATO is one thing, involving mainly the harmonization of military strategy and organization (though Kosovo showed how consequential for a country's foreign policy such a move might prove); entry into the EU is much harder, involving as it does the harmonization of laws and economies. Though the European Union has committed itself in principle to accepting new members from the former communist bloc, no such country has yet been considered ready for admission, despite considerable pressure from both within and without the EU. The reasons vary, ranging from a concern that the Central European economies would simply be overwhelmed if they entered in their current state to a fear that their entry would destroy the center of gravity of the European Union as originally conceived.[78]

Whether as a response to the perceived reluctance of Western European nations to accept them, or out of distrust of their politicians, or perhaps even from a sense that they are in some important ways different from the peoples of Western Europe, ordinary Central European people have been showing signs of a distinct disenchantment with the prospect of membership of the European Union. In a poll conducted in May 1999, only 35 percent of Czechs said they approved entry to the EU. In recent surveys Poland has registered 55 percent support, but that is down from 70 percent a few years ago, and Polish farmers, miners, and several other groups see disaster staring them in the face from EU membership. Hungary still shows 65 percent support, but that, too, is down compared with recent years. The initial euphoria, the rush to join "Europe and the West," has clearly received a check.[79]

Nor is it only the ordinary people who express reservations. Intellectuals turned politicians, such as Havel, may have become convinced Westophiles, but other Central European intellectuals are not so sure. Some retain the hopes and convictions of their dissident days that Central Europe still has something different to offer the world. In a defiant statement the Hungarian writer György Konrád, one of the most influential proponents of the Central European idea in the 1980s, has said: "No matter what we call it, and whether or not we speak of it as such, Central Europe was, is, and probably will continue to be. . . . Central Europe may well outlive us." For Konrád, Central Europe is "neither east nor west; it is both east and west. . . . It represents [its constituent countries'] mutual presence, all tension and irony: single-party habits and an attempt at pluralism; socialism and capitalism; state ownership and private ownership; the redistribution of wealth and the free market; state control and a civil society; paternalistic politics and a critical intelligentsia."[80]

This mixture of east and west "is truly unique and truly validates the Central European idea," according to Konrád. Its villages, towns, and cities resemble one another. It has "similar images, smells, personal relationships, and types of behavior." Konrád is prepared to envisage a Central Europe that goes its own way, especially if the European Union continues to drag its feet. Why not forge closer ties with the Commonwealth of Independent States (the countries of the former Soviet Union)—or Japan, or the United States, or the Near East? "If the much coveted marriage to fair Europa fails to come off," he says, "there are other fair maidens waiting in the wing." And if all these fail, there could be a much greater effort at Central European integration— "not so much to turn us all into winners as to help us support one another through hard times and preserve a modicum of sovereignty in the face of one or another powerful neighbor." The main thing is to refuse "to let the object of our concern, Central Europe, follow a path not of its own choosing; it means seeing our future open before us, a future dependent only upon our own wishes, our own work, our own selves."[81]

This may sound utopian indeed, especially in the current circumstances of NATO membership and continuing economic hardship. But even those, such as Adam Michnik, who contend that "Central Europe" was "a myth against the fact of Soviet domination" dreamed up by Kundera, Konrád, Havel, and others, accept that they were "fully justified in re-reading this region of borderlands—where nations, religions and cultures rub up against one another." They were "fully justified in presenting it as the realization of a multicultural ideal of society—a miniature Europe of Nations—founded on the principle of maximum diversity in minimum space." Michnik recognizes, too, that the resolutely "non-imperial character" of the small nations of Central Europe produced a distinctive tradition of thought and behavior: "Centuries of existence in an environment of oppression and repression produced a specific culture, characterized by honor and self-irony, the stubbornness to stand by values, and the courage to believe in romantic ideals. Here, national and civic consciousness developed as a result of human bonds—and not by the order of state institutions; here it was easier to devise the idea of civil society, precisely because the sovereign national state remained largely in the realm of dreams. The great cultural diversity of this region was to be—and frequently was—the best weapon of self-defense against the claims of ethnic or ideological power."[82]

This sounds scarcely less utopian than Konrád, at least in its picture of Central European culture and what it might have to offer the world. But Michnik is no utopian—he believes in the "grayness" of democracy, not the bright colors of absolutists' faiths—and what he wishes to point to is simply an alternative source of experience and values to add to the common European store. So, too, Czeław Miłosz has often felt the need to remind his Western audience that Central Europeans look East as well as West, that Central European imagining knows a world remote from the experience of most Western European nations, at least since the Middle Ages. He writes of his native Lithuania that with "its choral music, its green valleys, its oaks thought to be holy trees," it "sits deeply in me and I am not free of the pagan temptations that affect some of us from the last country in Europe to adopt Christianity."[83]

These and others like them may all be thought dreamers and unworldly intellectuals, though it would surely be unwise to disregard these voices, especially if they chime in with a popular feeling, born perhaps of different causes, of resentment toward the West. They are presented simply to show that "Westophilia" has not made the running all in postcommunist societies.[84] But of course in terms of current, day-to-day, politics the Westophiles have clearly seized the initiative. With Russia in turmoil, and their own societies wracked by ethnic conflict and suffering the stresses of radical economic change, there seems simply no alternative to the European Union as some sort of arena for the resolution of these problems. Certainly there is no lack of urging on this score from their friends in the West. Speaking, for instance, of Poland's "normal abnormality"—its turbulent history up to and including the communist period—and its transition to an "abnormal normality"—a more or less functioning democracy and market society today—Timothy Garton Ash presses the Poles to secure this achievement by finding their place in the EU and NATO: "Only if that is done will we, and the Poles themselves, begin to see what the Polish version of European 'normality' really looks like." He confesses that this new Polish normality, if achieved, "may well not be as interesting as the old abnormality. Indeed, it may at first look like a cheap copy of the West." But he considers it a price "worth paying."[85] It is not, of course, just the Poles, but all other Europeans, who may do the paying.

It was Milan Kundera who, with his 1983–84 article "The Tragedy of Central Europe," got the Central European debate going.[86] In that article Kundera proclaimed that Central Europe did not belong to "Eastern Europe"; it was a part of the West. Has the Westward turn of the postcommunist states of Central Europe vindicated him? It is interesting that in the early 1990s Kundera himself disavowed his earlier essay on the grounds that it had been written for Western consumption. He evidently did not wish to join in the chorus of Western triumphalism after 1989, or be counted among the Westophiles in Central Europe. His essay, he felt, had been used as a political weapon in a new war of Slavophiles and Westernizers.[87] Few readers of the essay had noted—or, at least, had cared to remember—that one of his targets was the West's neglect of its own best traditions. Central Europe had kept alive certain ways and values that the advanced capitalist West, in its single-minded pursuit of economic growth, had abandoned or relegated to the margins. Central Europe would remind Europe of what it had been, and what it could be again. In arguing for the concept of Central Europe, Kundera had not merely wished to protest at its annexation by the East; he had also hoped to open up the whole question of the meaning of Europe.

One of the consequences of the 1989 revolutions has indeed been to revive the question of Europe in its widest possible form. The development of the European Union would have stimulated that inquiry in any case, but with nothing like the scope and urgency that has been injected by the fall of communism. In that sense Kundera has succeeded in one of his aims, even if he now finds his work used in one-sided interpretations of the European tradition. There is now a rich and growing literature on the identity of Europe. Part of it continues to ask, Where does Central Europe fit in? Is Russia European? But some of it also asks, What have been the governing assumptions and ideologies about Europe in the West? How has the West come to be conceptualized? What links Portugal with Sweden? Why should Greece—but not Hungary or Poland—have come to be regarded as part of the West, when by geography and culture it so obviously belongs to the Balkan region of "Eastern Europe"? How did Europe come to be identified with the West?[88]

As regards the question of Europe, the 1989 revolutions provoked a divided reaction in the West. There were those who rushed to embrace the newly freed nations of Central and Eastern Europe, to proclaim them an essential part of Europe and indeed of the West. This line broadly followed the claims of those dissident Central European intellectuals who had felt the greatest antagonism toward the Soviet Union and perceived their countries as captives of an alien East. The other reaction was to stress the difficulties of accommodating the new nations in a newly expanded idea of Europe. They were seen as poor and backward, like "Third World" societies, generations behind the West in their political, social, and economic development. A new or revived "orientalism" arose in relation to Central and Eastern Europe, a new "Other" to take the place of the communist "Other."[89] Seen from this perspective, Central Europe might one day aspire to join Europe; but for the moment the obstacles were formidable and indeed might ultimately prove insuperable.

Some years ago Václav Havel suggested that we look at Europe in the twilight not of decline, but of contemplation—somewhat, presumably, in the spirit of Minerva's owl. If we did so, he went on, we would see that there were a number of Europes, or at least a number of overlapping meanings of Europe. For some time in this century many people identified Europe with noncommunist Europe, essentially the Europe of the European Union, and some still wished to do so. But this Europe, for all its freedom and prosperity, is limited and insufficient—a "self-centered Europe, concerned more for its immediate economic interests than for global philosophical considerations." This was his riposte to those Europeans who wished to exclude the countries of Central and Eastern Europe—which were, as he pointed out, European in *both* their communist and postcommunist (and, of course, precommunist) manifestations. Against this he proposed a concept of Europe as possessing "a common destiny, a common complex history, common values, and a common culture and way of life." The focus here is on Europe as "a place of shared values," on its spiritual and intellectual identity, on the "European soul": on "what Europe once was and what it believed in, what it is and believes in now, what it should be or could be, and what role it could play in the future."[90]

No doubt this idea can, for all its vagueness, be defended. But it raises an interesting question. Havel continues to see Europe as "a single indivisible political entity"; he places all his hopes for the realization of European values on an expanded European Union, and warns against the disastrous consequences for both sides of allowing Europe to remain divided. But is "Europe," however expanded, now the right vehicle for the realization of the European values that Havel cherishes—the values of individuality, diversity, freedom? Is "Fortress Europe," even if the fort is enlarged and more room found for newcomers, the right way forward? Many of Europe's citizens, especially those of non-European stock, have good reason to doubt this, and have been looking to organizations and institutions beyond Europe to sustain them in their struggle for civil and social rights.[91]

Moreover, the attempts to define Europe through the European Union open up all the old troubling questions. Few seem to regard Russia as a potential member. But, then, is Russia to be considered as "non-European," standing outside as the ever-present threat to "European values"? That would be to resurrect an old bogey whose baleful influence has surely been made plain by now. And what of those other problematic countries, in the Balkans especially? Slovenia will get into the EU, and probably so will Croatia; but some people, such as Samuel Huntington, would certainly want to deny EU membership to those of Orthodox descent—Serbia, Bulgaria, Romania—not to mention those, such as Albania, Bosnia and Macedonia, with strong Islamic heritages.[92] (Greece, of course, will remain the anomalous exception.) Faced with all these issues, it is not unreasonable to suggest that the idea of Europe has now become not a help, but a hindrance, to recognizing and resolving the problems of the continent. As Tony Judt says: "'Europe' is more than a geographical notion but less than an answer."[93]

The question of Europe is one of the great legacies of the 1989 revolutions. As with other aspects, there are more questions than answers. That is just another way of saying what a profound upheaval in our thinking they have caused. But it would not be the least of the many ironies surrounding those revolutions if, in raising the question of Europe, they put Europe itself in question.

*Four*

# The 1989 Revolutions and the Idea of Revolution

> *The events of 1989 in the East-Central European belt of satellite com-*
> *munist regimes was a most fitting finale for the twentieth century,*
> *bound to be recorded in history as the age of revolutions. They*
> *changed the political map of the globe, affecting even parts osten-*
> *sibly distant from the scene of the upheaval in ways which are still*
> *far from being fully grasped. They are also certain to be scrutinized*
> *for the updating they offer to our orthodox views of how revolu-*
> *tions come about and how they are conducted in a new socio-*
> *cultural context.*
>
> Zygmunt Bauman, Intimations of Postmodernity

## Annus Mirabilis

It is evident that what Chou En-lai is alleged to have said about the consequences of the French Revolution, that "it is too early to say," applies a fortiori to the revolutions of 1989 in East Central Europe. But no one has felt inhibited by this, and rightly so. It has seemed clear to the majority of observers that, whatever the precise and particular outcomes, the events of 1989 have a "world-historical" significance. "No politically literate person in the world," says Daniel Chirot, "can doubt that 1989, like 1789, will be remembered as one of those decisive years in which decades of slow political and economic change and development culminated in a series of unexpected, dramatic events that suddenly redefined the world." 1989, it became common to say, was "an earthquake in world politics," a "year of wonders," an annus mirabilis.[1]

It was, of course, first and foremost a year of wonders for the East Europeans themselves. For Janusz Ziolkowski, sociologist, Solidarity supporter, and, since 1989, Polish senator, the momentousness of the events swept aside any doubts that what had occurred was truly a revolution: "The term revolution aptly depicts the character of the changes which occurred in the last part of 1989 in East Central Europe. One should stop referring to what has been going on in the 'other Europe' as reform. It was revolution. By revolution I mean the overthrow of the existing political, economic and social order. The fact that the revolution has so far been peaceful does not make it any less genuine."[2]

Ziolkowski is responding to the views of those, such as Timothy Garton Ash, who question the use of the term *revolution*—"a word so closely associated with violence"—when the changes were carried through by means that were "almost entirely non-violent." Romania, Garton Ash concedes, clearly experienced revolution: blood was spilled. But Poland, Hungary, Bulgaria, and even Czechoslovakia and East Germany are more cases of what he calls "refolution" (a mixture of reform and revolution): "a mixture of popular protest and elite negotiation," reforms from above in response to revolutionary mass pressure from below. But there was, he admits, in all cases not just a change of government, but a profound "change of life." Moreover, the "astonishing speed" with which the change came, the "sudden and sweeping end to an ancien regime," may indeed "justify the use of the word 'revolution'"[3]

What are being raised here are classic questions in the study of revolution. Is violence a central criterion for revolution, as liberals have commonly held; or is it merely incidental, as most Marxists have argued? Is what matters the speed and depth of change rather than its forcible accomplishment? And if so, how might we gauge the depth of change? We generally look first at changes within society; but here the problem of time, of how long it takes for change actually to show itself at different levels of society, is acute. Chou En-lai's quip returns to harass us.

But we need to remember that the great revolutions of the past have struck most contemporaries—as opposed to later academic students of revolution—more from the point of view of their external impact than of their effects on their own society. The English Revolution of the seventeenth century was ambiguous in this respect, though there is no doubting its contribution to radical thought in the American colonies. But since the American and French Revolutions of the eighteenth century no one has questioned the international significance of revolution. It was largely in pointing to this that Hegel, Tocqueville, and Marx made their great contributions to the study of revolution.[4]

The 1989 revolutions have irresistibly sounded this note. It has been impossible not to think of 1989 in terms of its impact on the world as a whole. And, although the question of long-term effects on this scale poses difficulties even greater than those that apply to changes within society, the immediate effect has been clearer and more dramatic. The course of world history seems so obviously changed, despite deep uncertainties as to the ultimate outcome.

George Schöpflin emphasizes the largely European dimension of the 1989 revolutions: "[1989] was the year when Europe grew up and shook off the legacy of the Great European Civil War of 1914–45 and began to redefine itself in its own terms and against the now declining superpowers which had exercised tutelage over it for so long."[5] To this Fred Halliday adds the important and, as subsequent events were to show, prophetic rider: "The upheavals [of 1989] have placed in question not only Yalta and Potsdam, but also much of what was agreed at an earlier postwar conference, that of Versailles . . . and in some ways before."[6]

But to most observers the really important change was in the contest of ideologies and the world conflicts that flowed from it. 1989 meant the end of the communist challenge and, with it, the elimination of one of the two principal contenders for world hegemony. We could no longer speak of three worlds—as Ralf Dahrendorf says, "the very concept of a Third World presupposes two others"; we could speak only of one world, the world of liberal capitalist society.[7] For some, such as Francis Fukuyama, this outcome amounted to no less than "the end of history." It vindicated Hegel's contention that, with the French Revolution and the announcement of the principles of the modern liberal state, the dialectic of conflicting ideologies in history had reached an end and been resolved. There had been attempts since then to upset this fundamental settlement, but all had ultimately failed. The challenge of the Right, in the form of fascism and Nazism, had failed in 1945; that of the Left, initiated by the Bolshevik Revolution of 1917, had lasted longer, but with the collapse of communism in 1989 that, too, showed its inability to defeat liberalism.[8]

Ken Jowitt has, on the contrary, argued that "the Leninist extinction"—the "mass extinction of Leninist regimes" in 1989–91—will produce not stability, but an entirely new world "disorder." The liberal capitalist West may have won; but its victory opens the way not, as Fukuyama and others would have it, to the end of fundamental political and ideological conflicts, but to the start of a period of new conflicts and international turmoil. In the new environment Western civilization will be forced to reexamine its own premises based on the three revolutions—British, American, and French—that brought liberal capitalist democracy into being; it will face constant challenges both from within and from without. As Jowitt says: "For half a century we have thought in terms of East and West, and now there is no East as such. The primary axis of international politics has 'disappeared.' . . . In the immediate future, the Leninist Extinction is likely to dramatically, and in some instances traumatically, challenge and undermine the national boundaries and political identities of Third World nations, Western nations, and the character of the Western world itself, as well as create obvious and serious obstacles to stable and viable elite and regime replacements in the Soviet Union, Eastern Europe, and Asia."[9]

This is an international context in which revolution, far from having exhausted its appeal with the 1989 events, appears likely to flourish. For some, indeed, the striking thing about 1989 is that it has renewed the whole idea of revolution, after a period in which it seemed to have lost its force and relevance. In the West and the industrial world generally, revolution has for most of the twentieth century been in abeyance.[10] The work of revolution seemed to be over, the myth of revolution pernicious. 1989, the year of the East European revolutions, was also the year of the bicentenary of the great French Revolution of 1789. In the West it occasioned an outpouring of "revisionist" works on the French Revolution, questioning its historic meaning and significance and pointing to the disastrous consequences that flowed from it.[11] Even in France—indeed, especially in France—the celebrations were distinctly muted. Revolution was no longer, as it had been for two hundred years, an inspiration, a model of change by means of which societies might renew themselves. The revolution was over—not just in France, but throughout the Western world.

In 1989 the torch of revolution passed once more, as it had in

1917, to the East. If the West, sunk in the torpor of affluence, had lost the taste for revolution, in the East it still seemed to have the capacity to inspire popular feeling and mass action. The events of 1989, said Fred Halliday, "have restated, in a dramatic form, the most neglected facet of political life, one spurned in east as much as in west, namely the capacity of the mass of the population to take sudden, rapid and novel political action after long periods of what appears to be indifference. In their speed and import and the uncertainties they unleash, they can only be compared to a war, in which all established expectations and plans are swept aside, in the face of novel, and irrefutable, realities."[12]

And not just revolution, the form, but democracy, the content of the modern revolution, seems to have gained fresh life from 1989. This is seen most obviously in the rediscovery of the idea of civil society as a tradition that can regenerate the concepts and practices of democracy today.[13] More generally, the realization that democracy can still move men and women to take to the streets and risk their lives has reopened the debate about the forms and meaning of democracy, east and west, north and south.[14] 1989, argues Slavoj Žižek, reminded the countries of the West in particular of the democratic promise of their own societies; this is the chief source of the enthusiasm with which the West greeted the events of 1989: "What fascinates the Western gaze is the *reinvention of democracy*. It is as if democracy, which in the West shows increasing signs of decay and crisis, lost in bureaucratic routine and publicity-style election campaigns, is being rediscovered in Eastern Europe in all its freshness and novelty. The function of this fascination is thus purely ideological: in Eastern Europe the West looks for its own lost origins, for the authentic experience of "democratic invention."[15]

Revolution and democracy; 1789 and the revolutionary tradition; the "end of history" and new beginnings—all this returns us, as Zygmunt Bauman says, to "the age of revolutions." But, pace Bauman, this must take us back well beyond our own century. In fact, the revolutions of the twentieth century, notably the communist revolutions of 1917 and 1949, are for obvious reasons peculiarly unhelpful as points of departure (though for equally obvious reasons they remain important as points of reference). We need to go further back. The age of revolution is two hundred, perhaps even three hundred, years old. 1989 connects not only with 1789 and 1848, but also with 1776 and 1688. What

Václav Havel called "the chain of spectacular transformations" that took place in 1989 reaches back deep into the past.

What are the connections? What kind of challenge do the 1989 revolutions pose to "our orthodox views of how revolutions come about"? What is the "new sociocultural context" in which they occur, and how does that affect their character? What kind of "updating" may be necessary in understanding them?

## 1989 and Theories of Revolution

Some commentators on 1989 have simply reached for their Crane Brinton. Brinton's *Anatomy of Revolution* (first published in 1938) drew upon the "classic" revolutions of 1640, 1776, 1789, and 1917 to set out a "shopping list" of general causes of revolution: a downturn in a generally advancing economy, a government in financial difficulties, the "desertion of the intellectuals," the "loss of confidence among many members of the ruling class," and the "conversion of many members of that class to the belief that their privileges are unjust or harmful to society." Brinton cautioned that "some, if not most of these signs may be found in almost any modern society at any time," and that the extension of his "tentative uniformities" to other revolutions must be undertaken "with caution and humility."[16] This has not prevented students of revolution from using his list as the key to revolutions at all times and places. Usually the "structural strains" identified by Brinton are coupled with some set of "triggers" or "precipitants"—a bad harvest, a bungled use of force by the government—that explain the actual onset of revolution at a particular time.[17]

It has not proved difficult to find most of these factors at work in the 1989 revolutions.[18] A particular favorite is the "desertion of the intellectuals" in Eastern Europe and their uncovering and denunciation of what Daniel Chirot calls "the utter moral rot" at the heart of their societies.[19] Teodor Shanin similarly argues that the concept of a "moral economy" is necessary to make sense of 1989: "It was mass indignation and not mass hunger which made radicals . . . go on the offensive, drew masses of people into protest and broke the resolve of the rulers to hang on, come what may."[20] Nor is it hard to find plausible "precipitating factors" that brought matters to a head in 1989: popular candidates are Hungary's decision to open its borders with Austria, and General Jaruzelski's calling of the roundtable conference with Solidarity.

No one can doubt the importance of a factor such as the loss of legitimacy in bringing about revolution. But this very example illustrates what is wrong with a Brintonlike approach to 1989. For had not communist rule in Eastern Europe (outside Russia) always been regarded as more or less illegitimate—not just by the subject populations, but even, one might reasonably suppose, by many of the rulers themselves? Communist regimes throughout Eastern Europe had either been directly imposed by Russian arms or were sustained by them (the Balkan states to some extent excepted). Eastern European societies after 1945, as so often before in their history, were of the nature of conquest societies. Their rulers were satraps, like the provincial governors of the ancient Persian monarchy. The legitimacy of these rulers was in question from the very earliest days of communist rule. This is clear from the fact that, despite the enormous risks involved and the many chilling examples of what failure might mean, their rule was repeatedly challenged by movements of mass protest and rebellion—in 1953, 1956, 1968, 1970, 1976, and 1980–81. The question must be, Why did the movements of 1989 succeed when all the earlier ones failed? It clearly cannot do to answer this question by pointing to a loss of legitimacy of the ruling groups. Their illegitimate character was a constant throughout the period of communist rule.[21]

Other popular theories of the causes of revolution do not fare much better when confronted with 1989. Take James Davies' "inverted J-curve" theory. This argues that "revolutions are most likely to occur when a prolonged period of objective economic and social development is followed by a short period of sharp reversal," thus frustrating expectations of a steadily increasing level of "need satisfaction."[22] With some qualification, owing partly to the ambiguity of the concept of "need satisfaction," the theory holds up quite well for the classic revolutions of 1640, 1766, 1789, and 1917.

But does it hold up for the revolutions of 1989? The theory may work for some of the earlier East European rebellions, especially the long Polish sequence that began in 1956 (but it was precisely the message of the last attempt, Poland's "self-limiting revolution" of 1980–81, that revolution in the full sense was impossible against the organized communist state, which was here to stay for the foreseeable future).[23] In these cases it applies at best to unsuccessful efforts to reform or topple communist rule. But it can scarcely be persuasive in the case of 1989, when communist rule actually was overthrown. For what has been the common coin of observations on the East European economies before 1989 is to note their stagnation, their slow strangulation under the grip of increasingly inefficient and irresponsible centralized control (Hungary being the main exception—and, fittingly, the country where the communists were displaced, contrary to the theory's expectation, with the least disturbance). Not, then, the outrage of frustrated populations accustomed to steadily increasing standards of living and fearful of losing them, but stoic resignation in the face of a long-drawn-out deterioration in their conditions of life, characterized the attitudes of most East Europeans on the eve of 1989.[24]

But Davies does, nevertheless, give us a lead if we expand his theory to include political as well as economic change, and if we expand our horizons to consider the Eastern European societies within the context of the Soviet empire as a whole. This last is critical. It points to the main weakness of most of the usual theories of revolution, and in particular the reason for their failure in the face of 1989.

Most conventional theories of revolution, Marxist as well as liberal, focus on factors internal to society. They say it is the conflict of classes, or mass discontent, or struggles within the ruling class, that bring on revolution. This emphasis seemed satisfactory for most of the revolutions from the seventeenth century to the nineteenth. Increasingly, however, it has become clear that they leave out an important part of the story. The pressures that have brought about revolution have been at least in part the result of external, international factors.[25] This was true even for England's "Great Rebellion" of 1640, when fears of collusion between a Catholic-inclined king and the Catholic powers of continental Europe fueled revolutionary passions. It is truer still for the American and French Revolutions of the eighteenth century, which can scarcely be understood without reference to the rivalry and struggle for hegemony between Britain and France. With the Russian Revolution of 1917 we are squarely within the domain of world revolution. Neither the causes of the Russian Revolution nor its outcome can be separated from the international context. With every succeeding revolution of the twentieth century—those in China, Vietnam, Cuba— the importance of factors external to the society has grown. Revolution in our time has taken on the character of an "international civil war."[26]

The revolutions of 1989 confirm this picture. The situation of Eastern Europe since 1945 has been, as is well known, the result of superpower agreements, notably those reached at Teheran (1943) and at

Yalta and Potsdam (1945), where Eastern Europe was ceded to the Soviet "sphere of influence." Since 1945 its position as part of the Soviet bloc has determined its fate. Every effort to change its condition in any essential respect has been suppressed by the actual or threatened use of Soviet force. From 1985 onward that situation changed dramatically. The Soviet Union under Gorbachev, realizing that it could no longer compete successfully with the United States and the West either in the military or the economic sphere, began to reform. One consequence of the new thinking was to let Eastern Europe go (that is, the "Sinatra doctrine" replaced the Brezhnev doctrine).

The "Gorbachev factor" was therefore the essential external ("geopolitical") element that made the 1989 revolutions possible—made them, one might almost say, necessary.[27] Without the support of Soviet troops, the regimes of Eastern Europe tumbled one by one. The speed astonished everyone, participants as well as observers, but in retrospect it is not so surprising.[28] All the internal elements of revolution— alienated intellectuals, revisionist Marxism, delegitimized elites, disaffected populations—had been there for a long time, almost as long as the regimes themselves. By themselves, given the unwillingness of the West to interfere in the internal affairs of another superpower, they could do nothing—or rather, their expression in fitful movements of revolt led nowhere. They were elements sealed in a steel cauldron. Once Gorbachev had taken the lid off, their combined force easily swept the party state away.

Bronislaw Geremek, one of Solidarity's leading theoreticians in the 1980s, wrote after the events of 1989: "De Tocqueville's famous aphorism that for a bad government the most dangerous moment arrives when it starts to introduce reforms seems to be fully applicable to the situation in Central Europe." He further notes that Tocqueville also said, in *The Old Regime and the Revolution* (1856): "Patiently endured so long as it seemed beyond redress a grievance comes to appear intolerable once the possibility of removing it crosses men's minds."[29] Tocqueville's analysis anticipated Davies' formulation (as Davies, of course, acknowledges), with the critical difference that in the case of the East Europeans (unlike those of the French or Russians before their respective revolutions) the reforming government was not their own, in most cases, but that of the external power that had for so long made them "patiently endure" their grievances without hope of redress. Since

1985 a reforming government, that of Mikhail Gorbachev in the Soviet Union, not only showed that communism could be changed, thereby raising hopes and expectations throughout the sphere of Soviet influence, but also more or less guaranteed that a movement for change would not be put down by force. What is more, after 1985 the Soviet government took an active part in stimulating change throughout the region. This was the principal difference between 1989 and 1956 or 1968, when Khrushchev's denunciation of Stalin and the "thaw" that followed it established the essential conditions for the rebellions and radical reforms of those years in Hungary, Poland, and Czechoslovakia—but without affecting the resolve of the Soviet government to stay firmly in control. It was also the difference between 1989 and 1980–81 in Poland, when, as Geremek observes, "comprehensive economic and political reforms proved impossible because they were not accompanied by favorable international circumstances."[30]

It has struck many commentators on 1989 that, if they are looking for a classical theorist of revolution as a helpful guide, Tocqueville is their man.[31] It is not just that Tocqueville seized, with unparalleled insight, on the general forces that undermine governments; it is also because he was the incomparable analyst of the particular revolutions of 1789 and 1848 (and understood, better than anyone at the time, the principles of the revolution of 1776 in America). 1989, in the eyes of participants as much as observers, was connected with the revolutionary inheritance of the West. Its meaning, therefore, has to be sought, at least in part, by seeing where it stood in the revolutionary tradition.

## 1989 and the Revolutionary Tradition

The revolutions of 1989 can be seen to stand, to use Robert Redfield's terms, within a "great tradition" and a "little tradition" of revolution. The "little tradition" was the sequence of risings and attempted reforms within the communist world, from the East German rising of 1953 to the Polish Solidarity movement of 1980–81. Like all traditions, it had its symbolic heroes and specially charged events. Poland was the brave warrior that refused to accept defeat. It expressed the steady current of opposition throughout, swelling to a flood in the 1980s. The Hungarian Rising of 1956 and the Czech Spring of 1968 symbolize heroic but tragic endeavor. They teach bitter lessons; but they are also an inspiration to future generations. The greatest shame lies in not having tried.[32]

From the perspective of the "little tradition," the 1989 revolutions were the culmination of these efforts. The movements of 1989, the various Civic and Democratic Forums, helped each other; their leaders were in touch with each other; the success of one was the signal for renewed efforts on the part of others, so that there appeared to be an inexorable logic to the exhilarating chain of events that began with Hungary and Poland in early 1989 and was crowned by the spectacular overthrow of Ceausescu in December of that year.

The "great tradition" was the European or Western revolutionary tradition stretching from the English revolutions of the seventeenth century to the Russian Revolution of 1917 and its twentieth-century successors in the non-European world. Marx's category of "bourgeois revolutions" links many of these revolutions; but it was Tocqueville who made us most aware that the sequence of revolutions—including the "communist" revolutions—have a common theme. That theme is democracy. Reflecting in particular on the American Revolution of 1776 and the French Revolution of 1789, Tocqueville was convinced that they were part of a general "European revolution" that was sweeping the world. The ideology of that revolution is democracy.[33] Each particular revolution expresses different facets of the worldwide movement toward democracy; each can be scrutinized for what it shows of the varying forces in conflict. Every revolution therefore has a particular and a general aspect; differing according to the circumstances of time and place, they are nevertheless members of the same family.

The relation of the 1989 revolutions to the little tradition, the specifically East European tradition of revolt, is relatively straightforward.[34] Essentially it concerns the contribution of the dissidents. In retrospect, at least, there has been a clear movement among them, from attempts to reform the system—to establish "socialism with a human face"—to the development of the conviction that the system could not be reformed, but must be rejected altogether (although not necessarily by a head-on collision with the state). There has been a satisfyingly evolutionary and "progressive" quality to this movement that sits well with many conventional views of how revolution comes about. The fact that these views are, in this as in most other cases, mistaken should not lead us to ignore the importance of dissident thought and action in keeping alive the spirit of revolt within these societies. The dissidents, most of whom were intellectuals, did not overthrow communism, not even when they combined with the workers in Solidarity. But, like the philosophes of the Enlightenment, they were the gadflies of the ancien regime, the critics and tormentors whose constant undermining of the pretensions of their rulers is probably a necessary ingredient of all revolutions.

The basis of the relation of the 1989 revolutions to the great tradition, the centuries-old European revolution, is not so simple. The kinship was claimed again and again—not least in the declaration that the revolutions represented "the return to Europe."[35] For some, such as Ewa Kowalska, a young Slovak historian, the events of 1989 were "the culmination of the slow and continuous 'general revolution' of the western world, of the process that began economically and politically with the English and French revolutions and that is coming to an end spiritually and nationally with the upheavals of central Europe."[36] The desire to link 1989 with the Western revolutionary inheritance has been a common theme of nearly all accounts of these revolutions, from both East and West.[37]

But there has been an emphatic rejection of one part of that inheritance—that represented by the Russian Revolution of 1917 and its particular successors. East Europeans as much as Western liberals deny the validity of Lenin's well-known assertion that the Russian Revolution "merely recommences the French Revolution." For them the Russian Revolution was, if not a cynical repudiation of the European revolutionary tradition, at the very least a massive deviation from the mainstream of it.[38] Now that revolution has revealed its bankruptcy, the falsity of its claim to continue and complete the French Revolution. The Bolsheviks, said François Furet, "thought that with 1917 they had buried 1789. Here, at the end of our century, we see that the opposite is happening. It is 1917 that is being buried in the name of 1789."[39]

So the first aspect of the problematic relation of the revolutions of 1989 to the Western revolutionary tradition was its selectivity, its refusal to accept that the model of the communist revolution belongs to that tradition. This was, in effect, to reject Marxism and its whole account of the role of revolution in modern world history.[40] No surprise here; but we should be aware of the peculiarity of the claim being made in the name of 1989. It appeals to a highly truncated version of the revolutionary tradition—a version that denies the legitimacy of revolution to bring about economic and social equality (or "social" along with "political" and "legal" citizenship). The communist revolutions of the twentieth century stand condemned for precisely that, for what are seen as the disastrous political consequences of their stated objective of achieving a classless society.

The rejection of one part of the revolutionary inheritance is closely linked to another peculiarity of the 1989 revolutions: their unwillingness to announce anything new, their self-consciously backward-looking nature. Virtually every commentator has remarked on this. Jürgen Habermas has called the 1989 revolutions "rectifying revolutions," or "revolutions of recuperation." They sought to remedy, to recover, to restore, not to discover new principles of state and society. Habermas notes their "total lack of ideas that are either innovative or orientated towards the future." 1989, he says, "presents itself as a revolution that is to some degree flowing backwards, one that clears the ground in order to catch up with developments previously missed out on." The East European societies wished to restart their history, in the first place by going back to the political traditions of the interwar period that were cut short by Nazism and communism. At a deeper historical level they also wished to "connect up constitutionally with the inheritance of the bourgeois revolutions, and socially and politically with the styles of commerce and life associated with developed capitalism."[41]

Backward-looking revolutions are not new; in fact, most revolutionaries, according to Barrington Moore, like most generals, "march into the future facing resolutely backward."[42] But since the French Revolution, at least, what Hannah Arendt called "the pathos of novelty" has been a distinguishing characteristic of almost all revolutions. To be a revolutionary—itself a new type—has been to blaze a new path, to aim to start everything de novo. In turning their backs on the new, the revolutions of 1989 seem likely to return us to the premodern sense of revolution, as a return or a restoration.[43]

We shall consider in a moment what might be the significance of this unexpected turn in the ideology of revolution. But first we should ask: If the revolutions of 1989 looked backward, what precisely were they looking back to? What aspects of the revolutionary tradition mattered to them? What can we learn about the 1989 revolutions by comparing them with the various revolutions of the past that make up the revolutionary inheritance? 1917, we know, was no starting point, except negatively. But it has been the common practice of most commentaries on 1989 to look to one or more of the other great revolutions for the light they might throw on its meaning.

1789—the Great French Revolution—is a natural reference point. It is the revolution most commonly referred to by most East European participants in the revolutions of 1989 (including Russian reformers), and by many Western commentators as well. 1789 is almost impossible to avoid. Rightly or wrongly, it has long been regarded as the symbolic starting point of the whole modern revolutionary tradition. Since that tradition is about the struggle for democracy, and since the 1989 revolutions were in the first place about democracy and human rights, it has seemed well-nigh inevitable that homage should be paid to the revolution that resulted in the Declaration of the Rights of Man and the Citizen and carried out the first real experiments in democracy in the modern world.[44]

But there is another reason why 1789 is a popular parallel to 1989. It symbolizes mass action, and for many theorists, as we have seen, this is part of the significance of 1989. The 1989 revolutions, in this view, put back on the agenda the possibility of political change directed by the people. They demonstrated, says Habermas, "precisely the sort of spontaneous mass action that once provided so many revolutionary theorists with a model, but which has recently been presumed to be dead. . . . It was mass anger . . . that was directed at the apparatuses of state security, just as it had once been directed at the Bastille. The destruction of the Party's monopoly on state power could similarly be seen to resemble the execution of Louis XVI."[45]

I have discussed elsewhere the limitations of this view of the 1989 revolutions. The importance of mass action—even in Romania—has generally been exaggerated, to the neglect of the importance of maneuverings among the Communist Party elites, including those of the Soviet Union.[46] But seeing 1789 as parallel to 1989 is problematic for other reasons as well. That revolution connotes, beyond democracy and citizenship, Jacobinism, the Terror, and plebiscitary dictatorship. It evokes ideological fanaticism of the kind that was the principal target of the 1989 revolutions. It is the classic example of the revolution that, conceived in freedom, gave rise to tyranny and totalitarianism. It was in this, as in several other respects, the precursor and parent of 1917.[47] East Europeans do not reject 1789 as they do 1917. Its contribution to democratic theory and practice is seen as incalculable. But, enamored as they are of the liberal varieties of democracy, 1789 is bound to appear in their eyes highly equivocal.

1848 is another popular parallel. The reasons are obvious. The 1848 revolutions took place, to a good extent, in the very region of East Central Europe that is also the heart of the 1989 revolutions. They were the first European revolutions to raise seriously the questions of nationalism and ethnicity that have come to dominate the politics of the region since 1989. 1848 was also, like 1989, a "revolution of the intellectuals," in Lewis Namier's well-known phrase. These were, moreover, intellectuals who were mostly liberals. They were acutely aware of the dangers of democratic despotism and anxious to secure the rights of individuals through constitutions and the rule of law. In all these ways, 1848 offers the "obvious parallel" to 1989.[48]

Seeing 1848 as parallel to 1989 does, indeed, have many things to offer. Foremost among them might be the fact that many of the very same groups that contended in 1848—Czechs, Slovaks, Poles, Hungarians, Ruthenes, Rumans, Slovenes, Croats, Serbs—were once more resuming historic struggles, the sources of which were first revealed in 1848. And, as in 1848, there was the brooding presence of the two giants on their flanks—Germany and Russia. But this parallel also has problems. 1848 released not just nationalism, but also socialism. The "social question," first raised in the French Revolution, returned to haunt the liberals of 1848. This was the central point made by both Tocqueville and Marx in their incisive analyses of 1848. The 1848 revolutions were buried not just by nationalist conflicts, but by the class conflicts that erupted in the June Days in Paris and the workers' risings in Berlin and Vienna.

These comments might, if anything, serve to underline rather than question the parallel between 1848 and 1989. Is it not the theme of every journalistic commentary on Central Europe—and Russia—today that the societies of the region might succumb to the forces of nationalism and social unrest? And yet there was an important difference between the situations in 1848 and 1989. The men and women of 1989 lived through a social experiment—the system of state socialism—the very premise of which was the primacy of the "social question." Unlike the liberals of 1848, they did not confront the demands of the socialists as political innocents. Trotsky once wrote caustically of the bourgeoisie of 1848 as being "shabbily wise" with the experience of the French bourgeoisie during the French Revolution. Shabbily or not, we can say that the bourgeoisie of 1989 was wise with the experience of 1848 and

1917. Their whole concern was not to let the democratic revolution be "blown off course" by the urgent pressures for social and economic well-being. Hence their fervent and almost desperate espousal of strict liberal doctrines of the relation between state and society. For their part the socialists and communists in the region knew that they could not press their demands in the old way. They, too, had to speak the language of liberal constitutionalism, or risk being excluded from political society. None of these things, of course, has guaranteed success. Nationalism and social distress may very well undermine the precarious stability of current democratic regimes in East Central Europe. They are an old and powerful combination. But we can at least say that no one was more conscious of the danger than the liberals of 1989.

And what of 1776—and 1688 and 1640? What of the Anglo-Saxon revolutions? The literature on 1989 is noticeably thin on references to these revolutions, by comparison with later ones. But are there not good grounds for tracing the filiation of 1989 from these important ancestors? Not only is there the interesting parallel in that all these Anglo-Saxon revolutions, like those of 1989, claimed to be doing nothing new, but merely to be returning to an earlier, purer state of affairs, or restoring a constitutional agreement that had been wantonly disturbed by an "innovative" monarch. More important is the fact that, far more than the French Revolution, these revolutions were predominantly constitutional and concerned above all else with a political settlement that would guarantee liberal freedoms. If the 1989 revolutions were about democracy, constitutions, citizenship, the rule of law, the protection of individual rights, and the creation of a pluralist civil society, it is hardly possible to think of more suitable parallels than the English and American revolutions.

Some commentators have certainly been aware of this. Ralf Dahrendorf, for instance, has argued that in trying to understand the predicament of the East Europeans in 1989 we should go back to *The Federalist Papers* and the writings of Alexander Hamilton and James Madison on civil society and the rule of law ("As a manual of liberal democracy," he says, "*The Federalist Papers* are unsurpassed"). He also recommends Edmund Burke—not so much the Burke who wrote *Reflections on the Revolution in France* (1790), but "the great Whig who . . . had supported the American Revolution."[49]

Andrew Arato, searching for a concept of revolution to fit the events and ideology of 1989, also turned, initially at least, to America. "Generally speaking . . . if one is to speak of any revolution in the East perhaps it should be a 'conservative' one, in the spirit of Hannah Arendt's analysis of the American revolution where organized society (the state legislatures) came to represent the *pouvoir constituant,* rather than atomized individuals in a juridical state of nature, as in the views of Sieyès anticipating the French reality." He was dissatisfied with this, though, since in the case of the 1989 revolutions the constituent power was composed "not of legitimate provincial legislatures but illegitimate communist parliaments and entirely self-appointed round tables."[50]

This seems unnecessarily cautious and restrictive. In no revolution, not even the American, is there such a halo of legitimacy surrounding the actors that their opponents cannot plausibly accuse them of unlawful and reckless innovation. Moreover, what in this context has struck all observers about 1989 was the relative orderliness of the overthrow of the party state and the movement to some sort of parliamentary democracy. In many cases it was leading elements in the Communist Party who themselves negotiated the transition. Except in Romania, there was remarkably little violence. The smoothness of the transition—"the monster died in bed," as R. N. Berki observed of the Hungarian case—has, as we have seen, even caused some to doubt whether we should speak of revolution in 1989 at all. A similar question has always hung over the English and American revolutions, which, as is well known, were not so termed at the time and came to be called such only retrospectively, by analogy with the French Revolution of 1789. So the manner of change, and many of the arguments used to justify it, had revealing similarities in the cases of both 1989 and 1776, not to mention 1688 and even 1640.

But the more important thing, once more, is the content of the revolutions. Here the claims of the English and American revolutions are particularly compelling. No one can doubt, for instance, that the concept of "civil society" was central in the thinking of the East European dissidents who prepared the way for 1989. It can almost be said to have set the political agenda for the 1989 revolutions. Adam Seligman has shown that, if we wish to achieve the fullest and most farsighted discussion of the concept, the best places to look are England and, especially, America in the seventeenth and eighteenth centuries. Here were worked out the moral foundations and the political and social requisites for a functioning civil society. Seligman argues that in the case of one society, eighteenth-century republican America—the product of the American Revolution—the ideal of civil society found a real political and social expression. He also shows how fragile was its base and how, not just in America but also in Europe, the foundations of civil society were steadily eroded throughout the nineteenth and twentieth centuries. As Seligman makes clear, if the East Europeans want to rebuild their societies on the basis of a new or revived civil society, they will need to understand what the historical requirements of such a society have been.[51]

Seligman is not optimistic about the prospects for civil society in Eastern Europe. The point, though, is that his assessment is based on something more than the fleeting impressions and wishful thinking that mostly pass for considered judgments among commentators on Eastern Europe today. This is the real value of considering the revolutions of 1989 from the perspective of past revolutions. Comparisons can be frivolous as well as odious; but they can also be instructive. Revolutions in the West have a history. The revolutions of 1989 belong to that history. In deeds as well as words, the peoples of Eastern Europe have expressed the desire to "rejoin" the West, after a period (as they see it) of enforced exclusion. Their actions have been inspired by Western examples; their intentions have been proclaimed in terms drawn almost entirely from the vocabulary of the Western revolutionary tradition. It would be strange, indeed, if that tradition had nothing to teach them, or us, in our efforts to understand them.

## 1989: Continuity and Change

We have been concerned so far with the ways in which the revolutions of 1989 connect with previous revolutions and with the revolutionary inheritance in general. There are continuities of ideology, clearly, and to some extent of practice. But in what ways might the revolutions of 1989 represent something new? Were they, as Zygmunt Bauman says, conducted in a "new sociocultural context" and, if so, with what effect?

One important novelty, much commented on, is the role of television and the electronic media generally. The 1989 revolutions were, says Timothy Garton Ash, "telerevolutions," as must be all revolutions at the end of the twentieth century.[52] Every student has remarked on the importance of the print media—books, pamphlets, and newspapers—in all the great revolutions from that of England in 1640 to that of Russia in 1917. Now, with radio, television, cable, satellites, computers, videocassette recorders, photocopiers, and fax machines, there has been a qualitative leap in the expansion of the technology of information and communication. The media are now "global, instantaneous, simultaneous and total" in their effect. This, suggests Deirdre Boden, made the 1989 revolutions "like no others in human history." The rulers of Eastern Europe were confronted by populations educated, informed, and entertained by the mass media of the West. There was simply no way in which they could seal off the flow of images and sounds flooding in from outside. As Boden says, "The hearts and minds of the people of Eastern Europe were lit up by the kinetic effects of global communication." Especially in the key months from June to December 1989, there was a "chain reaction" triggered by the media images of events in China, Poland, East Germany, and other socialist countries. From the Baltic states to Bulgaria, the socialist countries were ringed by a belt of territories that insistently beamed images of protest and revolt into the living rooms of the people of Eastern Europe. The media messages "merged to become a seemingly unstoppable single signal of hope."[53]

Notoriously difficult as it is to assess the effects of the mass media, there can be no doubting their importance in the making of 1989. What they point to, moreover, is another feature of the 1989 revolutions that emphasizes their novelty: their place in global patterns of change. Again, it is clear that there was a global aspect to many earlier revolutions, as I have already discussed. Once more, however, the great increase in the range and intensity of globalization seems to indicate something new. The 1989 revolutions are impossible to understand without reference to some major currents of change in the world as a whole.

Economically, there has been the emergence of a global economy— more clearly than ever before dominated by the major capitalist powers— whose pressures on the stagnant economies of Eastern Europe were unquestionably one of the principal sources of change in the region. "Socialism in one country" never, as socialism, had much chance of success; industrial development under state socialist auspices, in relative isolation from the dynamic capitalist world economy, in the end proved equally bankrupt. What is now occurring, according to Leo Panitch and Ralph Miliband, is "the incorporation [of East European societies] as subordinate elements within the economic, cultural and military/ strategic networks of the international capitalist system."[54]

Politically, the 1989 revolutions seem to belong to an equally marked "global revolution" of democracy.[55] In the 1970s and 1980s, dictatorships gave way to democracies, of various kinds, on almost every continent of the world. It seemed obvious to consider the 1989 revolutions as what Bova calls "a sub-category of a more generic phenomenon of transition from authoritarian rule."[56]

The results of this comparison have yielded some genuinely interesting parallels and similarities—the importance of reforming elites, for one thing, and, less obvious, the role of religious opposition.[57] There is also the ubiquity of the communication revolution. But, as compared with the global economic pressures, it is less easy to discern at more than a superficial level a common pattern of "transition to democracy" across the globe. This is partly because the political sphere is always more marked by particular features of history and culture. But, more important, there is a fundamental difference between the political changes in Eastern Europe and those in the rest of the world. Only in Eastern Europe did democracy have to emerge from totalitarian societies—societies, that is, where economic, political, and cultural power were fused in a single center, to the exclusion of virtually all elements of pluralism. (Even the Nazi regime did not attempt such a total integration until the outbreak of war.) Nowhere else was there such a total politicization of society. The "transition to democracy" in Eastern Europe has features to which, as several scholars have pointed out, we simply have no parallels in either past or present experience. Not only do the sources of change differ in important respects from those of other transitions; the outcome of the change must be less easy to anticipate, and less secure, than elsewhere.[58]

The economic and political developments of the last part of the twentieth century have led to a strong revival of modernization theory—indeed, as Lucien Pye sees it, "a vindication of modernization theory."[59] This provides yet another way to understand the 1989 revolutions.[60] Here again there is a mixture of old and new. In one variety of the modernization theory, much favored by certain Sovietologists until recently, the theory accounted precisely for the stability of the Soviet system, and its likely persistence for a long time to come. State socialism and liberal capitalism were seen as alternative routes to modernity. There would be a degree of convergence between them, but both had their peculiar characteristics, and both were able, in a literal as well as a more metaphorical sense, to deliver the goods.[61]

Such an approach might appear to share in the collapse of state socialism. But it does not take very much modification to make modernization theory serviceable once more.[62] The new emphasis falls on the later stages of modernization, observable in late twentieth-century

Western societies. Soviet-type societies may have been capable of achieving the earlier levels of modernization—mass literacy, urbanization, and industrialization of the basic, Fordist, kind. But they have proved incapable of moving into the age of the "information society," "post-Fordist" practices in work and organization, and transnational patterns of production, trade, and finance. Nor are they in any way capable of responding to the new levels and types of consumption fed by these developments, though—dangerously—their populations are made only too aware of them. The dynamics of modernization have undermined the stability of the Soviet-style system. The party state has reached the limits of its ability to modernize. The old theorists were right: modernity, as the latest stages show, ultimately requires pluralism and a developed civil society, if not active democracy. Gorbachev understood this clearly; hence his desperate efforts to reform.[63] The reforms were not sufficiently far reaching and, in any case, opened the way to the collapse of communism throughout Eastern Europe.

There is a general plausibility to this picture that makes its appeal understandable. The problem is how far it explains the revolutions of 1989. Modernization theory has always moved at such a high level of abstraction as to fit any phenomenon it is applied to. It can explain both the persistence of the Soviet system and, with the merest modification, its dissolution. Such generosity in a theory is suspicious. In the case of the 1989 revolutions, it might account for some of the very general pressures on East European regimes. But it cannot account for the timing or the manner of their going. Theories of revolution drawn from the armory of structural functionalism—to which modernization theory belongs—always have the same weakness. They point to "strains" and "dysfunctions" in the system, but cannot explain why or when those strains become insupportable. There is, as we have seen, no difficulty in finding "strains" in East European societies. Many of these go back for decades. The populations of those societies had accommodated themselves in various ways to the system. Their efforts to change it had proved unavailing. What finally made it possible not just to try again, but to succeed? We need to understand the dynamics of modernization; but we also need to understand the dynamics of mobilization and political transformation.

If the revolutions of 1989 cannot, or not only, be explained by modernity, what of "post-modernity"? To what extent might these revolutions reflect not revolution's past, but its future, in a new, postmodern world? Zygmunt Bauman has suggested that the downfall of communism signifies the failure not just of a particular variety of modern society but of the modernizing project per se. Communism displayed, even more than capitalism, the Enlightenment ambition to construct a perfect, rationally ordered system of society: "Communism was modernity's most devout, vigorous and gallant champion. . . . Indeed it was under communist, not capitalist, auspices that the audacious dream of modernity, freed from obstacles by the merciless and seemingly omnipotent state, was pushed to its radical limits: grand designs, unlimited social engineering, huge and bulky technology, total transformation of nature." The 1989 revolutions, says Bauman, represent the failure and end of that dream: "What the affluent west is in fact celebrating today is the official passing away of its own past; the last farewell to the modern dream and modern arrogance. . . . With communism, the ghost of modernity has been exorcised."[64]

The sense of an ending, perhaps opening the way to something new, is to be found in a number of other comments on the 1989 revolutions. Shmuel Eisenstadt notes that, compared with past revolutions, there was in 1989 "no totalistic, utopian vision rooted in eschatological expectations of a new type of society. . . . There was no new revolutionary International; only a plethora of discussion groups, seminars, and the like. . . . Accordingly, the future is much more open."[65] For Octavio Paz, the Mexican poet and writer, the 1989 revolutions are testimony to "the end of the myth born with the French Revolution." As Paz says: "Both systems that came out of it are bankrupt. The liberal Western democracies have defended individual freedom, and given the developed countries . . . a high standard of living. But they haven't changed life. They haven't changed human beings. These societies lack fraternity. The failure of Marxism has been even more spectacular. The end of the two ideologies is a great thing. The coming century will surely bring with it a new fusion."[66]

Habermas has protested, in the name of "the still unfinished project of modernity," against the "postmodernist critique" that interprets the events of 1989 as "a revolution to end the epoch of revolutions." In this view, which Habermas contests, the 1989 revolutions represent a revolt against reason. They championed the claims of "a self-empowering subjectivity" against the Enlightenment dream of power and control based on objective knowledge.[67] The 1989 revolutions here take their place as not the least manifestation of that "death of grand narratives" that has been seen as the hallmark of our condition of postmodernity. No more can we believe in Truth, Progress, History, Reason, Revolution. What we are left with instead is irony, pragmatism, and the quiet pursuit of private purposes.[68]

Bauman, as we have seen, is sympathetic to this view. What for him has increasingly characterized the modern world, pushing it into the era of postmodernity, is the obsession with private choice and consumerism. It was the denial of this that was the undoing of communism, and the driving force behind the 1989 revolutions:

> What enraged the rebels against the communist command economy and eventually brought communism down was not the envious comparison with the productive successes of capitalist neighbours, but the enticing and alluring spectacle of lavish consumption enjoyed under capitalist auspices. It was the post-modern, narcissistic culture of self-enhancement, self-enjoyment, instant gratification and life defined in terms of consumer styles that finally exposed the obsoleteness of the "steel-per-head" philosophy stubbornly preached and practised under communism. It was this culture that delivered the last blow to abortive communist hopes of competition with the capitalist rival. And it was the overwhelming desire to share (and to share immediately) in the delights of the postmodern world, not the wish to tread once more the tortuous nineteenth-century road of industrialization and modernization, that mobilized the massive dissent against communist oppression and inefficiency.[69]

We might all share Bauman's disquiet at this situation if this is indeed our common condition; and we might wish to endorse the hope of his erstwhile compatriot, Czesław Miłosz, reflecting on the changes of 1989, that "the turmoil in these countries has not been a temporary phase, a passage to an ordinary society of earners and consumers, but rather the birth of a new form of human interaction, of a non-utopian style and vision."[70] Once more we have to fall back on the verdict, "It is too early to say," though the signs are not propitious. "Normalization" seems to be precisely what the citizens of the new democracies crave, and in the circumstances of the time one can hardly blame them.

But the meaning of the revolutions of 1989 is, after all, not so very clear. The very terms *modernity* and *postmodernity* are still being hotly debated, and even if we were to characterize the 1989 revolutions as "postmodernist," it would by no means necessarily be to consign them to the sphere of rampant consumerism. That would, in any case, make nonsense of some of their most obvious features. The language of the

1989 revolutions was the language of rights, democracy, and freedom. These are concepts whose meaning, as with all concepts, is historical. In different revolutions they have spelled different things. In the present case they may well, and justifiably, include the claims of private choice and private life. But that does not exhaust their current meaning. For instance, when East Europeans appeal to the idea of civil society, they are invoking a democratic inheritance with possibilities going beyond anything yet achieved in either West or East.[71] Those possibilities remain to be realized, but they are part of the revolutionary tradition to which the 1989 revolutions were heir.

The 1989 revolutions partook both of the old and the new. The novelties must be given their due. But the "backward-looking" character of the revolutions is also abundantly clear, as are their connection with the democratic legacy of the great revolutions of the West. This, far from suggesting that the epoch of revolutions is over, actually points to quite a different possibility. For are we not, in the West as much as in the East, still trying to fulfill the promise of the democratic revolution? Does the democratic revolution not have, as Tocqueville argued, the character of a permanent revolution? Can such a revolution be halted by postmodernist fiat?

## A Further Note

"Many years will pass before we have a firm grasp of what processes the revolutions of 1989 and 1991 have unleashed," wrote Gale Stokes in his accomplished account of those revolutions published in 1993.[72] Six years on, that verdict still stands. The politics, economics, and social life of the countries of the former communist world remain in a state of turmoil. At the end of 1995 it looked, indeed, as if former communists—if not communism—would return to power in the region. Socialist parties composed mainly of former communists swept back to power in Bulgaria, Lithuania, Poland, and Hungary. They remained dominant in Albania, Romania, Serbia, and Macedonia. They constituted the largest parliamentary grouping in Belarus and Ukraine. In Slovakia they ran the government in alliance with nationalists. In the territories of the former East Germany they scored large votes in regional *(länder)* elections. It was as if the populations of East Central Europe, disappointed with the changes and tired of struggling to remake their lives in the disturbed conditions of postcommunism, had decided to return to the leaders who at least promised to moderate the pace a little and to restore something of the former stability and security.

In past revolutions, when the radicalization of the revolution has been tempered, conservatives have taken over and prepared the way, sometimes, for reaction and even restoration, which has been called Thermidor. The 1989 revolutions had their Thermidor, or what Adam Michnik called their "velvet restoration," some five or six years after they began. But they did not rest there. In the next few years the socialists were kicked out in Bulgaria, Romania, and Slovakia. They lost their standing in all the states of the former Yugoslavia with the exception of Serbia (and even there, with the defeat of Serbia over Kosovo, their future looked precarious). In Poland a coalition dominated by former Solidarity members took back the government in 1997. Contrariwise, socialists made a strong showing in the 1997 elections in the Czech Republic, hitherto a bastion of the latest free market thinking. There have indeed been "deep ups and down" to break "the monotony of the evolutionary process" in the region, as Attila Ágh remarked.[73] The revolutions of 1989 are not over. Turbulent crosscurrents continue to mark their course, though no one expects a return to anything like the pre-1989 situation. What marks postcommunist societies is what Zygmunt Bauman calls the condition of "liminality": an ambivalent, underdetermined state "without clear time-span, obvious exit and authoritative guides."[74] If this is "transition," it is unclear what it is a transition to, or when (if ever) it will end.

In any case, it is clear that there are many aspects of the 1989 revolutions that still remain unclear, not the least their long-term consequences. But if we continue to fulfill the purpose of the present chapter, which is to see the 1989 revolutions within the context of the general revolutionary tradition, there are a number of areas where more recent writing has rounded out or contributed something new to the account given above.

## Concept

The first thing we need to discuss is whether the events of 1989 fit the concept of revolution. Is it right to call these events a revolution (or revolutions)? Here there seems to have emerged a reasonable consensus: these events do deserve the name of revolution. Stokes heads one of his chapters, "The Glorious Revolutions of 1989," and most commentators, whether or not they judge them glorious, have followed suit. "The revolutions of 1989" has become the standard term used to discuss the momentous events of 1989 in Central and Eastern Europe, and it seems unlikely that this consensus will be shaken in the foreseeable future, whatever fresh revelations emerge and whatever new developments take place in the region.[75]

But that does not mean there is no doubt or dissent. In a later discussion, Stokes was more cautious than he was earlier. The events of 1989 were indeed "revolutionary," he said, but, except in Poland, these were not "social revolutions in the way we have thought about them in the past." Outside Poland there was nothing to match the "self-activating workers' movement" that was Solidarity, no social mobilization of workers, peasants, or a commercial or technocratic middle class to take over power from the communist party and the communist bureaucrats. Moreover, there is the much-harped-upon fact of the lack of "a level of violence normally associated with the concept of revolution. Even the Romanian events were small potatoes compared to the bloody traditions of the great revolutions." Stokes, like others, is also disturbed that "in contrast to earlier social revolutions, the revolutions of 1989 were not progressive because they restored or sought to copy social and economic norms that had previously existed in Eastern Europe or that had proven successful elsewhere rather than opening new avenues for human development, as presumably the French Revolution did and as the Bolshevik Revolution claimed to be doing." Hence he rather primly proposes to "refer to the 1989 revolutions with a small 'r' and with adjectival prefixes, such as 'negotiated revolution.'" Ultimately what seems important to him about the 1989 revolutions is their negation of their recent past, and their acceptance of an open-ended "pluralism," rather than any affirmation of a radically new future: "If the events of 1989 can be understood as the recognition that the centrally planned system failed, then it seems appropriate at the very least to term those events revolutionary in the negative sense that they interred any realistic hope that the teleological experiment in the use of human reason to transform society in its entirety [i.e., Marxism or communism] might succeed."[76]

The signs of strain and struggle in the writing here are evident. They show that Stokes, like many others, though convinced of a revolutionary occurrence in 1989, remains uncertain as to what precisely constitutes its revolutionary character. The term "negotiated revolution," first employed by László Bruszt in the Hungarian case, has proved popular as a general description. This points to the element of compromise and bargaining between moderate, reform-minded communist leaders and various opposition groups, usually in the context of "roundtable" discussions. A corollary of this view is that, as Bruszt puts it with regard to Hungary, "Mass movements did not topple the old system."[77] The "negotiated revolution" involves the masses on its own, carefully orchestrated, terms; that is another meaning of the much-used term, "velvet revolution," whose main connotation is the absence of violence and bloodshed (the Czech case here being the exemplary one).[78]

But even the term "negotiated revolution" does not answer all the queries or still all the doubts. Claus Offe is troubled by "the distinctly 'a-theoretical' character of the upheaval. . . . Entirely absent are all analytical expressions and grandiose directives by revolutionary intellectuals." He saw the 1989 revolution as "a revolution without a historical model and a revolution without a revolutionary theory." As Offe says, "Its most conspicuous distinguishing characteristic is indeed the lack of any elaborated theoretical assumptions and normative arguments addressing the questions who is to carry out which actions under which circumstances and with what aims, which dilemmas are to be expected along the road, and how the new synthesis of a post-revolutionary order ought to be constituted, and what meaning should be assigned to the notion of 'progress.'"[79] Offe is of the view that "in all of the revolutions of the last two centuries some kind of answers to these questions had been available." This is highly questionable, and the argument is not much strengthened by Offe's quip that "most of them proved wrong." The Bolsheviks may have gone in for revolutionary theory (little of which, in truth, prepared them for the revolution in whose making they had very little hand), but can the same be said of the French Revolution of 1789 or the revolutions of 1848? Theorizing the revolution seems in most cases a highly retrospective affair, requiring a Tocqueville or a Marx. Revolutions, as Sir Lewis Namier said, "are not made; they occur." Once they have occurred, "groups or parties with elaborate programmes . . . try to stamp them with their own ideology and, if successful, claim to be their spokesmen or even their makers."[80] This seems to be a more realistic account of revolution than Offe's. It certainly fits 1989, as it fits 1789, 1848, and 1917. The difference is that not enough time has yet elapsed for the various parties to indulge in revolutionary myth making—perhaps because, like many observers, they too are unsure of the character of the revolution whose mantle they might wish to assume.

Apart from the qualified terms—"negotiated revolution," "velvet revolution," "nonviolent revolution," and so on—or the new ones coined—such as Timothy Garton Ash's "refolution" (pointing to the mixture of reform and revolution)—the main conceptual rival to revolution in describing the events of 1989 appears to be "transition." East Central Europeans themselves tend to be wary of the word *revolution* for historical reasons; as Andrzej Tymowski says of the Polish case, "since the Second World War, 'revolution' has been identified almost exclusively . . . with the imposition of Stalinist power and its rhetoric." Even in 1989, he says, "the word was used sparingly, usually in pejorative or ironic contexts."[81]

Andrzej Tymowski himself, in discussing the Polish revolution of 1989, hesitates between "revolution," "transition," and even "restoration." The slogans of 1989—"return to normality," "return to Europe"—strongly recall, he says, the old, pre-1789, meaning of *revolution* as restoration or return, and for many this was the primary meaning of 1989.[82] Politically, Tymowski is certain, "revolution" is the wrong word. The long drawn-out process of negotiation between communist elites and Solidarity leaders, the controlled and carefully supervised nature of the handover of power to noncommunist parties, the lack of real mass involvement, and the absence of "foundational" elections symbolizing the start of a new political era, all militate against "revolution" and point to "transition" as the right description. The parallel here is the negotiated post-Francoist transition to democracy in Spain in 1976–77. But matters are not so certain at the economic and social levels. Economically, especially with the introduction of the radically free-market "Balcerowicz plan" in 1990, there was a sudden and distinct rupture with the past—not just with the communist past of a command economy, but with Poland's precommunist past of strong state regulation and state welfare. In the economic sphere, there was something like a Leninist "administrative imposition" of top-down institutional change, a "shock therapy" that dismayed not only former Solidarity supporters, but many within the Mazowiecki government that sponsored the plan. This, in turn, was leading to an unanticipated and in many quarters unwanted "social revolution." The old social structure of peasants, workers, and intelligentsia—a social structure that survived the communist interlude—was finally being melted in the heat of the rapid transition to a market economy. "What forty years of Soviet ideology could not do," Tymowski says, "the Solidarity triumph accomplished at one stroke."[83]

So in the end, despite doubts and qualification, Tymowski comes down on the side of the term *revolution* (at least "the initial, destructive phase of revolution"). András Bozóki is equally convinced that this is a mistaken description with regard to most of the former communist world. For him the concept of "transition" expresses "an alternative to revolution." Transition is "controlled transformation," an orderly process of "systemic change" that "accomplishes the objectives of revolution while avoiding the sacrifices as corollaries of revolutionary change." The majority of East Central European countries experienced "democratic transition" in 1989–90, on the model of the "Glorious Revolution" of 1688–89 in England ("the first successful transition"); only in Romania—where there was considerable violence and bloodshed—could there be said to be an example of revolution in 1989, with the French Revolution of 1789–93 taken as the model of this form of systemic change.[84]

This distinction, based on the absence or presence of violence, is, as we have seen, a familiar one; and once more it is necessary to stress that it is an exaggerated aspect of the theory and practice of revolution. What matters is the speed and depth of the change; whether or not it is accomplished or accompanied by violence has seemed to most theoreticians—for instance, Marx—to be incidental.[85] Such considerations have, on further reflection, brought back waverers such as Piotr Sztompka who were earlier inclined to question the application of the designation *revolution* to the events of 1989. The "means of revolutionary action," concedes Sztompka, are "historically changing"; there is no warrant for excluding "massive changes by non-violent means." Not only was 1989 revolutionary; it properly belongs to the category of "great revolutions"—those that, like the British, American, French, Russian, and Chinese Revolutions, have had "world-wide, global, truly historical impact. . . . Like those," Sztompka declares, "the revolutions of 1989 have undoubtedly changed the world."[86] One must surely say "Amen" to that. If the events of 1989, in the perspective of history, are not considered revolutionary, it is difficult to imagine why one would want to preserve the word, or what one would usefully mean by it. It is heartening that Stokes, too, for all his reluctance to use the word *revolution* in its full-blooded sense, has no doubt about the

epoch-making character of the changes launched in 1989. "It is difficult to imagine a more sudden and more complete creation of the conditions of social transformation than the events of 1989."[87] In other
words, a revolution—no less.

## Causes

The next area conventionally dealt with in accounts of revolution is
causes. Earlier in this chapter I considered the theories of such individuals as Tocqueville, Brinton, and Davies as to their relevance to 1989.
More recent discussions continue to rely on these classic approaches.
Like Brinton, Gale Stokes, for instance, following such writers as
Daniel Chirot, stresses the loss of moral legitimacy on the part of the
rulers of Eastern Europe. "Utter moral rot," says Stokes in a direct
echo of Chirot, is ultimately what made the walls come tumbling
down in the region.[88] Hence the importance of the "antipolitical" opposition of Havel and the Charter 77 group in Czechoslovakia, and of
Jacek Kurón and Adam Michnik in Poland. As Stokes says, "For more
than a century Marxists had occupied the high moral ground in politics by claiming to be the true opponents of repression. When the antipoliticians began to show the hollowness of that pretension with their
simple but effective strategy of living in truth, they began to edge the
Communists off that high ground and to assume the moral leadership
of their societies. This process, more than any single political, economic, or military event, is what doomed the Communist regimes of
Eastern Europe."[89]

A new importance for antipolitical politics is also claimed by
Jeffrey Isaac. The antipoliticians may have largely disappeared from
the political scene after 1989, but what they offered—not just for their
own societies, but also those of the West—was a vision of politics that
went beyond conventional liberal democracy. Liberal democracy is
what it is commonly assumed the revolutions of 1989 were all about;
and spokesmen from the region have continued to speak as if that
were the ultimate goal of the movement of opposition. But antipolitics
cannot simply be glossed as liberal democracy. In its idea of the "parallel polis," in its concern with active citizenship and the independent
life of civil society, in its antipathy to official parties and their programmes, antipolitics suggested a model of political action and political life closer to the radical republican ideas of Hannah Arendt than to
the assumptions and practices of currently existing liberal democracies.

It was such a vision that animated much of the opposition in Eastern Europe; and if, in the event, that vision has faded, to be superseded by "politics as usual," that should not take away the importance of such a vision in undermining the legitimacy of the monolithic totalitarian state, or of its potential for reinvigorating politics in both East and West.[90]

Loss of legitimacy is clearly a feature of most prerevolutionary societies. It is part of the perception that revolution, in the sense of the change of heart and minds, is usually already accomplished among significant sections of the population before the actual outbreak of revolution as a political event. Insofar as the dissident intellectuals and their message of antipolitics contributed to the delegitimation of the communist regimes—and no one can doubt that—they played an important part in preparing the way for 1989.

But, as Stokes among others concedes, the dissidents were a small group that had a limited impact on the population at large.[91] Moreover, as I argued earlier, the communist regimes of Eastern Europe had in the eyes of their populations lacked legitimacy for a very long time—in some cases, from their very inception after World War II. Thus loss of legitimacy by itself is not very useful in helping us to understand the causes of the 1989 revolutions.

Economic causes are equally clear to see. The deteriorating economies of communist societies, their lack of desired consumer goods, their large measure of indebtedness to Western banks, their inability to keep up with the new developments, especially in information and communication, in the industrial world economy: all these continue to be the common coin of observations on the causes of the 1989 revolutions. "Above all," Philip Longworth says, "as with the French Revolution, it was a consequence of economic crisis."[92] But it was certainly not an "economic crisis" in the French sense, where a long period of prosperity was followed by the short, sharp shock of economic setback caused by, among other things, a run of bad harvests. It was this pattern, as we saw, that was the basis of Davies' theory that relative deprivation is the cause of revolutions. As I argued earlier in this chapter, this was precisely not the pattern of the recent economic history of communist societies. The period of economic stagnation and decline began in the 1970s; by the 1980s the populations of Eastern Europe were learning to live with it. Hence, although undoubtedly, as with the loss of legitimacy, the bad economic situation contributed to the sense of discontent in Eastern Europe, it was too diffuse and long term to be accounted an important cause of the breakdown in 1989.[93] Certainly there cannot have been that outraged sense of normal expectations denied that is so important in Davies' theory. Generally economic causes can be found in all revolutions; 1989 is no exception. But, as in the other cases, the precise contribution of the economic factor has to be specified, and weighed against others.

What remains of outstanding importance, and what is stressed in my account earlier in this chapter (and also in chapter 2), is the international or geopolitical dimension to the 1989 revolutions. Another way of putting that is to stress the "Gorbachev factor" in the causation of the events of 1989. The Soviet Union under Gorbachev did not directly cause the revolutions of 1989; certainly the Soviets were not pleased with the result, which brought about the end of communism everywhere in Europe, and ultimately in the Soviet Union itself. But first and most important, they made it clear in the late 1980s that they would no longer intervene in the affairs of neighboring communist states (that is, they abandoned the Brezhnev doctrine of "international proletarianism"). This meant that any reform movement that began—whether within the Communist Party, as was most common, or outside—would no longer receive the brutal check that reformers received in 1956, 1968, and 1981. Second, and more obscure, was the encouragement openly or covertly given by the Soviet Union to the reformers in the communist bloc. This was partly by the "demonstration effect" of what was going on in the Soviet Union itself under Gorbachev with his *glasnost* and perestroika; there was also the more or less direct intervention by various Soviet agents—including Gorbachev himself—in the internal struggles taking place between reformers and "hardliners" in the various communist governments in the region.

About this latter phenomenon not much is distinctly known or is ever likely to be. We are mainly reliant on hearsay, personal memoirs, and interviews with prominent individuals who, in the aftermath of 1989, are naturally concerned to give an account of events that put them in the most favorable—or the least compromising—light. But we are better informed now on strategy at the higher levels of the Soviet government, and especially Gorbachev's own thinking and action in the crucial years between 1985 and 1989. We know, above all, that Gorbachev gave a very clear "green light" to reformers in Hungary, Poland, Bulgaria, and Romania, and that he gave an equally clear warning to the hard-liners in Czechoslovakia and the German Democratic Republic that they would have to change their ways or be swept aside.[94] When we consider that every thinking East European was aware of the precedents of 1956, 1968, and 1981, when we remember that in the very year of revolution, 1989, the Chinese Communists were busy shooting down student democracy advocates in Tiananmen Square, it is impossible to exaggerate the significance of the Soviet response—or the lack of it—in the face of the momentous changes in 1989.[95]

There remains one further question concerning the causes of the revolutions of 1989. How far were the revolutions popular revolutions, brought about essentially by mass protest and mass action, and how far were they basically elite led and elite controlled throughout? Few question the important role of party reformers in the changes—especially in Hungary, Bulgaria, and Romania—but some commentators are concerned to stress the role of "people's power" as well, especially as expressed by Solidarity in Poland and by the large popular gatherings in Budapest, Prague, Leipzig, and Timisoara. In one of his accounts, Stokes is definite:

> Whatever specific events happened in the various countries involved, all of them were made possible by the people throwing off forty years of passivity. The popular revolutions of 1989 produced many potent visual images of the people in action: dancers on the Berlin Wall; thousands of people in Sofia maintaining candle-lit vigils; a Romanian demonstrator in Cluj baring his chest to armed soldiers. . . . Chanting words like "Freedom," "Democracy," and "Solidarity," 1989's equivalent to the "Liberty, Equality, and Fraternity" of 1789, hundreds of thousands of ordinary citizens, rarely mobilized before or since, toppled the rotted Communist regimes of East Germany, Czechoslovakia, and Romania, and to a certain extent Bulgaria too.[96]

But in a later analysis by Stokes, this euphoric account is tempered by the sober observation that "the key element in the revolutions of 1989 . . . was not so much the mechanisms of street demonstrations that provided the impetus for change but the fact that they were fomented by a leadership committed to a democratic outcome." This formulation does not, of course, necessarily deny the important role of popular protest; and Stokes, in fact, concludes with a reaffirmation of his original position: "In most of the revolutions of 1989 the main social element was people power, crowds on the street."[97]

Stokes's hesitations are symptomatic of much of the literature deal-ing with 1989. There is a reluctance to accept that the people may have played little part in the changes. It is part of the mythology of revolu-tion, especially in the West, that the people are the main actors in revo-lution, its essential driving force. And yet the evidence is that in none of the revolutions of 1989 was mass protest the decisive factor. This was true even in Poland, where Solidarity undoubtedly had a mass base, but where the Solidarity leaders were extremely careful to keep negotia-tions with the communists firmly in their own hands and, to a good ex-tent, in secret. Elsewhere—as, for instance, in Czechoslovakia, Bulgaria, or Romania, where the crowds were evident at key moments—there is a good deal of material to suggest that these crowds were carefully mo-bilized and controlled by opposition leaders—where indeed they were not being shamelessly manipulated by both incumbents and their op-ponents.[98] There is no question that large numbers of people in East Central Europe were anxious for change, and welcomed it deliriously when it came, at least in the early stages. But the people of this region had no tradition of active involvement in politics. Under the commu-nists they made their own private pact with the regime, turning their backs on it if they felt particularly hostile. But they knew the futility of attempting open opposition, even had they felt so inclined. 1989 con-tinued this pattern of passivity. The people were seen in the squares of the main capitals; they had to be. This was part of the legitimating myth of these revolutions, that they were revolutions of the people. But in few revolutions of the past two hundred years have the people played so minor a role. Hence, again, as with the absence of violence, the problem for some commentators in calling the events of 1989 "revolutions."

## Comparisons

A popular way of considering the revolutions of 1989 has been by comparing them with the other "transitions to democracy" that took place in the 1970s and 1980s. This term refers to the democratization in Southern Europe in the 1970s (in Portugal, Spain, and Greece), and to the collapse of authoritarian rule in South America in the 1980s (in Argentina, Brazil, Uruguay, Chile, and Paraguay). It also sometimes in-cludes a comparison with the transition to democracy in post-World War II Germany, Japan, and Italy. Commentators do not always stress uniformities or similarities in all the processes of transition; they are just as likely to stress differences. The point for these analysts, however, is the theoretical value to be gained from making the comparisons, and the illumination that each case may cast on the others.

Two of the acknowledged leaders in this field of comparative politics, Juan Linz and Alfred Stepan, have built on earlier work in producing a comprehensive and wide-ranging treatment that includes the changes in Eastern Europe as part of the comparative exercise. Though mainly concerned with developments after 1989, the account of Eastern European societies necessarily contains an analysis of the various factors responsible for the revolutions of 1989, as some sort of guide to the prospects for democracy in the different postcommunist societies.[99]

The common assumption of much of the "transition" literature is that, despite particular differences, there are uniformities and structural parallels in the movement from authoritarian regimes to liberal democratic market societies. Linz and Stepan, for all their caution and sophistication, share that basic assumption. But from a relatively early date dissenting voices were heard. Claus Offe argued that the conditions of the East European states meant that their revolutions were of a fundamentally different kind from those that marked the transitions elsewhere. Unlike in other parts of the world, what was being attempted in Eastern Europe was the simultaneous implementation of change at three different levels—political, constitutional, and economic—for which there were no earlier precedents and no existing models.[100] Others, too, stress unusual or unique features in the East European case—the absence of an entrepreneurial middle class, the low level of development of capitalism before the communist takeover, the lack of preexisting democratic traditions, the historic dependence on external forces, especially during the communist period, and the social and psychological legacy of the communist period itself, in which there was an unprecedented concentration and centralization of political, economic, and cultural life.[101]

This seems the direction to take, as I have argued earlier in this chapter. Comparisons within the communist bloc and between communist and postcommunist states seem altogether valuable, and indeed probably necessary; comparisons with "transitions" elsewhere will no doubt yield some illumination and the occasional striking insight, but on the whole are likely to mislead more than they enlighten. The communist experience was distinctive, perhaps unique. Unless this is acknowledged, the attempt to force the revolutions of 1989 into some common mold of "transitions" will produce the usual monstrous distortions and misunderstandings. Above all, it will leave us helpless in the face of the attempt to understand the current condition of postcommunism and the many peculiarities—some of them the result of the recent communist past, others of more distant historical provenance—that affect all current efforts to establish new political and economic institutions in the region.[102]

There remains another kind of comparison—not with contemporary "transitions" in other parts of the world, but with past revolutions in the Western world. At least in this case, unlike in that of universally conceived "transitions," we are dealing with a culture and a civilization—Europe and North America—shared between the societies of Central and Eastern Europe and those of the rest of the West— that is, between societies all of which can in some sense be considered "European" (see chapter 3 of this book). It is the argument of the present chapter that a great deal can be gained by seeing the 1989 revolutions within the context of the Western revolutionary tradition. Not only does this square with the self-understanding of many of the participants in these revolutions; it also provides the best basis for an understanding of the concept, causes, course, and consequences of the 1989 revolutions. The 1989 revolutions share much with the revolutions of 1688, 1776, 1789, 1848, even 1917—to mention only the best known. They are equally a response to those of 1956, 1968 (not only of Prague, but also of Paris), and 1981. There are continuities—as well, of course, as discontinuities—with those revolutions in terms of ideas, aspirations, examples, warnings, development, and outcomes. Many of the same social groups—as, for instance, intellectuals, students, workers, and dissident or discontented members of the ruling elites—were involved. The international environment was of the same importance.

Nothing could be more beneficial in furthering our understanding of the 1989 revolutions than this kind of comparison. But it is here that the literature is singularly lacking. For the dozens of studies comparing 1989 with contemporary transitions there are a mere handful comparing it with past revolutions.[103] Perhaps this simply reflects the fading of the interest in revolution in the contemporary West (see chapter 8 of this book). If so, it is a pity, because it is here that some of the most interesting work on the 1989 revolutions could be done, and remains to be done.

## Novelties

What might be new about the revolutions of 1989? In this chapter I have considered some of the views that point to the new importance of mass communications and information technology. I have also considered the character of these revolutions as "postmodern" revolutions. Nothing of much significance in these areas has appeared since this chapter was first written.[104] It is possible to see the fragmentation and divisions that have followed the revolutions as an instance of "postmodernist" tendencies, but one hardly seems to need to invoke postmodernism when one considers the very old-fashioned "modernist" forces of nationalism and ethnicity that have been responsible for these developments.[105]

Of the novelties that have been claimed for 1989, one that has attracted considerable attention has been the element of surprise. Most revolutions happen by surprise—as with Auguste Blanqui's "happy surprise" at the events of 1848—but there has been a sense that the 1989 revolutions were particularly unexpected, that they happened with a speed and suddenness that defied all rational expectation and surprised all seasoned observers of Eastern Europe. "At the time," says William McBride, "we were all astonished. Only later did some writers and thinkers begin to look back, *post festum,* and point out signs and symptoms that had been there to see. . . . But the proposition that traditional Communist Party dominance in Eastern Europe would end within a matter of just a few months was not one that anyone, to the best of my knowledge, was seriously advancing even shortly before the end came."[106]

The element of surprise in 1989 has led to a vigorous discussion that is itself somewhat surprising. One interesting strand has been conducted in the journal *Contention,* and began with a spirited piece by Nikki Keddie in which, basing her position on the unpredictability of the Iranian Revolution of 1979, she went on to argue for the basic unpredictability of all revolutions. For her, therefore, the element of surprise in 1989 was no surprise, nor should it have been. Countering this, Jack Goldstone argued that if area experts on Iran and Eastern Europe had been familiar with recent work in the theory of revolution, they should have been able to predict the revolutions in those regions. Goldstone accepted that "individual (or accidental) interventions can delay or accelerate the transformation of a potentially revolutionary situation into an overt revolutionary struggle." He saw Gorbachev's intervention in East Germany as bringing about Honecker's speedy downfall in what was otherwise an unpromising situation for the opposition. Hence, prediction in the strict sense may indeed be impossible. "But what *can* be done," Goldstone says, "and this is my meaning when I speak of 'predicting' a revolution, is to identify states that are moving rapidly toward a revolutionary situation, so that if trends continue unchecked a revolution is highly likely to break out when a triggering or accelerating event occurs." On the basis of a series of indicators— the state's loss of efficacy in commanding resources and obedience, the alienation of elites, and a populace primed for mobilization— Goldstone argues that the communist states, and specifically the Soviet Union, were in a clearly revolutionary situation by the 1980s, and revolution was therefore predictable—though the exact timing was not.[107]

Goldstone's contention depends on a questionable separation— unusual, as he admits, in scientific theorizing—of causality from prediction: we can *predict* revolution, though we cannot always give an account of its *causes* until after the event. His examples, and the factors he identifies as necessary for correct prediction, make one wonder whether he has really added much to Tocqueville and similarly minded theorists. A different line was taken by Randall Collins. Again focusing on the Soviet Union, but with implications for the revolutions of 1989, he argued that "geopolitical theory" would have enabled us to predict the demise of the Soviet Union, and that he did predict its demise in the late 1970s (even though he admitted, "I was surprised that it happened so soon").[108] Specifically arguing against Collins, Timur Kuran maintained his earlier view that revolutionary surprises will occur repeatedly and that social science has no way of predicting them.[109]

There is no space here to deal in detail with this very stimulating debate. It is a testimony to the continuing interest of 1989: for its historical importance, for the general theoretical issues it raises, above all for the number of ways it makes us rethink our understanding of revolution as a phenomenon and as a persistent fact in the development of modern societies.

*Five*

# Civil Society: An Inquiry into the Usefulness of a Historical Term

*Civil society is still only an idea; let us look at ourselves here in Budapest, as if from the island of Utopia.*
György Konrád, *Antipolitics* (1984)

## An Act of Recovery

It is undeniably the case that many Central and East European intellectuals have seen the construction or reconstruction of "civil society" as the salvation of their nations in their current predicament. Their example has inspired several Western thinkers to reconsider the concept of civil society, to ask whether it may not also speak to the condition of Western societies. In both cases it is the crisis of socialism, as an experience and an ideology, that has prompted this search for alternative concepts. The terms of civil society, its attractive combination of democratic pluralism with a continuing role for state regulation and guidance, make it appear hopeful to societies seeking to recover from the excesses of state socialism; at the same time it seems to offer help in the refashioning of radical politics in those societies where socialism has lost whatever appeal it once possessed.

The revival of the concept of civil society is a self-conscious exercise in remembering and retrieval. It is, says one of its proponents, to engage in "a type of future-oriented memory," "a rescuing or 'redemption' of the lost treasure of authors, texts and contexts" neglected as outdated or merely "bourgeois"; it is "a necessary condition of stimulating the contemporary democratic imagination."[1] Western scholars are perhaps more likely to stress this revivalism than their counterparts in Central and Eastern Europe. There the concern with "totalitarianism"—another concept latterly somewhat disregarded in the West—has kept alive the idea of civil society as the antithesis and alternative to the party state.[2] But even here it was the unexpectedly swift collapse of the party state, especially in the remarkable events of 1989, that gave a new relevance and a new currency to the idea of civil society. Here, too, in the sense of the recovery of certain traditions of the precommunist past, there is the element of revival and retrieval.

In both cases, then, we are dealing with a concept rich in historical resonances; a concept where a good part of the appeal is the sense of many levels and layers of meaning, deposited by successive generations of thinkers. With it, as most of its uses clearly testify, we are in the realm of the normative, if not indeed the nostalgic. "Civil society" sounds good; it has a good feel to it; it has the look of a fine old wine, full of depth and complexity. Who could possibly object to it, who not wish for its fulfilment?

Fine old wines can stimulate, but they can also make you drunk, make you lose all sense of discrimination and clarity of purpose. What is the case for reviving the concept of civil society? What can it offer that other concepts cannot? What is its theoretical reach, and how far can this be translated into practice? To answer these questions we must first look, however briefly, at the history of the concept. For doubts about the usefulness of reviving it spring in part from its perplexing history of varying, and sometimes contrary, meanings.

## The Career of a Concept

Up to the end of the eighteenth century, the term *civil society* was synonymous with the state or *political society*.[3] Here it reflected precisely its classical origins. *Civil society* was a more or less direct translation of Cicero's *societas civilis* and Aristotle's *koinônia politiké*. Locke could speak of "civil government" along with, and as an alternative term for, "civil or political society." Kant saw *bürgerliche Gesellschaft* as that constitutional state toward which political evolution tends. For Rousseau the *état civil* was the state. In all these uses the contrast has been with the "uncivilized" condition of humanity—whether in a

hypothesized state of nature—or, more particularly, under an "unnatural" system of government that rules by despotic decree rather
than by laws. *Civil society* in this conception expresses the growth of
civilization to the point where society is "civilized." It is, as classically
expressed in the Athenian polis or the Roman republic, a social order
of citizenship, one where men (rarely women) regulate their relationships and settle their disputes according to a system of laws—where
"civility" reigns, and citizens take an active part in public life.[4]

The connection of citizenship with civil society was never entirely
lost. It forms part of the association that lends its appeal to the current
championing of civil society. But there was a decisive innovation in
the latter half of the eighteenth century that broke the historic equation of civil society and the state. John Keane has argued that this was
an achievement of British and American thought. In the writings of
Locke and Paine, and also in those of Ferguson and Smith, he discerns
the basic elaboration of a sphere of society distinct from the state and
with forms and principles of its own. Although these writers continued to use the term *civil society* in its classical sense—as in Adam
Ferguson's *An Essay on the History of Civil Society* (1767)—they were
in fact establishing the distinction that was later to bring about a radical transformation in the meaning of the concept.[5]

The concern of these writers, argues Keane, was largely political.
Civil society was elaborated as a concept in the eighteenth-century debates about despotism and the means to counteract it.[6] Keane is here
reacting against the conventional "property-centered" view, derived
from Marx, that associates the distinction between civil society and
the state with the growth of capitalism and the development of the science of political economy. In this view the refashioned concept of civil
society was tied to the emergence of a distinct sphere of private property whose principal feature was an unprecedented degree of autonomy and independence from other social spheres.

Civil society *(bürgerliche Gesellschaft)*, said Marx, "embraces the
whole material intercourse of individuals within a definite stage of the
development of productive forces." In this general, analytical sense,
civil society as "the social organisation evolving directly out of production and commerce" is always and everywhere "the true source
and theatre of all history"; it "forms the basis of the state and of the
rest of the idealistic superstructure." But the discovery of this sphere,
and the recognition of its central importance in history, could come

about only at a particular stage in the development of the productive forces: the stage at which the bourgeoisie could establish an economy, in principle and to a good extent in practice, distinct from the state and all other regulatory bodies. Only then could civil society be named, only then its principles anatomized by the new economic science. As Marx said, "The word 'civil society' emerged in the eighteenth century, when property relationships had already extricated themselves from the ancient and medieval communal society. Civil society as such only develops with the bourgeoisie."[7]

Marx explicitly attributed this view of civil society to Hegel. He referred to "the material conditions of life, the sum total of which Hegel, following the example of the Englishmen and Frenchmen of the eighteenth century, combined under the name of 'civil society.'"[8] But an examination of Hegel's admittedly very abstract account of civil society does not really support this purely "materialist" interpretation. What it shows, rather, is that Hegel was closer to the eighteenth-century, pre-Marxist, concept of civil society and that Keane is right to insist on the richer, more complex, more political provenance of the concept.[9]

Civil society in Hegel, says Shlomo Avineri, "is nothing else than the market mechanism."[10] Nothing else? Certainly material interests belong here, in this "association of members as self-subsistent individuals." And Hegel was also, like Marx, clear that the crystallization of this sphere, as an institutionalized and differentiated entity, has occurred only relatively recently—for Hegel, in the period since the Renaissance. "The creation of civil society," he said, "is the achievement of the modern world which has for the first time given all determinations of the Idea their due." It is, moreover, indeed the case that civil society is a realm of "appearance," where particularity and egoism lead to "measureless excess," and ethical life, which is essentially social, seems to be lost in a riot of self-seeking.[11]

But the appearance is of course deceptive. Civil society, as a moment in the progress of the spirit toward the universality of the state, is not simply—as Marx would have had it—a cockpit of competing individuals pursuing their private ends. Civil society is a part of ethical life, the part that provides the middle term between the family and the state. It therefore partakes of that unity of "abstract right" and "subjective morality" that is the formal principle of ethical life. It goes, that is, beyond individuals and the relations between individuals to encompass the life of the community as a whole. At the core of civil society is a process of mediation. The "concrete person" of civil society differs from the isolated subject of the sphere of morality *(Moralität)* in that he gradually comes to recognize himself as a member of society and realizes that to attain his ends he must work with and through others. According to T. M. Knox, "Through working with others, his particularity is mediated; he ceases to be a mere unit and eventually becomes so socially conscious, as a result of the educative force of the institutions of civil society, that he wills his own ends only in willing universal ends and so has passed beyond civil society into the state. . . . The history of civil society is the history of the education of . . . private judgement until the particular is brought back to the universal."[12]

The term *bürgerliche Gesellschaft* encompasses the very ambiguity that needs to be explored in Hegel and Marx. It makes no distinction between the sphere of the bourgeois and the sphere of the *citoyen*. Marx interpreted it very much as synonymous with bourgeois society—the arena of the self-seeking economic actor. Hegel certainly included this—civil society is not the state—but, critically, he also included within it the impulse to citizenship, the passage from the outlook of civil society to that of the state. That is why the sphere of civil society encompasses not just economic, but social and civic, institutions. It includes not just the market, the system of production and exchange for the satisfaction of needs, but also classes and corporations concerned with social, religious, professional, and recreational life. One of these classes is the bureaucracy, "the universal class," the class that links the particularism of civil society with the universality of the state. The other mediating devices are the whole range of public institutions, such as courts, welfare agencies, and educational establishments, that are directly concerned with civic purposes. These noneconomic institutions are not peripheral or minor aspects of civil society, but are central to its function in Hegel's political philosophy. As Z. A. Pelczynski says: "Civil society in this sense is an arena in which modern man legitimately gratifies his self-interest and develops his individuality, but also learns the value of group action, social solidarity and the dependence of his welfare on others, which educate him for citizenship and prepare him for participation in the political arena of the State."[13]

Shlomo Avineri, perversely, having sought to narrow Hegel's concept of civil society, has elsewhere tried to inflate Marx's. Marx, says Avineri, clearly distinguished civil society "as a sphere of economic activity unlimited by political considerations," from "the bourgeoisie as a social class." This allowed him to give a political interpretation of the rise of capitalism. Civil society was the creation of the communal movement of the burghers of the late Middle Ages. The stuff of civil society were the urban corporations and communes. These cleared the space for the accumulation of capital and the rise of the bourgeois class. Thus it was "a socio-political revolution in late medieval Europe" that heralded the industrial revolution: "Countries which did not evolve a civil society were unable to develop on capitalist lines."[14]

This attempt to give civil society a largely sociopolitical character does not, however, really square with Marx's normal treatment of it. As Alvin Gouldner says, "Marx normally emphasized that the social structures of civil society were *not* independent entities generating bourgeois society but were, rather, forms in which bourgeois society had emerged; that is, *they were the products rather than the producers of the bourgeois class.*"[15] Marx's tendency to dichotomize, to assign all social phenomena to base and superstructure, meant that there was no place for an independent and distinctive realm of the social. The social practices and social institutions of civil society could be no more than the forms in which the essential life of capitalist society, the economic life, was played out. Hence Marx's claim that "the anatomy of civil society is to be sought in political economy."[16] The social structures of civil society were dissolved in the economic base; the economic dimension of society was expanded until it became coterminous with society itself. This left only the simple dichotomy "society-state." And it was quite clear which way the influence flowed. As Engels put it: "The State—the political order—is the subordinate, and civil society—the realm of economic relations—the decisive element."[17]

Marx's reductionist concept of civil society, argues Gouldner, led Marxism away from an engagement with the central subject matter of sociology, which has been precisely the social structures of civil society, conceived as a domain occupying the space between the individual and the formal institutions of the state. In the writings of Saint-Simon, Comte, Tocqueville, Durkheim, Tönnies, and Parsons (among others), Gouldner sees the attempt to grapple with the central problem of modern society: how to find a "third way" between "the atomization of competitive market society," on the one side, and "a state dominated existence," on the other. The solution has generally been seen to lie in a structure of "natural" or voluntary groups and organizations through which the individual develops the sense of social solidarity and civic participation. As Gouldner says, "Sociology conceives of civil society as a haven and support for individual persons, i.e. as de-atomizing; as a medium through which they can pursue their own projects in the course of their everyday lives; and as ways of avoiding dependence on the domination by the state."[18]

Gouldner sees weaknesses in this sociological tradition, which he views as a largely reactive and conservative response to what were perceived to be threats to social order posed by the French and Industrial Revolutions. In its pursuit of the "organic," "spontaneous," and "natural" forms of society, sociology, like Marxism, has been neglectful of the state and the political dimension generally. But at the same time Gouldner wishes to praise the sociological emphasis on the structures of civil society. Especially in an era in which the collectivist state has revealed the dangers and limitations of Marxism's "liberative aspirations," sociology has an important role to play in thinking through the problem of developing "a *self*-maintaining civil society, social organisations, and social systems." As Gouldner says, "No emancipation is possible in the modern world . . . without a strong civil society that can strengthen the public sphere and can provide a haven from and a center of resistance to the Behemoth State."[19]

This is, of course, the language of other recent proponents of the civil society idea, and we shall return to its claims. But we should note in passing that of all the contributions of the classic sociologists to the idea, it was probably Alexis de Tocqueville's that was the most incisive. What Tocqueville did was to refine the state-society dichotomy, common not just in Marxism but in much other discussion of the time, and introduce a third region, a third term, that kept alive the idea of a political culture below—or, perhaps better, around—the state. Though he did not spell them out in precise terminology, in *Democracy in America* (1835–40) and *The Ancien Régime and the Revolution* (1856) Tocqueville effectively identified three realms of society. There is the state, the system of formal political representation, with its parliamentary assemblies, courts, bureaucracy, police, and army. There is civil society, which is essentially the arena of private interest and economic activity, and which corresponds more or less directly to the capitalist economy that Marx also identified with civil society. But although Marx made this the whole of nonstate society, Tocqueville critically added another dimension, the dimension of "political society."[20]

Political society draws upon the fullest development of what Tocqueville called the most important "law" controlling human societies, "the art of association." In civilized societies there are political associations, such as local self-government, juries, parties, and public opinion; and there are civil associations, such as churches, moral crusades, schools, literary and scientific societies, newspapers and publishers, professional and commercial organizations, organizations for leisure and recreation. The life of all these associations, the "superabundant force and energy" that they contribute to the body politic, constitutes political society. Tocqueville noted that it is usually politics that spreads "a general habit and taste for association," so that "one may think of political associations as great free schools to which all citizens come to be taught the general theory of association." But he also argued that "civil associations pave the way for political ones." It is there that "feelings and ideas are renewed, the heart enlarged, and the understanding developed."[21] It is, in any case, through political society that the potential excesses of the centralized state are controlled, especially in democratic societies. Political society supplies "the independent eye of society" that exercises surveillance over its public life. It is what educates us for politics, tempers our passions, and curbs the unmitigated pursuit of private self-interest.

Something of Tocqueville's understanding of political society has returned with Antonio Gramsci, who has been called "the Marxist Tocqueville."[22] Gramsci also returns to the Hegelian roots of the idea of civil society. At one point in his *Prison Notebooks* he writes of "civil society as understood by Hegel, and as often used in these notes (i.e. in the sense of political and cultural hegemony of a social group over the entire society, as ethical content of the state)."[23] Elsewhere he says that "between the economic structure and the State with its legislation and its coercion stands civil society"—and it is the latter that must be "radically transformed" if revolutionary change is not to degenerate into "economic moralism."[24]

Gramsci here sets himself against the purely economic interpretation of civil society associated with Marx and his followers. Indeed, it is possible to go further, and to agree with Norberto Bobbio when he says that, in contradistinction to Marx, "civil society in Gramsci does not belong to the structural sphere [i.e., the "base"], but to the superstructural sphere."[25] Civil society for Gramsci is indeed to be found not in the sphere of production or economic organization, but in the state. The formula most commonly found in Gramsci is this: the state equals political society plus civil society. Political society is the arena of coercion and domination, civil society that of consent and direction (or "leadership"). The hegemony of a ruling class is expressed through the "organic relations" between the two realms.[26]

But, in opposing the "economistic" tendencies within Marxism, Gramsci is usually concerned to emphasize the central role of civil society in the manufacture and maintenance of hegemony. He therefore sometimes narrowly equates the state with political society, the system of direct coercive rule, leaving to civil society the main work of organizing hegemony.[27] A section of the *Prison Notebooks* is headed "Hegemony (Civil Society)." Even where Gramsci warns against the identification of the state with political society, as merely "dictatorship or coercive apparatus," he still singles out civil society as the area where hegemony is exercised. We must, he says, regard the state as "an equilibrium between political society and civil society (or hegemony of a social group over the entire national society exercised through the so-called private organisations, like the Church, the trade unions, the schools, etc.)." It is "precisely in civil society," he goes on, "that intellectuals operate especially." It is here that they perform their key function of supplying legitimacy and creating consensus on behalf of the ruling groups.[28]

"Force and consent; coercion and persuasion; State and Church; political society and civil society; politics and morality . . . ; law and freedom; order and self-discipline"—or again, "force and consent, authority and hegemony, violence and civilization, the individual moment, and the universal moment ('Church' and 'State')": these antinomies litter Gramsci's writings, and they make clearer than any elaborate discussion just how and where we are supposed to see civil society.[29] Civil society is the sphere of culture in the broadest sense. It is concerned with the manners and mores of society, with the way people live. It is where values and meanings are established, where they are debated, contested, and changed. It is the necessary complement to the rule of a class through its ownership of the means of production and its capture of the apparatus of the state. By the same token, it is the space that has to be colonized by any new class seeking to usurp the old, in the famous "war of position."

# Civil Society Today

In seeking to excavate the concept of civil society and put it to use in current conditions, contemporary theorists are evidently mining a rich but highly variegated vein. Civil society has been found in the economy and in the polity; in the area between the family and the state, or the individual and the state; in nonstate institutions that organize and educate citizens for political participation; even as an expression of the whole civilizing mission of modern society. Can any central meaning, more or less coherent and consistent, be discerned in this intellectual tradition? How far do current concepts derive from or depend on this inheritance? What kinds of policies and practices, in any case, follow from current usages?

It is clear that for most Western writers the classic inheritance is not simply important, but determining. It is seen as the source of a new politics to revitalize a bankrupt tradition, especially on the Left. That is why thinkers such as Keane urge on us an exercise in recovery and retrieval. The concept of civil society is proffered as a piece of "lost treasure" that will bring a much-needed luster to contemporary political thinking. Perry Anderson, too, advocates the classic concept, on both theoretical and practical grounds, despite the "multiple ambiguities and confusions" that he admits surround it as a result of its complex history. Civil society, he says, "remains a necessary *practico-indicative* concept, to designate all those institutions and mechanisms outside the boundaries of the State system proper. . . . Its function is to draw an indispensable *line of demarcation* within the politico-ideological superstructures of capitalism."[30]

If we abstract from the specifically Marxist content of Anderson's formulation, this suggests one common understanding of the concept. Civil society is the arena of nonstate institutions and practices that enjoy a high degree of autonomy. Classic Marxism would make economic institutions the heart of this region of society. But latterly, especially under the influence of Gramsci, and to some extent Althusser, the tendency has been for Marxists and non-Marxists alike to stress the specifically noneconomic dimension of civil society, and to concentrate instead on civic, cultural, educational, religious, and other organizations not directly related to the system of production. Trade unions and professional associations are included insofar as their influence goes beyond the immediate sphere of work and links their members to wider social and political purposes.[31]

This manifestly goes only so far. How, in the first place, are we to consider the issue of "autonomy"? We are confronted here with the problem not, as in the familiar debates, of the "relative autonomy" of the state, but of the relative autonomy of society. Pierre Rosanvallon, for instance, proposes to break out of the "nationalization/privatization straitjacket" in discussions of the welfare state by a strategy of "bringing society closer to itself": that is, by expanding the boundaries of civil society. "There must be," he says, "an effort to fill out society, to increase its density by creating more and more intermediate locations fulfilling social functions, and by encouraging individual involvement in networks of direct mutual support." The machinery of the welfare state, says Rosanvallon, has become increasingly "invisible" to citizens. It is "operating within a fog." We do not know what services we are paying for through our taxes, or why we are paying for them. Visibility can be increased by expanding "the sphere of the social"— formal and informal associations, long-term and temporary organizations, ranging from "informal cooperative initiatives" such as neighborhood and mutual aid groups to more permanent associations of welfare, such as housing groups and therapeutic communities.[32]

At the same time Rosanvallon admits that "there is no way in which the state itself can be instrumental in bringing about such a reconstitution of society."[33] That would be for the state voluntarily to reduce its scope and power, something that, whatever its rhetoric, the modern state does not do. This leaves society to pull itself up by its own bootstraps. Is it to bypass the state? How does it deal with the facts of state power, the state's evident desire and ability to maintain its control of society? Rosanvallon calls upon the state to be more "pluralist" in its conception of law, to bring in a new category of "social law" that would enable "segments of civil society" to be "recognized as legal subjects and enjoy the right to establish laws independent of state law."[34] Yet again he declines to offer an account of how or why the state should respond to this call to abandon its power as sovereign lawmaker. All he can do is paint a grim scenario, if the requisite initiatives are not forthcoming, of "a bastard society in which ever stronger market mechanisms will coexist with rigid statist forms and the growth of a selective social corporatism."[35]

John Keane does not ignore the question of the state. Indeed, he warns against those who feel that the whole solution to the problem of democracy and social justice lies in the nonstate sphere, in the institutions of civil society: "Civil society and the state . . . must become the condition of each other's democratization." Civil society must be boosted, certainly; this is the most urgent requirement today. And it must become "a permanent thorn in the side of political power." But in its turn it requires the constant surveillance of the state if it is not to degenerate into self-paralyzing conflict and "anarchy." Keane says:

> In short, I am arguing that without a secure and independent civil society of autonomous public spheres, goals such as freedom and equality, participatory planning and community decision-making will be nothing but empty slogans.
>
> But without the protective, redistributive and conflict-mediating functions of the state, struggles to transform civil society will become ghettoized, divided and stagnant, or will spawn their own, new forms of inequality and unfreedom.[36]

Whereas Rosanvallon largely ignores the state, Keane is, if anything, too eager to bring it back in. His formula of socialism "as equivalent to the separation and democratization of civil society and the state" turns out to give an enormous, potentially overwhelming, power to the state side of the balance. There will have to be "centralized planning and coordination" to offset the "poor coordination, disagreement, niggardliness and open conflict" that the pluralist structures of civil society invariably engender. Further, "since universal laws cannot emerge spontaneously from civil society, their formulation, application and enforcement would require a legislature, a judiciary and a police force, which are vital components of a state apparatus." Even "standing military institutions," the bugbear of all democratic theories, must be accepted as "a disagreeable necessity" so long as "the present system of nation states and empires remains a dangerous state of nature."[37]

It is difficult to see in what way this conception differs fundamentally from most conventional statements of liberal democratic theory. All of these grant some degree of autonomy to both sides of the state-society (or state-individual) dichotomy; all of them equally warn that neither side should expect total autonomy, but must act as the guardian of the other. A different conception, if that is the intention, must surely specify the balance in a novel way. This, however, Keane, like Rosanvallon, declines to do. In Keane's case the refusal is deliberate and considered. The state–civil society dichotomy, he argues, is of considerable value in reflecting on current developments in both Eastern and Western Europe. But, especially if we are concerned about forms of political action, we should not try to go beyond "generalizing terms" in discussing its relevance: "Beyond such generalizations not much can or should be said about the efficacy of the distinction in specific social and political contexts. Efforts to maximize the level of 'concreteness' of the idea of civil society for political purposes should be resisted."[38]

This really cannot be accepted. It is not that an unwarranted degree of specificity is demanded; it is, rather, that to leave the matter at this level of generality is to sidestep a central problem of state–civil society theorizing. For how, without specifying concrete mechanisms and actual resources, can we project a convincing picture of "a secure and independent civil society"? How can civil society protect itself against the state? Must its independence rest simply upon the disinterested benevolence of the state—a most insecure basis? If, however, the autonomy of civil society is, as Keane says, to be "legally guaranteed," who but the state will be the guarantor of this guarantee? And if it is derelict in this self-imposed duty, what kind of sanctions against the state do citizens possess?[39] It may be useful, in certain respects, to contemplate the state-society relationship philosophically, from lofty Hegelian heights; but, precisely as in the case of Hegel, it can also mean a cavalier disregard of key questions concerning the desired relationship.

Questions of this kind are even more acute for the Central and East European advocates of civil society. In this region, as we have noted, the embrace of civil society has been even more passionate, the hopes even more fervent.[40] It was above all the rise of Solidarity in Poland that sparked the enthusiasm. Writing with reference to the Polish dissident movement of the late 1970s that was the immediate prelude to Solidarity—Komitet Obrony Robotników (KOR)—Jacques Rupnik proclaimed "the end of revisionism and the rebirth of civil society."[41] With the formation and growth of Solidarity, Andrew Arato was even more emphatic. Whatever the differences within the democratic opposition in Poland, he wrote in 1981, "one point unites them all: the viewpoint of civil society against the state—the desire to institutionalize and preserve the new level of social independence."[42]

At the heart of the Solidarity experience—before the unexpected achievement of power in 1989—was seen a movement for the "self-defense" and "self-management" of society. The elevation of civil society meant not so much a new relationship between state and society as their virtual uncoupling. The state was not to be directly challenged; it was to be ignored. Civil society turned its back on the state, and sought to build a democratic pluralist order so far as it could within the confines of a still powerful party state. Civil society aspired to be an alternative society, a "parallel society" coexisting, for the time at least, with a delegitimized and weakened official state. But the emphasis was clear. Nowhere other than in the societies of "real socialism" did it seem more important to insist on the horizontal integration of civil society as against the vertical integration of the state.[43]

The strategy of "dual power" was perfectly understandable in the conditions of the party state in Poland and elsewhere. As Michnik argued, to engage the state head-on would be a suicidal venture for the opposition movement in these societies. Nothing that happened later, up to and including 1989, contradicted this. The rulers in Poland, Hungary, Czechoslovakia, and elsewhere in the erstwhile communist bloc, capitulated in 1989 not because of the irresistible force of the opposition movement but because, for reasons of its own internal problems, the Soviet government declined to support its client states and even went out of its way to undermine them.[44] Therefore, what Solidarity aimed for, and to a considerable degree achieved, reflected a realistic and sophisticated reading of the situation in its kind of society.[45]

In other respects, however, the linking of civil society to Solidarity has been unfortunate. It has tied the conception of civil society largely to a *social movement*—a spectacularly successful one, admittedly, but with characteristics that limit its usefulness as a general model. Solidarity sought to unite all the forces of civil society in a single all-encompassing movement that would offer itself as a sort of counter-power to the party state. But it had little idea how it would relate to the state, or, in the (unlikely) event that it supplanted it, what sort of state it could itself constitute. The question, What kind of civil society? left not merely unresolved, but unexamined, the question, What kind of state?

Solidarity lacked, in other words, an account of its ultimate political role. It had few ideas concerning the political institutions that would be necessary to accompany its takeover of power and to stabilize the new postcommunist regime. This was hardly surprising. The Solidarity leaders had had virtually no experience of the requisite kinds of institutions and practices—parties, political associations, electoral competition, a democratic constitution—in the previous forty years of communist rule. Equally important, a public sphere, in the sense of Jürgen Habermas's *"offentlichkeit,"* hardly existed. What Solidarity was able to provide, on a heroic scale, were the structure and practice of a social

movement whose hallmarks were national mobilization and monolithic solidarity. This served it well up to 1989—especially, we might say,
in its underground period following General Jaruzelski's imposition of
martial law at the end of 1981. But the strengths of its period of opposition became the weaknesses of its period of rule, and of its relevance
as a general model of civil society. By being the one and only (society-
wide) organization, it inhibited the creation of a genuine pluralism of
opinions and interests. It proved incapable of evolving the institutions
that would be necessary for a safe transition to democracy. After 1989,
Solidarity, the only possible ruling force, fragmented into sectional
squabbles and personal rivalries, leading many observers to fear for
the future of the new democratic state and to draw ominous parallels
with the 1930s.[46]

Civil society theorists in Central and Eastern Europe have been
well aware of the specific, and to some extent exceptional, features of
Solidarity. Solidarity operated in a context where any attempt to challenge the state directly invited Soviet intervention—constant and per-
vasive fear. Hence, the problematic concept of dual or parallel power
was more or less enforced.[47] The example of Solidarity has, nevertheless, remained mesmerizing. Poland was, after all, the one society in
the communist world to develop something like an independent civil
society, distorted as it had to be. Its experience must therefore, to societies even more lacking in traditions of independent association, appear exemplary. It has, in any case, proved impossible to depart too
far from Solidarity's basic conception of civil society as an organization (or "self-organization") of society against the state.

Given the nature of many of the postcommunist regimes, this may
turn out, in the end, to be not such a bad thing after all. But in the current situation, where some relation between civil society and the new
states has to be worked out, this conception of civil society is peculiarly
disabling. It pushes to an extreme degree the tendency, common to most
advocates in the West as well as in the East, to elevate civil society above
the state. Civil society becomes a utopia, or a panacea—the solution to
all the problems accumulated by "real socialism."[48] When the state has
to be considered, as after 1989, it is simply embraced by a more inclusive concept of civil society. A recent pronouncement on civil society by
the editorial board of the Romanian journal 22 reads: "Romanian civil
society is beginning to be configured. We have begun to talk with a
firmer voice, and the themes of our discussions are: pluralism, political

parties, free elections, independent unions, parliament."[49] These may indeed be, as the editors claim, "the signs of a democracy"; but such an inflation and conflation of institutions and practices make it impossible to maintain the distinctiveness of civil society as an entity, or to suggest any coherent relationship of it to the state. Civil society simply becomes all that is desired in the making of a democratic society (significantly—and typically in the East European usage—economic institutions are not mentioned).

The failure in Eastern Europe of revolution (Hungary 1956) and reform from above (Czechoslovakia 1968) led in the 1970s to the idea of a third way: reform from below, by the construction or reconstruction of civil society. The Polish experience of the 1980s seemed to confirm the validity of this strategy. But whatever its strength as an oppositional strategy—and this has been overestimated by both participants and outsiders—it offers little guidance to societies seeking to construct a genuine *political* society out of the debris of postcommunist systems. Solidarity as a social movement achieved something like "hegemony" in Polish society; it left open the question of how this hegemony should express itself in political terms, in terms of the organization of the state. One consequence of the concern with civil society is that the theory of the state in postcommunist societies is in total disarray.

## Democracy or Civil Society?

It is evident, as the example of Solidarity well illustrates, that the concept of civil society that is most widespread today is fundamentally Gramscian. The East has, in this as in other respects, caught up with the West. Gramsci's general position concerning bourgeois rule in the West was that it was mainly exercised through the "consent" ("hegemony") of civil society rather than the "coercion" of the state. This has appealed to Western radicals anxious to avoid both "economism" and Jacobinism (or what Gramsci called "statolatry"). It has, for quite different reasons, also appealed to East European thinkers, in the circumstances of whose societies a concentration on "society" rather than the state appeared not just theoretically desirable, but practically necessary. In both cases, as with Gramsci's own inclination, the right direction to move is seen in the fullest expansion of civil society, which is identified with the realm of freedom, and the greatest possible contraction of the state or "political society," which is identified with the sphere of coercion.[50]

The dangers of this position are clear, and have often been pointed out. It turns attention away from the real degree of coercion historically and potentially involved in the maintenance of political power in modern societies. Eastern European societies, in the post-1989 euphoria, need to be reminded of this as much as Western societies. The problem relates to all modern states, "democratic" as well as authoritarian, and cannot be wished away by a concentration on the institutions of civil society. Nor is it, as Perry Anderson points out, merely a question of noting the role of force or repression. We have to see the extent to which the form of the state, specifically the modern representative parliamentary state, is itself one of the most powerful agents of ideological hegemony. As much as the institutions of civil society—churches, schools, the mass media, and so on—the democratic state, with its juridical rights of citizenship and civic freedoms, also plays an indispensable "cultural-ideological" role.[51]

The second point also applies equally to Western and postcommunist Eastern European societies. Civil society is, no more than state power, a panacea. Its divisions and discontents remain a source of inequality and instability. The anatomy of civil society conducted by eighteenth- and nineteenth-century theorists, from Ferguson to Durkheim, was directed specifically by this perception: that society could be as pathological as the state. That, above all, was the lesson taught by Marx, and perhaps too well learned. But it is surely not a lesson to be discarded now, when states of both West and East seem eager to give civil society its head and to let it run away with itself. As Ellen Wood has said, "The new concept of 'civil society' signals that the left has learned the lessons of liberalism about the dangers of state oppression, but we seem to be forgetting the lessons we once learned from the socialist tradition about the oppressions of civil society."[52]

It might seem from this that Hegel's concept of civil society, as a realm of association interpenetrated by the state, remains the most satisfactory. It has the great merit of acknowledging the complementarity of state and civil society, of their need for one another in the maintenance of both individuality and sociability, private interest and communal purpose, freedom and regulation. But if civil society theorists today are apt to be too uncritical of civil society and too indifferent to questions of state power, Hegel notoriously had the opposite weakness. In his focus on the state as the true realm of reason and universality, he failed to consider carefully enough just how civil society can protect itself against the incursions of a potentially authoritarian and even totalitarian state.

One thing that might follow from all this is the need to avoid the use of civil society as a general category abstracted from particular social philosophies. In the uses of Hegel, Marx, Gramsci, and others we can see the reasons for using the term, and the particular value of doing so. Some of these reasons may still persist (although it is interesting that Marx found little use for the term in his later writings, being content simply with "society"). Nothing but confusion can follow, though, from the attempt to bundle all these uses together into some supposedly neutral social-scientific category for everyday sociological analysis. As with so many other concepts in modern sociology—alienation and anomie spring immediately to mind—the procedure is as arbitrary as it is generally arid. If we wish to continue to use the concept of civil society, we must situate it in some definite tradition of use that gives it a place and a meaning.

The deeper question, however, must be whether we need the concept of civil society at all. Is the resurrection of this old concept necessary, or profitable? We can understand why, in the recoil from a wholly alien and unresponsive state, intellectuals in Central and Eastern Europe felt driven to turn their attention to those areas of society that they could in some sense manage and seek to change. We can also understand why socialists in the West have sought to restore their morale and bring some credibility to their beliefs by attending to those problems neglected in the classic texts, and often ignored in the practices as much of West European social democracy as of those of the societies of "real socialism."[53]

But, apart from the difficulties with this position that we have already examined, we must ask what the concept of civil society adds that other more familiar concepts do not already cover, perhaps more adequately. If we are concerned with the abuses of state power, with recognizing and promoting pluralism and diversity, with defending rights and enabling individuals to act politically, what is wrong with the language and terms of such concepts as constitutionalism, citizenship, and democracy? None of these, it appears, needs to invoke the concept of civil society.[54] All deal, both in the traditional and in the newer literature, with precisely the problems that seem to preoccupy the advocates of civil society. This seems particularly the case in Eastern Europe, where both in the Soviet Union and in the former communist states the overriding problem seems to be democracy: how to achieve it, how to institutionalize it. The agreement on a democratic constitution, one might say, is the necessary condition of political progress in the region.

And it is not only in that region that this agreement is necessary. Throughout Western Europe there has been a renewed concern with citizenship and civic rights, with charters and contracts. There is an expressed sense that many of the gains of the democratic revolution—the legacy of the eighteenth-century American and French Revolutions—have been lost or are under threat. There has been a demand that these achievements be secured and expanded—perhaps by the addition of a "social charter"—by the enactment of concrete constitutional guarantees. And, specifically in Britain, it can hardly have escaped anyone's notice how much today there is a new awareness of constitutionalism, a new feeling of the inadequacy of relying on the informal conventions and practices of the British political tradition. For both nationalists in the non-English regions of the United Kingdom and democrats concerned at the erosion of civil liberties and the apparently unchallengeable power of the British state, an urgent requirement seems to be a new constitutional settlement. The agreements of 1688 have to be renewed; rights and powers must be entrenched, preferably in a written constitution accompanied by a formal bill of rights or citizens' charter.[55]

Tocqueville, we may remember, noted that it was politics that spreads "the general habit and taste for association." In other words, politics precedes civil society. A democratic polity and a public sphere of political debate and political activity are the primary conditions for a thriving civil society of independent associations and an active civic life. In Romania today, Gail Kligman observes, the attempt to revitalize civil society "from below," as it were, is premature and misguided: "The establishment of public life itself is prerequisite to constituting a civil society."[56] This would seem to be the general lesson taught by both the history of Western societies and the current efforts of Eastern European societies to restart their political life. It underlines the point that the central problems in both East and West relate not to the institutions of civil society, but to the institutions of the state and the reconstitution of a functioning political society. To rediscover civil society, to retrieve an archaic concept, may be an interesting exercise in intellectual history, but it evades the real political challenges at the end of the twentieth century.

## A Further Note

Introducing a recent volume of studies on civil society, Jeffrey Alexander rightly says that "almost single-handedly, Eastern European intellectuals reintroduced 'civil society' to contemporary social theory. Until they started writing about it [in the 1970s and 1980s], it had been considered a quaint and conservative notion, thoroughly obsolete."[57] The debt, we might say, has been repaid with a vengeance. Western social theory in the 1990s has embraced the concept passionately, at just the time when some Eastern European intellectuals are becoming wary of it, unsure that a concept elaborated essentially as a tool of opposition to the totalitarian communist state can serve the same useful purpose in rebuilding their societies.[58] For the West, however, the concept has played a key role in rethinking the nature of liberal democratic societies. If democracy seems to have stalled, if the citizens of democratic societies seem passive and alienated from political actors and institutions, the fault perhaps lies in the condition of the "support systems" of democracy—the structures and practices of civil society.

Certainly nothing seems to stem the flood of works dealing with civil society.[59] Nor is this confined to the West. If Eastern Europeans are showing some skepticism, this does not seem to apply to the rest of the world. In Africa and Latin America, the Middle and Far East, the concept has been taken up with marked enthusiasm, if not always with the greatest consistency or clarity. Surveying these developments, John Keane, who has good reason to claim some paternal and proprietary interest in the phenomenon, observes with satisfaction that "the language of civil society is now more widely used than ever before in the history of modern times, including the century of its birth and maturation (1750–1850)."[60]

Moreover, as in the past, most of the writing is celebratory rather than critical. The kind of skepticism I expressed in the article on which the earlier part of this chapter is based has been rare—rare enough for the article to be directly challenged, and to be singled out for citation on a number of occasions when some sort of dissenting voice was sought for the purposes of argument.[61] Interestingly, it is largely from disciplines outside those—sociology and politics—principally concerned with the idea of civil society that the most searching critical questions have been raised. Chief among these has been anthropology, whose practioners have rightly queried whether a concept with so determinately Western an origin and orientation can really aspire to universal analytical and prescriptive status. In thus situating the concept culturally, these scholars have also brought a fresh perspective to bear on the question of its value and usefulness in analyzing the contemporary Western condition.[62]

I shall return to this question of value, the central critical point of my original article. But first it may be helpful to reconsider briefly, in the light of the recent literature, some historical and analytical issues. I had complained about the conceptual looseness of the term *civil society,* its tendency to mean all things to all persons. John Keane, an ardent protagonist of the term, also writes with evident frustration of the "muddle and delirium" that is one consequence of the "increasingly polysemic signifier 'civil society.'" He says, "Its burgeoning popularity accelerates the accumulation of inherited ambiguities, new confusions and outright contradictions."[63] One does not, of course, unless one is an out-and-out positivist, ask for scientific precision in the case of concepts in the human sciences. All such concepts are, to use the hallowed phrase, "essentially contestable"—but some are, as it were, more contestable than others. W. B. Gallie's original point in coining the phrase was not simply to suggest that there was a certain ineradicable imprecision in concepts that are historically and socially formed. More particularly, he wished to argue that there were in the case of certain concepts—such as democracy or social justice—varying uses and meanings that were in inherent tension and even contradiction with each other, the inescapable result of their location and development within different intellectual traditions and social practices. Moreover, acknowledgment and recognition of these differences by different practitioners was a crucial component of the definition of essentially contested concepts. Hence, Gallie says, "to use an essentially contested concept means to use it against other uses and to recognize that one's own use of it has to be maintained against these other uses." One consequence of this is that "to use an essentially contested concept means to use it both aggressively and defensively." But this does not, or at least need not, mean one must engage in single-minded fanaticism. Gallie suggested in an optimistic vein: "Recognition of a given concept as essentially contested implies recognition of rival uses of it (such as oneself repudiates) as not only logically possible and humanly 'likely,' but as of permanent potential critical value to one's own use or interpretation of the concept in question."[64]

Gallie was perfectly aware that this was perhaps an overly rosy view, and that an alternative consequence of recognizing the essential contestedness of a given concept—that is, knowing that one's interpretation of it was inescapably partial and likely to remain so in the eyes of one's adversaries—could be "a ruthless decision to cut the cackle, to damn the heretics and to exterminate the unwanted."[65] Assuming that the scholars debating civil society are not so fanatical or bloodthirsty, we have in Gallie's account one reasonable and constructive way of dealing with what in the case of civil society is clearly an essentially contested concept. That is, we acknowledge that there are different interpretations and uses of civil society, that these derive from different intellectual and political traditions, that they point in different directions as to policy and practice, but that there is room for a critical dialogue and attempts at persuasion. This last hope, indeed, depends upon certain common assumptions, some basic agreement as to the rough terrain on which we are working. That, I would submit, is given by the more or less universal acceptance that civil society has to do with that area or arena of institutions and practices that lie between the family and the state. This is admittedly a purely negative demarcation; and beyond that there can be endless disagreement—and perhaps, in the end, insufficient room for compromise or even coexistence. But it seems to me that the history of the concept since the eighteenth century, up to and including its recent revival in Central and Eastern Europe, points to the possibility of a difficult but potentially rewarding dialogue (assuming that that is what we want, rather than to dispense with the concept altogether as hopelessly muddled and grotesquely inflated, beyond any practicable use. But, though tempting, that may no longer be a feasible option, given the immense popularity and currency of the term today).

The measure of the difficulty is provided by what seems to be the central disagreement in contemporary usage. This has to do with whether, and to what extent, the concept of civil society should include the market and, in general, economic life. In the tradition deriving from Hegel—and, more emphatically and restrictively, Marx—the market is at the heart of civil society in modern societies. Hence Marx's programmatic statement that "the anatomy of civil society is to be sought in political economy."[66] Gramsci, on the other hand, drawing on certain elements in the more complex account in Hegel, was concerned to emphasize the noneconomic aspects of civil society. For him civil society was distinct not just from the coercive apparatus of the state, but also from the economic institutions of society. At its center, the arena where "hegemony" was both promoted and contested, were the social and cultural organizations and activities of society (see the discussion of Gramsci earlier in this chapter).

Scholars have divided rather neatly along the lines of these two traditions. One is tempted initially to see a European–North American contrast. Europeans such as Ernest Gellner, John Keane, and Victor Pérez-Díaz, together with most East European theorists, tend to be what Pérez-Díaz calls "generalists."[67] That is, they include within the concept "civil society" not just markets, but a whole range of liberal political institutions. The full-blooded generalists, such as Gellner and Pérez-Díaz, see themselves as followers of the Scottish thinkers of the eighteenth century in conceiving civil society as the ideal-typical liberal, commercial society in all its manifestations. More restricted generalists, such as Keane, working within a broadly Marxist tradition, include the market and the public sphere, but tend to put the stress on nongovernmental institutions; that is, they exclude the state.

"Minimalists" are mostly Americans, such as Jean Cohen, Andrew Arato, and Jeffrey Alexander. But here the neat European-American distinction breaks down, because their mentor, in this respect at least, is the quintessentially European thinker Jürgen Habermas (though one could also derive this conception from Talcott Parsons). Habermas follows Gramsci in separating out the cultural and the social from the political and the economic realms. They each have their own logics—power and administration in the case of politics, accumulation in the case of the economy, and solidarity and free and open communication in the case of civil society or the "life-world" *(lebenswelt)*.[68] The crucial thing is that this concept of civil society excludes the market, which is seen as working according to a principle that, as much as the bureaucratic and coercive operations of the state, threatens the solidarity and self-reflexivity of civil society and the public sphere.

The danger, then, according to this conception, is when the logic of one sphere interferes with or intervenes in the logic of another—when, as Habermas puts it, "colonization" takes over. Alexander illustrates this well in his account of civil society. For him, civil society is an autonomous sphere of solidarity that is both analytically and empirically separable from other spheres of society—not just the polity and the economy, but also religion, science, the family, and several other spheres. Civil society does not exist in a self-contained vacuum any more than do the other spheres. It overlaps with these other spheres and draws much of its resources from them. But, by the same token, it is vulnerable to damaging incursions from these other spheres, which operate according to different logics and have their own criteria of justice and systems of rewards. The problem, then, is to balance the autonomy and independence of civil society against its need for the cultural and material resources that it derives from the other spheres.[69]

The theoretical elaboration is elegant and, to a degree, persuasive. The question is the empirical and historical plausibility of the conception, the extent to which the separation of spheres has existed, and can exist, not merely in principle, but to any real extent in practice. To put it more concretely, can civil society survive without the market?[70] The problem is not resolved, but only intensified, by Alexander's explicit acknowledgment of the "facilitating inputs" of the market—and, more generally, the capitalist economy—to the sphere of civil society:

> When an economy is structured by markets, behavior is encouraged that is independent, rational, and self-controlled. It was for this reason that the early intellectuals of capitalism, from Montesquieu to Adam Smith, hailed market society as a calming and civilizing antidote to the militaristic glories of aristocratic life. It is in part for this same reason that societies which have recently exited from communism have staked their emerging democracies on the construction of market societies in turn. . . . In so far as the capitalist economy supplies the civil sphere with facilities like independence, self-control, rationality, equality, self-realization, cooperation, and trust, the boundary relations between these two spheres are frictionless.[71]

But there are also the "facilitating inputs" from another important "noncivil" sphere, the state. The state regulates civil society, polices it (in the old sense of framing policies for it, as well as the newer sense of maintaining "law and order"), prevents it from degenerating into a cockpit of warring gangs and mafias. Left to itself, civil society has a tendency to become Hobbesian or, more benignly, neofeudal (as in the case of the "bastard feudalism" of fifteenth-century Europe).[72]

If, in addition to the economy and the state, we add the moralizing influences of religion and the socializing influences of the family, it becomes very unclear what is left for the sphere of "civil society" to do. What are the practices of the specifically civil sphere? What are the attitudes and behaviors learned there that are not primarily developed and practiced in other spheres? The danger is that civil society becomes a somewhat residual sphere, useful for certain rhetorical and normative, not to say utopian, purposes, but bereft of any real specificity and autonomy.

This, of course, relates to a more general problem with the model of differentiation that underlies the account of civil society provided by Alexander and other "minimalists." The different spheres—economic, political, cultural, familial, and so on—indeed seem to be so permeable, so interdependent, that it seems unrealistic to treat them as empirically separate entities. If, in practice, "civil society" derives so much of its "culture" from other spheres, if the way it works and sustains itself depends so much upon attitudes and attributes learned elsewhere, what is gained from insisting on its separateness? This is not to ask that all practices be collapsed back into some unitary entity called "capitalism" or "market society." Not only are there many different varieties of capitalist society; capitalist society in any form, like all modern societies, possesses an inescapable heterogeneity. The identification of "civil society" may be one way of recognizing and discussing this essentially plural character. But the task, then, is not to dwell on its separateness, but to understand and analyze its interrelatedness and interdependence with other elements in society. In doing so, "minimalists" may find that they are not so far removed from "generalists," who are so persuaded of the intrinsic relation between market institutions and civil society as to make markets integral to their understanding of civil society. This would precisely exemplify the dialogue or debate that Gallie thought implicit in the very idea of "essentially contested concepts."[73]

The generalists, for their part, pose a different kind of problem. If civil society includes not just markets, but the whole set of social and political institutions associated with eighteenth-century commercial and nineteenth-century industrial society, what is added by recognizing and naming a concept and sphere of "civil society"? What additional theoretical or empirical contribution does this make? Why not simply speak of "liberal society," or even "modern society"?[74] The question gains additional force from the fact, acknowledged by most, that the term *civil society* originated in eighteenth-century discussions of the birth of liberal or "commercial" society.[75] This suggests that, if we wish to retain the concept at all, it should be seen as one of an array of concepts linked in a common discourse about the birth of modernity. Civil society is kin, that is, to citizenship, democracy, constitutionalism, republicanism, individualism, trust, friendship, and a number of other such ideas and qualities linked to the development of modern capitalist societies. It may even be tied specifically and concretely to the discussion and defense of private property as the ground of modern individual liberties. In any case, it seems perverse and unhelpful to isolate it either conceptually or empirically.

This brings us back to the question posed in my original treatment of civil society: whether or not the concept, as a newly revived term, still possesses any value. Chris Hann, explaining why anthropologists have hitherto been largely dismissive of the concept, issues a stern warning: "There is something inherently unsatisfactory about the international propagation by western scholars of an ideal of social organisation that seems to bear little relation to the current realities of their own countries; an ideal which, furthermore, developed in historical conditions that cannot be replicated in any other part of the world today. I . . . suggest that the term is riddled with contradictions and the current vogue predicated on a fundamental ethnocentricity."[76]

Nevertheless, faced with the current popularity of the concept in so many parts of the world, and its explicit endorsement by many international agencies and organizations, Hann accepts that anthropologists need to work with it and to use their special skills to make the concept more supple and serviceable in the context especially of non-Western cultures.[77] I, too, am less convinced than I was earlier that we should simply discard the concept of civil society and view its establishment as a pointless and potentially distracting exercise in retrieval. For whatever reasons—not all of them good—it evidently appeals to many people in many different places and contexts, and presumably in some sense speaks to their condition. What we must do, therefore, is try to lay down a few guidelines to bring some order and purpose in what is an increasingly chaotic field.

The first thing is to insist that scholars (we cannot hope to legislate for anyone else) distinguish far more clearly than they do at present between descriptive and prescriptive uses of the term. For obvious reasons, most students of civil society tend to be enamored of the thing itself. They are anxious to promote it, and their analyses often amount to no more than a listing of all the good things—free association, a thriving public sphere, a vibrant discourse of citizenship and human rights—that they wish to see present or established in society. It is one thing to want civil society; it is another to understand what it is. Of course it will help accomplish the former purpose if there is some understanding of the conditions of civil society. But one cannot always control what politicians and publicists say and do. "Civil society" has become a slogan and a battle cry in many parts of the world. That may be no bad thing. But, however much we may wish to be involved in its strengthening or recovery, we should recognize that there is a separate task of analysis and description that is not necessarily tied to promoting the project of civil society.

The second thing is to be more historical in our understanding and approach. This seems to me sound advice in the case of *all* concepts in the human sciences; and civil society, so variously and divergently used, is one of those concepts that brings home with special force its desirability. It is not simply the meaning, but the social conditions, of its establishment and development that need to be understood historically. Is Adam Seligman right, for instance, in arguing that civil society in its original eighteenth-century setting depended on the existence of a particular kind of moral, and indeed religious, community that was its necessary underpinning?[78] If so, with the disappearance of that type of community is there any real hope of preserving or resurrecting civil society in anything like its classic form, as Seligman also pointedly asks? Of course, one could say that civil society means something else now, and that contemporary societies offer the conditions for its realization in newer forms. But unless one were to allow a concept to mean anything one liked, there is, at the very least, an obligation to show the connection between the newer and older forms, both in terms of meaning and in terms of the changing conditions that have made it necessary to reconceptualize the idea of civil society. In both cases, what is involved is a historical task.[79]

A different kind of historical task is to ask, Why now? Why has the old concept of civil society, which had more or less disappeared from the vocabulary of politics as well as of social theory, reappeared with such force in the closing two decades of the twentieth century? The Eastern European stimulus is obvious, and important. But what is not so clear is why the concept has been taken up so enthusiastically in the West. The answer presumably has to do with a concern with the concept and conditions of democracy, and a feeling that "civil society" is both more inclusive and perhaps a firmer base than formal democracy for securing the conditions of an enriched and more active citizenship.[80] But few of the theorists of civil society have explicitly addressed this question, showing either how (or whether) civil society was a response to a felt crisis in democracy, or why and in what respects so archaic and in many respects cumbersome a term should have been thought preferable to one with such a refined and respectable tradition of analysis and debate.

History comes in again in yet another way. In my original treatment I argued against some all-purpose, omnibus definition of the concept of civil society. There are clearly overlaps of meaning and use, deriving from a common storehouse of concepts elaborated in Europe between the seventeenth and nineteenth centuries. It is this that makes dialogue possible. But it is equally important to insist on the need to situate any concept of civil society within a definite intellectual tradition. English and Scottish thinkers of the seventeenth and eighteenth centuries; French thinkers such as Montesquieu, Rousseau, and Tocqueville; German thinkers such as Kant, Hegel, and Marx; later theorists such as Gramsci and Habermas: although many of these drew on and debated with each other, they also in many cases developed quite distinctive social and political philosophies. Their use of the concept of civil society relates directly to these philosophies, and we can add nothing but confusion if we attempt to sweep away all differences in the search for some neutral, all-inclusive, concept suitable for all people and all purposes.[81] The dialogue that takes place between different users will be the more fruitful for recognizing the different ancestries, the different traditions of meaning and intent, that underlie and frame the use of the term. Intellectual history must be the backbone of this effort.

To return finally to Central and Eastern Europe, the region that relaunched the concept of civil society on the world in the 1970s and 1980s and is mainly responsible for why we are all discussing it today, we must ask: How does civil society fare there today? Some intellectuals—and civil society was always an intellectuals' pet idea, not one in which the people played much part—are clearly less enthusiastic than they or their counterparts were in the 1980s and the early 1990s.[82] They are dismayed at the promiscuous use of the term as its geographical reach has widened; they are disappointed at the achievements so far, and are becoming aware of the deep-seated and stubborn obstacles placed in the way of civil society not just by the period of communist rule, but by the long centuries of their countries' histories before that. Efforts by well-meaning Western governments and international organizations to "stimulate" civil society in the region have only revealed how uncomprehending they are as to what it means to have or become a civil society, while the suspicion develops that these efforts have another, more sinister, meaning, designed to absolve the West of its responsibilities and to relieve it of its obligations to discharge its earlier promises to Eastern Europe.[83] At the same time, in their own efforts to develop democracy and to establish the framework of liberal and pluralist politics, they have become uncomfortably aware of the difficulties placed in their way by elements of civil society—for instance, the Catholic Church in Poland.[84]

Still, Eastern Europe certainly has not given up on civil society, either as a concept or as a goal (still less as a slogan or a rallying cry).[85] A recent conference in Prague, convened by President Václav Havel, found intellectuals such as Adam Michnik and Lezek Kolakowski engaged in full-blooded discussion of it, while, as if to underscore the importance of the concept not just to the region, but to the world as a whole, the conference was treated to an illuminating lecture on civil society by no less a political figure than Hillary Clinton.[86] Moreover, in one of those ironic twists that often characterizes East-West relations, Eastern Europe, having renewed the concept of civil society and passed it on to the West, now finds itself the recipient of advice and offers on all sides as to how to rebuild civil society in postcommunist societies. Seminars, conferences, and whole programs of aid make free play of the vocabulary of civil society, and woe betide those players who do not know the language. Whether it wants to or not, Eastern Europe cannot abandon the concept of civil society. It has become part of the texture of the cultural and political life of the region, part of the discourse of intellectuals and politicians of every kind. All the more reason, therefore, that scholars involved with the concept treat it with the care and delicacy that it deserves. That, at least, is our responsibility in handling a matter that clearly has repercussions well beyond the walls of the academy.

*Six*

# The End of Socialism?
# The End of Utopia?
# The End of History?

*Our country has not been lucky. Indeed, it was decided to carry out this Marxist experiment on us—fate pushed us in precisely this direction. Instead of some country in Africa, they began this experiment with us. In the end we proved that there is no place for this idea. It has simply pushed us off the path the world's civilized countries have taken.*

Boris Yeltsin

*Two years of unbelievable political change in Europe have been sufficient to proscribe the use of the word "utopia." No one talks about utopia any more.*

Wolf Lepenies

*I do not believe . . . that utopianism is at an end. Quite the contrary. Perhaps it is only now that we can invent utopian utopias.*

Immanuel Wallerstein

## Waiting for the End

"Endism" is rampant, and likely to become even more so as we end the second millennium and begin the third. Millennial endings, even more than centurial ones, give rise to millennial imaginings.[1] But there is a profound difference between the millennial thoughts of our time and those of earlier ages. For thinkers such as Joachim of Fiore, the "last days" marked a radically new beginning. They portended a new age of the Holy Spirit, a millennial age of love, freedom, and joy. What was contemplated was not simply an end, but a new beginning, a new dispensation based on radically different principles.

For our thinkers, on the contrary, the "end of history" brings nothing new. Quite the opposite. It announces the final victory of the old. Things that were thought to be new have failed. They were, in any case, delusions, unnecessary and destructive deviations. There is no need to imagine anything new. We already live in the millennial new age, the last age. The Messiah has already come, and fulfilled his mission; the everlasting Gospel is with us; all we can do now is wait wearily, like St. Augustine, for the sands of earthly time to run out. No wonder that even the most confident pronouncements of the end of history in our time are tinged with melancholy at the predicament of the "last man."[2]

It is not, of course, simply the end of a century and a millennium that inspires these oracular utterances. The idea that we may have reached some final point of historical development is linked to other, more familiar, notions. There is the announcement of the death of the socialist ideal that, already prominent in the writings of many East European dissidents in the late 1960s and 1970s, reached a crescendo in both East and West following the revolutions of 1989 in Central Europe and the collapse of the Soviet Union in 1991.[3] Even further back in the century was the widely held view that utopian thought, which for nearly five hundred years had fired the European imagination with dreams of a better future, was finally bankrupt.[4] Since socialism of one kind or another had become the central component of the modern utopia, the fate of socialism in the last part of our century might seem to have buried utopia even more comprehensively. In 1919, two years after the Russian Revolution, the American writer Lincoln Steffens returned from a visit to Russia and made the famous remark, "I have been over into the future, and it works." Now not only the Soviet Union, but all the other putative models of utopia, appears defunct. "The Soviet Union," says Anthony Sampson, "has finally gone the way of all Utopias; along with China, Cuba, Sweden and Tanzania, denounced and discredited by its own inhabitants."[5]

Together with the perception that the capitalist democracies of the West have, for all their faults, survived and prospered, and that they alone appear to have a continued appeal for the rest of the world, it is not so difficult to see why a general sense of self-congratulation, not to say complacency, should have overtaken the Western world. The West has won; its system, evolving steadily since the sixteenth century, has now triumphed over all rivals and competitors; there can be no further meaning to history than the elaboration and firmer implementation of Western principles throughout the globe.

I shall return to this later in this chapter. Here I am mainly concerned with the effect of the 1989 revolutions on the idea of utopia. Have they, as many claim, put the final nail in the coffin of utopia? Is the story of utopia, therefore, one of unremitting decline in this century? What further function might there be for utopia in a world where there no longer seems to be any place for radical alternatives to the present order?

## The Assault on Utopia

Utopia, in the twentieth century, has not had many friends. For left-wing thinkers, who might have been expected to be more sympathetic, it has been a standing reminder of their own origin in a form from which they were anxious to distance themselves. In any case, had utopia not been sufficiently realized in the Soviet Union? What need was there now for utopias? Was not the main task now the support, through propaganda and more practical ways (e.g., spying), of the country that was the spearhead of the Third International?[6] For those socialists who were less convinced that the Soviet Union was utopia made real, utopia was still unwelcome. It distracted from the main task of organization. Whether parliamentary or revolutionary, socialists in the twentieth century have been less interested in elaborating their view of the future society than in planning, like a General Staff, the tactics of gaining and maintaining power.

The Right and the Center have, not surprisingly, been even more virulent in their attack on utopia. For them utopia is, by definition, an affront. Even if they accept that utopias are not to be taken literally, that their authors are not in most cases writing blueprints for the perfect society, the whole enterprise is to liberals and conservatives deeply suspect. It is an act of hubris. It makes claims for human reason that are unreal and liable to encourage dangerous ventures in practice. History is littered with failed utopian experiments, many of them as unappealing in their lifetime as they were frequently bloody in their end.

This kind of response to utopia has been familiar from earliest times, for instance, in Aristophanes' mocking of Plato's *Republic* and Swift's satire on Francis Bacon's scientific utopia. But the attack has taken on a heightened urgency in the twentieth century, largely because of a presumed connection between utopian thought and the totalitarian regimes of this century. Fascism was a utopia; so, too, was communism in its Soviet form.[7] They were utopian, it is argued, precisely in their worst aspects, in their belief that they had discovered the secret of history and that, armed with this discovery, they were in a position to rule and regulate society totally, in all its aspects.

The most celebrated rendering of this view was George Orwell's antiutopia, *Nineteen Eighty-Four* (1949). Despite Orwell's protestation that the book was not meant to be antisocialist, his portrait of totalitarianism—often identified by careless readers with Stalin's Russia—was grist for the mill of antiutopian liberals and conservatives (and certainly upset many socialists, such as Isaac Deutscher).[8] It chimed in particularly well with the wide-ranging critique of radical politics provided by a group of brilliant and highly influential European emigré intellectuals who felt themselves the victims of the utopian politics of their native countries. In exile in France, Britain, America, Canada, and Israel, they launched a vigorous and often bitter and passionate polemic against the whole utopian tradition, seen as a pestilential inheritance.

One could say that this wave of protest began with Yevgeny Zamyatin's *We* (1924), a piercing satire on the new Soviet state, for which Zamyatin was lucky enough to be rewarded by no more than exile to Paris. But, largely owing to the exigencies of publishing, this novel did not become widely known until the 1950s, partly as the result of the success of *Nineteen Eighty-Four*.[9] A much greater impact was created by Arthur Koestler's *Darkness at Noon* (1940), another antiutopian novel that reflected bitterly on the author's experience of the communist mentality as an erstwhile member of the German Communist Party and as a journalist during the Spanish Civil War.[10]

These were novels, fictional treatments of totalitarianism.[11] Matching them, and indeed making very much the same kind of points, were a series of works in social and political theory written by the emigrés (there is a strong parallel here, not to say thematic continuity, with the conservative response to the French Revolution, in the writings of Burke, Bonald, de Maistre, and others). From a haven in Christchurch,

New Zealand, Karl Popper wrote *The Open Society and Its Enemies* (1945), about which Popper said, "the final decision to write [which] was made in March 1938, on the day I received the news of the invasion of Austria" by the Nazis.[12] Not just fascism, but, even more, Marxism, was denounced for its historicism—its belief in general laws of history that pushed societies inexorably along a predetermined path.

But Popper also reserved some of his fire for "Utopianism," which he saw as "a necessary complement to a less radical historicism" deriving from Plato and the utopian tradition. This Utopianism was pernicious for holding that it was possible to devise a "blueprint" of the Ideal State, to which all political activity should be subordinated. It was not, as in the common criticism, the "idealism" or unrealizability of utopia that Popper saw as its main weakness; it was its recommendation of "the reconstruction of society as a whole," in accordance with some supposedly absolute and rational ideal. It was this that must lead to violence and tyranny. Utopianism "with the best intentions of making heaven on earth . . . only succeeds in making it a hell—that hell which man alone prepares for his fellow-men."[13]

*The Open Society and Its Enemies* has remained the most thoroughgoing and influential critique of utopianism from the pen of a modern social theorist; it is, we might say, the nonfictional equivalent of *Nineteen Eighty-Four*.[14] But other emigré intellectuals have also made famous contributions to the same basic enterprise. Removed, like Popper, from his native Austria, Friedrich von Hayek sought to arouse controversy with the London publication of *The Road to Serfdom* (1944), a stinging attack on "the great utopia" of collectivism that he saw exemplified equally in German fascism and Russian communism. Like Popper, too, Hayek identified the enemy as the hubris of reason and the idea of a total reconstruction of society by political means. Jacob Talmon escaped the Central European Holocaust via London and Jerusalem; in *The Origins of Totalitarian Democracy* (1952) he traced the roots of modern totalitarianism back to the utopian ideas of Rousseau and other French thinkers of the eighteenth century.[15] Going further back, Norman Cohn, resuming an inquiry "first begun in the ruins of Central Europe fifteen years [earlier]," sought the seeds of totalitarian communism and Nazism in a different variety of utopianism: the millenarian beliefs and movements of the European Middle Ages.[16]

The inquiries of Popper, Hayek, Talmon, and Cohn were predominantly historical. They wished to show that the catastrophe of Europe in the twentieth century could be traced back to a set of thinkers and ideas deep in the European past. These ideas they equated with a long-standing utopian strand in European thought. Against this they set, with a reasonable degree of optimism, a tradition of thought that had come down from classic liberal thinkers such as Alexis de Tocqueville and John Stuart Mill. The problem of utopianism appears more intractable to Isaiah Berlin and Leszek Kolakowski, perhaps because of their provenance in a more easterly region of Europe than most of these others. It is seen as an almost natural distemper of the human mind whose cure probably lies well beyond the realm of the usual liberal remedies. Berlin, forcibly displaced by revolution from Riga and Petrograd to an English public school and Oxford, meditated on Kant's dictum that "out of the crooked timber of humanity no straight thing was ever made." The utopians, he said, from More to Marx, had flattened out human nature, had continued to "downgrade man's role as creator and destroyer of values . . . as a subject, a creature with an inner life denied to other inhabitants of the universe."[17] Utopia has declined in the twentieth century, but Berlin acknowledged its perennial appeal and the possibility that it can resurface in such forms as militant nationalism—and, he might now add, religious fundamentalism. Moreover, he admitted the limited attractions of the liberal model that he offered as an alternative.[18]

Kolakowski, a Polish dissident and Oxford don, was so struck by the recurrence of "the utopian mentality" that he wondered whether we might not have to do "with an everlasting form of human sensitivity, with a permanent anthropological datum for which an English thinker in the sixteenth century simply invented an apt name." He rejected this notion as supplying an unhelpfully wide definition of utopia. In any case, like Berlin, he thought utopia was in decline, that "utopian dreams have virtually lost both their intellectual support and their previous self-confidence and vigor." Utopia has been discredited by the realization that its attainment would bring "a perpetual deadly stagnation" and death of human creativity and striving. All change is a response "to dissatisfaction, to suffering, to a challenge"—precisely those aspects of human life that utopia seeks to expunge. Utopias were harmless, Kolakowski said, so long as they remained "literary exercises." In our century what has made them "ideologically pernicious" is the conviction of their advocates that they have discovered "a genuine technology of apocalypse, a technical device to force the door of paradise." Worst of all in this respect has been the Marxist utopia, which became "the main ideological self-justifying and self-glorifying support of the totalitarian cancer devouring the social fabric of our world."[19] No doubt Kolakowski rejoiced at the downfall of this utopia in his native Poland and the rest of Eastern Europe.

Kolakowski has observed, apropos the popularity of utopia, that "it is an interesting cultural process whereby a word of which the history is well known and which emerged as an artificially concocted proper name has acquired, in the last two centuries, a sense so extended that it refers not only to a literary genre but to a way of thinking, to a mentality, to a philosophical attitude."[20] It is equally interesting that Kolakowski does not appear to see the relevance of this observation to himself, or to most of the other twentieth-century critics of utopia. For what has been striking about their treatment of utopia has been precisely the tendency to turn it into an abstract current of thought, or a psychological or temperamental propensity. Utopia has become utopianism, the utopian mentality, the utopian impulse. Or it has been equated with a particular style of thought that thinks in terms of wholes and systems; so Popper could talk of "the Utopian planners," "the Utopian engineers," "the Utopian blueprint."[21] This does not necessarily lead to the view that utopianism is some universal, transhistorical human propensity—indeed, most of the critics are concerned to stress its historical origins. But it does make it easier to see utopianism at work in a host of modern ideologies, many of which have never been the subject of a formal utopia.

This is the important point. There is no harm in talking about certain forms of thinking, and certain thinkers, as utopian. It is almost impossible not to do so in the case of thinkers like Rousseau or Owen, perhaps even Plato and Marx. But it becomes dangerous when all forms of thinking about "the good" or "the best" society are labeled utopian, and given a systematic description such that they can hardly avoid being characterized as "totalitarian." Utopia has performed many functions in its long history, and promoting systematic thinking about the future society is only one of them. The same is true of "the design of the perfect society." The different forms of utopia—from Socratic dialogues and Biblical prophecies to proposals of ideal cities and ideal societies, from social and political speculation to satires and science fiction, from the realist novel to the popular culture of films and television—need to be treated with respect for those differences, and the different aims and meanings that they carry.[22] The fact that none of Plato, Rousseau, Owen, or Marx—not to mention Hitler— ever wrote a formal literary utopia should be as important in assessing their utopianism as doing so in the case of those of their disciples who did write such utopias. It may be useful for certain purposes to treat the *1844 Manuscripts* or the *Communist Manifesto* as utopian; but a comparison of these with, say, Edward Bellamy's *Looking Backward* or, again, William Morris's *News from Nowhere* should make us aware of the differences as much as any similarities.

One other confusion is particularly important for present purposes. It is one thing to conflate, as we have just noted, the fictional utopia with various forms of "utopian" social theory. It is even more dubious to treat as a unified entity utopian speculation and various forms of social experimentation that dub themselves or are dubbed utopian. This, too, is a common procedure of the antiutopian critique. The refusal to distinguish between these spheres, each of which has its own forms and logic, is one major reason why utopia can be made to seem dangerous. "Utopian" communities, such as Robert Owen's New Harmony in nineteenth-century Indiana, or many of the "counter-cultural" communes of the 1960s, often end in disillusion or débacle. Their repeated failure can then be used to discredit the utopian enterprise as a whole.[23]

The fate of both socialism and utopia has been partly determined by this kind of argument. In the last two centuries utopia has come to be closely connected to the socialist project, even to an extent identified with it. Socialism, in its turn, has been judged by the success or failure of certain kinds of social experiment, notably that carried out in the Soviet Union. The decisive failure, as it appears, of socialism in the closing years of this century has therefore brought with it the refrain that utopia, too, has died.

We shall turn to this idea in a moment. But, as a footnote to the twentieth-century assault on utopia, we should note the unexpected career of Aldous Huxley's *Brave New World* (1932). Huxley's anti-utopia is matched only by Orwell's for its fame. For it, too, there were important Continental precursors and influences, an important one being the thought of the Russian emigré Nicholas Berdyaev. *Brave New World* indeed carried as an epigraph an observation of Berdyaev's that summed up its central message: the tragedy of the modern world was not, as was often claimed, that the modern utopia—the utopia of science and socialism—was too idealistic to be realizable, but, on the contrary, that it had been realized, with disastrous consequences to the individual and society.[24] *Brave New World* portrayed a hedonistic paradise in which all needs and desires were painlessly satisfied—but also rigidly shaped by the ruling elite of scientific controllers in the interests of social stability. The casualties, Huxley suggested, were freedom, love, and creativity—indeed, all that made human life truly worthwhile.

It seems clear that, unlike Orwell's, Huxley's antiutopia has not been so threatening to the generations of the second half of the twentieth century. Perhaps this has something to do with Huxley's own recantation, in his utopia *Island* (1962), where something in many respects quite close to the Brave New World was presented in a utopian rather than antiutopian light. It is, in any case, an irony that, as reported by several American college professors, many young people read *Brave New World* as a utopia rather than an antiutopia. Huxley's attack on hedonism appears to them rather a celebration of sex, drugs, and effortless living—the very things that they crave.[25]

And are these students not, in a sense, right? Has not the society of *Brave New World* become the Western utopia in the second half of our century? Economic abundance and uninterrupted increases in one's personal standard of living—are not these the highest goals put before the populations of Western industrial nations? It is, indeed, precisely this consumerist utopia, in the opinion of observers like Ernest Gellner, that has been the principal dissolving force of the regimes of Eastern Europe.[26] Consumerism has killed communism; both East and West now inscribe on their banners, "Live now, pay later."

## Utopia, Socialism, and the 1989 Revolutions

The breakup of communism in Eastern Europe was bound to bring with it fresh denunciations of utopia. Dissident thought in the area had long identified the ruling systems with a misbegotten and disastrous utopian experiment. Solzhenitsyn in Russia, and even more out of it—Havel and Kundera in Czechoslovakia, Michnik and Geremek in Poland—all inveighed against the utopianism that had infected the politics of the region. The Soviet Union was the exemplary case of what Solzhenitsyn called "the Marxist-Leninist utopia, which was blind and evil at birth."[27] For the Czech philosopher Milan Simecka, "In the course of some sixty years, the hitherto greatest utopia of all has been turned into a social order whose immobility and intellectual sterility is reminiscent of the nightmares of the ancient utopias." The "real socialism" of Eastern Europe was for Simecka a standing reminder of the truth that all utopias must betray their ideals when put into practice: "All the indications are that utopias are nothing but the instrument of a historical deception, the bait set out for the desperate, a false rainbow beneath which the people is easily to be led into a new slavery."[28]

Simecka referred to Karl Popper as having powerfully put forth this view of utopia; at the same time, he invoked *Nineteen Eighty-Four*— "surely one of the most exciting books in world literature"—for its prophetic understanding of the nature of the communist utopia.[29] There is a clear indication here of the link between the earlier antiutopian critique and the present recoil from utopia. The current antiutopians also see utopia as a poisonous inheritance. Its burial by the revolutions of 1989 in Central and Eastern Europe is an event to be celebrated, not mourned, according to Hans Magnus Enzensberger. We should not fear that by bidding "farewell to utopia" we would be losing the element of dream or desire in society. These are, unlike utopia, anthropological constants. What we would have discarded "would above all be the most fatal elements of utopian thinking: the projective megalomania, the claim to totality, finality and originality."[30]

Yes, indeed. But is that the main legacy of utopia—a totalitarian aim and ambition? It might seem so, if utopia is equated with specific social experiments, in this case the state socialism of Eastern Europe. Scarcely less damaging is the claim, made by Jürgen Habermas, that "the exhaustion of utopian energies" is bound up with the perceived failure of modern social democracy and the welfare state—the more general expression of "the utopian idea of a laboring society" that included not just Marxism, but all hopes based on transforming the sphere of work and production.[31]

In both these cases the fate of utopia is tied to particular social philosophies and particular social practices. Although it is important to see that utopia has received specific embodiments in different periods of its history, that is quite a different matter from identifying it with any of those embodiments, however comprehensive. After the eighteenth century utopia certainly found its principal expression in socialism. But not only is socialism not one thing, but many things; even if socialism has lost its capacity to inspire utopian visions, that does not exhaust utopia. There is still much for it to do.

Even in the nineteenth century socialism was a multifarious project. It included—to name only the principal forms—Owenism, Saint-Simonism, Fourierism, and Fabianism in addition to Marxism, not to mention the anarchist and syndicalist varieties of socialism among the followers of Proudhon and Bakunin, or the decentralized socialism of John Stuart Mill. All these pointed in very different directions, as is well illustrated both by the socialist communities of nineteenth-century America and by the different kinds of socialist movements and parties that emerged in nineteenth-century Europe.[32] The different forms of the good life to which competing conceptions of socialism could lead were also vividly portrayed by two famous utopias of the late nineteenth century, those of Edward Bellamy's state-socialist *Looking Backward* (1888) and William Morris's ecosocialist *News from Nowhere* (1890).

In our century the Russian Revolution of 1917 and the Chinese Revolution of 1948 added yet other varieties to the mixture. And there have also been "African socialism" and the socialism of the Israeli kibbutzim. No doubt the Soviet Union—like America in the parallel case of liberal democracy—came to be seen as the exemplary expression of the socialist utopia. Its downfall equally poses the greatest challenge yet to the whole socialist enterprise. There is no telling now whether socialism can survive the challenge. Nor do its devotees take much comfort from the fact that the socialism of Eastern Europe can justly be held not to have been very socialist at all—not, at any rate, as its putative progenitor Marx envisaged it. André Gunder Frank says that "the real practicality" of this "well-meaning" argument "clashes with all world social-political-economic reality. . . . It is wholly unrealistic to think that the damage of the whole experience to the idea of socialism . . . can simply be wished away by latter-day professions of one's own purity against others' former sins."[33]

Is this being too pessimistic? Already there are commentators who have sought to rescue socialism from its productivist, factory-based orientation, as a "utopia of work," and to see its relevance to the organization of life beyond the world of work. Drawing upon Marx's well-known observation in the third volume of *Capital* that the "realm of freedom" lies beyond "the realm of necessity"—beyond, that is, economic life per se—thinkers such as André Gorz have elaborated a utopian vision of a socialism that encompasses family, community, and "own work" in the social space and free time that could be released by the prodigious capacities of modern industrial technology. "What is involved," said Gorz, "is the transition from a productivist work-based society to a society of liberated time in which the cultural and the societal are accorded greater importance than the economic."[34]

The issue here is not so much the immediate (or even ultimate) practicability of this vision as that it shows socialism's great capacity for renewal as an alternative to existing forms of society. And there are other current varieties, such as the "ecosocialism" of many contemporary Green thinkers, or the "market socialism" of many social democrats.[35] Indeed, one might go so far as to say that as long as there is industrial civilization there will always be socialism. Socialism was born in the eighteenth century at the same time as industrial capitalism. It has always accompanied the evolution of capitalism, as critic and "counterculture" to its values and practices. It is even possible to argue that, had socialism not been its alter ego, capitalism would have succumbed, as Marx predicted, to the contradictions of its development (though socialism would not necessarily have been its successor). Socialism has kept capitalism on its toes, has reminded it of its promises, has forced it to tone down its harshness and regulate its operation out of consideration for the social consequences that, disregarded, might have undermined its stability. Capitalism needs socialism; if it did not exist, it would have to invent it.[36]

Nowhere is this more relevant now, perhaps, than in the postcommunist societies of Central and Eastern Europe. In this region a veritable frenzy of procapitalist, promarket enthusiasm, urged on by the International Monetary Fund and sundry Western economists, has seized intellectuals and politicians. East Central Europe may think it has turned its back on utopia, but it has only too evidently exchanged one utopia for another, the capitalist and consumerist utopia. And America, still the world symbol of capitalism/consumerism, has, somewhat to its surprise, recovered something of its former utopian appeal, at least to non-Americans. Writing in the year of revolution, 1989, George Steiner observed: "It is a TV-revolution we are witnessing, a rush toward the 'California-promise' that America has offered to the common man on this tired earth. American standards of dress, nourishment, locomotion, entertainment, housing are today the concrete utopia in revolutions."[37]

But it is precisely in this sphere that socialism, not necessarily so named, is likely to see its resurgence. The capitalist cornucopia, even if it fills within a reasonable time in this economically shattered region, will not distribute its fruits at all equitably without active intervention by the state. That, after all, has long been the situation in Western capitalist societies, as John Kenneth Galbraith is fond of pointing out to East European free marketeers.[38] The populations of East Central Europe seem already to be realizing this. They are reacting with growing disillusionment and apathy to the power struggles taking place in the political arena, where social policies are looked upon with suspicion as smacking of the old discredited communist system. In Poland and Hungary participation in parliamentary elections has dropped to 40 percent. The massive group of nonvoters provides, it has been plausibly argued, a natural constituency for a renewed social democratic alternative.[39] The demand for economic security and social justice is also showing a more active, and in some ways a more disturbing, side. In the Polish elections of October 1991, the socialists (ex-communists) gained 12 percent of the vote; in the Bulgarian presidential election of January 1992, the socialist-backed candidate received 47 percent of the vote; and in Russia Boris Yeltsin's vice president, Alexander Rutskoi, found a heartfelt popular response to his fierce public criticism of the liberal free market policies of the government.[40]

If Eastern Europe once more rediscovers socialism, one might say that, whatever the fate of this or that socialist or labor party, it has never really left Western Europe. Communist parties may dissolve, but the social democratic presence remains strong in many Western European countries—France, Germany, Spain, Italy, Austria, and the Scandinavian countries especially. The changes in work and employment increasingly brought about by the microelectronic revolution and the intensified globalization of capitalism are likely to produce sizable constituencies for a serious challenge to unmodified free market philosophies. As André Gorz has shown, the "post-industrial proletariat" of the unemployed and the casually or insecurely employed is already close to 40 to 50 percent of workers in many Western countries. As Gorz says, "The two-thirds society has already been left behind"—and with it, perhaps, the automatic majority of right-wing parties.[41] Socialism will need to work energetically to be the beneficiary of the sea change in economic life; there are many other contenders for the voices and votes of the disinherited and dispossessed. But the material for the recovery is there.

R. W. Johnson has pointed to the deep entrenchment of socialism in the values and practices of Western Europe. Socialism, as much as capitalism, has become part of the fabric of European society. With communism seen off the stage, it has become easier to see the natural and necessary function of socialism in an economy and a society dominated by the institutions of private property. Socialism here returns, as it should, to the legacy of the great social democratic movements of the late nineteenth century. As Johnson says: "The world's leading social democratic party in 1992 is the same as in 1892, the German SPD. The lasting monument of this movement is a successful European tradition of mixed economies and extensive welfare nets which give concrete expression to the notion of a comprehensive citizenship in communities which, for all their faults, are closer to the Rawlsian ideal than any others on earth. The preservation, advancement and integration of these communities is, perhaps, the true vocation of Western socialists. In this they have large consensual majorities on their side, despite their current ragged state as parties."[42]

Even if socialism as a movement does not regain its vitality, at least for some time, must that also be true of socialism as a utopia? Even those, such as Frank Manuel, who are performing the obsequies over Marxism as a theory and a practice, are still aware of its power as the most compelling embodiment of the European Enlightenment: "The ideal of physical and psychic actualization as an individual human right, embedded in the Marxist utopia and long repressed, may yet find a place as a moral statement acceptable to both a secular and a religious humanism."[43] The downfall of Marxism as a system may paradoxically release suppressed elements in Marxism that could regenerate utopia— not the least in that part of Europe that has been most vehement in its rejection of both Marxism and utopia (which are seen as synonymous). Erazim Kohák has argued that "the absence of a legitimating vision may ultimately prove the biggest obstacle to building viable societies in the lands of the erstwhile Soviet empire."[44] Even Milan Simecka, one of the most passionate critics of utopias, arrived finally at the view that, for all their dangers, utopias are an indispensable component of a true politics: "A world without utopias would be a world without social hope, a world of resignation to the status quo and the devalued slogans of everyday political life. . . . We would be left with hopeless submission to an order which is only too natural, because it can, as yet, modestly feed the people, give them employment and a secure daily round.

It is unable to provide for the unnatural demands of man, for the utopian ideas of its beginnings such as justice, freedom and tolerance, and to carry them further. This order no longer understands such demands, considering them unnatural and utopian; a remarkable case of amnesia."[45]

With this we have, of course, moved a long way from the specifics of Marxism or socialism. But the house of utopia, like that of Marxism itself, contains many chambers. Even if the socialist utopia, in its many guises, proves unpalatable, that still leaves myriad possible forms for utopia to take. Ecologists, taking their cue from Morris's *News from Nowhere* and, more recently, Huxley's *Island* (1962) and Ernest Callenbach's *Ecotopia* (1975), have seized upon utopia as an admirable vehicle for the expression of their planetary concerns. Ursula le Guin's *The Dispossessed* (1974) has rightly been hailed not just as one of the best ecotopias, but even more for its rehabilitation of utopia as a literary genre. Le Guin also provided a bridge to the feminist utopia—the most thriving of the current reworkings of utopia, and one that has, as an important add-on, reestablished the connection with science fiction that lies at the root of the genre.[46]

There has even been, in a fittingly playful fashion, the elaboration of a "liberal utopia," postmodernist style, that proclaims the contingency of self, morality, and community, but which can imagine an ideal social order in which the recognition of this contingency—by "liberal ironists"—is the ground of private and public life.[47] This is attractive, but at first sight surprising. Have not the postmodernists generally been among the most scornful critics of utopia? Utopia for them is identified with the belief in Reason, Progress, and History, with the "metanarratives" encompassing all of these in some unified view of humanity and its destiny. As such, utopia belongs with all supposedly scientific theories of society on the scrap heap.[48]

But of course there is a utopia, or utopias, in postmodernism. The announcement of "the end of history" and the rejection of all future-oriented speculation merely displaces utopia from time to space. To this extent postmodernists are returning to the older, pre-eighteenth-century, spatial forms of utopia, the kind inaugurated by More. The postmodernist utopia has been described as "a vision of a neo-tribal paradise in which a set of spatially set forms of life carry on experiments, each in their own culture."[49] But there is a certain spatial dynamism also in the vision, commensurate with the global reach of postmodernism. One is free, indeed encouraged, to move between local cultures, like a tourist. Disneyland may, not unkindly, be taken as some sort of model of the postmodernist world: a range of cultural experiences drawn from different times and places that one can mix according to taste.

The "spatialization of the temporal" in postmodernism has indeed been seen by Fredric Jameson as a powerful force revitalizing the utopian impulse in our time. In spatial utopias "the transformation of social relations and political institutions is projected onto the vision of place and landscape, including the human body. Spatialization, then, whatever it may take away in the capacity to think time and History, also opens a door onto a whole new domain for libidinal investment of the Utopian and even the protopolitical type." Jameson professes to find today, especially among postmodernist artists and writers, "an unacknowledged 'party of Utopia.'"[50] If this is so, if the desire to restore "the broken unity" reasserts itself against all the forces of fragmentation currently ranged against it, not only is there no "death of utopia," but, on the contrary, we find an affirmation of the persisting vitality of a way of thinking that Isaiah Berlin has seen as "a central strand in the whole of western thought."[51]

## The Future of History

Does the likely persistence of socialism as an oppositional force, even an ideal, contradict the view of Francis Fukuyama and others that we have reached "the end of history"—the end, that is, of the competition between fundamentally different ideologies? Not necessarily, and not by itself. For Fukuyama's argument is that there is now nowhere in the world a realistic alternative to the idea of liberal democracy, still less to its economic counterpart, capitalism or the market. Socialism may continue to provide a critical counterpoint to capitalist development, but it cannot offer itself any longer as a systematic alternative to it. The collapse of communism since 1989 has, for Fukuyama, been the decisive thing. It has confirmed the worldwide movement toward democracy that, in the last decade or so, has toppled dictators on all continents. As Fukuyama says, "As mankind approaches the end of the millennium, the twin crises of authoritarianism and socialist central planning have left only one competitor standing in the ring as an ideology of potentially universal validity: liberal democracy, the doctrine of individual freedom and popular sovereignty."[52]

Despite some rude noises and scornful denunciations of Fukuyama, it is striking how few of his critics have answered his repeated challenge to them to show what might upset the hegemony of liberal democracy as a worldwide aspiration. Piotr Sztompka, for instance, calls Fukuyama's concept of the "universal homogeneous state," based on liberal principles, "a perverse, counter-utopian utopia." But he then goes on to admit that "there is a worldwide ideological and political trend toward liberal democracy . . . growing in salience and acceptance"—thus conceding the main point.[53]

The critics are probably right to say that Fukuyama smooths over persisting differences between contemporary states and nations, that he too readily embraces all of them with the cover-all term "liberal democracy." Alan Ryan observes that "it is only from an altitude so great that most of human life is invisible that Japan and the United States could be passed off as examples of the same socio-political system."[54]

But the existence of authoritarian capitalist regimes in Asia and elsewhere—Lee Kuan Yew of Singapore calls his system "East Asian Confucian capitalism"—does not appear to constitute a major contradiction to Fukuyama's thesis. Fukuyama is himself too anxious to distinguish the capitalist economy from the liberal polity, regarding their joint victory as the result of the triumph of fundamentally different principles.[55] Historically they have, in fact, been closely, if not indissolubly, connected.[56] One need not argue a full-blooded materialist position to say that it is capitalism that has given the general character to modern liberal societies. It is capitalist institutions and values— private property, profit seeking, individualism, consumerism—that color the attitudes and beliefs of the majority of the populations of modern societies.

Certainly these attitudes can partially be offset by the persistence of traditional cultural features—for instance, the often-remarked-upon "group" orientation of the Japanese, which mitigates the extreme individualism of capitalism. But this does not seriously qualify the fundamentally transformative effect—as Marx argued—of capitalist social relations across the whole society. One of these effects is a tendency toward individualism and political democracy, though sometimes of a somewhat illiberal kind. But this is, despite Fukuyama, perhaps not the most important thing; yet it is certainly the most fragile one. When Fukuyama talks about the worldwide spread of liberal democracy, he is really talking about the worldwide victory of capitalism. And there certainly seems, at the moment, no real rival in sight.

The real challenge that Fukuyama throws up is when he says that "we cannot picture to ourselves a world that is *essentially* different from the present one, and at the same time better."[57] This is, once more, a rejection of the classic utopian function, on the grounds of its obsoleteness. Enough has already been said to suggest that this rejection is misplaced, the result partly of a misunderstanding of utopia's traditional concerns. But there is a need, nevertheless, to state why one might think that the engine of history has not stalled, that history has not reached its *telos.*

Fukuyama is right, I think, to say that the recrudescence of ethnic and national passions is no contradiction of his claims. They are, after all, in however rough a form, no more than reassertions of principles—the principles of autonomy and "self-determination"—linked ultimately to the American and French Revolutions, the joint ancestors of liberal democracy. He is also right to point out that resurgent Islamic fundamentalism, a possibly competing ideology to liberalism, has had "no appeal in areas that were not culturally Islamic to begin with. Young people in Berlin, Tokyo, Rio or Moscow are not rushing to don chadors, as they were once tempted by Communism."[58]

But there are far greater challenges to liberalism and capitalism than these. Fukuyama is fully aware of the subjective and expressive discontents of the "last man." Liberal capitalism, he argues, undermines the sense of solidarity and community. It creates a culture of amoral hedonism and consumerism. It might bore us to death, because of its lack of challenge to our more active faculties. This is the price we pay for the freedom and plenty of the "universal homogeneous state" of capitalist liberal democracy.[59] If only this were all! For if so, most of us might settle for a quiet private life of comfort and consumption, and let those who wanted to do so worry about the higher things of the mind.

But capitalist industrialism does not only strip us of culture and community. More dangerously—with an impact we shall see in the immediate future—it is undermining the life support systems of the planet itself. This is where history comes back in, with a vengeance. If the challenges to liberal capitalism were no more than those Fukuyama indicates, it might indeed be plausible to say that it could see them off without too much trouble. But what if capitalism, consistent with its world-transforming potency, in its restless and relentless expansiveness consumes the very seed corn of its being and growth? What if it threatens the health and habitations of whole cultures across the globe? How can it possibly be held, not simply that there is no more for utopias to do, but that historical choices of the most fundamental kind do not face us more urgently now than ever before? What could be more challenging than the fate of the planet?

In facing this challenge we will have to see that liberal capitalism may not, after all, be the final form of history. Its excessive individualism may need to be severely restrained by national and international bodies concerned with regulating the use and disposal of the earth's resources. The invisible hand of the market may need to be made more visible and given more guidance in the interests of social stability and social justice. "Consumer choice," insofar as it is more than a myth of manufacturers and advertisers, might have to be curtailed out of consideration for the finitude or scarcity of particular materials (not to mention the battered sensibilities of supermarket shoppers), or because of the ecological damage inflicted in the making or consuming of particular products—for instance, hamburgers—on a world scale.[60] There may even be the need for the promotion of some sort of new religion, stressing mutualism and planetary solidarity, in the face of the impending catastrophe.[61] Not for nothing does Durkheim seem increasingly to be becoming the prophet of the twenty-first century.[62]

In all these ways liberal capitalism may have to undergo such extensive modification that it might become impossible to use the term with any real meaning in the not-too-distant future. Communitarianism and authoritarianism, not necessarily opposed to each other, could be our future as much as some variety of liberal individualism. Certainly there still seem to be some strong contenders for the soul of modern man, even if some of them appear in novel form. Our historical condition—one in which life itself is threatened with insupportable damage, perhaps even extinction—is unprecedented. There is nothing to guarantee that we will find our way out of this mess. But, at the very least, we can think about—we must think about—alternatives to the system that has gotten us into it.

East Europeans are very well aware of the poisoning of their land and the pollution of their atmosphere by unchecked industrialism. In their case it was called socialism, in ours capitalism. Some of them also see that the solution to their problems cannot, therefore, be the wholesale importation of market capitalism in all its unadorned glory.[63] In that sense East Europeans cannot, as some of them hope, go back to their past to "restart" their history. Not only has that history now been indelibly marked by the communist episode, so that they must interrogate and come to terms with that experience.[64] Even more important, to go back would be to do no more than imitate the pattern—probably as dependent or peripheral elements—of Western development. This pattern is now in several essential respects unviable. There is indeed an opportunity, as well as a need, for the "rebirth of history." That is one of the great consequences of the 1989 revolutions. But we must understand this not as the resumption of the sway of the past, but as the invention of something new, a rebirth that is also a renewal of history.

## A Further Note

No one seems to think that the socialist project, as conceived for most of this century, has much chance of being revived in the foreseeable future. The victory of a number of social democratic parties in Western Europe, the return to power of former communists in some of the countries of East Central Europe—the main political developments since this chapter was first written—have not fundamentally changed this view. The social democratic parties have made it clear that they have shed many of their traditional goals, not to mention some of their traditional allies, such as the unions. The former communists have renounced communism, and seek only to slow down somewhat the pace of change and the transition to a market economy. Tony Blair's "New Labor" in Britain, Lionel Jospin's Socialist Party in France, Gerhard Schröder's Social Democratic Party in Germany—all of which achieved electoral victory in the second half of the 1990s—have shown that they have learned only too well the lessons of the 1980s, when the New Right philosophy of Margaret Thatcher and Ronald Reagan was triumphant almost everywhere in the West. All are anxious to throw off the socialist heritage of big government, nationalization of the "commanding heights" of the economy, and even commitment to the welfare state. What they promise, instead, is a more caring, more just society. Chancellor Schröder perhaps spoke for all the new socialist leaders when he declared, "There is no longer right or left, there is only right or wrong."[65]

Still, just as socialism in general and communism in Eastern Europe (though not communism as Marx understood it or would have liked it) kept alive the idea of an alternative to capitalism, so we might say that the unexpected victory of social democratic parties in Europe has kept alive, however faintly, the idea that free market capitalism, the capitalism of Reagan and Thatcher, is not the only alternative. The crushing defeat of the Republicans in the United States by Bill Clinton's Democrats in 1992 and again in 1996 is also some indication of this. These events seem to go some way toward justifying the argument of this chapter, that whatever the fate of the socialist movement, a critical awareness of the limitations of capitalism, of the price we pay for its economic dynamism, will remain and return even amid the triumphant spread of capitalism across the globe. Today's social democrats may not want to nationalize the economy or run all the social services; but they are aware, just as are their counterparts in Eastern Europe, that an unregulated and untrammeled capitalism runs the risk of undermining itself by the material, social, and moral destruction it can wreak.[66]

In any case, whatever the future of socialism, the continuing spread and worldwide triumph of capitalism would seem to suggest the continuing and indeed heightened relevance of *Marxism*. It is often forgotten that Marx's principal work was called not *Der Sozialismus*, but *Das Kapital*. Marx's theorizing and expectations of socialism are one thing, and perhaps the lesser thing in his overall writing and thinking. What looms much larger in his writing, and is likely to prove his enduring contribution, is his analysis of the origins and development of capitalism. If, as is often claimed today, capitalism is the name of the only game in town, Marx is, par excellence, its anatomist and diagnostician. Capitalism's overthrow might not be on the horizon, as Marx had hoped and predicted; but he remains a powerful theoretician of its methods of operation and the social and political problems they create. Capitalism was always, for Marx, a global system. Current attempts to understand the globalization of capitalism, and its social consequences, remain indebted to him even if they seek to distance themselves from his predictions of capitalism's demise.[67]

Socialism, it is argued in this chapter, is the modern utopia. Its apparent failure and lack of appeal today also spell, for many, the death of the utopian project in the modern world.[68] 1989 is widely regarded as having put the final nail in the coffin of utopia.

I have argued that utopia is too many things, and serves too many functions, to be equated *tout court* with socialism, particularly if socialism is identified with only one of its varieties, the so-called societies of "actually existing socialism" in Central and Eastern Europe. At the beginning of a new century, and a new millennium, there is much for utopia to do. The world is being transformed in many ways: by the impact of the new communication technologies and the information revolution; by the emergence of a new international order with the breakup of the Soviet Union and the rise of China as a new world power; by the resurgence of nationalism and ethnicity, reshaping the territorial map of the world; by the spread of a global culture, often with its source in the West, but altered in many ways by the receiving societies. There are splendid opportunities here, and a pressing need, for utopian visions— or, as always and performing the same useful functions, dystopias or antiutopias.[69]

And "the end of history"? How does that fare some years on? Francis Fukuyama's pronouncement was initially greeted with a good deal of skepticism, not to mention—especially from academic commentators— contempt.[70] What is noticeable is how, with time, many of those critics have come to smuggle Fukuyama's views into their own accounts, often without acknowledging their change of mind. Certainly the Fukuyama thesis still seems to stand up quite well: namely, that there is not currently on the scene—nor is there likely to be in the foreseeable future— any real rival to liberal market societies for the allegiance of most of the world's populations.[71] What happened in China in the 1990s— when, despite retaining a communist regime, market reforms were introduced on a wide scale—confirms rather than contradicts Fukuyama's expectations. This is not to say, as argued in this chapter, that liberal capitalist societies do not face many challenges, some of which may force us to conceive of a fundamentally different way of conducting our lives and organizing our societies. It is simply to state what seems obvious to most observers at the present time: that, understood in the broadest sense, liberal capitalist societies seem the aspiration of most peoples in the world—nationalist fanaticism, fundamentalist regimes, and communist remnants notwithstanding.[72]

Finally, let us consider the end of one millennium and the birth of another. In this chapter I have suggested that "endism"—focusing on the end of history, the end of utopia, and so on—is partly bound up with millennial expectations of the end of time and a new beginning, a new era. In that sense the year 1989 has had a distinct millennial charge. The "end of socialism," supervening on the anticipation already aroused by the coming end of the millennium, has undoubtedly added a highly dramatic flavor to commentary on the events of that year. There is, of course, an element of pure accident, pure coincidence—or is there?—in all this. Nevertheless, it is only because everyone is aware of the momentousness of 1989, of the extraordinary changes that it portended not just in Eastern Europe, but the world at large, that it is possible for the revolutions of 1989 to be conceived in apocalyptic terms. It is a tribute, yet again, to the immense potency of those events in stimulating thought and the imagination on the widest possible scale.[73]

*Seven*

# History and Identity in the Revolutions of 1989

*Nowhere in the world does history have such importance as in Eastern Europe.*

Milan Simecka

*Forgetting, I would even go so far as to say historical error, is a crucial factor in the creation of a nation.*

Ernest Renan

*We face a future in which it cannot be guaranteed that histories will supply identities any longer.*

J. G. A. Pocock

## History and Memory in East Central Europe

History haunts all societies, only some, as it were, more than others. Jacques Rupnik has said that "to the peoples of Central Europe, the past, to use Faulkner's phrase, 'is never dead. It is not even past.'"[1] The past can be a presence to a greater or lesser degree in the social and political life of a nation. The British, as occasion suits, recall the great days of the Industrial Revolution and the time British power dominated the globe. Americans, like Norwegians, celebrate Independence Day, and the promise of their new or newly freed societies. Practically all modern societies remember, in solemn anniversaries, the fallen dead of their major wars.

But this kind of remembering is more akin to a reminder, or a warning, not to forget ("Lest we forget," the motto on many British war memorials). History here serves as a kind of spur to long-term reflection on the meaning and purpose of national life. It is not the irruption of the past into the present, the turning of the present into a battleground resounding with past cries. In the West, history has become largely a storehouse of memories for example and instruction, in the old tradition of *historia magister vitae*. The past has been tamed.[2] Even the French wish to bury their Revolution, for so long the pivot of their political conflicts.

Nothing of the sort applies to Central and Eastern Europe. Where else but here could a six-hundred-year-old battle mobilize fierce energies and evoke bloody passions, as does the battle of the Field of Blackbirds (1389) in shaping Serbian feelings toward the mainly Muslim Albanians of Kosovo?[3] Where else but in this region can one find—to take some recent examples at random—arguments such as that of the Romanians that, because they descend from the Roman Empire and speak a Romance language, they have an especially strong claim to NATO membership, and that exclusion now means "another Yalta for Romania"; or the similar claims of the Slovenians that their four-hundred-year membership in the Habsburg Empire entitles them to admission to the European Union? Where else but here could one find the Polish Pope John Paul II, speaking before an assembled group of Central and East European presidents on a visit to Poland, urging on them as a model of European cooperation the example of the missionary St. Adalbert, who preached to Slavs as well as Western Europeans a thousand years ago in a region stretching from France to Poland?[4]

The historical parallels and references flow effortlessly from the lips of politicians and intellectuals in the area as they reach back now to the distant past—the Second Bulgarian Empire of the thirteenth century, the battles of Mohács (1526) and the White Mountain (1620), the first Polish constitution (1791)—now to the endless crises and betrayals of the twentieth century—Versailles, Trianon, Munich, Yalta. The communist era added its own historical markers: 1953, 1956, 1968, 1981—and now 1989.[5] Such events and dates, scorched in the collective memory at least of intellectuals, speak of tragic conflicts and bitter divisions as well as of heroic strivings. They recall not simply external incursions, but, even more, internal enmities. As Tony Judt says, "For Eastern Europeans the past is not just another country but a positive archipelago of vulnerable historical territories, to be preserved from attacks and distortions perpetrated by the occupants of a neighboring island of memory, a dilemma made the more cruel because the enemy is almost always within."[6]

Andrew Janos has remarked that "it is one of the timeless clichés of East European studies that these peoples tend to live in their history," but his own account testifies to the truth of the observation.[7] For Eastern European peoples it is not so much a matter of choosing to be historically conscious as of having history thrust upon them. Many must heartily wish to be free of history, to be like "normal" (that is, Western) nations; happy is the country that has no history. The persistence of history, as a point of reference and an active presence, is an index of a troubled legacy. It reflects the most obvious fact about the region's character to date: its lack of control over its own destiny, its dependence on the politics of others. Where one is not in a position to make one's own future, one scrutinizes the past for the evidence of historic turning points, lost opportunities, perhaps memories of former glories. A country like the United States, its face always turned toward the future, can afford to be indifferent to its history. Not so the countries of Eastern Europe.

This is not only nostalgia; it is the necessary work of understanding. It may involve painful memories and mutual recrimination. It can even lead to despair in the face of what may seem overwhelming forces. But it can also provide the resources for hope. It can involve the search for buried traditions and alternative possibilities. It can supply rallying cries and inspiring examples. History cautions, but it also encourages and emboldens. Reflection on the Polish victory of 1920 over the Bolsheviks, says Adam Michnik, created for many generations the "cultural reserves" for resisting Sovietization in the period of communist rule.[8]

All this is true. But it leaves open the question of how far Eastern Europeans should be relying on the past in their present efforts to rebuild their societies and construct new national identities. Does the past liberate or entrap? The revolutions of 1989 in East Central Europe have raised this question in an urgent form, as the matter of everyday politics. For the past seemed to be what they were preeminently about. Participants and observers alike spoke of "the rebirth of history," or, more ominously, of "the revenge of the past." Eastern Europe's engagement with history seemed to enter a new phase, one full of hope as well as of foreboding.

What do these revolutions tell us about this? How did they see themselves in time? What historical examples and concepts of history did they appeal to? What do these reveal of their "self-understanding," and the directions in which they wished to move their societies? Revolutions are commonly moments of acute self-consciousness, when societies are forced to take stock of some of their deepest assumptions and make fundamental decisions about their future. The 1989 revolutions were no exception.

## The 1989 Revolutions and the Revolutionary Tradition

Revolutions in the modern world have often served as "identity-creating" mechanisms. They have been the founding events of new nations, displaying to the world the new national colors and the terms in which henceforward they wish their societies to be understood. Or they have been the regenerative convulsions of old societies in the throes of massive reordering, signaling a change of direction and purpose. The American Revolution of the eighteenth century is the best example of the first kind. It inaugurated a style of revolution that was to give national identities to a host of new nations in the breakup of European colonialism in the twentieth century. The French, Russian, and Chinese Revolutions are the outstanding examples of the second type. The French Revolution also set the example, both in style and substance, for many of the nationalist movements of nineteenth- and early twentieth-century Europe, and the emergence or reemergence of independent nations from amid the ruins of the Habsburg and Ottoman Empires.

The participants in the 1989 revolutions were also aware of the revolutionary inheritance. The Russian Revolution was, of course, no point of reference; but there were in 1989 many echoes of the French and American Revolutions, and even occasionally of Britain's seventeenth-century revolutions.[9] If "Liberty, Equality, Fraternity," in its elemental form, was too strong for some, with its reminder of the excesses of the French Revolution, there was no problem with the acceptance of the generally liberal legacy of the Western revolutions of the seventeenth century to the nineteenth century. The vocabulary of democracy, pluralism, human rights, the rule of law, constitutionalism, and citizenship was evidently drawn from its lexicon. In such a way, in the name of the "Principles of 1789," did the societies of East Central Europe decisively reject the ideology or "political morality" of Marxism.[10]

This rejection, then, provided one badge of identity. Societies newly freed from thralldom to the East declared themselves politically liberal societies. Their revolutions were liberal revolutions. But this raised a host of other questions. For one thing, was not the concept of revolution itself suspect to liberals? Had not nineteenth-century liberals, reflecting above all on the French Revolution, themselves wrestled with this troubling aspect of their inheritance? Western observers had been quick to pin the revolutionary label on the events of 1989 in East Central Europe, even where they had some doubts as to its full appropriateness.[11] And in the West the fashion has persisted, as the stream of books and articles on "the revolutions of 1989" amply testifies. The lack of violence in these revolutions worries some purists, as does the fact that the communist regimes were not so much overthrown as died by their own hands, or those of outside agents. But generally Western commentators are in agreement that if such dramatic and sweeping changes as occurred in the mass downfall of communist states cannot be called revolutions, perhaps the word has no useful meaning.[12]

Eastern Europeans cannot be so confident. For them the word *revolution,* at least in part, conjures up an oppressive legacy. It connotes 1917 as much as, and perhaps even more than, 1789. The rhetoric of revolution—"workers' revolution," "people's revolution," "world revolution"—had been an insistent part of the propaganda that had assailed them for the past forty years. Hence, although not unwilling to join in the euphoria that the word *revolution,* understood in a festive sense, can suggest, they have generally been careful to qualify it in the case of 1989 by using a whole series of moderating adjectives— "peaceful," "velvet," "negotiated," "bloodless," "legal." "The monster died in bed," as the Hungarians are fond of saying of their own peacefully negotiated *rendszerváltás,* or "exchange of systems"—a "strangely colorless term," says Andrew Arato, "capable of inspiring little passion or enthusiasm."[13] Here we are a long way from the bliss that the French Revolution inspired in the young Wordsworth. The "pathos of novelty" that Hannah Arendt saw as characterizing all revolutions since 1789[14] also seems conspicuously absent in the case of 1989.

These features of the Eastern European nations' understanding of their revolutions express a typically complex and somewhat ambivalent relationship to the Western revolutionary tradition. On the one hand, many passionately want to affirm their affiliation to it. If Western nations see themselves as heir to the revolutionary struggles of the eighteenth and nineteenth centuries, Eastern European nations also wish to place themselves within that heroic tradition. Their revolutions, says the Hungarian György Varga, may have been "postponed"; but what they did in 1989 was essentially to replay 1789, specifically in terms of the demands for democracy and pluralism.[15] Varga's more conservative compatriot Gáspár Tamás prefers to invoke the American rather than the French Revolution: for him what was at issue in 1989 was that "human rights," and the struggles of that time, "forced the ideas of the American Revolution on to the political agenda after two hundred years."[16] Others, both in Eastern Europe and elsewhere, have preferred to see 1989 in the mirror of the 1848 revolutions, the reflection in this case not just of "the Springtime of the Nations" but also "the revolution of the intellectuals."[17] All these points of reference have their particular problems for the liberals of 1989, as I have discussed elsewhere;[18] the impressive thing, however, is their testimony to the wish to establish the proper revolutionary credentials.

But there is also a rejection of the revolutionary tradition—or, more precisely, a sense that in many important respects the events of 1989 do not fit the classic pattern of the "Great Revolutions" of the West. For Piotr Sztompka, for instance, "the crucial fact about the revolution of 1989 is its basically atheoretical character." As he says:

> Great Revolutions were normally preceded, and to some extent prepared, by theoretical visions which provided legitimacy to the social forces carrying them out, as well as the goals to be achieved. There were always some chosen groups or social classes considered as revolutionary agency. . . . And there were always some, more or less utopian and always strongly normative images of the better society which the revolutions were to realize. . . . Nothing of the sort in 1989. That revolution just happened; it was carried out by the wide alliance of diverse social groups which cut across all traditional class, occupational, regional, or ethnic frontiers; and it was inspired more by the repulsion against the existing system and sharp negative awareness of what is no longer acceptable, than by any clear notion of what is to come in its wake. It was not a revolution in the name of another utopia, but rather against any utopia. It was not a revolution under the banner of ideology, but rather expressed disenchantment with any ideology.[19]

One might feel that Sztompka here has been carried away by certain, especially Marxist, models of revolution, and that the "Great

Revolutions" did not happen quite in the way he suggests.[20] His description of the revolutions of 1989 is, in fact, rather a good account of how many of those earlier revolutions came about, at least up to 1917. But that is not the point. The point is the perception on the part of many Eastern European commentators that their revolutions were in some essential sense different from those of the West. A similar sense of perplexity is shown by two other commentators, one Western, one Eastern, who remark that "the revolution in Eastern Europe was always an odd one in so far as there was no new revolutionary idea whose time had come." They are resigned to the use of the term *revolution* in relation to 1989, but consider that it has "the wrong associations to capture the character of the who, the what and the why of the changes in 1989 and after." Instead they offer a different interpretation: "Insistent demands for liberal democracy, and rather less insistent demands for a capitalist economy, might have been thought more a *counter-revolutionary* demand for the restoration of precommunist traditions."[21]

"Counter-revolutionary"? Once more our commentators show a certain narrowness in their understanding of the Western revolutionary tradition. For was not an accepted—indeed, the dominant—meaning of *revolution* until the end of the eighteenth century a turning back, a *return* to a previous (purer) state of things? This was why Clarendon could declare, without any fear of being thought eccentric, that the Restoration of the English King Charles II in 1660 constituted a "revolution," following the irregular and pernicious innovations of Parliament and the Puritans in the Civil War, and why Locke could similarly defend the English Revolution of 1688 on the grounds that it represented a return to the normal, preexisting relationship between crown, people, and Parliament, before its untoward disruption by James II.[22] It was not until, and during, the French Revolution, that the word *revolution* acquired its more recent meaning as the construction of a fundamentally new social order;[23] and there have been plenty of occasions since 1688 to which one might think it appropriate to reapply the older meaning—for instance, the Iranian Revolution of 1979.

So when commentators question or deny the application of the term *revolution* to the events of 1989, they usually have in mind certain conventional understandings: violence, class conflict, mass movements, proclamations of new systems of society. They do not see that the events of 1989 can fit into a longer and more complex tradition of use, one with many layers and levels of meaning, where the older levels by no means disappear as they are overlaid by newer levels. Like all historical—which is to say, all human—concepts, revolution is a palimpsest. New circumstances can disinter and refurbish old meanings. This is happening today with respect to *democracy* and *civil society*; why should it be resisted in the case of *revolution*?

We shall see soon what the idea of revolution as restoration might mean in the case of the events of 1989. But there is a deeper aspect to consider first. 1989 repudiates 1917, of course; but does that not also mean that it repudiates 1789 and, beyond that, the whole revolutionary epoch that is associated with it? If, as Lenin himself claimed, 1917 merely renewed the revolutionary impulses of 1789, 1848, and 1871, to reject Lenin's revolution might mean to reject the European revolutionary tradition as a whole. And that, in turn, could mean the need to rethink the whole framework of politics bequeathed to us by that tradition. "If," says Tony Judt, "we have reached the end of the revolutionary era set in motion by Lenin, then we have in an important sense also closed the era opened by his French predecessors in 1789. . . . The implications are startling in that both the language and the projects of European political life rest squarely upon the terms of reference in which the heritage of the French Revolution has hitherto been grasped."[24]

Not just socialism, but liberalism and even conservatism, lose their meaning once unmoored from this revolutionary tradition. This is not to proclaim—again—the "end of ideology," still less the "end of history." But it opens up the intriguing possibility that 1989 might spell the "end of revolution," at least as that project has been understood in the West for the past two hundred years. In what terms the new forms of political conflict might be fought out can yet only dimly be discerned, some of it in the language of ecology, some of it in that of postmodernity and other kinds of "post-Enlightenment" philosophy.[25] But it might not be the least part of the challenge posed by the 1989 revolutions to the concept and theory of revolution that they question the very future of revolution in an increasingly disenchanted world.

## Revolution As Return

Revolution looks back—as is reflected by the older meaning of *revolution* as restoration or return—and it also looks forward, to the creation of an absolutely new future, a *novus ordo saeclorum*. The 1989 revolutions pointed in both these directions simultaneously. On the one hand, they announced the "rebirth of history," the recovery of their own past, with its own principles of development. On the other, they aspired to go beyond their past: not just their immediate, communist past, but the older, precommunist past, which for various reasons was as disquieting as the period of communist rule. In that sense they turned their faces toward the future.

We will return to this future orientation later. More controversial—and more consequential—has been the idea of the recovery of history in East Central Europe, and what this might mean for the outlook of the societies of the region. We should note that the slogan, the "rebirth of history," is itself ambiguous. It can suggest that, after an enforced period of stasis or immobility, the engine of history has been restarted. But to make your own history is not necessarily to be governed by it. It can also mean to give yourself the freedom to determine your own future: you, rather than others, make your history. The "rebirth of history" here connects with the second, future-oriented, concept of revolution.

For most people, the association of revolution with the rebirth of history has pointed to a significant reengagement with the past of the region: revolution as return (or revenge). The 1989 revolutions meant the "exit into history"; they involved facing Eastern Europe's "ghosts," the memories of past deeds and misdeeds under communism.[26] "Far from coming to an end," said Misha Glenny in a riposte to Francis Fukuyama, "history is being reborn."[27] In a direct reference to the older concept of revolution, Giuseppe di Palma says that "the East European revolutions may be seen as revolution in its pristine meaning of 're-turn': an effort by East Europeans to appropriate-reappropriate distinctively Western ideas and principles from which they had been severed by communism."[28]

The return to history here means the recovery of past traditions and former paths of development. The argument is that the nations of East Central Europe were forcibly—and, as it were, artificially—deflected from their natural course of evolution. In Milan Kundera's evocative account, Central Europe was "kidnapped" and held in captivity for forty years by the Russian bear. Soviet-maintained communist rule was an alien imposition on the countries and cultures of the region.[29] The end of that rule means that those societies can resume the path from which they were violently plucked.

For some intellectuals, that path, and that past, is that of the region as a whole. Central Europe, the "lands in-between," has a distinct civilization, different from that of both the West and the East. Therefore, although there is a fervent desire to "return to Europe," the Europe they have in mind is a plural entity, made up of overlapping traditions. Intellectuals such as György Konrád and Czesław Miłosz do not wish Central European societies to throw off the statist communism of the East only to embrace the commercialism and consumerism of the West. Central Europe has its own traditions, formed partly by the very dependency that has been the political tragedy of the region. But out of that dependency, they argue, has come a culture of ironic detachment and dissent, of satire and humor, of resilience in the face of adversity and clear-sightedness in the face of cant. These elements can be the building blocks of a new identity for the region as a whole, in the context perhaps of a political federation of the kind that was much discussed in the declining years of the Austro-Hungarian Empire.[30]

Critics both from within and without the region have spoken sharply of this "Central European utopia."[31] It has variously been regarded as the nostalgic dream of an idealized Habsburg Empire and as a simple anti-Soviet device. Now, with the pressure of the Soviet Union removed, some even see it as modulating more dangerously into the traditional idea of *Mitteleuropa*. It becomes the covert form of German predominance in the region. As Geoff Eley sees it, "As soon as one separates East Central Europe from Russia . . . another much less congenial conception of Central Europe/*Mitteleuropa* comes into play, one that was hatched originally in the imperial dreams and expansionist logics of German nationalists in the period between the 1880s and the First World War."[32]

Domination by Germany might be the lesser of the threats to the Central European dream. There are more powerful, if less traditional and less direct, threats. The problem with the idea of a "Central European way" is not that it is wrong. Its account of a multilayered Europe is at least as convincing as those that would reduce Europe to the heritage essentially of Western Europe. Nor is its vision unattractive. It is simply that it is a vision not apparently shared by the bulk of the populations of the region. The people share the intellectuals' commitment to the idea of Europe, "but it is a commitment," says Robin Okey, "which brooks no Central European mediation, whether as power bloc, federal, or cultural pluralist model, or Viennese metropole." What they want is swift and direct "incorporation into the European Community."[33]

Moreover, theirs is a Europe seen increasingly through the eyes of America. It may be true that, in looking West, East-Central European intellectuals were initially drawn to the tradition of Western social democracy, that, in the words of Eric Hobsbawm, "Stockholm was their model rather than Los Angeles."[34] But for much of the rest of the population, especially the young, it is the dream of California rather than of Paris or London that draws them Westward. This is partly the effect of the international youth culture and the global, largely American, media culture, intensified by the new experience of foreign travel of many ordinary East Central Europeans. But it also reflects, at a deeper level, the ideological victory of free market economics in the West, and the sense that it is American-inspired models that are transforming thought and practice throughout Europe, if not the whole world.

Whatever the wishes of the people, the autonomy of the region is in any case severely qualified by a host of familiar outside pressures. International bodies such as the International Monetary Fund and the World Bank routinely link strict fiscal and other policy conditions to their offers of loans and financial aid. Foreign business organizations in the region impose their own culture of attitudes and practices. The strongly expressed desire of all the political elites in East Central Europe that their countries join the European Community and NATO as soon as possible implies conformity to a host of economic and political requirements laid down by those institutions. In short, if there is a "Central European way," it may simply not be an option in the current environment, or for the foreseeable future.[35]

If not a "Central European way," what of a national way? The pressures working against the autonomy of the region as a whole evidently affect that of any particular state within it. But that has not prevented an explosion of nationalist feeling whose principal feature is the claim of a distinctively national history and national culture, and whose principal aim seems to be to insist on the freedom of each nation to go its own way. Indeed, for most observers as well as participants, what most clearly defines the notion of the "rebirth of history" in the region is not the revival of ideas of Central Europe, but, on the contrary, the "return to diversity" and the decisive breakup of any concept of a unified region.[36] The Central European idea is seen simply as a nostalgic variant of the persisting tendency to treat the region as a "community of fate," defined by a common history and a common destiny.[37]

First the Habsburgs and Hohenzollerns, then the Nazis and the

Bolsheviks, imposed their ideologies and institutions on the societies of East Central Europe. Whether as *Mitteleuropa, Zwischeneuropa,* or "Eastern Europe," the countries of the region found themselves forcibly bundled together under the aegis of a suzerain with its own interests and agenda. A spurious unity was proclaimed, and enforced. Now, with the retreat and dissolution of the Soviet empire, the latest attempt at homogenization had passed. The East Central European countries were free to determine their destinies according to their own sense of their different traditions and cultures. When, in his 1990 New Year's Day address to the Czech nation, President Václav Havel quoted, in a somewhat adapted form, the words of the seventeenth-century Czech scholar Comenius, "People, your government has returned to you!" to many he might equally well have been saying, "People, your history has returned to you!"

"Nineteen eighty-nine," says Misha Glenny, "was the finest hour of East European nationalism, when the natural desire for liberation was expressed through a reassertion of national identity."[38] This is a generous interpretation, and no doubt captures well the mood of that annus mirabilis. There were misgivings even then, which subsequent developments have converted into something approaching anguish on the part of many commentators. And part of that concern has been about what it might mean to express national identity through a return to history. There is perhaps no clearer expression of the mixed feeling of hope and anxiety than was expressed in the speech by then–American President George Bush to the United Nations General Assembly in September 1991: "Communism held history captive for years, and it suspended ancient disputes, and it suppressed ethnic rivalries, nationalist aspirations, and old prejudices. As it has dissolved, suspended hatreds have sprung to life. People who for years had been denied their pasts have begun searching for their own identities, often through peaceful and constructive means, occasionally through factionalism and bloodshed. This revival of history ushers in a new era teeming with opportunities and perils."[39]

The problem with this national "revival of history" is that it begins an unending quest: Which history? Which traditions? From what part of the past? All societies have a multilayered history. At any one time there tends to be a particular selection of pasts available, usually one that allows the society to bask in a glow of self-satisfaction. For much of the past two centuries, the British have gloried in "the Whig interpretation" of their history; after 1871, the French canonized their Great Revolution; America harks back repeatedly to the utopian promise of its foundation.

But as for the countries of East Central Europe, what comforting myths of the past can they revert to? The Czechs have the democracy of the interwar period, but even that rang hollow in the ears of their erstwhile fellow citizens, the Slovaks, who speedily put into effect the "velvet divorce" when given the opportunity.[40] Few other countries in the region have even that fragile historical support—not, at least, in the terms in which they now wish themselves to be understood. Should Bulgaria, say, look back to the interwar years of King Boris and the terrorist "Internal Macedonian Revolutionary Organization"? Or to the peasant dictatorship of Alexander Stamboliisky (1919–23)? Should it look back to the "Greater Bulgaria" of the 1878 San Stefano Treaty, an ambition spasmodically pursued and briefly realized during World War II under Nazi auspices? Presumably, as with Romania or Serbia, the five hundred-year "Turkish yoke" offers few attractions; in the absence of stopping points there, Bulgarians are forced to refer back to the "Second Empire" created by the Asen brothers in the late twelfth century, the last time before the nineteenth century that Bulgaria could regard itself as an independent state. Memories of the medieval empire had kept Bulgarian national identity alive throughout the nineteenth century; now, after the end of communism, it has once more been called upon to play a legitimating role, as for instance in the curricula of secondary schools.[41]

Or what of Poland? In what part of its history must it seek its national identity, as currently defined? Though Walesa at times seemed to wish to emulate the interwar dictator Marshall Pilsudski, Pilsudski's Poland can hardly stand as a historical referent for a would-be democracy. Going further back brings little relief. Throughout the nineteenth century Poland was no more than a historical memory kept alive by exiled nationalists, and, inspiring though the poems of Mickiewicz might be to a current generation, a dismembered and dependent Poland is an example to see as a warning, not to imitate. But the elective monarchy of the eighteenth century, which was partly responsible for the tragedy of the partitions, is no model either. Poles sometimes refer warmly to the lost liberal constitution of 1791, which indeed embodied many of the values currently admired. But its cruelly brief life meant that it established no lasting tradition of liberalism. Finally, what historical memories can be relevant to a country so lacking of even a fixed geography? What would Mickiewicz, who began his most famous poem, "Pan Tadeusz," with an invocation to "Lithuania, my fatherland," feel about a Poland that in its latest displacement has been so rudely uprooted that it no longer occupies several of its most historic territories?[42]

The examples of Bulgaria and Poland serve to make the general point about the "return to history" in East Central Europe: in virtually no case is there any acceptable, legitimating, history to return to. Isolated episodes aside, there are simply too few historical resting places from which current efforts can derive inspiration and guidance.[43] This is partly due to the politics of tangled ethnicities within the region, and the uncomfortable history it has generated. But, more significant, it reflects, once more, the basic historical fact of the societies of the "lands in-between," their dependence on powers and forces on their periphery. Squeezed between and subordinated to the Habsburg, Hohenzollern, Romanov, and Ottoman empires, they have been shaped largely by Great Power rivalries and ambitions.[44] There has been scant opportunity to mark out an independent national history, on the lines of France or England, and to look to it for defining features and cherished traditions. For East Central Europe, the answer to the question of its history in the present instance might well be an echo of Archbishop Temple's celebrated reply to the question, "What is man?"—"Not yet." Put another way, East Central Europe has had a lot of history—too much—but not of the right kind.

## The Past As Communism

If the countries of the region can find their identity not in the remote past, the *longue durée,* what of the more recent past, the period of "actually existing socialism"? It might seem that, even if East Central European societies are faced with formidable problems in seeking an identity in preceding centuries, there should be no difficulty in asserting some kind of identity by the simple rejection of their immediate past, the forty or so years of communist rule. There is a widely expressed view in the region that this rule was in some deep sense "illegitimate," that it was profoundly hostile to the aspirations of the people. Communism was, it is often argued, imposed: either by the direct intervention of an outside power or by self-seeking elites from within. If the past cannot supply a positive identity, it might at least supply a negative point of reference: the comprehensive repudiation of yet another, the most recent, experience of alien rule.

We know the most obvious problem with this position. Communist rule was not an alien imposition throughout the region. In the election of 1946 in Czechoslovakia, communists took 38 percent (40 percent in the Czech lands) of the vote, the largest of any party and "the best showing ever by a Communist Party in a free election."[45] In Bulgaria the communists were the strongest and most popular of the postwar groups, the result partly of pro-Russian feeling and of the communists' strong presence as an opposition in prewar Bulgaria. Though strong-arm tactics were undoubtedly used, and Soviet pressure palpable, the communists' victory in the election of October 1946 was a reflection of their real strength in society. In Yugoslavia, Tito's communists took the lead in the partisan warfare against the Nazis, and their victory after 1945, achieved without Soviet support, was the natural consequence of this identification with the wartime resistance. A similar situation obtained in Albania, at that time closely linked to Yugoslavia. In all these countries, communist regimes could reasonably claim a real degree of legitimacy, in the sense of having significant popular support.[46]

Certainly there were countries—Poland, Hungary, Romania—where communism was more or less imposed by Soviet power, with varying degrees of internal collaboration. But these countries, like all others in the region, have to face the uncomfortable fact that communist rule was condoned by the bulk of the population throughout the subsequent forty years. Resistance was sporadic, and, apart from such high points as 1956 and 1980–81, confined to small minorities of dissidents. According to Tony Judt, "Most people, sooner or later, collaborated. . . . It is not for any real or imagined crimes that people feel a sort of shame at having lived under communism, it is for their daily lives and infinite tiny compromises."[47] Such experiences might make the people of East Central Europe wish to wipe the slate clean, to pretend that they never happened. But in doing so they should be aware that they are not reviving history, but denying it.

The view that communism was alien to the region *tout court* is in any case a gross oversimplification, which complicates any attempt to recover a national identity by a simple rejection of the communist past. Communism was grafted onto cultures and societies that in many cases were congenial to it. This was true not simply of such societies as those of Soviet Central Asia, but also of those of East Central Europe, especially those (most of them) with strong rural sectors. Traditions of bureaucracy, hierarchy, welfarism, étatism, elitism, corporatism, even collectivism—not to mention "backwardness" and allegiance to a foreign ruler—all made it possible for communist practice, if not precisely communist ideology, to be incorporated into the familiar ways of doing things.[48] The communist period of East Central European nations was not some sort of "aberration," some sort of unnatural deviation from their "normal" path of development. It was a part of their national histories, and must be encountered and understood as such.[49]

In doing so, it will not—or at least should not—always turn out that communism in Central and Eastern Europe was an unmitigated disaster. This is not the place to attempt to draw up any kind of balance sheet of the losses and gains of communist rule, although the losses in the sphere of culture and education as a result of its ending are immediately obvious to any visitor to the region. What is more important is to insist upon the need to interrogate the history of the past forty years as an integral part of East Central European experience, not as an alien excrescence to be scraped away as soon as possible. That would be not only wrong but foolish. Václav Havel is only one of the many who has emphasized that the line of division under communism did not run neatly between "Them" and "Us," but through the heart of every individual man and woman.[50] The communist legacy has to be scrutinized and made to reveal its persisting markers. Only then might we make sense of current attitudes toward work, welfare, and entrepreneurship; toward the family and feminism; toward civic participation; and toward politics and the state.[51]

Such considerations arise again in relation to the most vexing issue raised by current attempts to confront the recent past: the question of guilt. The parallel with "de-Nazification" after 1945 is evident, and raises the same hornet's nest of misattributed blame, unrewarded virtue, and rampant injustice in the treatment of perpetrators and victims alike. In Czechoslovakia, the draconian "lustration" law, designed to ban from public life past informers and collaborators with the communist state, caught in its comprehensive net a host of blameless individuals, briefly including President Václav Havel himself.[52] Commentators, in the West especially, have been well-nigh unanimous in their condemnation of this heavy-handed measure.[53] On the other hand, Poland's attempt to draw a "Thick Line" under the historical record of communism has equally brought accusations of unfairness to the victims of the past, especially those most resistant to communist threats and blandishments.[54] Calculated forgetting, if not forgiveness, has the obvious advantage that it avoids the dangers of McCarthyism and witch hunts. Moreover, as the Nuremberg trials and other attempts to put former Nazis in the dock showed, there are formidable obstacles in the way of trying to allocate individual responsibility for public acts, especially those carried out under state legality. The farce of the trials of former communist leaders such as Erich Honecker and Todor Zhivkov only serves, it seems, to underline the wisdom of the Polish way, imitated to a good extent by Hungary and Romania.[55]

But there are other considerations. What, asks Timothy Garton Ash, of the justifiable protests of the "conservative, Catholic, more or less nationalist anti-Communists who now feel cheated of any historical justice or catharsis"?[56] What might be the consequences of *not* confronting the past, treacherous as all such attempts must be? What will be the bitter resentments and irreconcilable oppositions left brooding in dark corners of society, biding their time to take, as they see it, a due revenge? To tackle the matter of past guilt risks opening a Pandora's box of odious smears and vindictive accusations, not to mention complicity and collaboration on a nationwide scale. Not to do so runs the risk of leaving the scars of injustice, and the sense that the society has too much to hide to dare face its past squarely.

One final example might illustrate the dilemmas of postcommunist societies trying to find some sort of anchorage in their past: the restoration of property in an attempt to return to the precommunist period. The "seizure" of private property by the state is seen as having been illegitimate and unjust. To settle one's accounts with the communist period means to reverse this act and restore the confiscated property, as far as possible, to its "rightful" owners. But not only has this raised predictable problems of missing deeds and absent or distant owners; more intractably, it has raised acute questions of entitlement that break down the neat distinction between the communist and precommunist past and lead to a bewildering variety of conflicting claims, moral and historical.

The question of dating is one source of conflict. Does one restore property to the owners who held it immediately before the communist takeover in 1945–48? That has been the common practice, at least in intention.[57] But why stop there? What of the changes of ownership that took place during World War II, often under duress or through forced seizure? Or, in the Czech and Slovak cases, the expropriations after 1938? Does that not make titles to ownership of property acquired in these ways as illegitimate as those of the communist period? And what of the possible, and historically justifiable, claims of the roughly fifteen million Germans forcibly expelled after the war from Poland, Czechoslovakia, Yugoslavia, Romania, and Hungary? Do these people not have some moral claims to their former property—their former homes? The list of possible claimants does not, of course, stop there. There are the Hungarians forcibly transferred from Slovakia after 1945, the dispelled Slovaks from Hungary, and the Italians dispelled from the coastal regions of Yugoslavia. At quite another level are the claims of millions of deported and murdered Jews and Gypsies throughout the region. The wisdom of Solomon himself would not be adequate to adjudicate claims of the scale and complexity presented by the recent history of East Central Europe. "Restitution" means the act of restoring something to its original state or form, often with the sense of a wrong righted. What is "original" in this context, and what is the "wrong" that has to be righted?

The historical record is not the only source of uncertainty and ambiguity in the attempt to restore property. The whole policy is shot through with perplexities. If, asks Ákos Róna-Tas, the communist state was not the legitimate owner of factories, houses, telephone lines, and the rest, "why does it have the right to sell them or even decide who will get them? And who deserves to get state property? Those who owned it before the state took it from them? Those who worked in them, maintained them, and improved them? Those who will pay the most for them? Those who will put them to best use?"[58] What has been called "nomenklatura privatization," for instance, which pays scant respect to the principle of original ownership, has sometimes been defended on the grounds that the new owners are those best placed to develop postcommunist economies in the peculiarly unfavorable circumstances in which they find themselves.[59]

The point of raising such questions is not to condemn the current policies of postcommunist governments. The situation urgently calls for action, even though virtually anything they do is likely to be unjust, and will certainly be invidious. The point at issue is a more general one. In East Central Europe today all attempts to use the past, whether remote or recent, as a source of identity end in hopeless confusion and contradiction. No doubt something of the kind could be said about any region or society, at any time. Once more, however, it is a matter of degree. To unravel the skein of history in East Central Europe is to meet at every turn with such ambivalence and antipathies, such reversals and relapses, as to render the past virtually useless for the purposes of constructing national identity. Some other strategy must be attempted.

## An Identity in the Past or in the Future?

"The social revolution of the nineteenth century cannot draw its poetry from the past, but only from the future." Thus, in the *Eighteenth Brumaire,* did Marx reprove the French revolutionaries of 1848 for allowing themselves to be transfixed by the memory of the 1789 revolution, delivering themselves in the process into the hands of the adventurer Louis Napoleon. The men and women of 1989 were not exactly revolutionaries of that kind—they had no wish to be—although much of what they strove for was implicit in the program of 1848. But they, too, seem to be transfixed by the past. They, too, seem to think that the recovery of their past is synonymous with the recovery of their freedom. No longer submerged in a common "Eastern Europe," they feel that the way to assert their individual national identities must be to return to the national histories that were abruptly cut short by Soviet-imposed communism after World War II.

We have seen how treacherous such an idea must be, and how uncertain a guide in the present and for the future. It leads to such dangerous absurdities as the rehabilitation and celebration of "anticommunist heroes" such as Monsignor Josef Tiso, head of the Nazi puppet state of the Slovak Republic from 1939 to 1944; General Ion Antonescu, the fascist wartime dictator of Romania who was executed for war crimes in 1946; and Ante Pavelic, leader of the murderous fascist Ustashe regime of wartime Croatia.[60] All anti-Soviet and anticommunist individuals and groups, however odious their activities, become candidates for canonization as national martyrs. The past comes to be rewritten or reinterpreted to suit the convenience of the present, no matter how far-fetched and incredible the inventions.[61]

It used to be said that under communism the future was known; the most difficult thing to predict was the past. The past was reinvented with sometimes bewildering speed to fit the political exigencies of the moment. Today the countries of East Central Europe face a most uncertain future, but the invention and reinvention of the past continues. This is understandable: no nation develops a sense of itself without recourse to the past. Moreover, that past is, as is well known, in all cases invented to a greater or lesser degree. But for East Central Europe such a strategy is strewn with such pitfalls that it may be wise to try to avoid it altogether, or at least as much as possible.

The reasons have to do with a history peculiarly marked by negative experiences and examples. The most recent, the experience of Nazism and communism, is only the latest in a succession of melancholy episodes whereby the countries of the region found themselves subject to external forces over which they had little control. For most of them, the experience of independent rule in modern times amounts to little more than the twenty years of the interwar period—and the memory of those years, for most of them, cannot but be disturbing. In East Central Europe, the past has abrogated its authority.

The countries of East Central Europe must look to the future, not the past. The "rebirth of history" must be understood as a new beginning, not as a return to a putative past or pasts. Here the 1989 revolutions will connect with the modern idea of revolution not as return or restoration, but as the creation of something new, something different from all that has gone before. Never mind that many of the ideas of 1989 are borrowed from the past of the Western revolutionary tradition. For the societies of this region the provenance of the ideas matters less than their practical realization in institutions and everyday practices. It is that that would constitute the real novelty of 1989.

It is a tragic irony, of a kind not so uncommon in history, that the past has prepared the way for its own abrogation and cleared the path to a new beginning in East Central Europe. But it was not communism, despite popular views to the contrary, that was the revolutionary force that launched the assault on age-old traditions and institutions. What made the impact of this force profound was that it supervened on societies already devastated and transformed by fascism and war. The first "East European Revolution," as Hugh Seton-Watson termed the communist takeover in 1945–48,[62] was as much Nazi as it was communist. As several commentators have pointed out, it was not communism, but Nazism, that made the decisive break with the past in East Central Europe.[63] It was Nazism that smashed the old elites and undermined traditional social structures. It was Nazism that made a mockery of the rule of law and regularized rule by party decree. It was Nazism that destroyed the Jews and so ended their historic presence in the region. It was the Nazi occupations that led to the subsequent expulsion of Germans—another historic element—from the area, and allowed the Allied leaders to engage in other acts of "ethnic cleansing" after 1945.

Poland, as so often in the region, supplies the exemplary case. As a result of World War II and the Nazi occupation, Poland lost a sixth of its prewar population; its capital city, Warsaw, lost two-thirds of its population and was razed to the ground after the 1944 rising. The whole of the interwar aristocracy was scattered, and something like a third of the intelligentsia was destroyed. The Potsdam agreement shifted Poland's borders hundreds of miles westward and northward to the Oder-Neisse line; six million Germans were displaced by three million newly settled Poles; at the same time nearly two million Poles were forced to migrate westward as a result of the loss of eastern territories to the Soviet Union. Roughly a third of the population was involved in this massive demographic shift.[64] By the time the communists took over, Poland was in effect already a new nation, at least *in statu nascendi*: socially reordered, geographically resettled, ethnically homogenized. The communists added their own dose of novelty. In seeking to remove that, however, what the Poles return to is not some traditional society, but a distinctly new creation. The national past they seek to restore is no more than half a century old. Poland really has nowhere to go but forward.

Such is also the case with the other societies of East Central Europe. They may not all have been so radically recast as Poland, but to a greater or lesser degree they are also new societies. What Nazism began, communism completed. Societies that on the eve of World War II were largely agrarian, by 1989 were predominantly urban and industrial.[65] They may have thrown off the political regime of communism, but they will not—nor do they wish to—dispense with the larger legacy of the communist period. Perhaps that is the real meaning of the widely accepted view of the 1989 revolutions as *nachholende revolutionen*, "revolutions of retrieval or recuperation" or "rectifying revolutions."[66] These revolutions expressed the aspirations of societies that had, finally, joined or rejoined the West. But the West means not only democracy and pluralism; it also means economic and social modernity. The societies of East Central Europe had become Western in the crucial sense that they had become modern industrial societies. That they have done so by different means should not obscure the fundamental transformation that has taken place. That might mean that in another sense, too, they may become Western: by being not the prisoners, but the makers, of their history.

*Eight*

# The Revolutionary Idea in the Twentieth-Century World

> *Can such a situation last? Will the end of communism deprive de-*
> *mocratic politics of a revolutionary horizon for long? With this*
> *question, I take my leave.*
>
> François Furet, final lines of his last lecture

## 1789 and 1989

In July 1989, as tourists poured into Paris for the celebration of the bicentenary of the fall of the Bastille, Parisians were to be observed setting off in droves for their country retreats. As had become increasingly clear in the preceding months, the French were disenchanted with
1789, bored with the very idea of revolution.[1] In this they reflected the
scholarly consensus that had built up steadily over the years after 1968
in the West. It was shown in the triumph of the "revisionist" historiography of the French Revolution, illustrated in the characteristically
engaging—and *engagé*—remark of Richard Cobb that "the French
Revolution should never have happened, possibly never did happen,
and in any case had no effect one way or the other on most people's
lives."[2] It was shown in the general disparagement of revolution as a
mode of transformation, the view that if revolutions had indeed once
been, as Marx put it, the locomotives of history, "in our industrial (or

post-industrial) age, the locomotive has become an outdated means of historical transport."[3]

Elsewhere things suddenly looked very different. In the very months that Western disillusionment with revolution was expressing itself in this sour attitude toward the bicentenary of the French Revolution, the idea of revolution was reborn in Eastern Europe. Between June and August 1989, the Polish workers' movement Solidarity emerged after years of repression to take over the reins of power. It was the signal for revolution throughout Central and Eastern Europe, eventually reaching the Soviet Union itself and bringing about its collapse in the last days of 1991. Revolution, apparently buried in Western Europe, had achieved a remarkable resuscitation in the East.[4]

But was what occurred in Eastern Europe in 1989 a "revolution"? And, if so, how does it connect with the Western revolutionary idea? Does it, as some have claimed, renew it, give it a new lease on life at a time when it appeared to have become moribund, at least in Europe? Or does it in some sense mark the end of revolution? Does it confirm a widely expressed view that the revolutionary tradition, as it has been understood in Europe, is played out?

We shall return to these questions at the end of this chapter. What we must examine first is the fate of the revolutionary idea, in Europe and the world at large, as it left behind the experiences of the eighteenth and nineteenth centuries that had given it its characteristic form and meaning.

## From Theory to Technique

"1789 and 1917 are still historic dates, but they are no longer historic examples," said Albert Camus. Contemplating the idea of revolution amid the ruins of Europe in 1946, Camus concluded that the classic concepts would no longer do. National revolutions, on the French or Russian model, were now out. The rise of the superpowers, America and the Soviet Union, had so transformed the conditions of revolution that the only kind of revolution worth serious discussion was world revolution. But that world revolution would bear little resemblance to the old Trotskyite dream of an international revolution brought about "by the conjunction or the synchronisation of a number of national revolutions—a kind of totting up of miracles." Stalin was the greater realist. World revolution, if it ever were to occur, must now mean a revolution carried on the bayonets of foreign armies across the world.

It would begin with a military occupation, or the threat of one, and would become significant "only when the occupying power has conquered the rest of the world."[5]

It has indeed been said that "all revolutions start in principle as world revolution," that they all aspire to universalize their aims and symbols.[6] No one can doubt this of the two "classic" examples cited by Camus, the French Revolution of 1789 and the Russian revolution of 1917. No less do they exhibit the characteristics of the "international civil war" that Sigmund Neumann, writing about the same time as Camus, noted as the hallmark of the wars and revolutions of the twentieth century.[7] The appeal to general principles of humanity and society, the summons to the oppressed groups of every nation, foreign intervention and international war: all of these can be seen as much in the French and Russian cases as in any later instances of revolution, such as the Chinese and Vietnamese revolutions.

So there are continuities as well as discontinuities between the past and present of revolution. The Russian Revolution probably illustrates this best. In its theory it looked back to the reflections of Marxists and others on the European revolutions of the seventeenth century to the nineteenth century. In its practice—in the conditions of society that made it, in the nature of the forces that contended for mastery, in the organizational forms that emerged from it—it looked forward to the "Third World" revolutions of the twentieth century (though, it must be said, Mexico in 1910 and China in 1911 had already partly inaugurated the pattern of Third World revolutions).[8]

But Camus was surely right to feel that as the century progressed the divide between the old and the new style of revolution had grown. The international dimension, always present to some degree in past revolutions, had swollen to unprecedented proportions.[9] It had proved to be so as much in the Spanish Civil War as in Central and Eastern Europe after World War II. It was clear in China, where Mao led the communist forces to victory largely through conducting a nationalist struggle against the Japanese, and where his main opponent, the Kuomintang, subsisted on American arms. It was clearer still in Vietnam, Algeria, and Cuba, where the attitudes and actions—or inaction—of the major international powers were critical to the outcomes of the internal conflicts in those countries. And in case anyone had forgotten the lesson of the Spanish Civil War, and thought external intervention a purely non-European phenomenon, the international factor showed its continuing force in largely determining the course of the Portuguese revolution of 1974, and in conditioning both the outbreak and the outcome of the revolutions of 1989 in East Central Europe.[10]

If the balance of forces on the international plane entered as a decisive element in revolutionary fortunes, the change in the relative strengths of the contending parties within the state was scarcely less significant. This was possibly of greater relevance in the advanced industrial societies, though by no means negligible in the less developed ones. Already in his 1895 Preface to Marx's *Class Struggles in France* Engels had drawn attention to the great growth in the military power of the modern state. Revolutionaries were increasingly disadvantaged in the struggle for state power. Rebellion in the old style, Engels concluded, with street fighting and barricades, had since 1848 progressively become obsolete.[11] The fate of urban insurrections in this century has proved him right. "The city," as Fidel Castro correctly observed from Latin American experience, "is a cemetery of revolutionaries and resources." Without peasant support, without the prior weakening or destruction of state power in international war, all purely urban insurrections have failed. And since Engels wrote, practically every new development in weapons technology and in systems of communication has benefited the government at the expense of insurgents.[12]

One consequence of this situation has been the retreat from theory to technique. The classics of nineteenth-century revolutionary theory—Tocqueville's study of the revolution of 1789, Marx's writings on those of 1848 and 1871—concerned themselves with the long-term causes of revolution, and with the prospects for revolution in changing social circumstances. Their framework was the evolution of whole societies in historical time. They were genuine sociologies of revolution. The twentieth-century classics of revolution have reflected an obsession with the techniques for making revolution. "How to Make a Revolution" might adequately sum up their burden. The existence of revolutionary forces, and of revolutionary situations, has been taken for granted—disastrously, in many cases. All states, it was assumed, could be overthrown, given the necessary will and preparation. The revolutionary, said André Malraux, "doesn't have to define the revolution, but to make it." Or, as Régis Debray put it: "A political line which, in terms of its consequences, is not susceptible to expression as a precise and consistent military line, cannot be considered revolutionary."[13] The outstanding successes of post-1917 revolutionism, the Chinese and Cuban revolutions, stood, it was felt, as witnesses to this.

Revolutionary thinkers consequently devoted themselves to the strategy and techniques for seizing state power. The formidable power of the modern state apparatus was acknowledged; all the more important, then, to analyze it, to find its possible weaknesses for exploitation by revolutionaries. Starting with some of the Comintern publications of the 1920s, the texts produced by twentieth-century theorists of revolution increasingly came to mirror the professional military manuals of their opponents. Revolution took from counter-revolution the view that military success was the overriding consideration; revolutionary thinking was converted into thinking about war. In the writings of Mao, Giap, Guevara, and Debray the modern techniques of counter-insurgency were coolly scrutinized and answered point by point. In producing counterstrategies for revolution, a military understanding seemed more important than an understanding of the society in which revolution was plotted. Worked out largely in relation to the conditions of Third World societies, and having some relevance there, such thinking took on overtones of fantasy when transplanted to the cities of the industrial world.[14]

New contexts imply—though they do not always necessarily get—new concepts. Several students have complained of the excessive dominance of the French and Russian cases in our approach to twentieth-century revolutions.[15] The changing conditions of revolutionary action, in the West and the wider world, have forced modifications in the traditional conceptions of revolution. It is not clear that anything new has taken their place, or even that it could or should. Postmodernists would wish to consign revolution to the dustbin of modernist ideas, along with truth and progress. Others, for other reasons, may also feel that revolution has had its time, that it no longer connotes any species of meaningful action. Before assessing the validity of that radical conclusion, we need to consider some of the attempts that have been made to redeem the concept of revolution.

## Utopia and Revolution

If, as many have held, ours is "the century of revolution," this can have little to do with the West. Revolution, as a concept and a practice, is a Western invention. The concept has taken on a career of its own. Like cricket or the English language, it is no longer under the control of its creators. The practice, though, has to date largely been absent from twentieth-century Western industrial societies. Not only has there not occurred the proletarian revolution hoped for and expected by Marx; there have been remarkably few revolutionary attempts of any kind.[16] The 1989 revolutions in East Central Europe may constitute an exception, but, as we shall see, it is by no means clear that they mark a departure from this general picture.

The dearth of revolutionary experience in the recent history of the West has, in a familiar pattern, accompanied and perhaps caused a conceptual inflation. As Western society—at least, the bulk of its population—forgets its revolutionary origins, its intellectuals have increasingly distilled some of their deepest longings into revolution. No longer merely a change in the political system, or even the social system, revolution has come to mean the transformation of humanity at its core.

This utopian conception of revolution was also present in the early Marx, of course, and in certain other nineteenth-century thinkers, such as Fourier.[17] But it did not predominate in societies that lived with the fact of revolution as a regular occurrence and an ever-present possibility. Revolution, a concept taken from astronomy and applied to society in the seventeenth century, until the mid-nineteenth century had a preeminently political meaning. This was, for all the secondary undercurrents, the main legacy of the English, American, and French revolutions. The slogan of the French Revolution, "Liberty, Equality, Fraternity," more or less adequately summed up the political goals. Variously interpreted, these could take on utopian dimensions; but for most revolutionaries the historic examples of England, America, and France suggested achievable ends and something of the institutional means toward them.

In 1848, as both Marx and Tocqueville observed, the "social question" raised its urgent voice. To the "national" or political revolution of the earlier tradition was now added the demand for a social revolution. After the further experience of the Paris Commune of 1871, and the official adoption by the Third Republic of the 1789 revolution as its founding event, the call intensified. The *Internationale,* the anthem of the workers' revolution, challenged the *Marseillaise,* the battle cry of the bourgeoisie. Marxists and anarchists warred over the precise form of the future socialist society; nihilists and populists added a new fervor to the debate. All agreed with Marx on the insufficiency of the "partial, *merely* political revolution" that left "the pillars of the building standing."[18]

But, up to and including the Russian Revolution of 1917, revolution remained primarily within the mold of the French Revolution of 1789—the "model" revolution for the nineteenth century. When the Second International was founded in Paris in the centennial year 1889, the founders were fully conscious of the homage they paid both to the date and the place. The new revolution would obviously have to go beyond the aims and accomplishments of that quintessentially "bourgeois" revolution, but it was accepted that the French Revolution still remained the cardinal point of reference. All revolutions aspired to imitate it, even as they hoped to go beyond it. "A Frenchman," said Lenin in 1920, "has nothing to renounce in the Russian revolution, which in its method and procedures recommences the French Revolution."[19]

It is the primacy of the French Revolution as the model revolution that has come under attack in the twentieth century. The Russian Revolution did not so much displace the French, at least in the West, as add to the doubts surrounding it. It did so not by deviating from the model, but by what appeared to be almost slavishly imitating it. In doing so—and doing so, moreover, with a success and a thoroughness that had evaded its great predecessor—it brought out with disconcerting clarity the elements of the model that had alarmed not just counter-revolutionaries but, increasingly, the friends of revolution.

The outcome of the Russian Revolution—the suppression of the Soviets, one-party rule, state socialism—threw into question all the principal features of the classic French model of revolution. No longer could one take for granted, as the necessary and desirable elements of all revolution, the revolutionary party, the seizure of power, "revolutionary terror," and the use of centralized state power to transform society. Trotsky's reflections on "The Soviet Thermidor" crystallized for many western Marxists their reservations about the Russian Revolution as the new model form.[20] Henceforth revolution must mean, over and above the question of gaining power, a concern with matters of democracy, ethics, education, and culture. The Bolsheviks and their allies had debated these things; in the event, their revolution denied them.[21]

Gramsci's and Luxemburg's prison writings, and those of Trotsky in exile, became the source of a comprehensive rethinking of the concept of revolution among Western Marxists. The relationship of intellectuals to the revolutionary party, and of the party to its mass following, were reexamined with an eye to avoiding the Russian precedent. The "incorporation" of the working class into bourgeois society, and the possible means of extricating it, was the subject of intense debate: here it was the Frankfurt school of "critical theory" that set the terms.[22] Hungary in 1956, Czechoslovakia in 1968, and Poland in 1980 added fresh material for reflection. For the New Left of the post-1945 era, revolution emerged as a category in which the political and economic dimensions of past revolutions were overlaid, redefined almost, by cultural aspirations. If an example was sought as a model for this conception, it was not Russia, but China and Mao's "Cultural Revolution."[23]

But education and culture, the hallmarks of the new concept of revolution, were not enough for some. Or, rather, as generally understood, they did not go far enough. This, in the end, was what in Western eyes disqualified the Chinese and Cuban revolutions, for all their elements of novelty, as true exemplars. There persisted in the minds of many Western radicals the conviction that revolution still concerned itself mainly with external forms. The repeated failure of revolutions to realize their promise was attributed to their indifference to the human material that carried through the revolution. Regarded alternately as cannon fodder for the revolution and as the readily reeducated citizens of the new society, the human masses went through the revolution carrying most of the baggage of their unreconstructed past with them. The political and economic forms changed; "human nature" remained the same. Oppression and submission persisted, perhaps literally, in the minds and bodies of men. Hence the common fate of all revolutions hitherto. Conceived in freedom, they ended by restoring despotism. The revolutionary cycle from freedom to despotism seemed a mocking echo of the original astronomical meaning of the term. Like the revolutions of the heavens, human revolutions seemed destined to go through unvarying cycles that would always bring them back to their starting point. And so they would so long as human needs and desires remained mired in their prerevolutionary past.

Reflection on this phenomenon drove many intellectuals away from revolution altogether. Revolution, along with the communism with which it has been associated for much of this century, was the god that had failed. Others, however, were inspired by the early Marx and by "utopian socialists" such as Fourier to rethink the concept of revolution along the lines of what Aldous Huxley called "The really revolutionary revolution: the revolution in the souls and bodies of human be-ings."[24] The ultimately revolutionary program of the Marquis de Sade, to reconstruct bodily desire, was here recalled; so, too, the aesthetic and sensuous utopia of William Morris. The Surrealists' exploration of the unconscious, and their emphasis on spontaneity, supplied another building block. Above all there was Freud, as purged of his conservative philosophy by "Freudo-Marxists" such as Wilhelm Reich and Herbert Marcuse.

Freud's importance lay in pointing to the "instincts" as the crucial stumbling block to revolutionary designs. He threw down the ulti-mate challenge: selfishness, aggression, and war were inherent in the biological nature of humans; revolution could no more change that than it could change the color of their skins. In seeking to show that that was not so, that acquisitiveness and aggression were the products of historically formed social systems, the Freudo-Marxists aimed to strengthen the concept of revolution at its most vulnerable point. They accepted the importance of the "instincts"; no revolution could suc-ceed that ignored their power. The limited achievements of past revo-lutions were a testimony to this. But the energy of the instincts was not, as Freud had thought, forever frozen in antisocial drives. It could be harnessed and redirected to serve revolutionary ends. Pleasure, the principle of sex, could (and should) become the principle of work and politics as well. Eros could conquer Thanatos.[25]

The common theme in the new Western concept of revolution was the insistence that revolution, if it were to be successful, must ulti-mately work at the level of everyday life. Revolution must come down from the high thrones of politics and economics and enter the humble abode of the family, the home, and the sexual and emotional lives of individuals. It must transform not just the political and economic realms, but the "biological" and "instinctual" need structures of indi-viduals. It must acknowledge the importance of the beautiful. Work and leisure must be given the character of artistic creativity and enjoy-ment; society itself must be regarded as a work of art.[26]

Many of these themes came together riotously in the French "May Events" of 1968, especially as expressed in the thinking and practice of the group of radicals known as the Situationist International. The Situationist graffiti and manifestos proclaimed a conception of revolu-tion that made it synonymous with a total change in the human and social order: "Be realists—demand the impossible," "All power to the imagination," "It is forbidden to forbid." As one of the leading Situationists, Raoul Vaneigem, wrote, "Those who speak of revolution and class struggle without referring explicitly to daily life, without understanding the subversive element in sex and the positive element in the rejection of constraints, have a corpse in their mouths."[27] The variety of influences in this concept of revolution is sufficiently indicated by the titles of some of the action committees that sprang up in Paris in these weeks: "the Freud-Che Guevara Action Committee," "the Committee of Permanent Creation," the "*Comité Révolutionnaire d'Agitation Sursexuelle.*"[28]

The boundary between revolution and utopia, precariously enough maintained even in the nineteenth century, here fairly obviously dissolved. This does not mean that utopian conceptions of revolution, any more than utopianism in general, are worthless. But it does raise acutely the question of how such a revolution will, or can, occur. The students in Paris appeared to act at times as if they felt the state could simply be ignored, its power bypassed as being of no moment. They learned that although they might ignore the state, it had no wish to ignore them. It is not even clear how seriously they contemplated or hoped for revolution in these months. They seemed to think it more important to raise the standard of a different kind of revolution from the past—to put down a marker, as it were, for future revolutions.[29] But this does little to clarify the question of future forms of revolutionary action. We know reasonably well what people mean to do when they say "We want land" or shout "Down with the tyrant," as Leszek Kolakowski said shortly after the events. "But supposing they were to shout, 'Down with alienation?' Where does one find the palace of Alienation and how does one destroy it?"[30]

There is a further problem with what we might call the "totalistic" concept of revolution, revolution as total transformation of the individual and society.[31] Past revolutions provided, both for themselves and for future imitators, a distinctive imagery and iconology of revolution. Delacroix's *Liberty Guiding the People,* with its symbolism of the barricade, supplied a powerful myth of revolution for the national and bourgeois revolutions of the nineteenth century.[32] The storming of the Winter Palace in Eisenstein's film *October,* and posters such as El Lissitsky's *Beat the Whites with the Red Wedge,* played a similar role in the iconography of the proletarian revolution.[33] What are the icons of the totalistic concept of revolution, the revolution against alienation?

Since there have been no actual revolutions of this kind to give rise to them, not surprisingly they are hard to find. The elements that lie at hand—Situationist posters from 1968; some of Jean-Luc Godard's "Maoist" films of the 1960s, such as *La Chinoise*; the sexual politics of Dusan Makavejev's *WR: Mysteries of the Organism*—are mostly couched in a mocking or ironic vein, lacking the full-blooded commitment necessary for the achievement of iconic status. The lack of any convincing image of the future revolution is not the least of the problems surrounding the concept of revolution in the West.

## Salvation by the Third World?

If the advanced industrial West failed to provide any clear instance of revolution in the twentieth century, a failure that was reflected in an increasingly desperate search for a new and more inclusive concept, this manifestly does not apply to the societies of the undeveloped "Third World." The theoretical works dealing with twentieth-century revolutions give us a rich variety of cases to contemplate; almost all of them are from the Third World. Among them we might list those of Mexico in 1910, China in 1911 and again in 1949, Vietnam in 1945, Algeria in 1954, Cuba in 1959, and Iran and Nicaragua in 1979. This is a woefully incomplete list; Fred Halliday has said that "if we look at the 120 or so countries of the Third World, up to two dozen of them can be said to have had social revolutions . . . since the end of the Second World War."[34] Moreover, there are disputes about the dates, about the classification "Third World," and about the very designation of "revolution" as applied to all of these. Nevertheless, putting these aside, there can be no doubt that if ours is indeed the century of revolution, this can have little to do with Europe or the West and almost everything to do with non-Western or Third World societies.

A discussion of these revolutions in a volume of this sort might seem out of place. But nothing could be more mistaken. In the twentieth century, to a greater degree than ever before, all revolutions have been world revolutions. This statement applies as much to the rare instances of revolution in Europe—such as the Portuguese revolution of 1974, stimulated by the anticolonial struggles in Angola and Mozambique, as to revolutions outside it, where the participation of European or North American powers has been only too clear (as in Algeria or Nicaragua). Revolution in the twentieth-century world has been a matter of global politics. Influences have flowed reciprocally from the center to the periphery and back again.[35]

But it seems unnecessary to belabor the point. The link between revolutions in the Third World and the European or Western revolutionary tradition is plain for all to see. The West supplied the revolutionary conditions, in the form of colonialism and world war. It also supplied the revolutionary theory. What, after all, is Marxism, the legitimating ideology of so many Third World revolutions, but a Western invention? What, too, of imperialism, democracy, revolution itself: are these not also Western exports that, as concepts and practices, fueled the revolutionary struggles in the Third World? Most Third World revolutions were led by Western-educated intellectuals, or by intellectuals in close contact with Western sources—Sun Yat-Sen, Mao, Ho Chi Minh, Castro, Sukarno. The European revolutionary tradition provided them with the categories through which to see their revolutions, even when they had to engage in some fairly unorthodox interpretations (a lesson already taught by Lenin). When Kwame Nkrumah cried, "Seek ye the political kingdom and all the rest shall be added unto you," or when Achmed Sukarno confessed to being "obsessed by the romanticism of revolution," they were both reflecting the legacy of European revolutionism.[36]

For many Third World revolutionaries the models of revolution inspired by the classic European revolutions remained, unlike in the case in Europe itself, highly relevant. In his trial speech after the failure of the assault on the Moncada barracks in 1953, Fidel Castro ransacked the entire European revolutionary tradition in justification of his actions.[37] The French and the Russian revolutions, in both their theory and their practice, remained guiding models for countries that still had to achieve national independence and to establish modern political and economic institutions.

Nevertheless, as in twentieth-century Europe, there has also partly been a revulsion from these models, and what they may connote by way of theory and action. The reasons are also much the same: the models, it is felt, do not go deep enough into the structures of exploitation and oppression. If this is true for groups within European societies, how much more likely it is to be true for groups subjected to entirely alien rule, as the societies of the Third World have been.

But in reacting against these European models of revolution, Third World revolutionaries have not, for the main part, reacted against European thought. Rather, they have engaged in the same act of retrieval and reinterpretation attempted by their Western counterparts. They have turned to the very thinkers—Hegel, Nietzsche, Freud, and Marx as seen through the eyes of these other thinkers—who have been influential in the reformulation of the revolutionary project in the West. This is especially the case of Frantz Fanon, the most important of the theorists of Third World revolution in the recent period.

Fanon, a French-trained psychiatrist and supporter of the Algerian revolution, rejected most of the terms of classic European revolutionism—the class struggle, the leadership of the proletariat, the revolutionary party led by the intelligentsia. However relevant these might still be in Europe, the situation in the Third World was different, and in need of a new kind of understanding. The colonies and former colonies had to fight against themselves as much as against their European masters. Their subjugation was by now at least partly self-imposed. The effect of colonial rule was to infect the native populations with a colonialist and racist mentality. Unless they rid themselves of this, national revolution would mean simply a continuation of dependence. The traumas and neuroses engendered by colonialism, the self-hatred and self-estrangement, could be purged only through violence. "Violence," said Fanon, "is a cleansing force." Through collective violence the colonized populations would find themselves; through violence they would liquidate the legacy of colonialism not just in its political and economic, but, more important, in its psychological, manifestations. In his preface to Fanon's *The Wretched of the Earth* (1961), Jean-Paul Sartre wrote: "The native cures himself of colonial neurosis by thrusting out the settler through force of arms. When his rage boils over, he rediscovers his lost innocence and he comes to know himself in that he himself creates his self. . . . To shoot down a European is to kill two birds with one stone, to destroy an oppressor and the man he oppresses at the same time: there remain a dead man, and a free man." [38]

In Fanon, said Sartre, himself a key influence on Fanon, "the Third World finds itself and speaks to itself." But there was a paradox here. Fanon wrote in French, in the passionate rhetorical style of the committed French intellectual. His works drew upon much the same set of thinkers—Lukacs and Sartre as well as Marx and Freud—as were currently informing the thinking of Western radicals. Moreover, though he developed an influential theory of Third World revolution, he was always better known in Europe and North America than in the Third

World itself. This impact was not restricted to Western intellectuals. "Every brother on a rooftop can quote Fanon," it was said in the Chicago riots of 1967, and *The Wretched of the Earth* was a revered text in the Black Panther movement in America.[39] As with other Third World revolutionaries such as Mao and Guevara, Fanon found himself incorporated into the very revolutionary tradition from which he had sought to free himself.

There is a further problem. Despite Fanon's undoubted prestige among Third World intellectuals, the kind of revolution he envisaged nowhere fits the actual pattern of Third World revolutions—not even in Algeria, where he threw himself into the struggle. Fanon put his trust in the poorest and most marginalized of the peasants, as the groups least contaminated by the colonialist mentality. Certainly he seems to have been right in rejecting the revolutionary potential of the urban proletariat. But Third World revolutions have not been in any real sense peasant led. Westernized middle-class intellectuals have in all cases provided the leadership, and their organization of a nationalist struggle has in most cases also been indispensable to success (not to mention the effect of world war in weakening or destroying the power of colonial elites). Moreover, it is not the most wretched of the peasantry who have been the mainstay of revolutionary struggle; it has been the "middling" peasants—as we would expect from the well-attested theory of relative deprivation and social action.[40] Fanon provided a powerful myth for Third World revolutions; but, as with current concepts of revolution in Western industrial societies, its relationship to actual practice remains problematic.

In arriving at his concept of Third World revolution, Fanon refused to have any truck with theories of negritude, the "African cultural heritage," and similar ideas current among his fellow radicals from Africa and the West Indies. These smacked to him of racism, and black racism was as unacceptable as white. The Third World would be regenerated not by such backward-looking "primitivist" conceptions, but by looking to an entirely new future. It would be a future that rejected not just Europe but its own precolonial past, now in any case irretrievably lost. As Fanon said, "It is a question of the Third World starting a new history of Man . . ."[41] Fanon was vague about the "new man," but he never wavered in his conviction that he would be in some sense socialist. For all his antipathy to Europe, Fanon remained indebted to European social thought and the European revolutionary tradition.[42]

Others, however, have been at pains to deny the universalism of European categories of thought and practice, and to stress instead native particularisms. In several varieties of Third World theory, revolution has been seen as an affair as much of recovery as of new creation. The nineteenth-century Russian *narodniks* were perhaps the first to speculate along these lines. Lenin sternly stamped such as "reactionary" thinking, but in other versions of socialism, such as Maoism, it became an increasingly pronounced feature. It gained a particular prominence in the "African socialism" of such national leaders as Senghor, Touré, Nkrumah, and Nyere. Here an allegedly classless traditional African society was seen as the fortunate legacy that permitted the creation of a "communal" socialism representing, Rousseaulike, the will of the whole people rather than of a particular class. Latterly, the departure from Western models was even more profound in the Islamic fundamentalism of the Iranian revolution of 1979. Iran's example has been infectious. Currently there are probably more revolutionary movements in the world agitating under the banner of Islamic fundamentalism than of any other ideology.[43]

Attempts have been made to deny the validity of some of these non-Western cases as authentic instances of revolution. Revolution, it is said, as a theory and a practice, is historically linked to the effort to establish a new order of freedom and equality. What Condorcet said of the French Revolution is held to apply, with suitable modifications, to revolution as such: "The word 'revolutionary' can only be applied to revolutions which have liberty as their object."[44] In this view not only "revolutions of the Right," such as the Nazi revolution, but also religious revolutions, such as the Iranian revolution, are misnomers. Calling them "revolutions" abuses a concept too important to be abandoned to the vagaries of demagogic rhetoric.

There may be solid grounds for trying to hold to such a normative definition of *revolution*. Certainly within the revolutionary tradition of the West there has been a continuity of ideas and aspirations that supports the view of a common project. Liberal and Marxist varieties of revolution share a common inheritance. They are both heirs of the European Enlightenment, and their concepts of revolution are in various ways directed to the realization of Enlightenment ideals. Movements that consciously turn their backs on such ideals—the ideals of reason, freedom, equality—cannot therefore be called revolutionary. So, at any rate, it can be maintained.

But no part of the globe can permanently lay claim to a political or moral vocabulary. Christianity discovered this very early; more recently, and equally painfully, Marxism and democracy have had to come to terms with it. Revolutionism is clearly a Western principle, born of Western practice. But along with industrialism and other Western ideas and institutions, it has been freely exported to the non-Western world, which has interpreted it as it saw fit. We can no more legislate against that than we can against the Grand Canyon.

Had there been a greater experience of revolution in the West in this century, it might have been possible to insist on a stricter use of terms, to point to a dominating and defining tradition of revolution in the Western mold. The revolutions of this century, however, have been not here, but mostly in the Third World. The absence of a relevant experience to reflect on in twentieth-century industrial societies has meant that we are compelled to acknowledge that revolution in our time may depart sharply from the norm established by nineteenth-century revolutionism, up to and including the Russian revolution. It can take other, sometimes strange and exotic, forms. The Nazi revolution may be an example of one such form; the Iranian revolution of another. Some have argued that recent Latin American revolutions, such as the Cuban and the Nicaraguan, with their absence of a mass peasant base and their reliance on guerrilla cadres—a new type of "social banditry"—have represented a new species of revolution, different from all those of the past. There is also the category, familiar since the Meiji Restoration of 1868, of "revolutions from above": the largely military-led revolutions of Turkey in 1922, Egypt in 1952, North Yemen in 1962, Peru in 1968, and Portugal in 1974. The risings in the communist world—East Germany in 1953, Hungary in 1956, and Poland in 1980—again seem to be phenomena requiring their own form of analysis. And one still does not quite know what to do with the events of May '68.[45]

In the face of such conceptual luxuriance, sensible scholars may feel driven to reject the concept of revolution altogether, at least as applied to contemporary forms. And there are certainly signs of such a reaction. But though we must accept the variety of revolutions in the contemporary world, we need not feel that there must be, or has been, a lapse into total arbitrariness. There have been at least "family resemblances" between European revolutions and the revolutions of the

Third World, even those seeking to appeal primarily to non-Western traditions. This is no less than we should expect, given the wholesale penetration of the globe by Westernizing ideologies and institutions. With the possible exception of the Iranian revolution—though even here strong claims in support of its "modernity" have been made[46]— the impress of Western revolutionism can be found in practically every instance of Third World revolution. "African socialism," "Islamic socialism," and "South Yemeni Marxism" do, after all, by their very names proclaim their kinship with Western revolutionary thought. There are also opposite but equally relevant examples of the importation of Third World revolutionary ideas—Mao's in China, Guevara's in Cuba—into Western conceptions. None of this, so far, adds up to a coherent synthesis; but it does indicate the degree of overlap and convergence that is part of the complex picture of revolution in our own time.

About one thing, however, we may be clear. The further away we go in time and space from the Great French Revolution of 1789—still for many purposes the "model" revolution—the less we should expect revolution to resemble it. Peter Kropotkin was certainly right to claim that "whatsoever nation enters on the path of revolution in our own day, it will be heir to all our forefathers have done in France."[47] The contribution of the French Revolution to the ideology of revolutionism, in Europe and the rest of the world, has been unmistakable and incontrovertible. But Kropotkin did not live to see the great wave of Third World revolutions that broke over the world, especially after 1945. In this development not only the French Revolution, but increasingly the Russian, came to be seen as remote and unhelpful models. They remained, undoubtedly, a great source of emotional inspiration— in revolution always a great thing. But as models for practical imitation they could be dangerously anachronistic.

This distancing from European models of revolution has affected not just how the Third World regards the West, but increasingly how Western radicals regard the Third World. It used to be more or less taken for granted that Western radicals were enthusiastic supporters of Third World revolutions—the more so as they had none of their own to support. Mao, Ho, Castro, even Nasser and Sukarno, were at various times the objects of admiration, verging sometimes on adulation. More recently Western radicals have found it less easy to warm up to revolutionary movements in the Third World. The Sandinistas of

Nicaragua pose relatively few problems, as does the socialist guerrilla movement in neighboring El Salvador. But what of the Islamic Hezbollah of Lebanon or the Taliban of Afghanistan? What of the Revolutionary Council of Ethiopia or, for that matter, the National Liberation Front of Eritrea? What of Hamas, the Islamic wing of the Palestine Liberation Organization? As even earlier heroes, such as Mao and Castro, are critically reexamined, a certain disillusionment about Third World revolutions seems to have come upon a sizable portion of the Western radical intelligentsia. The outcomes of many of these revolutions, the Iranian revolution in particular, make them unattractive models to wish upon other Third World societies. At the same time, they have lost their capacity to inspire—however bizarrely in some instances—revolutionary fervor in the industrial societies. Taken together with the absence of revolutionary initiatives in these societies for much of this century, and the sense that their populations have lost interest in revolution, the revolutionary project in the West might appear to languish as at no time since it was launched upon the world in 1789.

## 1989: The Rebirth of Revolution?

Have the 1989 revolutions in East Central Europe changed this perception? Do they signal the rebirth of the revolutionary idea in Europe? Some have certainly been prepared to see them in this light. If the West, sunk in the torpor of affluence and "postmodernist" inertia, has lost the taste for revolution, in the East it still seems capable of arousing popular passions. The 1989 revolutions, says Fred Halliday, "have restated, in a dramatic form, the most neglected facet of political life, . . . namely the capacity of the mass of the population to take sudden, rapid and novel political action after long periods of what appears to be indifference."[48] Mass action is also the phenomenon that strikes Jürgen Habermas, who further draws a direct parallel with the revolution of 1789: "It was mass anger . . . that was directed at the apparatuses of state security, just as it had once been directed at the Bastille. The destruction of the Party's monopoly on state power could similarly be seen to resemble the execution of Louis XVI."[49]

It is not just the manner, but the matter, of the change that to these thinkers harks back to the revolutionary legacy of 1789. The 1917 Russian revolution might not, for obvious reasons, have been an inspiration to the revolutionaries of 1989; but, says François Furet, the "universal principles of 1789" were what animated the revolutions of

1989. "The Bolsheviks thought that with 1917 they had buried 1789. Here, at the end of our century, we see that the opposite is happening. It is 1917 that is being buried in the name of 1789."[50] The themes of 1989 were the great themes of 1789: liberty, democracy, civil society, nationhood.

That the participants in the 1989 revolutions—the historically minded among them, at least—were aware of the European revolutionary tradition is undoubted. In November 1989, "1789–1989" was the slogan on the banners of the demonstrators in East Berlin.[51] To the young Slovak historian Ewa Kowalska, the events of 1989 were "the culmination of the slow and continuous 'general revolution' of the western world, of the process that began economically and politically with the English and French revolutions and that is coming to an end spiritually and nationally with the upheavals of central Europe."[52] Bronislaw Geremek, one of the leading theoreticians of the Polish Solidarity movement, is fond of quoting Tocqueville and offers *The Old Regime and the Revolution* as the best guide to both the causes and the animating spirit of the 1989 revolutions.[53] Again and again, before, during, and after 1989, East European intellectuals paid homage to the French Revolution as the parent of their hopes and aspirations. For many intellectuals, the declaration that the revolutions represented a "return to Europe" meant precisely the recovery of the lost revolutionary inheritance.[54]

At the same time we recall Ewa Kowalska's remark that 1989 marked the end of a long European revolution. There have been repeated comments in a similar vein. Observers have been struck by the backward-looking nature of the 1989 revolutions, their unwillingness to announce anything new. Habermas calls them "rectifying revolutions," revolutions that sought to retrieve or restore, not to announce any new principles of state and society. The 1989 revolutions desired no more than "to connect up constitutionally with the inheritance of the bourgeois revolutions."[55] If, as Hannah Arendt once said, revolutions are distinguished by "the pathos of novelty," the 1989 revolutions were most unrevolutionary. In turning their back on the new, in wishing to do no more than "return to their history" and catch up with the process of Western constitutional and commercial development, they almost seem to have aspired to recall the old premodern sense of revolution, as a return or a restoration.[56]

The singularity of the 1989 revolutions appears in another way.

Unlike in most earlier revolutions, "the people," despite appearances, played a relatively minor role. There were indeed courageous dissidents in the region; Solidarity, the Polish workers' movement that swept to power in the summer of 1989, was a powerful inspiration; there were mass demonstrations and some violent clashes in Leipzig, Prague, Budapest, and Bucharest. But it is quite clear that on their own these would never have succeeded in toppling the communist regimes. They seem scarcely to have been intended to. When attempts of a similar kind had been made before—in 1953, 1956, 1968, and 1980—the use, or the threat, of Soviet tanks had been sufficient to crush them. Against Soviet resolve popular protests seemed futile, as Solidarity throughout accepted. In 1989 the unexpected and unhoped-for happened: Mikhail Gorbachev made it clear that Soviet troops would not be at the disposal of the communist rulers of Eastern Europe. More daringly, Soviet influence was put to work to undermine the power and authority of the old hard-liners at the top—Honecker, Kadar, Husak, Zhivkov, Ceausescu. Deprived of Soviet backing, their regimes crumbled one by one, usually through the machinations of reform-minded communists within their own parties who were emboldened by Soviet support and encouragement. The 1989 revolutions, despite their undeniable significance, increasingly have the appearance of *frondes,* or palace revolutions.[57]

In this, of course, they are not so unusual. Nearly all revolutions, the French and Russian no less than more minor ones, begin from a split within the ruling class or ruling elite. The peculiar aspect of the 1989 revolutions was the high degree of control excercised by the ruling *nomenklaturas* throughout the period of transition to democracy and market society. Except in Romania, there was remarkably little violence, and even in Romania the violence was to a good extent deliberately provoked by dissident members of the ruling group. It is this, coupled with the well-known success of old members of the *nomenklatura* in retaining their elevated positions within the new market dispensation, that has made some people question whether what happened in 1989 can properly be called a revolution.[58]

Such definitional disputes can be the bugbear of all discussions of revolution; and this is not the place to engage in them, at least not in the formal sense. The important question may be not so much whether the events of 1989 fit conventional notions of revolution as what they may tell us about the future of revolution. Assuming that the momentousness and the speed of the change—nothing less than the sudden and sweeping end to an ancien regime—sufficiently justify the epithet "revolutionary," did 1989 signal a renewal of revolution in Europe, after nearly a century of quiescence? Is revolution now once more on the agenda of advanced industrial societies? Or does 1989 in some way confirm the "sense of an ending," the feeling that it has merely completed some unfinished business, merely restored one section of Europe to the modernizing path taken by most other industrial societies, from which it had unfortunately deviated? If so, that might suggest that, to the extent that Central and Eastern European societies develop democratic institutions and achieve a reasonable standard of living for the bulk of their populations, they too, like the more affluent societies of the West, may make themselves relatively safe from revolution.

"Relatively" is the crucial word here. The 1989 revolutions at least remind us of one important thing, that no society, the most developed no less than the least developed, is immune from revolution. No one is in a position to write off revolution as a mode of transforming society—nor will anyone be in such a position in the future. Observers and participants alike were caught by surprise in 1989—at the speed and success of events; at the fact, disbelieved almost up to the day, that fundamental change was possible. Revolutions have always had this capacity for surprise; one remembers Lenin's famous remark in 1917, only a month before the February revolution brought down the czarist regime, that "we, the old, may not live to see the decisive battles of the coming revolution."[59] Revolution, as an idea and a practice, has become firmly lodged in the fabric of modern societies. No matter how long its absence, no matter how apparently unpromising the circumstances of its occurrence, it remains capable of convulsing society. And, as in the past, it is likely to do so when least expected, either by its enemies or its friends.

This is a different matter from saying that revolution is unaffected by social and historical changes. The virtual absence of revolution in the West in the twentieth century is clear testimony to the fact that the conditions that made it relatively common in the nineteenth century no longer exist, or exist in much modified form. Revolution is still—and will be always—possible; it is simply less likely to happen, at least in its familiar forms.[60] The result has been that conceptual inflation that we have noted. Revolution as a concept has come to be filled to the bursting point with projects for human liberation on a vast scale. Not just the external, but the internal, forms of life are to be renewed.

Human instincts must be redirected and freed from repression; a mentality of dependence and inferiority must be transformed into one of self-respect and daring in the face of the future. Transformation must be total or it will be nothing, the replacement of one form of tyranny by another.

As a concept, revolution has achieved a sort of theoretical completion and closure. It now embraces all aspects of the human condition, from politics to psychoanalysis, having taken in on the way economics and culture. It includes the "politics of the nervous system" along with the politics of the social system. The cost of this theoretical filling out has been to take revolution out of the sphere of political action and to place it in the realm of metaphysics. This is really what is meant by all the talk of the "end of revolution."[61] Revolution is no longer about changing the social order in any determinate time and place by conscious, collective human action. It has been detached from history and "universalized." Revolution takes place in a timeless present. It now symbolizes eternal protest against oppression and unfreedom as such, as more or less constant features of the human condition.

We return to Camus, with whom we started this chapter. For Camus, the revolutions of history stand condemned by their repeated consummation in murder and new forms of tyranny. Against revolution Camus counterposed the act of "metaphysical rebellion." He said, "It is metaphysical because it disputes the ends of man and creation. . . . The metaphysical rebel protests against the human condition in general."[62] Like many contemporary theorists of revolution, Camus followed a tradition of thinking that started with Sade and continued with Baudelaire, Stirner, Nietzsche, Lautréamont, and the Surrealists (all particular heroes of the revolutionaries of May '68). Revolution, a historical invention that gave rise to a specific tradition of theory and practice, ends in rebellion, a metaphysics of protest against the arbitrary injustices and hypocrisies of social existence. Existential rebellion has its place, of course; but it is a place alongside, rather than as a replacement for, revolution. If it has, indeed, substituted itself for revolution, we may well feel that revolution has ceased to have any useful meaning, or to be in any real sense a program of action.

It is too early to say whether the 1989 revolutions in the East have fundamentally changed this situation, so marked in the West. Their outcomes are still uncertain, and reversals are by no means yet ruled out. Even their forms are, as we have noted, ambiguous, partaking both of the classic pattern of popular revolution and of the more familiar type of palace revolution. But enough is already clear to enable us to make some reasonable predictions. Once the inevitable disappointment and disillusionment with democracy and the market have set in, East Europeans are as likely as their Western counterparts to turn their backs on revolution—perhaps even, as seems increasingly to be the case in the West as well, on politics in general. In Eastern Europe the intellectual tradition of "metaphysical rebellion," born of centuries of autocracy and empire, is, if anything, even stronger than in the more pragmatic West. On the other side is a tradition of detached irony and political passivity, both encouraged by the experience of communist rule. If these traditions reassert themselves, no more in the East than in the West would there seem to be much room for revolution.

But it would, to repeat, be unwise to rest on such a conclusion. The end of revolution has been proclaimed on numerous occasions in this century, in the 1930s as well as the 1950s and the 1980s. In each case a surprise was in store. We will be surprised again; of that we can be sure.

*Nine*

# The Return of the Repressed: Social Theory after the Fall of Communism

*The fact that we are in a post–Cold War period of transition, of ambiguity and uncertainty as much in terms of theoretical paradigms as in terms of world politics, should be welcomed by sociologists everywhere. It is a setting where new worlds emerge. . . . It is a challenging and dynamic period for sociology.*

Edward Tiryakian

*The repressed has returned.*

Michael Ignatieff

## A New World Order?

No one can speak with any great assurance about the future shape of the world after the fall of communism. We cannot even be sure that the fall will not, in some measure, be reversed. The return to power—or at least to parliamentary power—of former communists in many of the countries of East Central Europe does not by itself signify this reversal. There is no evidence that, whatever the regrets and sense of lost security of the population at large, any major group or party aims to restore communism. But the popularity of parties that wish to slow down the rate of change, and retain or restore elements of the welfare systems that existed before 1989, is some indication that the political landscape of East Central Europe will not be a carbon copy of that in the West.

238

Taken with the slowing, and in some cases reversal, of the industrial growth of previous times in the region, it suggests that some traditional distinctions—"East" and "West," regulated and laissez-faire economies, perhaps even authoritarian and democratic—may continue to be meaningful. The assumption of a homogeneous global capitalism as the form of the future seems as naïve now as it probably always was, even in the heady days of triumphalism after 1989.

Nevertheless, we must consider the fall of communism in the late 1980s and the early 1990s as the starting point of all our reflections on the contemporary world. It is the decisive fact of the second half of the twentieth century, as the Russian revolution of 1917 was the decisive fact of the first half. Considered more broadly within the whole history of modernity, both events can be seen as significant markers of that history. The Russian revolution signified the triumph of the rationalist, utopian strand of Enlightenment thought, the strand that found its most powerful expression in Marx's critique of the irrationality and inhumanity of capitalist industrialism. The 1989 revolutions signaled an important rejection of that tradition, and an affirmation instead of the liberal, individualist currents of Enlightenment thought. Karl Popper's "open society" has become the emblem of this worldwide victory.[1]

That the fall of communism entails an "end of history," in the sense of the cessation of all serious speculation in political theory, is of course a contentious claim. For many participants in the former communist countries, what it has rather meant is the return or the "rebirth" of history, the restarting of particular national histories that were, as they now regard it, "interrupted" by the period of communist rule. The two claims are not incompatible if what is meant by the rebirth of history is fundamentally a continuation of patterns of development that had been formed in the liberal capitalist mold. The argument could then be that what happened in 1989–91 simply showed that the communist era was a deviation from the normal course of modern development— which, in this view, is essentially the working out of the political principle of liberalism and the economic principle of capitalism.

We have seen (in chapters 1 and 7 of this book) that this interpretation involves a considerable distortion of the actual history of East Central Europe. But whatever our feelings about this particular debate, it is clear that one of the most significant features of the period since 1989 has been the return, or revival, of some of the central themes and ideas of modernity. There may be some sense in which the 1989 revolutions can be considered "postmodern," and undoubtedly they took place in a context in which postmodern thought and culture had become prominent throughout the developed world.[2] But the overwhelming impression, and the general consensus of opinion, is that these were events that carried the hallmarks of modernity in some of its most characteristic aspects.

Jürgen Habermas, as we have seen, has considered the 1989 revolutions *"nachholende revolutionen,"* "rectifying revolutions" or "revolutions of recuperation."* The societies of East Central Europe, he says, are restoring the project of modernity after a period during which their development was forcibly derailed from the tracks along which, more or less in parallel with Western Europe, they had been moving.[3] So, too, a number of thinkers, such as Jeffrey Alexander, have argued that, far from chiming in with the postmodern idea of "the death of grand narratives," the revolutions of 1989 have given a fresh lease on life to the grand narratives of Western modernity. These are the narratives of democracy, constitutionalism, capitalism, progress, perhaps even revolution itself. In removing communism, the peoples of Central and Eastern Europe have reaffirmed a faith in the central principles of modernity, at a time perhaps when this faith had weakened in the West. They have modernized modernity, given it a fresh vitality.[4]

Not surprisingly, going along with this refurbishing of modernity has been a rediscovery of modernization theory. Modernization theory, popular in the 1950s and 1960s, came in for something of a thrashing in the late 1960s and 1970s, particularly at the hands of left-wing theorists. Now it is enjoying something of a renaissance.[5] The "catching-up" that the countries of Central and Eastern Europe are supposed to be engaged in can readily be expressed within the terms of classic modernization theory. One can then speak of "accelerated" and "retarded" modernization, "leads" and "lags," "pioneers" and "late-comers," and the whole battery of other such concepts drawn from the theory.[6]

Modernization theory, in turn, leads us to world systems theory, and the current concern with "globalization." Modernization theory, whether in its Marxist or liberal form, has always had a worldwide scope (here clearly showing its origins in classic nineteenth-century social theory). The end of the Cold War has, for the moment at least, brought to an end the existence of a bipolar world and created, at least in principle, one world. It has also, it would appear, removed the necessity for the category of the "Third World," a theoretical convenience invented for the purpose of describing societies dependent on one or another of the world superpowers. Distinctions between "north" and "south" still make sense, and the inequalities between rich and poor nations are, if anything, greater than in the past.[7] But all this is now within the context of a unified world order.

Since this one world is also, to a predominant degree, a capitalist world, the analysis of capitalism as a global system would seem to be a central requirement for understanding the world after 1989. Some, such as Immanuel Wallerstein, have argued that this was always true, that state socialist societies had always been part—a "semi-peripheral" part—of the capitalist world system.[8] In this view the revolutions of 1989 can be the result only of the further evolution of that system, a reshuffling of its parts and a renegotiation of its international division of labor. This highly determinist view is disconcerting, and certainly ignores the key role played by the calculation of political elites in the communist world. But in any event, whatever the case before 1989, the open accession of a large number of new states to the global market economy must surely have the effect of further extending and complicating the capitalist world system.[9] Concepts such as "core" and "periphery" become more relevant than ever before, capturing more closely the new reality than the old "Three Worlds" framework. It should also be obvious that, as a result of this global economic unification, Karl Marx—as the supreme analyst of the world system of capitalism (rather than as the prophet of socialism)—becomes more (rather than, as many have too hastily assumed, less) relevant in understanding today's world.

All of these themes, whether or not one fully accepts them, suggest some of the ways in which social theory might have to reorientate itself in the world after the fall of communism. The most obvious casualty is the capitalist-communist opposition that structured so much work in the social sciences as well as, equally evidently, the machinations of global politics.[10] This involves, in one sense, a renewal of the cosmopolitan project of the eighteenth-century Enlightenment. The world can once more be considered a unity. Its fate can be considered as a whole. There is potentially a new enabling role for international institutions such as the United Nations. This does not necessarily mean we will have a more secure or happier world, as the bloody conflicts in the Persian Gulf and the former Yugoslavia testify. But perhaps Habermas is right in seeing in the part the United Nations played in those conflicts a normative gesture in the direction of international cooperation, in a way virtually unthinkable in the era of the Cold War.[11]

Of all the social sciences, and despite the lead given by Marx in particular, sociology has been most bounded by the perspective of the nation-state.[12] Comparative sociology tends to take a bundle of nation-states and compare them as to class structure, rates of social mobility, educational systems, and the like. Despite talk of "social systems," "capitalist societies," and so on—all concepts that point beyond historically defined nation-states—the practice has been to equate modern societies with specific examples such as English, French, and German society, and so on. Even Marx could fall victim to this practice, which meant that he made the mistake of reading the development of all modern societies through the English case, seen as the exemplar of capitalist modernity.[13]

National differences exist and will continue to do so. But it is time for sociologists to put the emphasis on the other side, to consider the global system as a whole and the way it is shaping developments within nation-states, in economics, politics, and culture.[14] This is one of the principal consequences of the fall of communism and the end of the bipolar world. Probably a global perspective would have been forced on social theorists in any case, by the growth and dynamism of the global economic system that was increasingly pressing on state socialist societies; but the collapse of those societies and their incorporation into the world economy make the imperative of a global perspective even clearer.

Talk of modernization, globalization, cosmopolitanism, and similar processes tends to carry an air of optimism, even utopianism, about it. It is not that commentators are unaware of the dangers and difficulties ahead. But these tend to be seen as a matter mainly of sound statesmanship aided, where necessary, by a stern crack of the whip. The ideas and institutions of Western societies are taken as firmly vindicated by the verdict of history. West is best. Other countries, including the former communist ones, have now recognized this and should be encouraged and helped to follow the Western path as speedily as possible (modernization theory *redivivus*).[15] There is an air of "business as usual," of uncomfortable and regrettable lapses (communism, fascism) from normal development now put firmly behind us and perhaps best forgotten. Basing itself on a dynamic capitalist system and liberal political institutions, the world can get on with the unfinished business of modernization. Much of Central and Eastern Europe can be brought within the ambit of the European Union; other key players on the world stage—the United States, Japan, probably also China—can oversee the development process within their respective regions. International institutions and organizations such as the World Bank, the International Monetary Fund, the World Trade Organization, the United Nations, and the North Atlantic Treaty Organization can provide additional increments of the necessary financial and military discipline.

Merely to state the matter like this is to make one aware of the enormous political and theoretical assumptions being made. It is not simply the hierarchical nature of the new world order that stands out. It is also an unreflecting confidence in the ideas and institutions of modern societies, specifically those of Western societies that are taken to be the most advanced version of the modern model available. If it is true that modernization has resumed its world course, we need to ask which aspects of modernity are most salient. What are the modern concepts and developments that have a renewed appeal? What are their implications for orderly development? To what extent are they renewals in the same form as before, and to what extent are they operating in a new environment, with a new meaning and significance? To examine the issues raised by these questions is to realize that the victory of a particular version of modernity is a highly ambiguous matter, one fraught with uncertainties and anxieties.

## Citizenship and the Return of the Repressed I: Democracy, Civil Society, Human Rights

It is possible to consider a number of important features of the post-communist, post-1989, world as the "return of the repressed" of modernity. By this I mean that features that had been taken for granted, and hence no longer examined, come for various reasons to appear problematic and in need of scrutiny. Additionally, features that had apparently disappeared or lost their hold make a reappearance, with a new vitality and in some cases in new forms.

The end of communism has stimulated this inquiry in two ways. First, the postcommunist societies themselves needed to work out the meaning of certain terms—democracy, constitutionalism, and so on—in seeking to apply them and to develop appropriate institutions and practices, in some cases where they were thin or nonexistent. Second, their efforts, both practical and theoretical, have forced Western scholars to rethink concepts long taken for granted. In doing so they have been led to turn the spotlight on the working of their own institutions, and to ask how far they match up to the promise of their ideals. In both cases, East and West, it has come to be realized that ideas need constant reexamination and refurbishment if they are to be meaningful and useful in contemporary conditions. This is partly because of the natural tendency toward inertia and routine, partly also because new or resurgent developments in the world bring fresh challenges that insist on a response.

One must necessarily be schematic here, for reasons of space. All that I can do is indicate the ideas and movements that seem to have presented themselves with unusual force, and that, in consequence, have come in for renewed scrutiny. Some are venerable ideas that have suddenly appeared problematic. Others are processes that had apparently disappeared or lost their force, and whose reappearance therefore forces a reconsideration of their place in modern societies.

First in precedence by virtue of its honored, not to say revered, status in modern society is *democracy.* The rehabilitation of democracy, as an object for investigation, is nothing short of astonishing. Here was a concept that had slumbered quietly in the arms of a few political scientists since the late nineteenth century. All the important things seemed to have been said: by Tocqueville in *Democracy in America,* by Mill in *Considerations on Representative Government,* by Bryce, Ostrogorski, and Michels at the turn of the century. Graham Wallas's *Human Nature in Politics* (1908) marked a convenient *terminus ad quem* of this phase of the classic discussions of democracy. After that came mainly technical accounts of political behavior and empirical analyses of voters, parties, leaders, and so on. Marxism contributed its storehouse of contemptuous epithets to what it regarded as a bourgeois sham, a facade behind which the ruling class got on with the real business of running society. Like a familiar and long-lasting spouse, democracy had become boring, if not despised, at least in the West. We thought we knew it so well that we did not expect it to say anything interesting or to surprise us in any way.

It took developments outside the West to rekindle Western enthusiasm for democracy—as if another man had shown an interest in one's wife. First came the worldwide turn to democracy in southern Europe,

South America, and southern Asia in the 1970s and 1980s. In 1989 it was the turn of East Central Europe. Between 1974 and 1990 some thirty states entered or reentered the democratic fold. Later, in 1991, the Soviet Union also broke up into fifteen independent states, most of which at least formally adopted democratic constitutions. Later still, in 1998, Indonesia, the world's fourth most populous state, returned to democracy after a thirty-year dictatorship. A "democratic revolution" seemed clearly under way in the late twentieth century.[16]

Faced with such a wealth of material, and an urgent need to understand the causes and likely outcomes of current efforts at democratization, scholars have poured forth a stream of studies and inquiries. New journals have appeared specifically devoted to democracy and democratization. Old concepts have been looked at afresh, and current practices scrutinized with a newly critical eye. Democracy's coexistence with capitalism, and the possible conflict between them, has come in for renewed attention. Venerable schemes of "cosmopolitan democracy" have been revived, to match the new realities of global politics. Marxists, reversing their traditional disdain for democracy, have rediscovered its radical potential in alternative traditions of socialism. Feminists have debated it within the context of ideas of diversity and difference. At no time since the beginning of the twentieth century has democracy been so intensively studied, or so subtly, perhaps oversubtly, theorized. Whatever comfort might be taken from its worldwide acceptance as the ideal form of government has had to be matched by a sober awareness of the complexity and competing nature of its claims, and the difficulties of realizing them in practice.[17]

Even more remarkable than the revival of democratic theory has been the retrieval of an archaic form of Western social thought: the idea of *civil society*. So ancient was this that not much had been heard of it since Gramsci wrote of it the early twentieth century—and that, too, was a revival of a concept that had more or less dropped out of the Western political vocabulary in the second half of the nineteenth century. Of all the concepts stimulated by the 1989 revolutions, that of civil society has undoubtedly been the most challenging—and problematic. Since this matter is extensively discussed in chapter 5 of the present volume, no more need be said here. It is necessary simply to mention it as a prime instance of the labor of excavation and recovery that has been going on, in both East and West, for the past decade. The events in Central Europe may have been the immediate stimulus to its rediscovery; but Western theorists have had no difficulty in claiming it as their own, and in applying it vigorously to the conditions of their own societies.

If civil society is recovered, can *citizenship* be far behind? That, too, has been another notable concern in recent years. Once more, urgent Eastern European interest in constructing viable democratic polities has fueled the inquiry, but it is fair to say that Western theorists had also been preoccupied with this for some years prior to the 1989 revolutions. T. H. Marshall's seminal essay "Citizenship and Social Class" (1950) was the springboard for a renewed sociological concern with the conditions of full and active citizenship, whereas legal and political theorists have been preoccupied with rights and civic participation in an era that has made both highly problematic. Equally noticeable is the new interest in trust as a key condition of a thriving civic and capitalist culture—a matter of even more urgency in the East than in the West.[18] A relatively novel feature in the Western case is the pressure put on traditional concepts of citizenship by the arrival of large numbers of immigrants and migrants, some of non-European stock, in the societies of Western Europe and North America. In examining the forms and manner of incorporation of these new groups, theorists have been led to conduct a wide-ranging examination of the whole basis of citizenship, and to consider new varieties of social inclusion and exclusion. The lessons are as clearly applicable to the societies of Eastern Europe, with their historic minorities, as to the newly "multicultural" societies of the West.[19]

Discussions of citizenship have tended to focus on the nation-state. "Transnational citizenship"—the search for spaces and identities beyond the nation-state—has evidently built on that while rejecting one of its fundamental premises.[20] Likewise, naturally a renewed concern with the terms and conditions of citizenship has brought *human rights* to the forefront of contemporary debates. Here the end of the Cold War has been decisive. So long as the two superpowers, the United States and the Soviet Union, confronted each other in the Security Council of the United Nations, and their allies faced off in the General Assembly, any concept of universal human rights was virtually impossible to implement. Whatever the evidence, and however massive the protests, whether it was the United States in Vietnam or the Soviet Union in Afghanistan, the two superpowers quietly ensured that no one was allowed to intervene in their "sphere of influence."

The Helsinki Accords of 1975 marked the first breach in that united front, and incidentally gave dissidents in the communist bloc, such as Václav Havel and the Charter 77 movement, something to rally around. But it was not until 1991 and the emergence of the virtual hegemony of the United States in world affairs that human rights could be made an instrument of international policy. Human rights became a slogan to brandish, and a declared reason for the international community to intervene, throughout the 1990s: in the Gulf War, the civil war in Rwanda, the war in Bosnia, the war in Kosovo, and the independence struggle in East Timor.

Commentators were right to point to an element of hypocrisy and self-serving in all this. Because of American anxieties about stability in Russia, nothing was done about Russian repression in Chechnya, nor, because of similar concerns about NATO member Turkey, was anything urged against the Turks for their treatment of the Kurds. All of this was only to be expected in the novel situation in which one superpower was dominant in the world. The "international community" was mainly the American-led community, whether in the United Nations or in NATO. The point, however, was that human rights, long a matter mainly for international lawyers and human rights groups such as Amnesty International, was put firmly on the agenda of international affairs because of Western insistence. It became a hot issue, debated on television and in the national press. There were international symposia, which were attended by presidents and prime ministers and given intensive mass media coverage. A striking example of the new climate was the decision of a Spanish court to indict General Augusto Pinochet, the former dictator of Chile, for human rights abuses, and of the British police to arrest Pinochet during a visit to Britain in 1998. The arrest of Pinochet, declared a French human rights jurist, responds to "an almost universal clamor today that those who commit crimes against humanity must be pursued to the ends of the world, wherever and whenever they can be found, and brought to justice."[21]

"Human rights," says Michael Ignatieff, "has become the major article of faith of a secular culture that fears it believes in nothing else."[22] Social theory has had to struggle to deal with this fact of contemporary life, revisiting an issue that in recent times it had left to lawyers and constitutionalists. Questions with a pressing practical importance arise: Are there such things as "universal human rights"? Whence do they come? Is the whole discourse of human rights ethnocentric, reflecting the bias of Western development and Western attitudes? Might "Asian values," or the traditions of other religions such as Hinduism and Islam, suggest different ways of conceiving the relation of the individual to society, ways less individualistic and "rights-oriented" than those suggested by Western forms of thought? Once again, an attempt to answer these questions has driven theorists back to some old classics in natural and international law from the seventeenth and eighteenth centuries, and to even earlier sources in medieval thought. Indeed, the medieval world, with its idea of "the peace of God," its internationalism, and its refusal to accept concepts of absolute or undivided sovereignty—at least on earth—is fast becoming an invaluable storehouse of ideas and precedents.[23]

## The Return of the Repressed II: Nationalism, Religion, Revolution

Democracy, civil society, citizenship, and human rights represent a forgotten or neglected legacy, a return to some of the founding ideas and institutions of Western societies. They were repressed in the sense of sinking below the threshold of Western consciousness, either because they were thought resolved and unproblematic or because they had been pushed to the margin. Nationalism, religion, and revolution represent the return of the repressed in a more obvious sense. Here are ideas and forces that the West thought it had dealt with. They had, it seemed, ceased their haunting. Nationalism was a nineteenth-century movement that, progressive for its time, had overreached and destroyed itself in the bloated nationalism of Fascism and Nazism. Religion was everywhere giving way to secularism (with the mysterious exception of the United States). Revolution had reached its apogee in the Bolshevik Revolution of 1917, and then moved rapidly out to the non-Western world, leaving but a myth and a memory in Western societies.

The end of the twentieth century has seen a vengeful return of all three, in the West and the world at large. Perhaps they had never really gone away, but simply been buried in the Western subconscious biding their time. That time has come. The repressed have resurfaced. They already showed signs of returning strength before the fall of communism; the 1989 revolutions and the breakup of the Soviet Union have given them a new surge of energy.

*Nationalism* is the most obvious of these phenomena. Already causing major political upheavals in the 1970s and 1980s in the West—in the United Kingdom, in Spain, in Canada—it broke out with fresh force in Central and Eastern Europe in the wake of the anticommunist revolutions. Communism, especially in the Soviet Union, had kept the wraps on nationalism. But it had also in several ways kept it alive and even, by some of its institutional arrangements such as the system of ethnically defined republics in the Soviet Union and Yugoslavia, stimulated its growth. It was not so much slumbering nations that awoke after the fall of communism as newly grown varieties.[24] It is easy (as I argue in chapter 1) to exaggerate the extent of the nationalist upsurge in the former region of communism. Other parts of the world are showing it in an even more acute form. But undoubtedly the return of nationalism to the heart of Europe was a powerful stimulus to renewed reflection on a phenomenon that many had thought was in terminal decline.

Once more, social theory found itself floundering. This was partly because, as already noted, the "founding fathers" of sociology took the nation-state for granted and were incurious about the phenomenon of nationalism. For Marxists in particular, nationalism, like democracy, was a bourgeois ideology whose main function was to deflect working-class feeling away from the class struggle, and which therefore it was more important to denounce than to analyze. Those theorists who took nationalism seriously, such as Friedrich List, Heinrich von Treitschke, and Charles Maurras, were mainly men of the Right and so were the casualties of the antinationalist feeling that swept the intellectual scene after World War II.[25] For more than a generation after the war, there was little interest in nationalism among Western scholars.[26]

But, as with democracy, theorists have been making up for lost time. Since the early 1980s, in response first to the nationalist movements in the West and then, even more so, to those in Eastern Europe and the Balkans, there has been a frenzy of scholarly activity around the subject of nationalism. Rarely has an area of scholarship established itself more rapidly or more completely. Journals proliferate; centers are set up; courses flourish in the universities; books pour forth from all the leading presses. The study of nationalism has drawn in scholars from East and West; in no other sphere of contemporary work in the social sciences has there been such a convergence of interests.[27]

The return of *religion* has perhaps been less a surprise than the return of nationalism. In some sense religion has never gone away. It was an assumption of many European sociologists in the 1960s that the secularization they witnessed in their own societies was the norm, and that exceptions such as the United States needed special explanation.

American sociologists always knew otherwise: it was Europe that was the exception. In America as in the world at large, religion had undergone many changes, but showed no signs of disappearing.[28] Therefore, the upsurge of Protestant fundamentalism and evangelicalism, the renewed activism of the Catholic Church, and, most spectacularly, the resurgence of militant Islam across the globe in the 1970s and 1980s should have been no occasion for surprise. Nor should it have been disconcerting to see similar revivals among Jews, Sikhs, Hindus, and Buddhists.[29]

Nevertheless, social theory, preoccupied with poststructuralism and postmodernity, seems to have been caught by surprise by the religious revival and, as with nationalism, has been struggling to come to terms with it.[30] It has been seen partly as a response to the crisis of identity brought on by globalization, the weakening of the nation-state, and cultural homogenization. In that sense it shares in the qualities expressed by the ethnic revival, and in the rediscovery of "place" and similar markers of identity. "Jihad" confronts "McWorld."[31] It can also be seen as a rejection of certain aspects of modernity, thus linking, for instance, Protestant revivalism in the West with Islamic fundamentalism in the Middle East and elsewhere. Although this is generally linked to a harking back to old forms of morality, as well as family and community life, it can also in some accounts tie in with the eclecticism and freer forms of identity proclaimed in postmodernity.[32] Most convincingly, what is called "fundamentalist" religion can be shown to be a species of modernity, "an attempt to recreate religion within the limits of modernity."[33]

The end of communism has arguably contributed its own share to this renewal of religion, and of our need to understand it. The church itself, especially in Poland, East Germany, and Romania, played an important role in the overthrow of communism, and has continued to have a vigorous, if somewhat controversial, career in postcommunist society.[34] Everyone, too, acknowledges the significance of the election of a Polish pope (Karol Wojtyla, John Paul II) in 1978 as a counter to communism, and the enhanced prominence of the papacy that resulted from the defeat of communism. More fundamentally, there is the possibility that the end of the ideological conflict between communism and capitalism has opened the way for other cultural differences to surface. Religion is clearly one of these; the end of the Cold War has therefore been a great boost to religion. For Eastern Europe itself this can be seen not just in the revived Orthodox and Catholic churches—and the consequences in conflicts such as those in Croatia, Bosnia, and Kosovo—but more generally in the spread of Protestant sects into the region and in a surge of proselytism. In the world as a whole, what conceivably has taken place is the reemergence of old civilizational "fault lines," many of which run along traditional religious divides, and the possibility of major conflicts based on them.[35] What cannot be doubted is that in the world "after the fall"—of communism, that is—religion seems likely to play as lively a role as in many an earlier period of world history. This is not the least striking of the many unexpected effects of the "return of the repressed."

Finally there is *revolution*. We have looked at this extensively throughout this volume; it is, in a sense, its main theme. There is therefore no need to add much here. What we might say is that it is the most ambiguous of the trio—nationalism, religion, and revolution. The return of the former two, often with fire and sword, is in no degree uncertain. In the case of revolution, we cannot be so sure. Undoubtedly it is, in some sense, back on the agenda. Quiescent in Western societies for most of this century, with partial exceptions such as May '68 in Paris, it has had a stronger presence in Eastern Europe, as in 1956 and 1980–81. In 1989 it returned in full force, or so it appeared.

But the manner of its return leaves many things unclear. For one thing, since its return was in essence in the form of a rejection of one kind of revolution, the Bolshevik Revolution of 1917, which could legitimately claim to be the heir of the revolutionary tradition launched by the French Revolution, 1989 could stand as evidence that in Europe, at least, revolution had indeed been buried. The events of 1989, says Fred Halliday, "can be said to have confirmed something that, in retrospect at least, had long been the case: revolution had ceased to be a viable option in Western Europe for a century and a half, since the failure of the upheavals of 1848."[36] There was also the more obvious fact of the relatively peaceful, nonviolent, nature of the 1989 revolutions, leading some observers to question whether they should be called revolutions at all.[37]

I have argued that they *were* revolutions, and that 1989 did spell some sort of return of the revolutionary idea to the twentieth-century world. At any rate, whatever was the case in the West, the revolutionary principle has been alive and well in the non-Western world. For good reasons, it shows no sign of disappearing there, even though the forms it takes may differ significantly from the "classic" forms of the Western revolutionary tradition.[38] The revolutions of 1989 brought the idea back home, to Europe, where it all began two hundred years ago. Here, too, the future of revolution need not be a slavish imitation of its past. Globalization, the information technology revolution, the rise of new social movements around issues of ecology, sexuality, and personal identity—all are changing the content and context of revolutionary action. Perhaps the new forms in the future will be so different from those of the past that we will cease to talk of revolution at all. But they will still be the "radical rejection of the given," still the aspiration to something different from the present.[39] In that sense, the revolutionary impulse will live on, albeit under different names.

## Alternative Modernities?

We return, finally, to the point made in the first paragraph of this chapter: the possibility that the patterns of modernity achieved in Central and Eastern Europe may differ in significant respects from those of the West. What we have so far discussed—the renewed debates about democracy, civil society, citizenship, and human rights; the return or revival of nationalism, religion, and revolution—all evidently apply to the West as much as the East. But they may work themselves out in different ways. They may lead to very different outcomes. We have seen, in chapter 1, that the development of East Central Europe diverged in several fundamental ways from that of the West. If we add to this the experience of Russia, with its more pronounced "Eastern European" character, the possibility of a continuing East-West divide becomes even stronger. What emerges in Central and Eastern Europe, after the fall of communism, may loosely resemble the West. There may be markets, democracy, constitutionalism, and other features of Western society. But what they mean, how they work, what effect they have on the majority of the people in the region, may be very different from their role in the West.

Piotr Sztompka has cautioned against drawing too close a parallel between the modernizing processes in the Third World and those in the postcommunist Second World. The crucial difference is the legacy of "real socialism." He says, "Whereas in the post-colonial countries, the starting point was usually the traditional, pre-modern society, preserved in more or less unchanged shape, in the Soviet Union and Eastern Europe, both the ruling ideology and the highly politicized, centralized and planned economic system, were for many decades involved in the promotion of modernization." He calls this a "fake modernity," a combination encompassing contradictory and inharmonious elements of "imposed modernity"—the vestiges of premodern society, with its national and ethnic resentments—and "symbolic ornamentations pretending to imitate Western modernity."

Sztompka also points to the fact that the renewed modernization drive of Eastern Europe is taking place at a time when significant sections of Western societies seem to have lost their enthusiasm for modernity: "Acute awareness of the side-effects and unintended 'boomerang effects' of modernity produces disenchantment, disillusionment and outright rejection. At the theoretical level, 'Post-Modernism' becomes the fashion of the day. It seems as if the Western societies were ready to jump off the train of modernity, bored with the journey, just at the moment when the postcommunist East frantically tries to get on board."[40] Göran Therborn also notes this phenomenon, but for him this disaffection with the fruits of modernity was also present in the 1989 revolutions, and so lends them a postmodern character. The 1989 revolutions questioned all modernist notions of linear progress:

> Eastern European 1989–91 was a star moment of postmodernism. The emplotment was neither a morality of counterrevolution, nor a high ideological drama of Liberation nor a romance of Capitalism, but irony and farce. The oppressive master narrative of Communist socialism was no longer taken seriously. For all its vices and flaws, Communist rule was a modernist project. . . . Eastern European post-modernism was part of a fundamental challenge of modernity's central tenets. . . . 1989–91 was the end neither of modernity nor of history, but its manner of occurrence was postmodern. Modernity's arrow of time has been bent crooked. It may go off in various directions, but perhaps not very far in either.[41]

Both Sztompka and Therborn exaggerate the uniformity and consistency of modernization elsewhere, whether in the First or the Third World. Contradiction and unevenness are the normal, not aberrant, features of modernization, whether in England or Egypt. There are plenty of "fake modernities" around, some of them in the West. Nor is an enthusiasm for modernity or a belief in progress necessary for modernization. There was not much of either present in early nineteenth-century England or early twentieth-century Russia, at least among the population at large. Yet both countries embarked, in their different ways, upon some of the most ambitious programs of modernization yet seen.

Sztompka and Therborn are right though to draw our attention to the different circumstances of postcommunist Eastern Europe, as compared with modernization experiences at other times and other places. These suggest that "Second World" modernization might continue to be different from examples elsewhere, despite the "Westernizing" turn in many of the societies of the region. There is no necessary "logic" to the process of modernization. It was done differently in England, France, and the United States, differently again in Germany, Russia, and Japan, and, as currently appears, it is being done differently yet again in China, Taiwan, and Singapore, not to mention Africa and South America. There is "Confucian" as well as "communist" and "capitalist" modernity; there may well be a variety of "theocratic" modernity, as practiced, for instance, in Iran and Afghanistan. "Modernization" is not the same thing as "Westernization," if by the latter we understand the liberal market form of modernity that has come down from the Enlightenment.[42]

If that is so, perhaps we should not be so disturbed by the apparent slowness of Western models of economy and polity to "take" in Eastern European societies. Those societies will find their own way to develop, based on their own histories. We should not expect, or wish for, a slavish imitation of the West. In any case, the whole framework of world politics and economics is changing. Western societies as much as Eastern European societies are going to have to find a new place in the evolving global order. That order is capitalist, and currently, at least, it is governed by a liberal ideology. To that extent, Western conceptions, if not necessarily the West itself, still dominate. But the end of the Cold War has fundamentally shaken up ideologies and alliances. It has opened the way for the renegotiation of power and domination in the world. The centuries-long hold of the West may be waning. Not only will Western societies now have to compete on new terms with powerful new nations in the East; it may be that Western ideologies, too—of which liberalism and socialism are closely related varieties—will find themselves increasingly challenged.[43]

This chapter, and this volume, has concerned itself mainly with the way in which this coming new world can be viewed from the perspective of what happened in Central and Eastern Europe in 1989. It was there that the first breach was made in the world order that was constructed after 1945. Closely following upon that was the dissolution in 1991 of the Soviet Union itself, whose internal problems were chiefly what had led to the anticommunist revolutions of 1989. Since that time, there has been a further unraveling of the old order: the end of white rule in South Africa, and the collapse of long-standing political arrangements in Italy and Japan, for instance; political settlements in Ireland and between Israel and Palestine; civil wars in Europe and elsewhere on a devastating scale; the rise of a dozen new nations; repeated international military intervention in the affairs of formally sovereign states. These are indeed new times, hopeful and alarming in equal measure. They present, as Edward Tiryakian says, a particularly exciting challenge to sociologists. They should seize the day.

# Notes

## 1. The Relevance of the Past

1. I have throughout this chapter tended to use the term *East Central Europe* to refer to the countries and region that are its main subject. This is because it is the term that seems to be now the normal one in the scholarly literature on the subject. But, in this chapter and even more in the later ones of the book, I sometimes use the term *Central Europe* and even *Eastern Europe* to refer to the region, since these terms were, and often still are, commonly employed instead. Usually the context makes clear what is meant. For helpful discussions of terminology, see the contributions to the special issue of *Daedalus* 119, no. 1 (winter 1990), subsequently reprinted as Stephen Graubard, ed., *Eastern Europe . . . Central Europe . . . Europe* (Boulder, Colo.: Westview Press, 1991); see also Robert Bideleux and Ian Jeffries, *A History of Eastern Europe: Crisis and Change* (London and New York: Routledge, 1998), 8–15.

2. See Peter F. Sugar and Donald W. Treadgold, "Foreword" to Paul Robert Magocsi, *Historical Atlas of East Central Europe,* corrected edition (Seattle and London: University of Washington Press, 1995), ix. Magocsi immediately breaks with this, and thereby illustrates the difficulties of any firm delineation, by declaring that his atlas (volume 1 in the series) will have a broader geographical scope, to include not just these countries, but also "toward the west, the eastern parts of Germany (historic Mecklenburg, Brandenburg, Prussia, Saxony, and Lusatia), Bavaria, Austria, and northeastern Italy (historic Venetia), and toward the east, the lands of historic Poland-Lithuania (present-day Lithuania, Belarus, and Ukraine up to the Dnieper River), Moldova, and western Anatolia in Turkey." Ibid., xi. The inclusion of Greece points to another tricky problem. Clearly a part of the region geographically ("the Balkans"), and historically especially so during the four centuries of Ottoman rule, it repeatedly jumps out of the category by virtue of its own self-understanding as the birthplace of the West, and by the fact that after 1945 it was a capitalist, "Western," island in an overwhelmingly communist sea.

Its perception—at least that of its elites—of itself as Western is of course strengthened by philhellenic sentiment among the educated classes of the Western world.

3. Gale Stokes, "Eastern Europe's Defining Fault Lines," in his *Three Eras of Political Change in Eastern Europe* (New York and Oxford: Oxford University Press, 1997), 21–22. For the finer fault lines within the region, on a country-by-country basis, see also Gale Stokes, "The Social Origins of East European Politics," *East European Politics and Societies* 1: 1 (1987): 30–74. A similar notion of "fault lines" is used by Dennis P. Hupchick, *Culture and History in Eastern Europe* (New York: St. Martin's Press, 1994); for Hupchick, though, the religious dividing lines—Catholic versus Orthodox, both against Islam—are the overriding things. Such a view has also recently been restated, with special reference to the post-Cold War era, by Samuel Huntington, *The Clash of Civilizations and the Remaking of the World Order* (New York: Touchstone Books, 1997), especially 157–63. For further discussion of this and related questions, see chapter 3 of this book.

4. Not that there is not a long tradition of "orientalizing" Eastern Europe. See, for example, Larry Wolf, *Inventing Eastern Europe: The Map of Civilization on the Mind of the Enlightenment* (Stanford: Stanford University Press, 1994), and, for the most recent period, Adam Burgess, *Divided Europe: The New Domination of the East* (London: Pluto Press, 1997). It is simply that such an approach, with its characteristic stereotyping, is not necessary in treating East Central Europe in a unitary way.

5. Ian McEwan, "An Interview with Milan Kundera," *Granta* 11 (1984): 26. Kundera quotes the opening phrase of a letter between the Polish writers Witold Gombrowicz and Czesław Miłosz: "In a hundred years—if our country still exists." He comments: "No English, American, German or French person could ever write such a phrase." Ibid., 27. For an account that stresses the making of East Central Europe by the pressure of the surrounding empires, see Michael G. Roskin, *The Rebirth of Eastern Europe* (Englewood Cliffs, N.J.: Prentice-Hall, 1991).

6. One of the earliest writers to employ the expression was Alan Palmer, *The Lands Between: A History of East Central Europe since the Congress of Vienna* (London: Macmillan, 1970). See also Melvin Croan, "Lands In-Between: The Politics of Cultural Identity in Contemporary Eastern Europe," *Eastern European Politics and Societies* 3, no. 2 (1989): 176–97, especially 177, n. 4.

7. Cf. Jerzy Jedlicki: "If all those peoples who live in the narrow space between the old Russian, German, Austrian, and Turkish empires share any basic experience and any common wisdom, it boils down to this: that no victory is ever final, no peace settlement is ever final, no frontiers are secure, and each generation must begin its work anew. There is no linear development in East European history, but rather a Sisyphus-like labor of ups and downs, of building and wrecking, where little depends on one's own ingenuity and perseverance. This sort of mild resignation—social psychologists call it 'learned helplessness'—has been conditioned by a very real historical experience and has nothing in common with any fatalistic 'Oriental metaphysics.'" "The Revolution of 1989: The Unbearable Burden of History," *Problems of Communism* 39 (July–August 1990): 40.

8. Jacques Rupnik, *The Other Europe* (New York: Pantheon Books, 1989), 3.

9. Jenö Szücs, "The Three Historical Regions of Europe," *Acta Historica Academiae Scientiarum Hungaricae* 29, nos. 2–4 (1983): 131–84.

10. Szücs, "The Three Historical Regions of Europe," 155.

11. For accounts that substantially follow Szücs, see Philip Longworth, *The Making of Eastern Europe: From Prehistory to Postcommunism*, second edition (New York: St. Martin's Press, 1994), especially chapters 7 and 8; George Schöpflin, "The Political

Traditions of Eastern Europe," in his *Politics in Eastern Europe 1945–1992* (Cambridge, Mass.: Blackwell, 1993), 5–37; Rupnik, *The Other Europe*, 9–20; Bideleux and Jeffries, *A History of Eastern Europe*, 15–25. There is a good discussion of Szücs, with a qualified endorsement, in C. M. Hann, "Boundaries and Histories," in his *The Skeleton at the Feast: Contributions to East European Anthropology*, CSAC Monographs 9 (Canterbury: University of Kent Centre for Social Anthropology and Computing, 1995), 1–28. An earlier account that makes many of Szücs's points is to be found in the contributions to Geoffrey Barraclough, ed., *Eastern and Western Europe in the Middle Ages* (London: Thames and Hudson, 1970); see also Antoni Maczak, Henryk Samsonowicz, and Peter Burke, eds., *East Central Europe in Transition from the Fourteenth to the Seventeenth Century* (Cambridge, U.K.: Cambridge University Press, 1985). Oscar Halecki, in *The Limits and Divisions of European History* (New York: Sheed and Ward, 1950), established the general typology of Europe—Eastern, Western, East Central, and so on—that was later refined by other scholars, including Szücs.

12. Piotr S. Wandycz, *The Price of Freedom: A History of East Central Europe from the Middle Ages to the Present* (New York: Routledge, 1992), 3. It is not usually recognized how important a role the region as a whole, not just its "core" countries, played in both transmitting and contributing to the Renaissance, the Reformation, and the Enlightenment. For a fascinating account of its impact in southeastern Europe—in "the region between Vienna and Constantinople," an area not normally treated in this context—see Victor Neumann, *The Temptation of Homo Europaeus*, translated by Dana Miu (New York: Columbia University Press, 1993).

13. Schöpflin, "The Political Traditions of Eastern Europe," 11. Cf. Stokes, "Eastern Europe's Defining Fault Lines," 7. A similar emphasis, distinguishing East Central Europe even more sharply from the West, is found in a statement by Bideleux and Jeffries: "We see more justification for treating East Central Europe as the most Westernized part of the East than for regarding it as the most easterly part of the West." *A History of Eastern Europe*, 15.

14. Széchenyi was in particular an admirer of England, which, like many other famous continentals—notably Tocqueville and Marx—he visited and studied. "What a happy country," he wrote to his father in 1816, "where so few are the unfortunate. We have to bow before her greatness." Quoted in Andrew C. Janos, *The Politics of Backwardness in Hungary 1825–1945* (Princeton: Princeton University Press, 1982), 50; also see p. 51 for Széchenyi's remarks about his countrymen's backwardness. Not for nothing was Budapest's grand new parliament building, constructed in the late nineteenth century on the east bank of the Danube, modeled on the Palace of Westminster on the Thames.

15. Quoted in Rupnik, *The Other Europe*, 11.

16. Janos, *The Politics of Backwardness in Hungary*, 314. A similar view of East Central Europe's peripheral or semiperipheral position in the global capitalist economy, and of the social and political consequences flowing therefrom, is to be found in Wandycz, *The Price of Freedom*, 3–9; Hann, "Boundaries and Histories"; Schöpflin, "The Political Traditions of Eastern Europe"; Longworth, *The Making of Eastern Europe*, especially 323–34. The theme of dependence and "incomplete Westernization" is also stressed in Robin Okey, *Eastern Europe 1740–1985: Feudalism to Communism*, second edition (London: Hutchinson, 1986). An eloquent restatement, in the context of post-1989 hopes, is Jedlicki, "The Revolution of 1989: The Unbearable Burden of History." See also Iván Berend and György Ránki, *The European Periphery and Industrialization 1780–1914* (Cambridge, U.K.: Cambridge University Press, 1982); Iván T. Berend, *Decades of Crisis: Central and Eastern Europe Before World War II*

(Berkeley: University of California Press, 1998), especially chapters 1 and 2. For a stimulating collection of essays that discusses the whole thesis of the region's backwardness, see Daniel Chirot, ed., *The Origins of Backwardness in Eastern Europe: Economics and Politics from the Middle Ages until the Early Twentieth Century* (Berkeley: University of California Press, 1989). Although the idea of backwardness as applied to the region is an old one, its current usage largely derives from the work of Alexander Gershenkron on Russian and East European economic history. See, for example, Alexander Gershenkron, *Economic Backwardness in Historical Perspective* (Cambridge, Mass.: Harvard University Press, 1962).

   17. Janos, *The Politics of Backwardness*, 314–20; for the persisting legacy, see also Janos, "Continuity and Change in Eastern Europe: Strategies of Post-Communist Politics," *East European Politics and Societies* 8, no. 1 (1994): 1–31; and cf. Berend, *Decades of Crisis*, 48–83. Note also Longworth's characterization of the Eastern European pattern: "Its population's attachment to democracy has been both uncertain and of brief duration; its institutions were weaker than the West's, its legal formation less developed. Certain distinctive inclinations and habits of mind also arose: tendencies to bureaucracy and collectivism; stronger urges to national self-realization than to personal autonomy; a disposition to ideology." He noted that a "love of poetry, idealism and cynicism" are also characteristic East European traits; later he adds "a disinclination to compromise and tendencies to both utopianism and romantic excess." All these qualities are seen as "contributing to the revolutions of the later 1980s," including the difficulties of "adjusting to democratic pluralism and the market economy." Longworth, *The Making of Eastern Europe*, 5–6, 323. This is, of course, the heart of the matter.

   18. Rupnik, *The Other Europe*, 13.

   19. For brief accounts, see Berend, *Decades of Crisis*, 20–22; Stokes, "The Social Origins of East European Politics," 37–40. Largely owing to the industrialization of its Czech parts, Austria-Hungary on the eve of World War I was the fifth largest industrial power in Europe and the fourth in world trade, surpassed only by Britain, France, and Germany.

   20. But see Daniel Chirot, "Causes and Consequences of Backwardness," in Daniel Chirot, ed., *The Origins of Backwardness in Eastern Europe*, 1–14. Chirot points to the great variety of outcomes in the region, especially owing to different political systems and relations.

   21. Stokes, "Eastern Europe's Defining Fault Lines," 8.

   22. Hans Kohn, *The Idea of Nationalism* (New York: Macmillan, 1945), 330–31. And cf. Bideleux and Jeffries, on "the curse of 'ethnic' nationalism" in the region, as contrasted with the "civic" nationalism of the West, in *A History of Eastern Europe*, 25–28. See also the contributions to Peter F. Sugar and Ivo J. Lederer, eds., *Nationalism in Eastern Europe* (Seattle: University of Washington Press, 1969); John A. Armstrong, "Toward a Framework for Considering Nationalism in East Europe," *Eastern European Politics and Societies* 2, no. 2 (1988): 280–305; Liah Greenfeld, *Nationalism: Five Roads to Modernity* (Cambridge, Mass.: Harvard University Press, 1992), chapters 3 and 4; Peter F. Sugar, ed., *Eastern European Nationalism in the Twentieth Century* (Washington, D.C.: American University Press, 1995). "Backwardness," and the importance of imported Western models of nationalism, but in very "un-Western" conditions, is also the *leitmotiv* of Gale Stokes, "Dependency and the Rise of Nationalism in Southeastern Europe," in his *Three Eras of Political Change in Eastern Europe*, 23–35. For a more varied picture, see *Social Research* 58, no. 4 (1991), a special issue on "Nationalism in Central and Eastern Europe."

   23. There is a useful brief description of the ethnic makeup, past and present, of the

region, in Berend, *Decades of Crisis,* 32–47. See also Magocsi, *Historical Atlas of East Central Europe,* 97–110; the relevant entries in Felipe Fernández-Armesto, ed., *The Peoples of Europe* (London: Times Books, 1994); Andrew C. Janos, "Continuity and Change in Eastern Europe," 6.

24. Jedlicki, "The Revolution of 1989," 40. Cf. Janos: "Ethnic tensions remain salient and acute because . . . Eastern Europe went to sleep at mid-century, and awoke nearly fifty years later with deeply entrenched conventional attitudes concerning the nation state." Janos, "Continuity and Change in Eastern Europe," 7. For the backward-looking anti-urban, anti-modern character of much of the nationalism of the region, see Armstrong, "Toward a Framework for Considering Nationalism in East Europe."

25. For some useful studies, see Paul Latawski, ed., *Contemporary Nationalism in East Central Europe* (Basingstoke, U.K.: Macmillan, 1994); Ray Taras, ed., *National Identities and Ethnic Minorities in Eastern Europe* (London: Macmillan, 1998).

26. See Stokes, "The Social Origins of East European Politics," 48–49, 57–58.

27. Berend, *Decades of Crisis,* 37–38.

28. For a good account of the differences between Western and Eastern absolutism, see Perry Anderson, *Lineages of the Absolutist State* (London: Verso, 1974). The most illuminating pictures of the social and political structure of the region up to 1914 are to be found in the great novels of and about the Austro-Hungarian Empire, notably Jaroslav Hašek, *The Good Soldier Svejk* (1918–23), Robert Musil, *The Man Without Qualities* (1930), and Joseph Roth, *The Radetzky March* (1932). Franz Kafka's novels, interpreted in a certain way, also give a striking impression of this culture. See the interesting discussion in Milan Kundera, "Somewhere Behind," *Granta* 11 (1984): 78–91. Kundera sees Kafka not just giving a "poetic" account of late imperial Habsburg society but also anticipating later totalitarianism.

29. For more on this, see chapter 5 of this book.

30. Gale Stokes, "Modes of Opposition Leading to Revolution in Eastern Europe," in his *Three Eras of Political Change in Eastern Europe,* 184.

31. There is a good summary of the differences between communist regimes, especially those in "Habsburg" Central Europe and those in the Balkans, in Fatos Tarifa, "The Quest for Legitimacy and the Withering Away of Utopia," *Social Forces* 76, no. 2 (1997): 454–57.

32. This seems to be the view, for example, of George Schöpflin, "The End of Communism in Central and Eastern Europe," in his *Politics in Eastern Europe 1945–1992,* 226; see also 37, 75.

33. For an informative discussion of this question, see Jacques Rupnik, "Totalitarianism Revisited," in John Keane, ed., *Civil Society and the State: New European Perspectives* (New York: Verso, 1988), 263–89. See also Abbott Gleason, *Totalitarianism: The Inner History of the Cold War* (New York: Oxford University Press, 1995).

34. Cf. Bideleux and Jeffries: "One of the primary tasks of this book is to offer hard-headed analyses of some of the historic differences between western Europe on the one hand and East Central Europe and the Balkans on the other. These emerged long before the advent of communist rule and the Cold War partition of Europe and they will long outlive the legacies of that more recent, vividly remembered but relatively ephemeral experience." Bideleux and Jeffries, *A History of East Central Europe,* 11. A similar view of the overriding importance of precommunist differences between the West and the "other Europe" informs the account in Z. A. B. Zeman, *The Making and Breaking of Communist Europe* (Oxford: Basil Blackwell, 1991).

35. See M. E. Yapp, "Europe in the Turkish Mirror," *Past and Present* 137 (1992): 134–55.

36. Ivo Andrić's novel *The Bridge on the Drina* (Chicago: University of Chicago Press, 1977) gives a vivid picture of the mutually respectful and peaceful coexistence of Orthodox, Islamic, and Jewish communities in the Bosnian city of Visegrad during Ottoman times and later. The old bridge, in both a literal and metaphorical sense, was one of the casualties of the Bosnian war of the 1990s.

37. See, for example, Huntington, *The Clash of Civilizations and the Remaking of World Order.*

38. For example: "Why, for instance, had the Prague Spring originated in Czechoslovakia? Almost certainly, because it had a long tradition of liberal freedoms and had been the only one of the East European democracies that survived throughout the interwar period." William L. Miller, Stephen White, and Paul Heywood, *Values and Political Change in Postcommunist Europe* (London: Macmillan, 1998), 41.

39. See Magocsi, *Historical Atlas of East Central Europe,* 133. For the difficulties of Czech democracy in relation to the minorities, see R. J. Crampton, *Eastern Europe in the Twentieth Century—and After,* second edition (New York: Routledge, 1997), 57–77. For an interesting discussion of Western attitudes toward the treatment of minorities in the region between the wars and later, concluding that the West displayed a patronizingly "orientalist" disposition toward Eastern Europe, see Adam Burgess, "National Minority Rights and the 'Civilizing' of Eastern Europe," *Contention* 5, no. 2 (1996): 17–35.

40. One might add that the Czechs' treatment of their Gypsy population today remains a source of much concern to Western liberals, though Burgess is probably right to see a certain Western hypocrisy in this. In November 1999, to the relief of many Czech liberals such as Václav Havel, the local authority of the northern town of Usti nad Labem removed a wall that had been built to separate Czechs from their Gypsy neighbors. See the report in the *New York Times,* November 25, 1999, A16.

41. For the history of these states in the interwar period, see Joseph Rothschild, *East Central Europe between the Two World Wars* (Seattle: University of Washington Press, 1974); Crampton, *Eastern Europe in the Twentieth Century—and After,* chapters 2–11; Bideleux and Jeffries, *A History of Eastern Europe,* 407–516. There is also a good short survey in Joni Lovenduski and Jean Woodall, *Politics and Society in Eastern Europe* (Indianapolis: Indiana University Press, 1988), 15–47. See also Berend, *Decades of Crisis,* 113–202, for a full account of authoritarian and nationalist movements and ideologies in the region during this period.

42. Cf. this typical comment on Poland, which can stand for many of the other countries of this region: "It can be argued that Poland has no authentic tradition of a modern market economy. Even in the interwar period the economy was based on traditionalist agriculture, state control and support of industrialization, and state ownership of railroads and one-third of banking. In addition, Poland at that time had a strong social welfare system and a widespread network of cooperatives." Andrzej W. Tymowski, "Poland's Unwanted Social Revolution," *Eastern European Politics and Societies* 7, no. 2 (1993): 185; and cf. also Edmund Mokrzycki, "Eastern Europe after Communism," *Telos* 90 (winter 1991–92): 130, on the widespread system of state ownership and control in the region before the communists took power.

43. On the varying degrees of popularity of the communists in the immediate postwar period, see Jerzy Tomaszewski, *The Socialist Regimes of Eastern Europe: Their Establishment and Consolidation 1944–1967* (New York: Routledge, 1989). See also Tarifa, "The Quest for Legitimacy and the Withering Away of Utopia," 441–46; Schöpflin, "The Communists on the Road to Power," in *Politics in Eastern Europe 1945–1992,* 57–74; Joseph Rothschild, *Return to Diversity: A Political History of East Central*

*Europe Since World War II*, second edition (New York: Oxford University Press, 1993), 76–123; Crampton, *Eastern Europe in the Twentieth Century—and After*, 211–39; Sten Berglund and Frank H. Aarebrot, *The Political History of Eastern Europe in the 20th Century* (Aldershot: Edward Elgar, 1997), part 2; Norman Naimark and Leonid Gibianski, eds., *The Establishment of Communist Regimes in Eastern Europe, 1944–1949* (Boulder, Colo.: Westview Press, 1998). And see further chapter 7 of this book.

44. Cyril (ca. 826–869) and his brother Methodius (815–885) were born in Thessalonika, at that time part of the Byzantine Empire. Undoubtedly, though, Bulgarians contributed greatly to the spread of Slavonic culture and the Orthodox religion, especially through the work of Cyril and Methodius's disciples Klement and Naum from their bases in the monasteries of Preslav, Rila, and Ohrid in the Bulgarian Empire. See Magocsi, *Historical Atlas of East Central Europe*, 10–12.

45. R. H. Lord, quoted by Wandycz, *The Price of Freedom*, 88. Nor have Poles forgotten that it was a Polish king, Jan Sobieski, who led the forces that repelled the Turks when they were at the gates of Vienna in 1683, and so, allegedly, saved Christian Europe from Turkish domination.

46. For the actual events and episodes, see Jean W. Sedlar, *East Central Europe in the Middle Ages, 1000–1500* (Seattle: University of Washington Press, 1993); Wandycz, *The Price of Freedom*, chapters 1 and 2; Longworth, *The Making of Eastern Europe*, chapters 9 and 10; Bideleux and Jeffries, *A History of Eastern Europe*, 111–261.

47. For more on this, see chapter 7 of this book.

48. There are some interesting thoughts on this, concerning mainly the communist period, in J. F. Brown, "The Legacy and the Revolution," in his *Hopes and Shadows: Eastern Europe after Communism* (Durham, N.C.: Duke University Press, 1994), 1–21.

49. See, for example, Czesław Miłosz, "Central European Attitudes," *Cross Currents* 5 (1986): 101–8; György Konrád, "Is the Dream of Central Europe Still Alive?" *Cross Currents* 5 (1986): 109–21. See also the discussion in Rupnik, *The Other Europe*, 41–55, and chapter 3 of this book.

50. Cf. Norman Naimark: "Now that the Wall—and communism—is gone, East European societies and the peoples who are part of them can come to an understanding of who they are without the distortions of both the reality and images of communist oppression and Soviet domination. . . . East Europeans now have the opportunity to shape their institutions and policies in accordance with their own national ethos and sense of common purpose. This is not a matter of sudden discovery and institutionalization, but of a long-term process of change, growth, and national introspection and argument." Norman Naimark, "Ten Years After: Perspectives on 1989," *East European Politics and Societies* 13, no. 2 (1999): 325–26.

51. For more on this, see chapter 3 of this book.

52. Diversity of experience, and the recovery of that diversity after 1989, is the theme of Joseph Rothschild's history of the region since World War II, *Return to Diversity*.

53. On these themes, see chapters 2, 4, and 6 of this book.

54. See Alex Callinicos, *The Revenge of History: The Revolutions of 1989* (Cambridge, U.K.: Polity Press, 1991).

## 2. The Revolutions of 1989

1. Robert Heilbroner, "The Triumph of Capitalism," *New Yorker* (January 23, 1989), 98. See also note 18 to this chapter.

2. Ralf Dahrendorf, *Reflections on the Revolution in Europe* (London: Chatto

and Windus, 1990), 38, 103. And cf. François Furet: "Today we are experiencing the be-ginning of an irreversible process—the end of an idea [socialism] that was one of the pil-lars (perhaps the principal one) of the European Left during the last 100 or 150 years." François Furet, "From 1789 to 1917 and 1989: Looking Back at Revolutionary Tradi-tions," *Encounter* (September 1990), 5.

3. Timothy Garton Ash, *We the People: The Revolution of '89* (London: Granta Books/Penguin, 1990), 131.

4. William Rees-Mogg, "A Wrong Theory with the Wrong Results," *The Indepen-dent* (February 19, 1990). Cf. Ralf Dahrendorf: "Communism has collapsed; social democracy is exhausted." Dahrendorf, *Reflections*, 71; see also 52–53.

5. Eric Hobsbawm, "Goodbye to All That," *Marxism Today* (October 1990), 19. See also the interview with Hobsbawm, "Waking from History's Great Dream," *The Independent on Sunday* (February 4, 1990).

6. Shortly after this the British Communist Party followed suit. It now also calls it-self the Party of the Democratic Left. It is not altogether inappropriate to cite, as an ex-ample of this worldwide trend, the case of the West African socialist state of Benin. At the end of 1989, the ruling Party for the Popular Revolution of Benin announced: "From now on Marxism-Leninism is no longer the official ideology of the state of Benin. Consequently, and with effect, use of the term 'comrade' is no longer obligatory for cus-tomary and administrative use in our country." *The Independent* (December 9, 1989).

7. "The End of Socialism," *The Independent* (November 28, 1989), p. 7. Jacques, though, specifically rejected the notion that "because the old forms of socialism are dead, then so is socialism."

8. Stuart Hall and Martin Jacques, eds., *New Times: The Changing Face of Politics in the 1990s* (London: Lawrence and Wishart, 1989), 137, 453. This is a collection of articles, most of which first appeared in *Marxism Today*. It includes extracts from the *Manifesto for New Times*. Its work of conversion completed, *Marxism Today* itself gracefully retired from the scene in December 1991—the month in which the Soviet Union was also dissolved.

9. Zygmunt Bauman, *Socialism: The Active Utopia* (London: Allen and Unwin, 1976), 36. See also my *Utopia and Anti-Utopia in Modern Times* (Oxford: Basil Black-well, 1987), chapter 2.

10. Wolf Lepenies, "Melancholy of Utopian Shadows," *Times Higher Education Supplement* (January 12, 1990), 17.

11. Norberto Bobbio, "The Upturned Utopia," *New Left Review* 177 (September/ October 1989): 37. And cf. Peter Jenkins: "We are witness to the fall of the world's great modern religion." Peter Jenkins, "The Death of a Modern Creed," *The Indepen-dent* (February 6, 1990).

12. Gareth Stedman Jones, "Faith in History: A Cambridge Sermon," *History Work-shop Journal* 30 (autumn 1990): 63.

13. Alexander Solzhenitsyn, *Rebuilding Russia: Reflections and Tentative Proposals,* translated by Alexis Klimoff (London: Harvill, 1991), 9. And cf. Richard Sakwa: "Perhaps the greatest achievement of Gorbachev and his reforms is that they set the U.S.S.R. and its peoples on the path of 'normal' development, renouncing utopianism and messianism." Richard Sakwa, *Gorbachev and His Reforms 1985–1990* (Hemel Hempstead, U.K.: Philip Allan, 1990), 402.

14. Václav Havel, "Politics and Conscience" (1984), in J. Vladislav, ed., *Václav Havel: Living in Truth* (London: Faber and Faber, 1989), 156, 140.

15. Václav Havel, "An Anatomy of Reticence" (1985), in Vladislav, ed., *Living in Truth*, 174–75.

16. Ibid., 176–77, 192–93.

17. Francis Fukuyama, "The End of Hysteria?" *The Guardian* (December 15, 1989). Fukuyama was, at the time of writing this article, deputy director of the U.S. State Department's policy planning staff. For an example of the responses from the Right, see Anthony Hartley, "On Not Ending History," *Encounter* (September–October 1989), 71–73, and, from the Left, the symposium by J. Steele, E. Mortimer, and G. Stedman Jones, "The End of History?" *Marxism Today* (November 1989), 26–33.

18. Francis Fukuyama, "The End of History?" *The National Interest* (summer 1989), 3–4. Many on the Left agreed; cf. Fred Halliday: "the end of the cold war . . . and the prevailing climate of detente in Europe and most of the third world, are being achieved not on the basis of a convergence of the two systems, or of a negotiated truce between them, but on the basis of the collapse of one in the face of the other. This means nothing less than the defeat of the communist project as it has been known in the twentieth century and the triumph of the capitalist." Fred Halliday, "The Ends of the Cold War," *New Left Review* 180 (March/April 1990): 12. Cf. also the pseudonymous "Soviet" writer "Z," "As 1989 draws to a close, it is clear that it will enter history as the beginning of communism's terminal crisis . . . and this not just in Russia, but from the Baltic to the China Sea, and from Berlin to Beijing." "Z.," "To the Stalin Mausoleum," *Daedalus* (winter 1990): 333. "Z" was later revealed to be the Berkeley Russian specialist Martin Malia.

19. Fukuyama, "The End of Hysteria?" A number of people have commented critically on Fukuyama's use of Hegel and his reliance on Kojève. See, for example, Stedman Jones, "The End of History?" and Nathan Rotenstreich, "Can There Be an End of History?" *History and Memory* 2 , no. 2 (1990): 136–41. I do not think these criticisms affect Fukuyama's main argument.

20. See, for example, Dahrendorf, *Reflections,* 33–5.

21. Dahrendorf, *Reflections,* 36, 57 ff.

22. Timothy Garton Ash commented on Dahrendorf's view that Marx deliberately, and mistakenly, conflated the two "cities" of modernity, the fruits of the Industrial and the French Revolutions, the bourgeois and the *citoyen.* For the people of East Central Europe, said Ash, Marx was in this respect right. They seemed to be saying that "the two are intimately connected—and we want both! Civil rights and property rights, economic freedom and political freedom, financial independence and intellectual independence, each supports the other. So, yes, we want to be citizens, but we also want to be middle class, in the senses that the majority of citizens in the more fortunate half of Europe are middle class." Garton Ash, *We the People,* 148–49. For a similar view of the intrinsic connection between "formal democracy" and capitalism—but one that draws quite different conclusions from the East Europeans—see Ellen Meiksins Wood, "The Uses and Abuses of Civil Society," in Ralph Miliband and Leo Panitch, eds., *Socialist Register 1990* (London: The Merlin Press, 1990), 67–74. I do not think the "mixed economies" of Social Democratic regimes such as that of Sweden constitute an exception, since they are still market driven, still fundamentally capitalist.

23. Stedman Jones, "The End of History," 33.

24. Fukuyama was well aware of these. He referred, for instance, to "the emptiness at the core of liberalism" and to the danger that the lack of a challenge to it will mean the worldwide diffusion of materialism, consumerism, and technicism. "The End of History?" 14, 18.

25. See Dahrendorf, *Reflections,* 26, 70. The point was reinforced by Dahrendorf's choice of modern heroes, Keynes and Beveridge. Both of these were, of course, notable liberals who wished to save capitalism, as the economic bedrock of political liberalism, by purging it of its historic errors.

26. Hobsbawm, "Goodbye to All That," 21, 23.

27. Jürgen Habermas, "What Does Socialism Mean Today? The Rectifying Revolution and the Need for New Thinking on the Left," *New Left Review* 183 (September/October 1990): 5. Cf. Timothy Garton Ash: "The ideas whose time has come are old, familiar, well-tested ones. (It is the new ideas whose time has passed.)" Garton Ash, *We the People,* 154.

28. Furet was quoted in Dahrendorf, *Reflections,* 23, 27.

29. Hobsbawm, "Goodbye to All That," 21.

30. See Jean-Francois Lyotard, *The Postmodern Condition,* trans. G. Bennington and B. Massumi (Manchester: Manchester University Press, 1984).

31. It had been argued by some that one further effect of the elimination of the communist alternative has been the decline of the concept, and perhaps even the reality, of the "Third World." The Third World was in effect a residual category—those countries that were not developed and were divided in their allegiance to the First (capitalist) and Second (communist) worlds. But it also suggested the idea of a moral and political alternative, a "third way" between capitalism and Soviet-style socialism. The collapse of communism, by effectively removing one of the models, has weakened the force of this idea. It may also be that this collapse itself gives testimony to the unreality today of the idea of "three worlds." There is only one world, the world of global capitalism. See, for example, Dahrendorf, *Reflections,* 22. This is, of course, a different sense from the "one world" preached by the ecologists. See, for example, *Our Common Future,* Report of the U.N. World Commission on Environment and Development (Oxford: Oxford University Press, 1986).

32. G. F. W. Hegel, *Philosophy of Right,* translated T. M. Knox (Oxford: Clarendon Press, 1945), 13.

33. Some doubts have been expressed about this. For example, Garton Ash, while acknowledging that what happened in Romania was a revolution, was not so sure about Poland, Hungary, Bulgaria, and even Czechoslovakia and East Germany. "Should popular movements which, however spontaneous, massive and effective, were almost entirely non-violent, really be described by a word so closely associated with violence?" But on the whole he feels that the "sudden and sweeping end to an ancien regime," and the fact that it occurred in all the countries of Eastern Europe within the space of a few months, justifies the term *revolution.* Ash, *We the People,* 20. For one of the strongest and clearest statements of the view that what happened in Eastern Europe in 1989 must be called a revolution—its peaceful nature notwithstanding—see Janusz Ziolkowski, "The Roots, Branches and Blossoms of Solidarnosc," in Gwyn Prins, ed., *Spring in Winter: The 1989 Revolutions* (Manchester: Manchester University Press, 1990), 40. Cf. also Hugh Trevor-Roper: "The revolutions of 1989 have been real revolutions: popular revolts before which armed governments, one after another, have collapsed; the recovery, by nations, of lost liberty." Hugh Trevor-Roper, "Europe's New Order," *The Independent Magazine* (December 30, 1989), 14.

34. See Robert H. Dix, "The Varieties of Revolution," *Comparative Politics* 15 (1983): 281–93, and Elbaki Hermassi, "Toward a Comparative Study of Revolution," *Comparative Studies in Society and History* 18 (1976): 211–35.

35. There are some groups, in the Soviet Union especially, who have seen the change in terms of a return to the "original" principles of 1917, the principles of socialist democracy, before their distortion not simply by Stalin, but also by Lenin (or at least Leninism). For an example of their thinking, see Boris Kagarlitsky, *The Dialectic of Change,* trans. Rick Simon (London: Verso, 1990), and for a discussion of what he calls "New Left perestroika," see Sakwa, *Gorbachev,* 200–07, 360–61. For the return to Lenin, the Lenin of the New Economic Policy, see Tatyana Zaslavskaya, *The Second Socialist Revolution: An Alternative Soviet Strategy,* translated by Susan M. Davies and Jenny Warren (London: I. B. Tauris, 1990).

36. Habermas, "What Does Socialism Mean Today?" 4–5. For the backward-looking nature of the 1989 revolutions, see also Jerzy Jedlicki, "The Revolution of 1989: The Unbearable Burden of History," *Problems of Communism* 39 (July–August 1990): 39–45. See also note 91 to this chapter.

37. Furet, "From 1789 to 1917 and 1989," 5. Fukuyama's Hegelian argument, noted earlier, also of course related the 1989 revolutions to the 1789 French Revolution. Cf. also Richard Sakwa on the aims of the "second Russian revolution," as understood by the radical proponents of perestroika: "The East European revolutions and the second Russian revolution . . . appeared to demonstrate not only the failure of the Bolshevik path of development but of the Marxist critique of Hegel in its entirety. These revolutions returned not only to the principles of the February 1917 'bourgeois democratic' revolution but to the French revolution itself. The Russian revolution of February 1917 . . . had only been the long-delayed triumph in Russia of the agenda set by the French Revolution over a hundred years earlier. . . . From this perspective the Bolshevik Revolution had only been a long and tragic hiatus before perestroika once again made possible a return to the challenge of the French revolution, and with it of liberal democracy and economic individualism." Sakwa, *Gorbachev,* 373–74; see also 388–89.

Linked to this view is the "Stolypin alternative" popular with some Russian reformers, including Solzhenitsyn: the return to the attempt begun by Stolypin at the beginning of the century to establish a functioning capitalist system in Russia on the basis of individual land ownership. See R. W. Davies, "Gorbachev's Socialism in Historical Perspective," *New Left Review* 179 (January/February 1990): 20–21. It need hardly be said how much additional force all this lends to the celebrated reply that Chou En-lai is reported to have given to the question, What were the consequences of the French Revolution?—"It is too early to say."

38. Habermas, "What Does Socialism Mean Today?" 7. And cf. Fred Halliday, who said of the events of 1989: "They have restated, in a dramatic form, the most neglected facet of political life, one spurned in east as much as in west, namely the capacity of the mass of the population to take sudden, rapid and novel political action after long periods of what appears to be indifference." Halliday, "The Ends of Cold War," 5. Timothy Garton Ash, though qualifying the point somewhat, also saw "the gentle crowd against the Party-state" as "both the hallmark and the essential domestic catalyst of change in 1989." Ash, *We the People,* 133.

39. Habermas, "What Does Socialism Mean Today," 7. Sakwa, too, noted that what Gorbachev was attempting in the Soviet Union had to be seen as a "profound reaffirmation of modernity" rather than as expressing any "post-modernist" values: "The very notion of 'reform,' of 'change' and 'renovation,' of 'progress,' speak of modernity rather than post-modernity. . . . Under Gorbachev the Soviet Union adopted the modern concept of political philosophy and the individual, the modernity proclaimed by the French Revolution." Sakwa, *Gorbachev,* 377.

40. For a good survey of the recent historiography of the revolution, see William Doyle, *Origins of the French Revolution,* 2nd edition, (Oxford: Oxford University Press, 1988), 7–40.

41. See Ronald Paulson, *Representations of Revolution (1789–1820)* (New Haven: Yale University Press, 1983); Noel Parker, *Portrayals of Revolution: Images, Debates and Patterns of Thought in the French Revolution* (Hemel Hempstead, U.K.: Harvester Wheatsheaf, 1990).

42. Leon Trotsky, *The History of the Russian Revolutions,* 3 volumes, translated by Max Eastman (London: Sphere Books, 1967), volume 1, 15.

43. See E. H. Carr, *A History of Soviet Russia,* volume 1, *The Bolshevik Revolution 1917–1923* (London: Macmillan, 1960), 25. For a discussion of the general point, see

my introduction to Krishan Kumar, ed., *Revolution: The Theory and Practice of a European Idea* (London: Weidenfeld and Nicolson, 1971), 40–70.

44. Plato, *The Republic,* translated by F. M. Cornford (Oxford: Clarendon Press, 1941), 262.

45. For an admirably wide-ranging discussion of "Gorbachevism," see Sakwa, *Gorbachev and His Reforms.* See also the arresting essay by "Z," "To the Stalin Mausoleum," note 18; Andrei Piontkowsky, "The Russian Sphinx: Hope and Despair," in Prins, ed., *Spring in Winter,* 164–90, especially 187–89; Stephen White, *Gorbachev in Power* (Cambridge: Cambridge University Press, 1990); S. White, A. Pravda, and Z. Gitelman, eds., *Developments in Soviet Politics* (London: Macmillan, 1990); Karen Dawisha, *Eastern Europe, Gorbachev and Reform,* 2nd ed. (Cambridge: Cambridge University Press, 1990); Davies, "Gorbachev's Socialism in Historical Perspective"; Zaslavskaya, *The Second Socialist Revolution;* Halliday, "The Ends of Cold War," 14–20; Wlodzimierz Brus, "'Perestroika': Advance or Retreat of a Revolution?" in E. E. Rice, ed., *Revolution and Counter Revolution* (Oxford: Blackwell, 1991), 171–87; Angus Roxburgh, *The Second Russian Revolution* (London: BBC, 1991).

For a discussion of the impact of the changes in the Soviet Union on the East European revolutions, see the symposium "Post-Communist Eastern Europe: A Survey of Opinion," *East European Politics and Societies* 4, no. 2 (spring 1990): 171–77. For developments before and after the attempted coup of August 1991, see Martin Malia (the pseudonymous "Z"), "A New Russian Revolution?" *New York Review of Books* (July 18, 1991), 29–31, and "The August Revolution," *New York Review of Books* (September 26, 1991), 22–28; see also Peter Reddaway, "The End of the Empire," *New York Review of Books* (November 7, 1991), 53–59; Ronald Suny, "Incomplete Revolution: National Movements and the Collapse of the Soviet Empire," *New Left Review* 189 (September–October 1991), 111–25. A cynical view of the aims of Yeltsin and his supporters is supplied by Boris Kagarlitsky, "The Coup That Worked," *New Statesman and Society* (September 6, 1991), 18–20.

46. Yugoslavia and Albania were the other countries where the communist regimes had for several decades made themselves independent of Moscow and did not depend on Soviet troops for the maintenance of their power. (Albania formally withdrew from the Warsaw Pact in 1968, although the break with Moscow came earlier, in 1961, owing to Albania's pro-China stance in the Sino-Soviet rift.) The slowness and difficulty of reform in these countries, as compared with other communist states in Eastern Europe, serve to underline the importance, as in Romania, of the "Gorbachev factor" in the East European revolutions. For good brief accounts of developments in these countries since 1948, see Misha Glenny, *The Rebirth of History: Eastern Europe in the Age of Democracy* (London: Penguin Books, 1990), chapters 5 and 6; Keith Sword, ed., *The Times Guide to Eastern Europe: The Changing Face of the Warsaw Pact* (London: Times Books, 1990), chapters 1 and 8; Joseph Rothschild, *Return to Diversity: A Political History of East Central Europe Since World II* (New York: Oxford University Press, 1989), passim; J. F. Brown, *Surge to Freedom: The End of Communist Rule in Eastern Europe* (Twickenham, U.K.: Adamantine Press, 1991), 221–45. Bulgaria was another Balkan country where the communist regime ruled without the need to invoke the help of Soviet troops. This was not because of its independence of Moscow, but for the opposite reason: its great loyalty to Moscow and the historic attachment of the Bulgarian people to Russia as their liberator from the Ottoman yoke.

47. On Romanian developments, see Glenny, *The Rebirth of History,* chapter 4; *The Times Guide to Eastern Europe,* chapter 7; Brown, *Surge to Freedom,* 199–220.

48. On the coup plot, see the report from the Romanian newspaper *Adevarul* in *The*

*Independent* (August 24, 1990). The details are based on an interview with two prominent National Salvation Front members, Silviu Brucan and Nicolae Militarau (the latter the former defense minister), both of whom had been involved in the plot as former members of the Politburo of the Romanian Communist Party. See also Mark Frankland, *Patriots' Revolution: Reports on the Liberation of Eastern Europe* (London: Sinclair Stevenson, 1990), 311.

49. The couplike character of the "Romanian Revolution" became clearer day by day, as the ruling National Salvation Front increasingly revealed itself as the victorious faction in a struggle for power within the former Romanian Communist Party of Nicolae Ceausescu. The leading members of the National Salvation Front—Ion Iliescu, Dumitru Mazilu, Roman Petre, Silviu Brucan—had all been former high-ranking officials of the party who at one time or another had quarreled with Ceausescu. According to Jonathan Eyal, "They all belonged to a ruling elite, a caste which sought redemption simply by eliminating a wayward member [Ceausescu] from its midst. . . . Romania's revolution therefore represented a paradox from the beginning: the first successful and seemingly complete overthrow of a Communist regime, produced leaders devoted to the resuscitation of Communism as an ideal and principle of government." Jonathan Eyal, "Why Romania Could Not Avoid Bloodshed," in Prins, ed., *Spring in Winter,* 158.

Eyal did not fully accept that the revolution was simply "hijacked by a team of Communists," with one unrepresentative clique replacing another—"as most Romanians fear." But that view has been forcibly put forth in two very good "docuthrillers" on British television: Peter Flannery's *Shoot the Revolution,* broadcast on BBC 2 December 16, 1990, and Robert Dornhelm's *Requiem for Dominic,* broadcast on channel 4 December 26, 1990. Both of these plays, based on real-life interviews, suggest that Iliescu, Roman, and company were pro-Gorbachev reformers opposed to Ceausescu who were encouraged by Moscow to depose Ceausescu. The National Salvation Front was constituted by "the men who had come back from Moscow": Iliescu and the others had indeed just returned from a trip to Moscow at the time of the Timisoara rising. This suggests a degree of complicity in the rising, and an exploitation of it for their own ends, that is still murky in its details.

Even the idea of a simple opposition between the army and the Securitate is questionable. General Vlad, the head of the Securitate, was one of the leaders of the war council that organized the resistance to the Securitate's "counter-revolution"; and there is a strong suggestion that a deal was struck between the National Salvation Front and the Securitate to protect Securitate officers after the revolution. Certainly former Securitate members, along with many other former communist officials, have so far been left remarkably untouched since the revolution.

50. The evidence of direct Soviet involvement (indirect is self-evident) in the deposition of East European leaders is not clear or complete, but overall appears pretty conclusive. **East Germany:** Andrei Piontkowsky has written: "It is known now from various sources that the Soviet military advisers in Berlin were instructed to dissuade Honecker on 9 October, 1989 from using force against the 50,000 demonstrators in Leipzig that day; in fact they took Krenz's position when Honecker wished to authorise the use of live ammunition against the demonstrators. Some sources believe that they were even ordered to prevent by intervention a repetition of the Tiananmen Square massacre in East Germany." Piontkowsky, "The Russian Sphinx," 169–70; see also Jens Reich: "We escaped a Romanian or a Chinese solution by the skin of our teeth." Jens Reich, "Reflections on Becoming an East German Dissident," in Prins, ed., *Spring in Winter,* 81, 88.

Timothy Garton Ash observed that "the 'Gorbachev effect' was strongest in East Germany because it was more strongly oriented towards—and ultimately dependent on—the Soviet Union than any other East European state. . . . For several years East Germans had been turning the name of Gorbachev, and the Soviet example, against their rulers. And Gorbachev personally gave the last push—on his visit to join the fortieth-anniversary celebrations of the G.D.R. on 7 October—with his carefully calculated utterance that 'Life itself punishes those who delay,' the leaked news that he had told Honecker Soviet troops would not be used for internal repression and . . . his direct encouragement to the likes of Egon Krenz and the Berlin Party chief Gunter Schabowski, to move to depose Honecker." Garton Ash, *We the People,* 65–66; see also Mary Kaldor, "After the Cold War," *New Left Review* 180 (March/April 1990): 27; Brown, *Surge to Freedom,* 140–47.

**Czechoslovakia:** The Hulik Commission, set up by the new Czech government, has provided important new evidence of what happened on the crucial night of November 17, 1989, when student demonstrators in Prague were set upon and badly beaten by police: the event that sparked off widespread popular disturbances and led to the downfall of the Husak regime. According to Gwyn Prins, "The Hulik Commission suggests that the course of events on November 17 was carefully planned and orchestrated jointly by General Lorenz, Head of the StB [*Statni Bezpecnost,* the state security police], in collaboration with the K.G.B. Their plan was to create the violence in which the marchers were beaten in Narodni Street. To this end, *agents provocateurs* who were actually StB officers but posing as student leaders led the demonstrators into the confined space where the beatings took place. One of the StB officers then impersonated a mathematics student, Martin Smid, and a further conspirator, Dragomira Drazska, carried the news of Smid's supposed death at the hands of the security forces to dissident sources. . . . The primary purpose was to cause the overthrow of the Jakes and Husak regime as a result of popular fury and to open the way for the installation of a moderate reformist communist, Zdenek Mlynar, as president in place of Husak. If this was the intention, it certainly bears marked similarity to the substitution of Krenz for Honecker in the D.D.R. [A] BBC report on Mlynar asserts that he went to Moscow where Mr. Gorbachev, with whom he had been a student and friend in the 1950s, failed to persuade him to take office. The conspiracy failed firstly because Mlynar did not wish to take on the role and second because the popular revolution developed its own momentum and found its own authentic presidential candidate in Václav Havel." Editorial note by Gwyn Prins to Jan Urban, "Czechoslovakia: The Power and Politics of Humiliation," in Prins, ed., *Spring in Winter,* 116–17; see also Edward Lucas, in The *Independent* (May 15, 1990); Sword, ed., *The Times Guide to Eastern Europe,* 63–69. The radicalness of Gorbachev's gamble is indicated by the fact that Mlynar was a prominent signatory of Charter 77.

On the more general issue of Soviet support of the Czech opposition, Timothy Garton Ash, in a piece written before the final toppling of Communist Party rule, said: "Behind everything there was the benign presence of Gorbachev's Soviet Union: the Soviet embassy in Prague receiving a [Civic] Forum delegation with ostentatious courtesy, Gorbachev himself giving marching orders to Party leader Urbanek and Prime Minister Adamec during the Warsaw Pact post-Malta briefing in Moscow, the renunciation of the 1968 invasion. Others will have to assess how far (and how) Gorbachev deliberately pushed the changes in Czechoslovakia. . . . Yet of course in a larger historical frame the Soviet attitude was fundamental." Garton Ash, *We the People,* 92–93; see also 122.

**Hungary:** As early as 1987, at the annual celebration of the October Revolution in Moscow, the Kremlin had made clear its declining support for Janos Kadar. A defiant speech by Kadar in March 1988, denying that there was any crisis in Hungary, further alienated the Soviet leadership. At the special conference of the Hungarian Socialist Workers' Party in May 1988, the Soviet Union gave its blessing to the removal of Kadar and his replacement by Karoly Grosz. During a visit to Hungary in November 1988 the Soviet

Politburo reformer Alexander Yakovlev went further. He told his hosts that the Kremlin had no objections to the Communist Party's abandoning its monopoly in Hungary. In March 1989 Grosz visited Moscow, and on his return he reported that Gorbachev had pledged not to intervene in Hungary's reform process. Nor had Gorbachev objected to the report of the Historical Commission of the Hungarian Socialist Workers' Party, publicized for tactical reasons by the radical reformer Imre Pozsgay in January 1989, that the events of 1956 were not, as the Kadarists had always insisted, a "counter-revolution," but rather a genuine "popular uprising."

In April 1989 Soviet troops began a phased withdrawal (already announced in January 1989) from Hungary. On June 16, 1989, the body of Imre Nagy, the executed leader of the 1956 government, was exhumed and formally reinterred in Heroes' Square in Budapest. All Warsaw Pact leaders (except Romania) sent delegations to the ceremony, thereby symbolically giving their acquiescence and approval to Hungary's bloodless revolution. On July 7, 1989, the same day on which Kadar's death was announced, Nagy was officially rehabilitated by the Hungarian Supreme Court, and in October 1989, on the anniversary of the 1956 uprising, Hungary was declared to be no longer a "people's republic," but simply a republic. The same month the Hungarian Socialist Workers' Party renamed itself the Hungarian Socialist Party and committed itself to a "social market" economy. Also in October, the Hungarian parliament adopted a transitional constitution legalizing a multiparty system and announced forthcoming elections. Elections to the National Assembly were held in March 1990. For this account see "Hungary: From Kadarism to Democracy," in Sword, ed., *The Times Guide to Eastern Europe,* 104–07; Sarah Humphrey, "A Comparative Chronology of Revolution, 1988–1990," in Prins, ed., *Spring in Winter,* 211–41; Garton Ash, *We the People,* 47–60; R. N. Berki, "The Monster Dies in Bed: Some Aspects of the Disintegration of Hungarian Communism in the Late 1980s," paper presented to the Sofia symposium "Building the One Europe," November 24–27, 1990; Nigel Swain, "Hungary's Socialist Project in Crisis," *New Left Review* 176 (July/August 1989): 3–29; Brown, *Surge to Freedom,* 99–123.
**Poland:** As Richard Sakwa wrote: "In Poland, more than in any other country, it was Gorbachev's reforms which provided the key to unlock the door to escape from the tragic cycles of history since 1945. By removing the excuse for the prevarications of the [Polish] leadership, who claimed that 'geopolitical realities' limited their freedom of action, the possibility of genuine change appeared." Sakwa, *Gorbachev,* 37. Sakwa also pointed to the significant influence on all East European countries, Poland especially, of the March 1989 elections—"the first semi-free elections in some seventy years"—for the new Congress of People's Deputies in the Soviet Union. "The Soviet leadership appeared willing to tolerate defeat and diversity, and thus encouraged East European countries to be bolder in dismantling Soviet-type socialism." Ibid., 140.

Poland's own first "semifree" elections were held only two months later, in June 1989, resulting in the annihilation of the Communist Party in all contested seats (Solidarity candidates won 99 percent of the contested seats). Janusz Ziolkowski noted how remarkable it was that not only the Polish Communist Party, but the Russian leadership, accepted the verdict: "And that was most important. It seems that at that moment, for practical reasons, Gorbachev wrote off Eastern Europe." Ziolkowski, "The Roots, Branches and Blossoms of Solidarnosc," 60. Timothy Garton Ash, present in Poland during the June elections, recorded the fear that greeted the news of the Tiananmen Square massacre, the report of which came through on the day that the election results were announced: "The tanks. The tear-gas. Corpses carried shoulder high. We had been here before; in Gdansk, in Warsaw." The *absence* of a Soviet response to the victory of Solidarity was a source of anxiety, but also of relief. Ash, *We the People,* 32.

When in August 1989 General Jaruzelski invited a leading Solidarity member, Tadeusz

Mazowiecki, to become the first noncommunist prime minister in Eastern Europe for over forty years, there was again great anxiety on the score of Moscow's attitude. This anxiety was allayed by a "crucial" telephone conversation between Gorbachev and the Polish United Workers' Party's new leader, Mieczyslaw Rakowski, on August 22. Garton Ash, *We the People,* 41. Even more crucially, Gorbachev rejected the call from the Romanian leader Ceausescu, at the Warsaw Pact meeting in Bucharest in July 1989, to intervene against the Solidarity government. It is clear, in fact, that throughout the critical months of 1988 and 1989, and especially during the Round Table talks between Solidarity and the Polish authorities from February to April 1989, General Jaruzelski kept himself fully informed as to the attitude of Moscow toward Polish developments. See "Poland: A Step-by-Step Revolution," in Sword, ed., *The Times Guide to Eastern Europe,* 117–19; see also the contributions to George Sanford, ed., *Democratisation in Poland, 1988–1990* (London: Macmillan, 1991); Brown, *Surge to Freedom,* 81–98.

*Bulgaria*: As Keith Sword wrote: "The collapse of the old regime in Bulgaria . . . was the result of a palace coup, not a popular revolution." Sword, ed., *The Times Guide to Eastern Europe,* 46. Leading the palace coup of November 10, 1989, was an anti-Zhivkov cabal within the Bulgarian Communist Party headed by the foreign minister, Petar Mladenov. The plotters not only secured the support of the military for deposing Todor Zhivkov, the long-serving communist leader; they were also assured of the support of the Soviet Union. The Soviet Union had been particularly concerned at Zhivkov's handling of the sensitive question of the Turkish minority in Bulgaria. The attempt to force assimilation on the Turks was accelerated in the summer of 1989. It led to widespread rioting and the killing of dozens of Turks by the Bulgarian police. The affair led Mladenov and his supporters to act. According to Misha Glenny, Mladenov "was very careful to include the Soviet leadership in his plans. On his return from a visit to China in November 1989 he stopped off in Moscow for a final briefing on the forthcoming denouement of the Bulgarian leadership crisis. He appears to have been given the final go-ahead, and Zhivkov's fate was sealed." Glenny, *The Rebirth of History,* 172. On the significance of "the prompting of Moscow" in the overthrow of Zhivkov, see also Jeri Laber, "The Bulgarian Difference," *The New York Review of Books* (May 17, 1990), 34; Brown, *Surge to Freedom,* 182–97.

*Romania*: On the role of "the men who had come back from Moscow," see note 49 to this chapter. There is certainly no doubt that Moscow had long wished for the removal of Ceausescu; Soviet antagonism toward his policies was made clear at the Warsaw Pact meeting in Bucharest in July 1989. No clearer signal could have been given to his enemies. Generally the "Gorbachev effect" is mentioned in most accounts of the 1989 revolutions, but usually as simply one in a "shopping list" of causes. For a more considered view, see Zvi Gitelman, "The Roots of Eastern Europe's Revolution," *Problems of Communism* 39 (May–June 1990): 89–94; R. J. Crampton, *The Revolutions of 1989 in Eastern Europe* (Coleraine, Ireland: University of Ulster, 1990), 6–9. Cf. Fred Halliday: "Gorbachev's change of policy was the indispensable precondition for the changes [in Eastern Europe] to occur." Fred Halliday, "The Ends of Cold War?" 19. Cf. also Mary Kaldor: "Gorbachev was the trigger for the revolutions of 1989. He signalled his unwillingness to underwrite the old regimes." Mary Kaldor, "After the Cold War," 27.

Some valuable material on Soviet involvement in the East European revolutions was presented in two documentaries broadcast on British television: *And The Walls Came Tumbling Down,* transmitted on channel 4 on November 5 and 12, 1990. On this see also Timothy Garton Ash, "Gorbachev's Gamble," *The Independent* (November 8, 1990). Garton Ash suggests that not even the "unanticipated consequence" of German reunification was necessarily unpalatable to Gorbachev: it might have made it easier for Germany to invest in the Soviet Union.

One more point. Even if the "Gorbachev factor" is discounted, for purposes of argument, the extent to which the 1989 revolutions remained an affair of competing elites rather than of mass popular risings is still remarkable. This has always been clear in the cases of Hungary and Bulgaria, and is increasingly clear in the case of Romania. Solidarity was certainly a mass movement in Poland, but even there the role of General Jaruzelski in negotiating an orderly handover of power has been admitted by all to have been critical. It was "pivotal," says Timothy Garton Ash, in *The Uses of Adversity: Essays on the Fate of Central Europe* (Cambridge: Granta Books/Penguin, 1989), 283–84; see also Adam Michnik, "The Two Faces of Europe," *New York Review of Books* (July 19, 1990), 7. In East Germany, such high-ranking party officials as Egon Krenz, Hans Modrow, and Gunter Schabowski were instrumental in forcing Honecker's hand. It was above all Czechoslovakia that lent the 1989 revolutions the air of a "people's revolution." But, as we have seen, elements of the Czech elite had already been set against each other by Gorbachev; their struggles usefully fueled popular protest.

51. Sakwa, *Gorbachev*, 326, 341.

52. This is what vitiates the many writers who seemed to think that they could simply slap Crane Brinton's classic account of revolution, drawn mainly from the 1789 French Revolution, more or less directly onto the events of 1989. The categories of Brinton's *Anatomy of Revolution*, revised edition (New York: Vintage Books, 1965)—financial bankruptcy, desertion of the intellectuals, growing popular disaffection, loss of nerve on the part of rulers—are easily imposed on the revolution of 1989, but they tell only half of the story, and perhaps not the most important half. For an example of this procedure (though Brinton is not mentioned), see George Schöpflin, "The End of Communism in Eastern Europe," *International Affairs* 66 (1990): 3–16. A more sophisticated approach, also stressing internal factors, is Grzegorz Ekiert, "Democratization Processes in East-Central Europe: A Theoretical Reconsideration," *British Journal of Political Science* 21 (1991): 285–313. It is evident that theoretical approaches to revolution that emphasize the international context are likelier to come closer to the perspective offered in this chapter. See, for example, Theda Skocpol, *States and Social Revolutions* (Cambridge: Cambridge University Press, 1979); Immanuel Wallerstein, "The French Revolution as a World-Historical Event," *Social Research* 56, no. 1 (1989): 33–52.

53. See Vernon Snow, "The Concept of Revolution in Seventeenth-Century England," *The Historical Journal* 5, no. 2 (1962): 167–90.

54. See Garton Ash, *We the People*, 134ff.; Hugh Trevor-Roper, "Europe's New Order," *The Independent Magazine* (December 30, 1989); Michael Howard, "Impressions from a Journey in Central Europe," *London Review of Books* (October 25, 1990), 3; Ziolkowski, "The Roots, Branches and Blossoms of Solidarnosc," 41–42. Most of these writers, referring to 1848, also turned to Alexis de Tocqueville for their understanding of the 1989 revolutions: the Tocqueville who, writing of 1789 and 1848, stressed the role of reforming monarchs in the causation of revolution, and the subversive effects of "new ideas" among the ruling elites. For the relevance of Tocqueville to the revolutions of Central Europe for the whole period since 1956, see Bronislaw Geremek, "Between Hope and Despair," *Daedalus* (winter 1990): 99. The typical response of the 1989 activists also echoes that of the activists of 1848: "We were surprised just how rotten the regime was. We just gave it a push and it crumbled." Czech dissident in BBC 2 television documentary *Absurdistan*, transmitted May 11, 1990. Cf. Teodor Shanin: "In Eastern Europe the communist regimes of 'actual existing socialism' dissolved and fell apart as a fruit rotten to the core falls off the tree." Teodor Shanin, "The Question of Socialism: A Development Failure or an Ethical Defect?" *History Workshop Journal* 30 (autumn 1990): 72.

55. For more on the revolution of 1848, see Sir Lewis Namier, *1848: The Revolution of the Intellectuals* (London: Oxford University Press, 1946); for more on the revolution

of 1989, see Timothy Garton Ash: "The politics of the revolution were not made by workers or peasants. They were made by intellectuals: the playwright Václav Havel, the medievalist Bronislaw Geremek, the Catholic editor Tadeusz Mazowiecki, the painter Barbel Bohley in Berlin, the conductor Kurt Masur in Leipzig, the philosophers Janos Kis and Gaspar Miklos Tamas in Budapest, the engineering professor Petre Roman and the poet Mircea Dinescu in Bucharest. History has outdone Shelley, for poets were the acknowledged legislators of this world." Garton Ash, *We the People,* 136. The Solidarity movement in Poland was led by an electrician and trade unionist, Lech Walesa, who was almost defiantly a nonintellectual, but until recently he surrounded himself with intellectuals such as Michnik, Geremek, and Mazowiecki.

56. The scale can be further indicated by the addition of the following other "minorities" (often majorities in their particular regions): Slovaks in Czechoslovakia, Romanians in Soviet Moldavia, Germans in Poland, Poles in Russia, Turks in Bulgaria, Albanians in Yugoslavia (Kosovo), Macedonians in Yugoslavia, Bulgaria, and Greece. The difficulties were probably greatest in Yugoslavia, where ethnic rivalries have been so entrenched and so intransigent as constantly to threaten the unity of the state. For some useful discussions and data, see P. F. Sugar, ed., *Ethnic Diversity and Conflict in Eastern Europe* (Santa Barbara, Calif.: ABC-Clio, 1980); Sword, ed., *The Times Guide to Eastern Europe,* appendix 8, "Nations and Languages of Eastern Europe"; Neil Ascherson, "Old Conflicts in New Europe," *The Independent on Sunday* (February 18, 1990); Glenny, *Rebirth of History*; Slavoj Žižek, "Eastern Europe's Republics of Gilead," *New Left Review* 183 (September/October 1990): 50–62; Paul Lendvai, "Eastern Europe: liberalism vs. nationalism," *The World Today* 46, no. 7 (July 1990): 130–33; Ernest Gellner, "Nationalism and Politics in Eastern Europe," *New Left Review* 189 (September/October 1991): 127–34.

57. Which it duly did in December 1991, when the Soviet Union, accepting the *fait accompli* of breakaway republics, dissolved itself and proclaimed in its place a "Commonwealth of Independent States." On the ethnic problem in the former Soviet Union, see P. Goble, "Ethnic Politics in the USSR," *Problems of Communism* 38 (July–August 1989): 1–14; G. Smith, ed., *The Nationalities Question in the Soviet Union* (London: Longman, 1991); Ernest Gellner, "Ethnicity and Faith in Eastern Europe" *Daedalus* (winter 1990): 279–94; Ronald Suny, "The Revenge of the Past: Socialism and Ethnic Conflict in Transcaucasia," *New Left Review* 184 (November/December 1990): 5–34; Suny, "Incomplete Revolution," note 45; Sakwa, *Gorbachev,* 231–67; Viktor Kozlov, *The Peoples of the Soviet Union* (London: I. B. Tauris, 1988).

58. The split in Solidarity between Walesa, speaking for the workers, and his erstwhile middle-class allies, such as Adam Michnik and Tadeusz Mazowiecki, symbolized the growing social divide in the region. So also did the conflict between miners and students in Bucharest. As in 1848, the conflict between liberalism and populism threatened to undo the constitutional achievements of the early stages of the revolution. For some interesting reflections on this, see Andrzej Walicki, "From Stalinism to Post-Communist Pluralism: The Case of Poland," *New Left Review* 185 (January/February 1991): 93–121.

59. Karl Marx, "The June Revolution" (1848), in S. K. Padover, ed. and trans., *Karl Marx: On Revolution* (New York: McGraw-Hill, 1971), 148.

60. *The Independent* (November 20, 1990).

61. Juan Linz has suggested that the remarkable speed with which East European societies moved to democracy can be explained "as a result of the successful examples in transition to democracy in Southern Europe and Latin America. This process was very visible and to some extent forged the techniques that could be implemented elsewhere. Linz, "Post-Communist Eastern Europe: A Survey of Opinion," 158.

62. Dahrendorf, *Reflections*, 74. A similar point was made by "Z" in "To the Stalin Mausoleum," 34. And cf. Václav Havel's account of the fundamental difference between the communist states and traditional dictatorships in Václav Havel, "The Power of the Powerless" (1978), in Vladislav, ed., *Living in Truth*, 37–41. See also Ekiert, "Democratization Processes in East Central Europe," 310–11, and note 66 to this chapter.

63. Dahrendorf, *Reflections*, 93; Garton Ash, *We the People*, 147–48. Timothy Garton Ash says elsewhere that "one could write the history of East Central Europe over the last decade as the story of struggles for civil society." Garton Ash, *The Uses of Adversity*, 174. Cf. Jan Gross: "The notion of civil society introduced by dissidents in East Central Europe in the seventies was for real. The process of emancipation of East Central Europe from Soviet imperial domination (unlike the movements of *national* liberation in the fifties and sixties) is about empowering society. The assertion of national identity is less of a problem than the enfranchisement of people into the body politic—the key term of this revolution is *citizen*, not Pole, Hungarian, or Czech." Jan Gross, "Post-Communist Eastern Europe: A Survey of Opinion," 176; and see also Piontkowsky, "The Russian Sphinx," 166.

64. On civil society, East and West, see chapter 5 of this book. For East Europeans, the idea of civil society was fundamentally one of social groups capable of self-organization independent of the state. To that extent, civil society was pitted against the state: the state seen as the totalitarian enemy. For an influential statement of this position, based on the example of Solidarity, see Adam Michnik, "A New Evolutionism," in Adam Michnik, *Letters from Prison and Other Essays*, translated by Matya Latynski (Berkeley: University of California Press, 1985), 135–48; see also Adam Michnik, "Towards a Civil Society: Hopes for Polish Democracy," *Times Literary Supplement* (February 19–25, 1988), 188, 198–99. For East European views of civil society in general, see the contributions to part 3 of John Keane, ed., *Civil Society and the State: New European Perspectives* (London: Verso, 1988); Garton Ash, *The Uses of Adversity*, 244–47; György Konrád, *Antipolitics: An Essay*, translated by Richard E. Ellen (London: Quartet Books, 1984), 133–48, 166–207; Vladislav, ed., *Living in Truth*; A. Arato, "Civil Society against the State: Poland 1980–81," *Telos* 47 (1981): 23–47.

65. See, for example, William Kornhauser, *The Politics of Mass Society* (London: Routledge and Kegan Paul, 1960)—though of course he did not use the term *civil society* any more than did anyone else at that time.

66. Václav Havel, "Letter to Gustav Husak" (1975), in Vladislav, ed., *Living in Truth*, 4–14. *Post-totalitarian* refers to societies that are "totalitarian in a way fundamentally different from classical dictatorships, different from totalitarianism as we usually understand it." Václav Havel, "The Power of the Powerless," in Vladislav, ed., *Living in Truth*, 40–41. For a defense of the idea that totalitarianism in this sense is the key to Soviet-type societies, see "Z," "To the Stalin Mausoleum," 298–301. For a discussion of the concept of totalitarianism in East European social and political thought, see Jacques Rupnik, "Totalitarianism Revisited," in Keane, ed., *Civil Society and the State*, 263–89. Rupnik emphasized the Orwellian understanding of totalitarianism in Eastern Europe, especially after 1968: living the lie, the corruption of language, the destruction of memory, and so on. This affects not just thought, but action: "The chief characteristic of totalitarianism is the ongoing capacity to limit all scope for independent action in every possible sphere of social activity." Ibid., 272. This indicates the difficulties of developing the practices of civil society once the principal restraints are removed. For a good example, see R. N. Berki on the depoliticization of Hungarian society under Kadarism and the problems this poses for postcommunist politics: "One must conclude that the greatest damage done to Hungary during the long ascendancy of the HSWP [Hungarian Socialist

Workers' Party] was not the well-nigh total discrediting of socialist values and ideas but the . . . disillusionment with public life as such, and without faith in and concern with public affairs political freedom and a democratic system are scarcely sustainable." Berki, "The Monster Dies in Bed," 31.

Finally, we should remember that the problem of the absence of a genuine civil society in Eastern Europe is a long-standing one. For instance, speaking of the modernizing efforts in these countries in the eighteenth and nineteenth centuries, George Schöpflin commented: "From the outset the East European modernizers were involved in a contradiction, that of having to construct civil society from above." George Schöpflin, "The Political Traditions of Eastern Europe," *Daedalus* (winter 1990): 64. The long-term legacy of the failure in Eastern and East Central Europe—unlike in the West—to constitute a sense and a sphere of "society" separate from the "state" is also powerfully brought out in Jenö Szücs, "Three Historical Regions of Europe: An Outline," in Keane, ed., *Civil Society and the State,* 291–332. East European socialism confirmed this historical legacy: "The sad fact is that socialism has created in the East European states an array of *domestic* barriers against the transformation to liberal-democracy-cum mixed economy quite as formidable as those that existed in recent West or South European dictatorships. . . . These barriers lie not only in the system of politbureaucratic dictatorship . . . , and not merely in the character and interests of the *nomenklatura* ruling class, but also in the interests, attitudes, and fears of many of the ruled." Garton Ash, *The Uses of Adversity,* 269.

67. On the "seminal" importance of the example of Solidarity, see Garton Ash, *We the People,* 134, and also Timothy Garton Ash, *The Polish Revolution: Solidarity* (London: Jonathan Cape, 1983); see also Konrád, *Antipolitics,* 136–45; Geremek, "Between Hope and Despair," 105. Z. A. Pelczynski pointed out that in 1980–81 Solidarity attempted to go beyond the "evolutionism" mapped out by Michnik, and that its attempt to force the pace brought on martial law. This argument is sustainable despite Solidarity's later success in 1989. See "Solidarity and 'The Rebirth of Civil Society' in Poland," in Keane, ed., *Civil Society and the State,* 369–78. For Michnik's views during 1980–81, see *Letters from Prison,* 103–31. See also the stimulating discussion in Jadwiga Staniszkis, *Poland's Self-Limiting Revolution* (Princeton: Princeton University Press, 1984); Jadwiga Staniszkis, "The Obsolescence of Solidarity," *Telos* 80 (1989): 37–51.

68. See "More Velvet than Steel: An Interview with Václav Havel," *The Guardian* (December 21, 1990). The formal split duly came on February 8, 1991, when it was announced that henceforward the Civic Forum would divide into two political parties, a right-wing party led by Václav Klaus and a liberal party led by Pavel Rychetsky, the deputy prime minister. See *The Independent* (February 9, 1991). Solidarity, too, fragmented irretrievably, with the election of Lech Walesa as president of Poland in January 1991, after a bitterly contested election in which he resoundingly defeated former Prime Minister Tadeusz Mazowiecki. For the elections in Hungary and East Germany, see Glenny, *Rebirth of History,* 74–85; Sword, ed., *The Times Guide to Eastern Europe,* 90.

69. See Norbert Elias, *The Civilizing Process,* 2 volumes, translated by Edmund Jephcott (New York: Pantheon Books, 1982); T. H. Marshall, "Citizenship and Social Class," in Marshall's *Sociology at the Crossroads* (London: Heinemann, 1963), 67–127.

70. Dahrendorf, *Reflections,* 97; and, for a similar view of the uniqueness of the American experience, see Daniel Bell, "'American Exceptionalism' Revisited: The Role of Civil Society," *The Public Interest* 95 (1989): 38–56.

71. Konrád, *Antipolitics,* 202, 227, 229, 231.

72. Ibid., 224; and on the two spheres generally, 216–33.

73. For these quotations, see Havel, *Living in Truth*, 55–62, 155–56.

74. Havel, *Living in Truth*, 70–71. Elsewhere he says: "Above all, any existential revolution should provide hope of a moral reconstitution of society, which means a radical renewal of the relationship of human beings to what I have called the 'human order,' which no political order can replace. A new experience of being, a renewed rootedness in the universe, a newly grasped sense of 'higher responsibility,' a new-found inner relationship to other people and to the human community—these factors clearly indicate the direction in which we must go." Ibid., 117–18. For a good general discussion of the antipolitical philosophy of Central Europe, see Timothy Garton Ash, "Does Central Europe Exist?" in Garton Ash, *The Uses of Adversity*, 161–91; Tony Judt, "The Dilemmas of Dissidence: The Politics of Opposition in East-Central Europe," *Eastern European Politics and Societies* 2, no. 2 (1988): 191–99, 236–38. Judt noted the "anti-Enlightenment" aspect of Havel's philosophy, as did Aviezer Tucker in tracing the roots of Havel's thinking to the Czech philosopher Jan Patocka and to Martin Heidegger, Patocka's contemporary at Freiburg. Tucker also remarked on the affinities between Havel and Solzhenitsyn. See Aviezer Tucker, "Václav Havel's Heideggerianism," *Telos* 85 (1990): 63–78. See further Tony Judt, "To Live in Truth: Václav Havel and the Privatizing of the Intellectuals," *Times Literary Supplement* (October 11, 1991), 3–5.

75. See, for example, Václav Havel, *Disturbing the Peace*, translated by Paul Wilson (London: Faber, 1990). See also Havel's "New Year's Day Presidential Address to the Czechoslovak Nation," reprinted in *Newsweek* (January 15, 1990), 42.

76. The relatively low turnout in several of the elections of 1989–90—the first more or less free elections in Eastern Europe for over forty years—was simply one indication of the difficulties that lay ahead. See the special issue of *Electoral Studies*, "Elections in Eastern Europe," *Electoral Studies* 9, no. 4 (December 1990).

77. Glenny, *The Rebirth of History*, 80.

78. Havel is quoted in *The Independent* (November 6, 1990).

79. See, for example, Jens Reich, "Reflections on Becoming an East German Dissident," in Prins, ed., *Spring in Winter*, 97. Timothy Garton Ash also recorded the disappointment of the activists who led the October revolution in East Germany: "For their starting-point had always been that they did not want reunification. Rather, they wanted to work for a better, a genuinely democratic German Democratic Republic. They did not regard the Federal Republic as the best of all possible Germanies. They thought there were some achievements and values in the G.D.R. worth preserving: less inequality and exploitation than in West Germany, a greater human solidarity, a more caring attitude, elements of something they still wished to call 'socialism.'" Garton Ash, *We the People*, 73. And cf. George Schöpflin's observation that "a certain kind of collectivism or corporatism appears to be a near-ineradicable component of the reigning political ethos in Eastern Europe." Schöpflin, "The Political Traditions of Eastern Europe," 88.

80. Glenny, *The Rebirth of History*, 84. As Glenny wrote: "Has social democracy collapsed in Eastern Europe? On the contrary. . . . Socialism—or, more properly, social democracy—is the ideology that dares not speak its name in Eastern Europe, although across the region it is probably still the most influential." Ibid., 200. And cf. Edward Thompson: "How can we know yet how political consciousness may be changing 'on the other side,' and what struggles over priorities, basic defences of the rights to work, housing and health, the allocation of resources, the social control of public wealth, will ensue when working people over there really come to understand what 'free' market forces mean? . . . Why should we prejudge the play's last act when the first act is not yet concluded?" Edward Thompson, "The Ends of Cold War," *New Left Review* 182 (July/August 1990): 145. On the felt need for social democratic representation in Central

Europe, as illustrated particularly by the high level of nonvoting in the Hungarian elections, see Ivan and Szonja Szelenyi, "The Vacuum in Hungarian Politics: Classes and Parties," *New Left Review* 187 (May/June 1991): 121–37. See also Peter Bihari, "From Where to Where? Reflections on Hungary's Social Revolution," in Ralph Miliband and Leo Panitch, eds., *Socialist Register 1991* (London: The Merlin Press, 1991), 279–301.

81. John Kenneth Galbraith, "Revolt in Our Time: The Triumph of Simplistic Ideology," in Prins, ed., *Spring in Winter*, 7. Cf. Mary Kaldor: "What has won? Liberal values have certainly won. But has capitalism won? In what sense can the West be described as 'capitalist'? In Western countries, including the United States, government spending averages 40 percent of Gross Domestic Product [and, in the more successful economies of Japan and Germany, as compared with the United States or Britain,] much greater emphasis is placed on education, social services, public investment, local planning, worker participation, and so on. . . . Europe (and the world) took the wrong direction because of a commitment to capitalist orthodoxy." Mary Kaldor, "After the Cold War," *New Left Review* 180 (March/April 1990): 26, 36. Edward Thompson also said: "One does not have to be an 'expert' to know how bookish are some of the notions of 'market economies' held by dissidents (old-style) in their book-lined apartments in Prague, Budapest and Moscow: obsessively fixated by the profound pessimism of 1984 and notions of 'totalitarianism' (which have been refuted in part by their own actions), committed to laughably abstract prescriptions from Hayek, Milton Friedman or American neo-conservatives—prescriptions which have no serious relevance to Western capitalist realities, let alone to the as-yet-undiagnosed ailments of command economies in decomposition." Edward Thompson, "The Ends of Cold War," 144.

82. Garton Ash, *The Uses of Adversity*, 282. For the rejection of a "third way" by another prominent Hungarian intellectual, see Janos Kornai, *The Road to a Free Economy: Shifting from a Socialist System—The Example of Hungary* (New York: W. W. Norton, 1990). Ralf Dahrendorf also dismissed the idea of a "third way"as a "Central European utopia" that is as illusory and dangerous as all other utopias." Dahrendorf, *Reflections*, 53–57. And cf. "Z," "There is no third way between Leninism and the market, between bolshevism and constitutional government." "Z," "To the Stalin Mausoleum," 335.

83. Michnik was quoted in Gitelman, "The Roots of Eastern Europe's Revolution," 94. For a similar warning to the East Europeans, see Bogdan Denitch, "The Triumph of Capitalism?" *Dissent* (spring 1990), 177–80. And cf. Timothy Garton Ash: "One might almost say that the free market is the latest Central European utopia." Garton Ash, *We the People*, 152. On the East European intelligentsia's "obsession" with the free market economy, and the danger this poses to social stability, see Juan Linz and Marcin Krol, in "Post-Communist Eastern Europe: A Survey of Opinion," 180–81.

84. See the exchange between Edward Thompson and Fred Halliday, "The Ends of Cold War," *New Left Review* 182 (July/August 1990), 139–50. Thompson (like Kaldor) appealed to the influence of the European peace movement in the 1989 revolutions and proposed it as a possible alternative model, a "third way," for the East Europeans. Halliday commented on this: "Those who have propounded a third way, as in East Germany, have, quite simply, been swept aside by the combined pressures of their own populations and Western state and financial intervention." Ibid., 149–50. This seems right, although of course it did not rule out the possibility of a third way's being looked upon with more favor at some time in the future—possibly when the social consequences of the "free market" had become more apparent.

85. Fred Halliday, "The Ends of Cold War," *New Left Review* 180 (March/April 1990): 22. And cf. Jürgen Habermas: "The liberal interpretation [of the changes in Eastern Europe] is not wrong. It just does not see the beam also in its own eye." Habermas,

"What Does Socialism Mean Today?" 9. For some spirited restatements of the relevance of socialism today in both East and West and the dangers of the current capitalist triumphalism, see the essays in Miliband and Panitch, eds., *Socialist Register 1990* and *Socialist Register 1991*. See also Robin Blackburn, "Fin de Siècle Socialism after the Crash," *New Left Review* 185 (January/February 1991): 5–66.

86. See Bauman, *Socialism: The Active Utopia*, note 9; also Zygmunt Bauman, "From Pillars to Post," *Marxism Today* (February 1990), 20–25. A somewhat similar role for socialism was implied in Habermas's contention that the achievement of the West European left had been the "transforming [of] socialist ideas into the radically reformist self-criticism of a capitalist society, which, in the form of a constitutional democracy with universal suffrage and a welfare state, has developed not only weaknesses but also strengths. With the bankruptcy of state socialism, this is the eye of the needle through which everything must pass. This socialism will disappear only when it no longer has an object of criticism." Habermas, "What Does Socialism Mean Today?" 21.

87. See the final chapter of my *Utopianism* (Buckingham: Open University Press, 1991).

88. Garton Ash, *We the People*, 130 (though the reference here is specifically to Czechoslovakia as the most representative East European case). Cf. George Schöpflin: "The countries of the region had embarked on their own, often rather fitful roads to modernity. . . . These processes were cut short." Schöpflin, "The End of Communism in Eastern Europe," 4. And see especially Glenny, *The Rebirth of History*, 183–236. For further discussion, see chapter 7 of this book.

89. Quoted in Glenny, *The Rebirth of History*, 216. And see chapter 3 of this book.

90. Thompson, "The Ends of Cold War," 144.

## 3. The 1989 Revolutions and the Idea of Europe

1. See Sigmund Neumann, "The International Civil War," *World Politics* 1, no. 3 (1949): 333–50. See also Baruch Knei-Paz, "The National Revolution As an International Event," *Jerusalem Journal of International Relations* 3, no. 1 (1977): 1–27; Peter Calvert, *Revolution and International Politics* (London: Frances Pinter, 1984).

2. A brilliant early study of the international character of the Russian Revolution is Franz Borkenau, *World Communism: A History of The Communist International* (1939; reprint Ann Arbor: University of Michigan Press, 1962). See also Ernst Nolte, *Der Europaische Burgerkrieg 1917–1945: Nationalsozialismus und Bolschewismus* (Berlin: Propylaen Verlag, 1987). It might be added that the Iranian Revolution of 1979 has also intensified the international character of revolution, though in a wholly different way from the Russian Revolution.

3. For more on this, see chapter 2 of this book.

4. See Misha Glenny, *The Rebirth of History: Eastern Europe in the Age of Democracy* (London: Penguin Books, 1990).

5. Václav Havel, "Preface" to Gwyn Prins, ed., *Spring in Winter: The 1989 Revolutions* (Manchester: Manchester University Press, 1990).

6. On these features of the 1989 revolutions, see chapter 2 of this book.

7. Cf., for instance, Jacques Rupnik: "From Prague to Budapest, from Cracow to Zagreb, the rediscovery of Central Europe will remain one of the major intellectual and political developments of the 1980s, and will no doubt be a vital ingredient in the reshaping of the political map of Europe in the post-Yalta era." Jacques Rupnik, "Central Europe or Mitteleuropa?" *Daedalus* (winter 1990): 250.

8. For the mix of contradictory tendencies in the politics and culture of the Empire

in this period, see Allan Janik and Stephen Toulmin, *Wittgenstein's Vienna* (New York: Simon and Schuster, 1973); Carle E. Schorske, *Fin-de-Siècle Vienna: Politics and Culture* (New York: Alfred A. Knopf, 1980); Erich Heller, "Art at the End of Empire," *The American Scholar* 56, no. 1 (1987): 87–93. Heller quotes, as expressing the characteristic mood of the time, Kafka's remark, "There is an abundance of hope, but not for us." See also Czaba G. Kiss, "Central European Writers about Central Europe," in George Schöpflin and Nancy Wood, eds., *In Search of Central Europe* (Cambridge: Polity Press, 1989), 125–36. Several commentators on the Central European idea observe in the proponents of the idea an unwillingness to acknowledge that, as François Bondy put it, "if Kafka was a child of Central Europe, so too was Adolf Hitler." See Timothy Garton Ash, "Does Central Europe Exist?" in *The Uses of Adversity* (Cambridge: Granta Books/Penguin, 1989), 166. See also Egon Schwartz, "Central Europe—What It Is and What It Is Not," in Schöpflin and Wood, eds., *In Search of Central Europe*, 150–51.

The dark side of the Central European legacy, and the neglect or suppression of it by Milan Kundera and his followers, is stressed by Milan Simecka and debated by others in their responses to Kundera. See note 53 to this chapter. And cf. Tony Judt: "To suppose that this part of the Continent was once a near-paradise of cultural, ethnic, and linguistic multiplicity and compatibility, producing untold cultural and intellectual riches, has been part of the Western image in recent years. Yet such imaginings take us back to Kakania again, when in truth Central Europe, from the battle of the White Mountain down to the present, is a region of enduring ethnic and religious intolerance, marked by bitter quarrels, murderous wars, and frequent slaughter on a scale ranging from pogrom to genocide." Tony Judt, "The Rediscovery of Central Europe," *Daedalus* (winter 1990): 48.

9. Quoted in Rupnik, "Central Europe or Mitteleuropa?" 251.

10. Quoted in Janik and Toulmin, *Wittgenstein's Vienna*, 68. Franz Werfel's own life echoed this conception. He spent the first third of it in Prague, the second third in Vienna, and the last third as an emigrant, first in France, then in America—"a typically Central European biography," says Milan Kundera, in "The Tragedy of Central Europe," *New York Review of Books* (April 26, 1984), 36.

11. The following comment on Kakania gives the flavor of Musil's account: "By its constitution it was liberal, but its system of government was clerical. The system of government was clerical, but the general attitude to life was liberal. Before the law all citizens were equal, but not everyone, of course, was a citizen. There was a parliament, which made such vigorous use of its liberty that it was usually kept shut; but there was also an emergency powers act by means of which it was possible to manage without Parliament, and every time when everyone was just beginning to rejoice in absolutism, the Crown decreed that there must now again be a return to parliamentary government." Robert Musil, *The Man without Qualities*, translated from the German by Eithne Wilkins and Ernst Kaiser, 3 volumes, (London: Picador, 1979), vol. 1, 33.

12. "The Austrian Empire had the great opportunity of making Central Europe into a strong, unified state. But the Austrians, alas, were divided between an arrogant pan-German nationalism and their own Central European mission. They did not succeed in building a federation of equal nations, and their failure has been the misfortune of the whole of Europe. Dissatisfied, the other nations of Central Europe blew apart their empire in 1918, without realizing that, in spite of its inadequacies, it was irreplaceable." Milan Kundera, "The Tragedy of Central Europe," 34.

13. Rupnik, "Central Europe or Mitteleuropa?" 260. Rupnik quotes Ernest Gellner's observation that "Central Europe before the war resembled a painting by Kokoschka, made of subtle touches of different shades; after the war it was turned into a painting by

Modigliani, made of solid single-color patches." See also Istvan Deak's contribution to the symposium "Post-Communist Eastern Europe: A Survey of Opinion," *Eastern European Politics and Societies* 14, no. 2 (1990): 183. For similar policies of ethnic homogenization in the Soviet Union, see Ronald Suny, "The Revenge of the Past: Socialism and Ethnic Conflict in Transcaucasia," *New Left Review* 184 (November/December 1990): 5–34.

14. Tony Judt, "The Dilemmas of Dissidence: The Politics of Opposition in East-Central Europe," *Eastern European Politics and Societies* 2, no. 2 (1988): 213, 215–16. And cf. Hans Tütsch on the change in Austria itself: "No longer is Vienna the second most populous Czech city after Prague and the second biggest Magyar settlement after Budapest, as it was in the days of the Empire." Hans Tütsch, "Mitteleuropa II: From Nostalgia to Utopia," *The American Scholar* 56, no. 1 (1987): 95.

15. For a good brief account, see Melvin Croan, "Lands In-between: The Politics of Cultural Identity in Contemporary Eastern Europe," *Eastern European Politics and Societies* 3, no. 2 (1989): 176–87.

16. Franz Neumann, *Behemoth: The Structure and Practice of National Socialism 1933–1944* (1944; reprint New York: Harper and Row, 1966), 130–51. See also Henry Cord Meyer, *Mitteleuropa in German Thought and Action* (The Hague: Martinus Nijhoff, 1955); Jacques Droz, *L'Europe Centrale. Evolution historique de l'idée de "Mitteleuropa"* (Paris: Payot, 1960). It is worth pointing out that one basic difference between the old and the new concept of *Mitteleuropa* was that Neumann allowed a central (commercial) role for the Jews in the new Central European state.

17. Mackinder's concept of Central Europe is discussed by Neumann, *Behemoth*, 140–41. Mackinder formulated it as part of his famous "heartland" thesis. See Sir Halford Mackinder, "The Geographical Pivot of History," *Geographical Magazine* (April 1904), 434–37. A concept of Central Europe very similar to Mackinder's was formulated by the Hungarian Oszkar Jászi in the last years of the Austro-Hungarian monarchy. He, too, argued that the successor states to the empire would be too small and vulnerable, too riven by nationalist and ethnic conflicts, to stand up to the pressures from Germany and Russia. His solution, echoed by several other Central European thinkers, was a "United States of the Danube Region," a non-national, federative answer to the problems of the collapsing Habsburg Empire. On Jászi, see Ferenc Fehér, "On Making Central Europe," *Eastern European Politics and Societies* 3, no. 3 (1989): 421–22. The Alpen-Adria intergovernmental organization, which was founded in 1987, and which includes Bavaria, five Austrian provinces, the two most westerly districts of Hungary, the Yugoslav republics of Slovenia and Croatia, and four northerly and northeasterly districts of Italy, might be considered a faint echo of this conception. See *The Economist* (December 26, 1987), 51–52.

18. For Masaryk's conception of Central Europe, see Roman Szporluk, "Defining 'Central Europe': Power, Politics and Culture," *Cross Currents: A Yearbook of Central European Culture* 1 (1982): 30–32. Masaryk defined "East Central Europe," or what he also called "the New Europe" of the post-1918 settlement, as "the lands between the East and West, more particularly between the Germans and the Russians." The threat to the region had historically come from the "reactionary regimes" of Vienna, Berlin, and St. Petersburg.

There is a general tendency to forget about the eastern and southeasterly countries of Europe in discussions of Central and East Central Europe. Large parts of Romania (Transylvania) and Yugoslavia (Slovenia, Croatia) were important components of the old Austro-Hungarian Empire. On this see Predrag Matvejevic, "Central Europe Seen from the East of Europe," in Schöpflin and Wood, eds., *In Search of Central Europe*, 183–90. Timothy Garton Ash, conceding this, nevertheless argues for the central and, as it were, exemplary importance of Poland, Hungary, and Czechoslovakia in the present endeavors to find a political solution to the problems of postcommunist societies. See Timothy Garton Ash, "Eastern Europe: Après le Déluge, Nous," *New York Review of Books* (April 16, 1990), 54, 57.

19. See Ferenc Fehér, "Eastern Europe's Long Revolution against Yalta," *Eastern European Politics and Societies* 2, no. 1 (1988): 1–34. "Yalta," says Fehér, "created a geopolitical entity, 'Eastern Europe,' which as a polity or a community of destiny had never before existed." Ibid., 20. And cf. Tony Judt: "It is one of the enduring achievements of socialism that it has succeeded, in the course of little more than a generation, in placing Russia at the center of the agenda in East-Central Europe, where for so long the problem had been Germany." Judt, "The Dilemmas of Dissidence," 222. Cf. also Marcin Król: "The Central European utopia really has only one referent—the Soviet Union as a negative influence." Król, "Post-Communist Eastern Europe: A Survey of Opinion," 193.

20. See Agnes Heller, "The Great Republic," in Ferenc Fehér and Agnes Heller, *Eastern Left, Western Left* (Cambridge, U.K.: Polity Press, 1987), 187–200. Heller admits that her Central European model is utopian, but "in the least possible degree."

21. István Bibó states his position briefly in "The Meaning of the Social Evolution of Europe," in Schöpflin and Wood, eds., *In Search of Central Europe*, 47–56. Ferenc Fehér notes that for Bibó "the principle of unification" of Central Europe was "the region's common set of historical and political miseries." Fehér, "On Making Central Europe," 423. See also Jenö Szücs, "Three Historical Regions of Europe," in John Keane, ed., *Civil Society and the State: New European Perspectives* (London: Verso, 1988), 291–332; Mihály Vajda, "East-Central European Perspectives," in Keane, ed., *Civil Society and the State*, 333–60. The mixed character of the Habsburg Empire in this respect is seen by Szücs as the key to the character of the region. Szücs, "Three Historical Regions of Europe," 326–28. For a similar placing of the region as a whole, see George Schöpflin, "The Political Traditions of Eastern Europe," *Daedalus* (winter 1990): 55–90. Cf. also Péter Hanák: "The [Austro-Hungarian monarchy] as a system of state powers and of politics, stood in the middle between the fully-fledged parliamentary democracy in the West and autocracy in the East. This is precisely the meaning of the term: Central Europe." Péter Hanák, "Central Europe: A Historical Region in Modern Times," in Schöpflin and Wood, eds., *In Search of Central Europe*, 68. Hanák also makes a carefully argued case for the distinctive economic—more classically capitalist—development of Central Europe as compared with Eastern Europe (Russia). In general his argument places Central Europe in "the Eastern zone of the West" rather than "the Western zone of the East," but he stresses "the historical reality of the region as an entity." Others have accepted this while denying that Central Europe any longer has a common identity—especially since it was incorporated in "Eastern Europe." See Miroslav Kusy, "We, Central-European East Europeans," in Schöpflin and Wood, eds., *In Search of Central Europe*, 91–96.

22. Quoted in Tütsch, "From Nostalgia to Utopia," 97.

23. György Konrád, *Antipolitics: An Essay*, translated from the Hungarian by Richard E. Allen (London: Quartet Books, 1984), 91–114, 195. For a discussion of Central European "antipolitics," see Garton Ash, "Does Central Europe Exist?" 161–91; Judt, "The Dilemmas of Dissidence," 191–99; and chapter 2 of this book.

24. Konrád, *Antipolitics*, 197–99, 216–33; György Konrád, "Is the Dream of Central Europe Still Alive?" *Cross Currents* 5 (1986): 110, 113–15. Cf. also Czesław Miłosz, "Central European Attitudes," *Cross Currents* 5 (1986): 107, where he speaks of Central European writing as having "a tinge of nostalgia, of utopianism, and of hope." On the critical role of intellectuals in East Central Europe, cf. Zygmunt Bauman: "For a long pe-

riod in national history [Central European intellectuals] played the role of a substitute for the absent national state and thereby gained acute political significance through their cultural, ideological, and generally symbolic activities." Zygmunt Bauman, "Intellectuals in East-Central Europe: Continuity and Change," *Eastern European Politics and Societies* 1, no. 2 (1987): 172.

25. Konrád, *Antipolitics*, 89.

26. Ibid., 116.

27. Ibid., 186–87, 191. And cf. Adam Michnik, who in speaking of a "return to Europe" sees it as the return to the (Western) tradition of "liberalism and open-mindedness," which, along with conflicting traditions of xenophobia and intolerance, has equally characterized the history of Central Europe in the twentieth century. Adam Michnik, "Notes on the Revolution," *The New York Times Magazine* (March 11, 1990), 38–45. Ferenc Fehér suggests that, whether with a positive or, as in the case of many German-inspired concepts, a negative evaluation of the West, most theories of Central Europe are "designed against the West (even if a rejection of a 'despotic' or 'backward' East is implicit)." Ferenc Fehér, "On Making Central Europe," 427. In the case of the positive evaluation of Western traditions of democracy and pluralism, the view is that if Central Europe "wants to regenerate itself, it has to complete the work of self-westernization. It has to emancipate civil society from the state." Ibid., 433.

28. Vajda, "East-Central European Perspectives," 333–35.

29. Ibid., 349. This is a view endorsed by a number of Western scholars as well. See, for example, George Schöpflin: "Central and Eastern Europe is an organic part of Europe as a whole, and its detachment from the mainstream of European development has been highly deleterious for all the peoples of the area who have to live with the socio-political systems which work against rather than with the grain of tradition and the aspirations derived from those traditions." George Schöpflin, "Central Europe: Definitions Old and New," in Schöpflin and Wood, eds., *In Search of Central Europe*, 17.

30. Or even the West, if the West is forgetful of itself. Mihály Vajda suggests that, with the gradual "Americanization of Europe" and a general "spirit of uncertainty and hesitation" on the part of Western Europe, it may be the distinctive mission of Central Europe to remind Western Europe of its true character and inheritance: "Precisely because we in East-Central Europe are nonconformists, we may also strike a blow for the renascence and creativeness of European culture. In my view, Western Europe seems to be in danger of throwing these very values overboard in order better to protect its pragmatic and rationalistic individuality. We who live in that region have much less to lose." Vajda, "East-Central European Perspectives," 336. This is similar to Kundera's lament in "The Tragedy of Central Europe," 37–38; see also note 66 to this chapter.

31. Václav Havel, "The Power of the Powerless," in Jan Vladislav, ed., *Václav Havel: Living in Truth* (London: Faber and Faber, 1987), 115–17.

32. Havel, "An Anatomy of Reticence," in Vladislav, ed., *Living in Truth,* 175. Czesław Miłosz also picks out irony, and the representative figure of the "brave soldier Svejk," as the distinctive Central European attitude. Miłosz, "Central European Attitudes," 103. And on the "concrete" imagination of East Europeans, who are skeptical of abstract labels like "socialism" and "capitalism," see Josef Skvorecky, "An East European Imagination," in *Talkin' Moscow Blues* (London: Faber and Faber, 1989), 136.

33. Václav Havel, "Politics and Conscience," in Vladislav, ed., *Living in Truth,* 149–50, 155; see also Havel, "An Anatomy of Reticence," 192–93. On the difficulties of translating the antipolitics of opposition to the politics of postcommunist rule, see Garton Ash, "Eastern Europe: Après le Déluge, Nous," 51–52; see also chapters 2 and 5 of this book.

34. See the interview with Havel in *The Independent* (March 30, 1991); and also the

report "Havel and Walesa Woo the West," *The Independent* (March 21, 1991). As early as April 25, 1991, NATO formally considered the application of several Central European states, Czechoslovakia included, to join the alliance but deferred a decision.

35. Address to the 28th Congress of the Soviet Communist Party, reported in *The Independent* (June 23 and July 3, 1990).

36. See Gale Stokes, "The Social Origins of East European Politics," *Eastern European Politics and Societies* 1, no. 1 (1987): 30–74; Robin Okey, *Eastern Europe 1740–1985: Feudalism to Communism*, 2nd ed. (London, Hutchinson, 1986).

37. Garton Ash, "Does Central Europe Exist?" 165–66. A related strategy is to define *the West* in a selective and idealized way—for example, as the home of political and ethnic pluralism—and to lament Central Europe's long-standing inability to incorporate the particular principles in its traditions. Only when it does so, the argument goes, can it return to Europe, that is, the West. See, for example, Miklós Duray, "The European Ideal," in Schöpflin and Wood, eds., 97–115.

38. Kundera, "The Tragedy of Central Europe," 33. This is probably the point at which to mention that it was Kundera's article, first published in the French journal *Le D'ébat* in November 1983, that revived interest in the Central European idea. The article opened with a reference to an anguished telex message sent by the director of the Hungarian News Agency just before the Russian tanks came in in 1956: "We are going to die for Hungary and Europe."

39. Ibid., 33.

40. Kundera's article was, of course, written before the 1989 revolutions. But it remains a valuable point of reference for considering the aspirations of those revolutions; and it certainly reflects the attitudes of many of the principal actors in those revolutions. The Hungarian sociologist Ferenc Miszlivetz says that, especially as the result of Kundera's article, the concept of Central Europe "was in the air everywhere before the storm of 1989." Ferenc Miszlivetz, "Central Europe—The Way to Europe," paper presented to the 1991 Congress of the Hungarian Sociological Association, Budapest, June 24–28, 1991. The Princeton historian Robert Darnton noted, as the common theme in the responses to some questions about the 1989 revolutions that he put to a group of young Eastern European scholars, the fervent desire for "reintegration in Europe"—that is, the West. Robert Darnton, "Runes of the New Revolutions," *The Times Higher Education Supplement* (September 6, 1991), 17.

41. Kundera, "The Tragedy of Central Europe," 34.

42. See Croan, "Lands In-Between," 188. Tony Judt also stresses that Kundera's view of Russia is not only popular among Central European intellectuals of the present time, but has been so for some considerable time in the region. See Tony Judt, "The Dilemmas of Dissidence," 222–23. See also Miszlivetz, "Central Europe—The Way to Europe," which is especially valuable for its discussion of Hungarian views of Central Europe.

43. Sir James Eberle, "Understanding the Revolutions in Eastern Europe," in Gwyn Prins, ed., *Spring in Winter: The 1989 Revolutions* (Manchester: Manchester University Press, 1990), 197.

44. For a brief outline of this tradition of thought, see Geoffrey Barraclough, "Is There a European Civilisation?" in Barraclough's *History in a Changing World* (Oxford: Basil Blackwell, 1957), 46–53. Most of the other essays in this volume contain critical discussions of the theme of a unified European (that is, Western) civilization. A good example of the genre is Christopher Dawson, *Understanding Europe* (1952; reprint New York: Image Books, 1960).

45. Oskar Halecki, *The Limits and Divisions of European History* (London: Sheed and Ward, 1950), 11.

46. For a radical statement of this kind, see Martin Bernal, *Black Athena: The Afro-asiatic Roots of Classical Civilization,* 2 volumes (London: Free Association Books, 1987 and 1991).

47. Hugh Seton-Watson, "What Is Europe, Where Is Europe? From Mystique to Politique," in Schöpflin and Wood, eds., *In Search of Central Europe,* 33.

48. George Schöpflin, "Central Europe," 10; and, for the general argument that Russia did not share in the common European experience, see ibid., 7–18. See also, especially on political differences, Szücs, "Three Historical Regions of Europe," and Vajda, "East-Central European Perspectives," (note 21). And, for an earlier statement from Central Europe, cf. the view of Russia of the Czech intellectual Radoslav Selucky: "It is a country which did not pass through the phase of civil society, did not absorb the intellectual trends of antiquity, Roman Christianity, Renaissance and Enlightenment, a country taking over Marxism without the experience of its original sources and integrating Marxism first of all from the angle of its internal needs and state interests." Radoslav Selucky quoted in Peter Hruby, *Fools and Heroes: The Changing Role of Communist Intellectuals in Czechoslovakia* (Oxford: Pergamon Press, 1980), 114. For a more balanced assessment of the differences between Russian and Western European history, see Geoffrey Barraclough, "Russia and Europe," in Barraclough's *History in a Changing World,* 185–202.

49. Seton-Watson, "What Is Europe, Where Is Europe?" 33.

50. Geoffrey Barraclough, "The Continuity of European Tradition," in Barraclough's *History in a Changing World,* 35, 36–37. See also "The Fall of Constantinople," ibid., 131–34; Arnold Toynbee, "Russia's Byzantine Heritage," in *Civilization on Trial* (London: Oxford University Press, 1948), 169–71. Barraclough adds that Russia's position on the extreme eastern edge of Europe made it more, not less, European: "Russia's position on the Asiatic 'march' or frontier of Europe, and (arising therefrom) the sense of differentiation from the peoples who swept across the steppe from Asia, was, over centuries, a factor cementing Russia's attachment to Europe." Barraclough, "Russia and Europe," 187. For the view that "the religious issue does not qualify as a principle of radical separation of Eastern Europe," including Russia, see also Fehér, "On Making Central Europe," 419–20. In this sense there is much justice in Mikhail Gorbachev's repeated claims of Russia's Europeanness, though he sometimes stretched things a bit; for example: "We are Europeans. Old Russia was united with Europe by Christianity. . . . The history of Russia is an organic part of the great European history. . . . Europe 'from the Atlantic to the Urals' is a cultural-historical entity united by the common heritage of the Renaissance and the Enlightenment." Mikhail Gorbachev, *Perestroika* (New York: Harper and Row, 1987), 191–97, passim. For Gorbachev's ideas on Europe generally, see Karen Dawisha, *Eastern Europe, Gorbachev and Reform,* 2nd ed. (Cambridge: Cambridge University Press, 1990), 197–227, 230–31.

51. Barraclough, "The Continuity of European Tradition," 40–41.

52. Seton-Watson, "What Is Europe, Where Is Europe?" 36. Seton-Watson considers Bolshevik Russia to have revived in many respects sixteenth-century Muscovy under Ivan the Terrible—only now the schismatics (the Chinese Communists) were in the East, and the infidels (the capitalists) were in the West. We may remember that Sergei Eisenstein, in his film *Ivan the Terrible,* proposed a similar historical parallel, to Stalin's displeasure.

The theme of the continuity of Russian history is of course an old and familiar one. For a clear and powerful statement, see Toynbee, "Russia's Byzantine Heritage," 164–83. See also Tibor Szamuely, *The Russian Tradition* (London: Fontana, 1988). Kundera, to the question of whether "communism is the negation of Russian history or its fulfillment," answers: "Certainly it is both its negation (the negation, for example, of its religiosity) *and* its fulfillment (the fulfillment of its centralizing tendencies and its imperial dreams)." Kundera, "The Tragedy of Central Europe," 33.

53. Barraclough, "Russia and Europe," 198. Much the same sort of point can be made by seeing Marxism, as Arnold Toynbee has done, as "a Christian heresy." See Toynbee, "Encounters between Civilizations," in *Civilization on Trial*, 221. And cf. Milan Simecka: "As a doctrine, Communism was cultivated in the West, researched in Germany, tested in combat in the French revolutions, and assigned to the shelves of the British Museum." Milan Simecka, "Another Civilization? An Other Civilization?" in Schöpflin and Wood, eds., *In Search of Central Europe*, 160. For Simecka's repudiation of Kundera's view of Russia's alienness, see ibid., 157–62; see also the debate between Simecka, Jane Mellor, and Mihaly Vajda, in *In Search of Central Europe*, 163–82.

54. The Petrine Revolution has been endlessly debated. There is a good discussion in Paul Dukes, *The Making of Russian Absolutism 1613–1801*, 2nd ed. (London: Longman, 1990). For the view stated here, see, for example, Fehér, "On Making Central Europe," 436–39.

55. Seton-Watson, "What Is Europe, Where Is Europe?" 34.

56. See Andrzej Walicki, *The Slavophile Controversy* (Oxford: Clarendon Press, 1975); see also Barraclough, "Russia and Europe," 196–97.

57. One might say that, whatever one's opinion on this point, the 1990s were hardly the time to be attempting to separate Russia from Europe, as many Central Europeans were trying to do. Certainly if we can contemplate admitting Turkey—the historic land of the infidel—to the European Community, Russia's case is much more compelling. Indeed, in the wake of the failure of the coup against Gorbachev in August 1991, and the subsequent dissolution of Communist Party rule in Russia and elsewhere in the Soviet Union, several commentators expressed the hope that not only would Europe "from the Atlantic to the Urals" become a practical possibility, but that "we should be starting to think of a European home stretching from Vancouver to Vladivostok." See William Rees-Mogg and Peter Jenkins in *The Independent* (September 2–3, 1991). And cf. Konrád: "I would like to think of myself as some utopian son of Europe able to touch the Pacific at San Francisco with one outstretched arm and Vladivostok with the other." Konrád, *Antipolitics*, 129.

58. See Fehér, "On Making Central Europe," 425. And cf. Barraclough on Europe as a whole: "The conception of European unity certainly is a high ideal, worthy of effort and sacrifice; but it draws its strength from our hopes for the future and not from our interpretation of the past. If it is to become a reality, it will be through our determination to grapple realistically with the hard facts of the present, as we find them, and not through the revival of the illusory unity of an imaginary golden age." Barraclough, "The Continuity of European Tradition," 45.

59. Konrád, "Is the Dream of Central Europe Still Alive?" 113, 115–16.

60. Kundera, "The Tragedy of Central Europe," 35.

61. Miłosz, "Central European Attitudes," 101, 107.

62. Egon Schwarz, "Central Europe—What It Is and What It Is Not," in Schöpflin and Wood, eds., *In Search of Central Europe*, 153–54. Something of the same attitude is revealed in the preference of Central Europeans for the more spiritual concept of *Kultur* to describe themselves, rather than the more historically concrete and "external" *Zivilization*. See György Csepeli and Anna Wessely, "The Cognitive Chance of Central European Sociology," paper presented to the 1991 Congress of the Hungarian Sociological Association, Budapest, June 24–28, 1991.

63. Fehér, "On the Making of Central Europe," 434. See also Hanak, note 21 to this chapter.

64. Kiss, "Central European Writers about Central Europe," 125.

65. Miłosz, "Central European Attitudes," 107–08. It is noteworthy, as Timothy Garton Ash observes, that Polish intellectuals have been the least inclined to follow Kundera in seeing Central Europe as "really" Western. Miłosz, with his Lithuanian background, is unlikely to be indifferent to Poland's other, Eastward-looking, face; and this is generally true of most Poles. Miłosz, "Does Central Europe Exist?" 168. See also Croan, "Lands In-Between," 188. And cf. Judt: "Many of Poland's poets and writers look East rather than West for their roots, to Vilna rather than Vienna." Judt, "The Rediscovery of Central Europe," 47. On Poland's "historic ties to the East," see also Roman Szporluk, "The Burden of History—Made Lighter by Geography?" *Problems of Communism* 39 (July–August 1990): 46–48. On what one might call the struggle between Slavophiles and Westernizers in Poland—and elsewhere in Eastern Europe—today, see Adam Michnik, "The Two Faces of Europe," *New York Review of Books* (July 19, 1990), 7.

Pope John Paul II, on a visit to Poland in 1991, declared himself incensed by the arrogant assumption of West Europeans, with their materialism and sensuality, that they best represent "Europeanism": "I wish as Bishop of Rome to protest at such a perception of Europe, of Western Europe. . . . This offends the great world of culture from which we [East Europeans] have drawn and which we have co-created. We do not have to enter Europe because we helped to create it and we did so with greater effort than those who claim a monopoly of Europeanism." Christendom was the true source of European culture, and the East had contributed at least as much as the West to it. See the report in "Pope on Visit to Poland Criticizes West," *The Independent* (June 8, 1991).

66. Kundera, "The Tragedy of Central Europe," 38. Cf. Konrád: "If there is no Central Europe, there is no Europe. . . . If there is no Central European consciousness, there is no European consciousness. . . . If we don't cling to the utopia of Central Europe we must give up the game." Konrád, "Is the Dream of Central Europe Still Alive?" 114. See also Kiss, "Central European Writers about Central Europe," 131, and note 30 to this chapter.

Writing of the 1989 revolutions in East Central Europe, Timothy Garton Ash said that "they have offered us, with a clarity and firmness born of bitter experience, a restatement of the value of what we already have, of old truths and tested models, of the three essentials of liberal democracy and the European Community as the one and only, real existing common European home. Intellectually, dare I say spiritually, '1989' in Eastern Europe is a vital complement to '1992' in Western Europe." Timothy Garton Ash, *We the People: The Revolution of '89* (Cambridge: Granta Books/Penguin, 1990), 156. Garton Ash's later reflections were somewhat less euphoric, and less confident; see "Eastern Europe: Après le Déluge Nous," *New York Review of Books* (April 16, 1990), 51–57.

Finally there is George Schöpflin's Mannheimian suggestion, that "those coming from the edge of Europe have a better view of what it is than those who live in the centre. . . . Central Europeanism can . . . become an instrument for interpreting traits in all parts of Europe and can be a way of recognizing the main sources of the threats to Europeanness." Schöpflin, "Definitions of Central Europe," 21.

67. Karl Marx, "The Eighteenth Brumaire of Louis Bonaparte," in Karl Marx and Frederick Engels, *Selected Works in Two Volumes* (Moscow: Foreign Languages Publishing House, 1962), vol. 1, 249.

68. Quoted in Kiss, "Central European Writers about Central Europe," 135–36.

69. "President Václav Havel's Speech to the Polish Sejm and Senate, January 21, 1990," *East European Reporter* 4, no. 2 (1990): 56–57.

70. On these developments, see Leslie Holmes, *Post-Communism* (Durham, N.C.: Duke University Press, 1997), 98, 318.

71. Robert Bideleux and Ian Jeffries, *A History of Eastern Europe: Crisis and Change* (New York: Routledge, 1998), 636; see also Timothy Garton Ash, *In Europe's Name: Germany and the Divided Continent* (New York: Vintage Books, 1994), 653. Most of their foreign trade is now, in fact, with the West (especially Germany); trade with Russia, with whose economy they were once fully implicated, now amounts to only 3 percent of exports in the case of the Czech Republic, 5 percent in the case of Hungary, and 8 percent in the case of Poland. See Bill Wallace, "Central Europe and Russia," *The Prague Post* (October 17–13, 1998), A11.

72. For some examples, see Steven Sampson, "The Social Life of Projects: Importing Civil Society to Albania," in Chris Hann and Elizabeth Dunn, eds., *Civil Society: Challenging Western Models* (New York: Routledge, 1996), 121–42. An illustration of the tension between locals and "outsiders" is the fate of the Central European University (CEU) in Prague. Though strongly supported by President Havel, it was regarded with hostility by many of the academics of the Charles University, and it incurred the displeasure of Prime Minister Vaclav Klaus. Unable to resolve the issue, Soros transferred the CEU to Budapest.

73. Reported in the *New York Times* (March 13, 1999), A5. And see there and the report in the *New York Times* (March 12, 1999), A1, A10, for the statements of the other Central European leaders. Few of those leaders were as frank as the Polish soldier who, celebrating the event in Warsaw, said, "At last we are with the West, with the Americans, whom we can trust." *New York Times* (March 13, 1999), A5. And cf. this engaging account of Hungary's return—or at least her long journey—to the West given at the independence ceremony by Tom Lantos, a naturalized American of Hungarian origin and now a U.S. congressman: "A pagan Hungarian king, St. Stephen, embraced Western civilization in 1001 by accepting a crown from Rome. But it has taken a millennium to complete the process. In the interim, we missed the Renaissance because we were occupied by the Turks. We spent centuries as an appendage of Vienna, clinging to the West through the hyphen that connected us, humiliatingly, to Austria. We stumbled through the 20th century, cut off from the mainstream. . . . After a thousand years of desperate craving to be part of the West, today it's official—we're in, we get the imprimatur of NATO." *New York Times* (March 13, 1999), A1.

74. In 1993, in response to the question, "Why should the postcommunist countries seek membership in NATO?" Havel answered, on behalf of the Czech Republic, Hungary, Poland, Slovakia, and Slovenia, that it was because "we share the values on which NATO was founded and which it exists to defend. We are not just endorsing such values from the outside; over the centuries we have made our own contribution to their creation and cultivation. Why then should we not take part in defending them?" Moreover, he added, the countries on whose behalf he spoke "clearly belong to the Western sphere of European civilization. They . . . are simply declaring an affinity with an institution they belong to intrinsically." *International Herald Tribune* (October 20, 1993), 4. It is such remarks as these that make some people feel that Havel has gone back on his earlier commitment to a distinctive Central European identity, with its own special contribution to make to the European idea.

75. See Czesław Miłosz, "Swing Shift in the Baltics," *New York Review of Books* (November 4, 1993), 12–16. Latvia and Estonia, colonized by Germans in the Middle Ages, have a largely Protestant inheritance; Lithuania threw in its lot with the kingdom of Poland and, as the Polish-Lithuanian commonwealth, shared with Poland a common Catholic culture. The common element among all Baltic peoples is the anti-Slav senti-

ment. As Miłosz observes, "None of these peoples is Slavic and their national feelings are exacerbated by their antipathy to everything Slavic." This continued into Soviet times; Russians were regarded as uncouth and inefficient. Russians seem to have acknowledged the differences: "The Baltic republics were regarded by the Russians with envy, as 'the West,' more prosperous than the rest of the Empire. Even the collective farms seemed to work." Miłosz, ibid., 12, 14; see also Anatol Lieven, *The Baltic Revolution: Estonia, Latvia, Lithuania and the Path to Independence* (New Haven: Yale University Press, 1993).

76. Blaga Dimitrova, "Walking in the Fog and Missing One Another," in Ludmilla Kostova, Margaret Dobing, Nick Wadham-Smith, and John Allen-Payne, eds., *Britain and Europe* (Veliko Turnovo, Bulgaria: Petrikov Publishers, 1994), 14.

77. See the *New York Times* (March 12, 1999), A1. When faced with the prospect of contributing troops from the region during the NATO engagement in Kosovo, popular enthusiasm was dampened even further. Havel's popularity in the Czech Republic was seriously diminished by what was seen as his uncritical championing of NATO actions. See *The Prague Post* (June 3, 1999), A3.

78. For the history of the tortuous negotiations between the European Union and the former communist countries of Central Europe since 1989, see Bideleux and Jeffries, *History of Eastern Europe*, 620–40; see also Milada Vachudova, *Revolution, Democracy, and Integration: The Domestic and International Politics of East Central Europe since 1989* (Oxford: Oxford University Press, 1999). The fear that the entry of the former communist countries would alter the whole character of the European Union is reflected in the report of an EU "reflection group" charged with preparing the agenda for an intergovernmental committee to review the Maastricht Treaty: "By deciding to enlarge the European Union with just about all the countries of Central and Eastern Europe, the EU leaders have signed a death warrant for the European community as conceived by Jean Monnet, Robert Schuman and Walter Hallstein. . . . Most of the new candidates are very different from the current member states. They are much less rich. They have only limited experience in democratic government (and even less in negotiating in supranational institutions)." Quoted in Bideleux and Jeffries, *History of Eastern Europe*, 622; see also Tony Judt, "Europe: The Grand Illusion," *New York Review of Books* (July 11, 1996), 8; Perry Anderson, "The Europe to Come," *London Review of Books* (January 25, 1996), 6–8. All this is part of a much wider debate about "deepening" or "widening" among member states of the EU. Though no formerly communist country has been admitted to the EU, several have been admitted to the Council of Europe, the much looser grouping of European states that exists largely to coordinate educational and cultural policies and to set certain standards of civic life, particularly those to do with human rights.

79. For the poll reports, see *The Prague Post* (June 16, 1999), A9, and the *International Herald Tribune* (June 22, 1999), 1, 4.

80. György Konrád, "Central Europe Redivivus," in Konrád's *The Melancholy of Rebirth: Essays from Post-Communist Central Europe, 1989–1994,* translated by Michael Henry Heim (San Diego, Calif.: Harcourt Brace and Company, 1995), 156–57.

81. Ibid., 158–59, 162–63.

82. Adam Michnik, "Gray Is Beautiful: Thoughts on Democracy in Central Europe," *Dissent* (spring 1997): 14–15. On the Central European idea as a myth or symbol, cf. Iver B. Neumann: "The debate about 'Central Europe' was and is a moral appeal to Western Europe on behalf of an imagined community, born of frustration with the Soviet hegemony in Eastern Europe." Iver B. Neumann, "Russia as Central Europe's Constituting Other," *East European Politics and Societies* 7, no. 2 (1993): 366. At the present time it is clear to many that the concept of "Central Europe"continues to perform

a political function, its very definition being dependent not so much on its cultural or historical heritage as its fitness or otherwise in the eyes of the West. According to Timothy Garton Ash, "To be 'Central European' in contemporary political usage means to be civilized, democratic, cooperative—and therefore to have a better chance of joining NATO and the EU. In fact the argument threatens to become circular: NATO and the EU welcome 'Central Europeans,' so 'Central Europeans' are those whom NATO and the EU welcome." Timothy Garton Ash, "The Puzzle of Central Europe," *New York Review of Books* (March 18, 1999), 18. Hence Slovakia, for instance, can move out of "Central Europe"—when under the authoritarian rule of Vladimir Meciar—and back in again when Meciar is defeated (in September 1998) by a coalition of opposition parties. One can imagine a similar to-and-fro with the Balkan states.

83. Miłosz, "Swing Shift in the Baltics," 16. There is a whole tradition in Lithuania and Poland of "looking Eastward," based on the experience and outlook of the great Polish-Lithuanian Commonwealth of the sixteenth century to the eighteenth century. The gentry who ran this multiethnic entity, reaching from the Baltic to the Black Sea, referred to this realm as "Sarmatia," and they saw themselves as descendants of the ancient Scythians of Eastern Europe. For the long-lasting influence of this conception, which envisaged a federation of Central and East European peoples rather than ethnic nationhood—as was so often claimed for this region—see Andrew Carpenter, *Sarmatia: Poland's Historical Blueprint for East-European Union* (Portsmouth, U.K.: University of Portsmouth, Nation and Identity in Contemporary Europe Research Group, 1997).

84. Another example is provided by Balint Magyar, the former minister of culture and education in Hungary. In an address to incoming students at the Central European University in Budapest, he urged them not to follow the example of countries like Slovenia and "some Czech politicians" who have too hastily concluded that their destiny lies with the West. Hungary, at least, wishes to remain a Central European country, by which it recognizes its position "as a meeting place of Eastern and Western cultures," drawing upon Catholic, Protestant, and Orthodox experiences, among others. Magyar wished that Central European University would see itself as "the embodiment of a virtual region," a region of the mind to match the concrete region of Central Europe. See the report of his speech in the *CEU Gazette* 6, no. 2 (1996–97): 3–5.

85. Timothy Garton Ash, "'Neo-Pagan' Poland," *New York Review of Books* (January 11, 1996), 14. See also Garton Ash, "The Puzzle of Central Europe," 18–23, where he argues that the "core"countries of Central Europe have now more or less been accepted as part of the West, and that that is the best strategy for others in the region to pursue, if they can, by adopting Western patterns of democracy, the rule of law, tolerance for minority rights, and so on. At present the eastern edge of the West has shifted eastward but stops at the border of the old Soviet Union; that is, it excludes Ukraine, Belarus, and European Russia. There is no reason, though, why the westward move cannot continue, though it will take time. Can all the Balkan states, then, become "Central European" and thus part of "the West"? Garton Ash balks at this, at least in the case of Serbia. Ibid., 23. And what of Russia?

86. See Edward Mortimer, "The Rebirth of Central Europe," *Financial Times* (June 27, 1989), 12. Kundera did not, of course, do it by himself; Konrád, for instance, was equally active in propounding the idea in these years. But most people agree that it was Kundera's essay, originally published in French in Paris, that set the ball rolling among Central European intellectuals, including those resident in the West.

87. See Neumann, "Russia as Central Europe's Constituting Other," 357–8. Kundera's comments are made in a postscript of 1991 to the Czech version of his novel *A Joke*.

88. Among the contributions to this literature one might note Neumann, "Russia As Central Europe's Constituting Other" (see note 13 to this chapter); also Iver B. Neumann, *Russia and the Idea of Europe* (New York: Routledge, 1995); Iver B. Neumann, *Uses of the Other: The "East" in European Identity Formation* (Minneapolis: University of Minnesota Press, 1998); Edward Timms, "National Memory and the 'Austrian Idea' from Metternich to Waldheim," *Modern Language Review* 86, no. 4 (1991): 898–910; Jacques le Rider, "Hugo von Hofmannsthal and the Austrian Idea of Central Europe," in Ritchie Robertson and Edward Timms, eds., *The Habsburg Legacy: National Identity in Historical Perspective* (Edinburgh: Edinburgh University Press, 1994), 121–35; Robin Okey, "Central Europe/Eastern Europe: Behind the Definitions," *Past and Present* 137 (1992): 102–33; Garton Ash, "The Puzzle of Central Europe" (see note 13 to this chapter); Larry Wolff, *Inventing Eastern Europe: The Map of Civilization on the Mind of the Enlightenment* (Stanford: Stanford University Press, 1994); Jan Nederveen Pieterse, "Fictions of Europe," *Race and Class* 32, no. 3 (1991): 3–10; Brian Nelson, David Roberts, and Walter Veit, eds., *The Idea of Europe* (New York: Berg, 1992); Kevin Wilson and Jan van der Dussen, eds., *The History of the Idea of Europe* (New York: Routledge, 1995); Gerard Delanty, *Inventing Europe: Idea, Identity, Reality* (London: Macmillan, 1995); Maryon McDonald, "'Unity in Diversity': Some Tensions in the Construction of Europe," *Social Anthropology* 4, no. 1 (1996): 47–60; Peter Gowan, ed., *The Debate on Europe* (New York: Verso, 1997).

89. On the new orientalism, see C. M. Hann, "When West Meets East: The Skeleton at the Feast," in C. M. Hann, *The Skeleton at the Feast: Contributions to East European Anthropology* (Canterbury: University of Kent Centre for Social Anthropology and Computing, 1995), 195–208; Adam Burgess, *Divided Europe: The New Domination of the East* (London: Pluto Press, 1997). On the earlier "orientalizing" of Central and Eastern Europe, see Wolff, *Inventing Eastern Europe*; Maria Todorova, *Imagining the Balkans* (New York: Oxford University Press, 1997); also on the Balkans, see Vesna Goldsworthy, *Inventing Ruritania: The Imperialism of the Imagination* (New Haven: Yale University Press, 1998).

90. Václav Havel, "The Hope for Europe," *New York Review of Books* (June 20, 1996): 38–39. And cf. Jaques Rupnik: "Economically the East needs the West, but culturally today the West needs the East, precisely because it is there that the soul of Europe, the idea of Europe as a culture that transcends political divides, has been preserved." *The Other Europe* (New York: Pantheon Books, 1989), xi.

91. See, for example, the study by Yasemin Nuhoglu Soysal, *Limits of Citizenship: Migrants and Postnational Membership in Europe* (Chicago: The University of Chicago Press, 1994). Such a concept of "postnational citizenship" might indeed make it easier to realize the "metaphysically anchored sense of responsibility"—which lifts us above "our party, our electorate, our lobby, our state" to take in the interests of humanity as a whole—that Havel sees as the "cornerstone of the values that underlie the European tradition." Havel, "The Hope for Europe," 41. For what that points to is a set of practices and institutions that transcend not just the nation state, but any political grouping, such as the European Union. This is just one of the many places where there seems a distinct tension between Havel the thinker and Havel the politician, head of a Central European state.

92. See Samuel P. Huntington, *The Clash of Civilizations and the Remaking of the World Order* (New York: Touchstone Books, 1997).

93. Judt, "Europe: The Grand Illusion," 9.

## 4. The 1989 Revolutions and the Idea of Revolution

1. Daniel Chirot, "Introduction," in Daniel Chirot, ed., *The Crisis of Leninism and the Decline of the Left: The Revolutions of 1989* (Seattle: University of Washington Press, 1991), ix; Fred Halliday, "The Ends of Cold War," *New Left Review* 180 (1990): 5; Timothy Garton Ash, *We the People: The Revolution of '89* (Cambridge, U.K.: Granta Books/Penguin Books, 1990), 156; Ralf Dahrendorf, *Reflections on the Revolution in Europe* (London: Chatto and Windus, 1990), 5; George Schöpflin, "The End of Communism in Eastern Europe," *International Affairs* 66 (1990): 3; Lucien Pye, "Political Science and the Crisis of Authoritarianism," *American Political Science Review* 84 (1990): 5–6. And cf. Ellen Rice: "1989 may prove to be one of the great Years of Revolution in history." Ellen Rice, "Introduction," in Ellen Rice, ed., *Revolution and Counter-Revolution* (Oxford: Basil Blackwell, 1991), x.

2. Janusz Ziolkowski, "The Roots, Branches and Blossoms of Solidarnosc," in Gwyn Prins, ed., *Spring in Winter: The 1989 Revolutions* (Manchester: Manchester University Press, 1990), 40.

3. Ash, *We the People*, 14, 20, 139; for justification of the term "revolution" applied to 1989, see also Dahrendorf, *Reflection on the Revolution in Europe*, 5, 74, 103; Andrew Arato, "Revolution, Civil Society, and Democracy," *Praxis International* 10 (1990): 27; Giuseppe di Palma, "Legitimation from the Top to Civil Society," *World Politics* 44 (1991): 50; Sasha Weitman, "Thinking the Revolutions of 1989," *British Journal of Sociology* 43 (1992): 12.

4. Among later students of revolution who have emphasized the international aspect, the most prominent have been Albert Sorel, *Europe and the French Revolution*, translated and edited by A. Cobban and J. W. Hunt (1885; reprint London: Fontana, 1969); Lord Acton, *Lectures on Modern History* (1906; reprint London: Fontana, 1960); R. R. Palmer, *The Age of the Democratic Revolution*, 2 volumes (Princeton: Princeton University Press, 1970); see also Theda Skocpol, *States and Social Revolutions* (Cambridge: Cambridge University Press, 1979).

5. Schöpflin, "The End of Communism in Eastern Europe," 3; see also Ash, *We the People*, 156.

6. Halliday, "The Ends of Cold War," 9.

7. Dahrendorf, *Reflections on the Revolution in Europe*, 22; see also Ken Jowitt, *New World Disorder: The Leninist Extinction* (Berkeley: University of California Press, 1992), 261.

8. Francis Fukuyama, *The End of History and the Last Man* (New York: The Free Press, 1992). Ken Jowitt remarks that "historical 'exceptions' of this order (the Nazi and Bolshevik revolutions) don't prove the 'liberal rule'; one almost destroyed it, and the other had the nuclear power to do it." But at the same time he admits: "I have no quarrel with Fukuyama's observation that liberal capitalism is now the only politically global 'civilization.'" Ken Jowitt, *New World Disorder*, 263. The fullest discussion of Fukuyama's thesis, which was first stated in 1989, is in Perry Anderson, "The Ends of History," in Perry Anderson, *A Zone of Engagement* (New York: Verso, 1992), 279–375. And see also chapter 6 of this book.

9. Jowitt, *New World Disorder*, 260, 263–64; see also 306–31.

10. See Krishan Kumar, "Twentieth-Century Revolutions in Historical Perspective," in Krishan Kumar, *The Rise of Modern Society* (Oxford: Basil Blackwell, 1988), 169–205. And see also chapter 8 of this book.

11. See, for instance, Simon Schama, *Citizens: A Chronicle of the French Revolution* (London: Penguin Books, 1989).

12. Halliday, "The Ends of Cold War," 5; cf. Jürgen Habermas, "What Does Socialism Mean Today? The Revolutions of Recuperation and the Need for New Thinking," in Robin Blackburn, ed., *After the Fall: The Failure of Communism and the Future of Socialism* (London: Verso, 1991), 29–30; Bruce Cumings, "Illusion, Critique, and Responsibility: The 'Revolution of '89' in West and East," in Chirot, ed., *The Crisis of Leninism and the Decline of the Left*, 101; T. Kuran, "Now Out of Never: The Element of Surprise in the East European Revolutions of 1989," *World Politics* 44 (1991): 36; Weitman, "Thinking the Revolutions of 1989," 13.

13. See Jean Cohen and Andrew Arato, *Civil Society and Political Theory* (Cambridge, Mass.: MIT Press, 1992). See also chapter 5 of this book.

14. See, for example, David Held, ed., *Prospects for Democracy: North, South, East, West* (Cambridge, U.K.: Polity Press, 1993).

15. Slavoj Žižek, "Eastern Europe's Republics of Gilead," *New Left Review* 183 (1990): 50.

16. Crane Brinton, *The Anatomy of Revolution*, revised and expanded edition (New York: Vintage Books, 1965), 7, 68.

17. See, for instance, Neil Smelser, *Theory of Collective Behavior* (New York: The Free Press of Glencoe, 1963).

18. See Schöpflin, "The End of Communism in Eastern Europe"; Andras Bozóki, "The Hungarian Transition in Comparative Perspective," in Andras Bozóki, Andras Körösènyi, and George Schöpflin, eds., *Post-Communist Transition: Emerging Pluralism in Hungary* (London: Pinter Publishers, 1992), 170–72; S. N. Eisenstadt, "The Breakdown of Communist Regimes and the Vicissitudes of Modernity," *Daedalus* 121, no. 2 (spring 1992): 21–22.

19. Daniel Chirot, "What Happened in Eastern Europe in 1989?" in Chirot, ed., *The Crisis of Leninism and the Decline of the Left*, 20; see also di Palma, "Legitimation from the Top to Civil Society."

20. Teodor Shanin, "The Question of Socialism: A Development Failure or an Ethical Defeat?" *History Workshop Journal* 30 (1990): 71.

21. See Bronislaw Geremek, "Between Hope and Despair," *Daedalus* (winter 1990): 93–94; and cf. Geremek's observation: "In an extended time perspective, the successive crises of [East European politics] may be viewed as the spasms of an organism seeking to reject an alien body." Ibid., 108. On the insufficiency of the concept of legitimacy to explain regime change in general, see Adam Przeworski, "Some Problems in the Study of the Transition to Democracy," in G. O'Donnell, P. C. Schmitter, and L. Whitehead, eds., *Transitions from Authoritarian Rule*, 4 volumes (Baltimore: Johns Hopkins University Press, 1986), vol. 3: 47–63; R. Bova, "Political Dynamics of the Post-Communist Transition," *World Politics* 44 (1991): 113–38. According to Przeworski, "What matters for the stability of any regime is not the legitimacy of this particular system of domination but the presence or absence of preferable alternatives." Przeworski, "Some Problems in the Study of the Transition to Democracy," 51–52. One might also add, *possible* alternatives.

22. James C. Davies, "Toward a Theory of Revolution," *American Sociological Review* 27 (1962): 6.

23. The significance of Poland's role in the overthrow of communism has been everywhere remarked upon. For some commentators, the effective beginning of the 1989 revolutions was the election of a Polish pope in 1978—the mass enthusiasm for which, especially after the Pope's visit to Poland in 1979, led to the formation of Solidarity. See Timothy Garton Ash, *The Uses of Adversity: Essays on the Fate of Central Europe* (Cambridge, U.K.: Granta Books/Penguin Books, 1989), 42–54; Garton Ash, *We the People*, 133–34. Leszek Kolakowski puts this in the grander perspective of post-1830

"Polish messianism," the idea of Poland as "the Christ of nations" whose suffering and crucifixion would redeem mankind. Noting Poland's prominence in opposing communism throughout the twentieth century, he argues that "its pioneering role in the slow decomposition of Sovietism cannot be denied." Leszek Kolakowski, "Amidst Moving Ruins," *Daedalus* (spring 1992): 50–51. See also Geremek, "Between Hope and Despair."

24. On the economies of Eastern Europe in the 1970s and 1980s, see J. Vanous, "East European Economic Slow-Down," *Problems of Communism* 23 (July–August 1982): 1–19; Alec Nove, *The Economics of Feasible Socialism* (London: Allen and Unwin, 1983), J. Kornai, *The Road to a Free Economy* (New York: W. W. Norton, 1990); M. Lavigne, ed., *The Soviet Union and Eastern Europe in the Global Economy* (Cambridge: Cambridge University Press, 1992). It could be argued that "rising expectations" were fueled by the "demonstration effect" of Western consumerism, as witnessed on the television screens of East Europeans. But such an effect had been in evidence for decades without leading to the overthrow of communism. Once the system collapsed, of course, the pent-up desire for Western-style goods was given full reign. But it did not cause the revolutions of 1989: like the loss of legitimacy of the rulers, it was constant more or less throughout the whole period of communist rule.

A further economic argument has been that the revolutions were caused by the increasing articulation of East European economies with the capitalist economies of the West. This, it is claimed, explains in particular the sequence of revolutions in 1989, with the more articulated (those in Hungary, Poland, and East Germany) the first to go, and the least articulated (those in Czechoslovakia, Bulgaria, and Romania) the last. See R. G. Hill, "Revolutions Waiting to Happen? An Analysis of the Revolutions of 1989," paper presented to the Annual Conference of the British Sociological Association, University of Kent at Canterbury, April 1992. This is unconvincing not only for its reliance on the very shaky economic statistics of Eastern Europe, but for its economic determinism, which fits 1989 even less well than it does earlier revolutions. Generally Bronislaw Geremek's verdict seems right: "Political crises tend to break out in Eastern bloc countries in all kinds of economic conditions. The timing of events in Poland and Hungary in 1956 and those of 1968 in Czechoslovakia and Poland, can hardly be explained in economic terms alone." Geremek, "Between Hope and Despair," 107. This applies a fortiori to 1989.

25. See, for example, Skocpol, *States and Social Revolutions*; and see also Immanuel Wallerstein, "The French Revolution as a World-Historical Event," *Social Research* 56, no. 1 (1989): 33–52. The whole of this special issue of *Social Research*, "The French Revolution and the Birth of Modernity," makes the point about the international character of the French Revolution and of revolution in general.

26. See Sigmund Neumann, "The International Civil War," *World Politics* 1 (1949): 333–50.

27. For the evidence of this, including the role of the Soviet Union in fostering change in the region, see Krishan Kumar, "The Revolutions of 1989: Socialism, Capitalism, and Democracy," *Theory and Society* 21 (1992): 322–34, 345–49 (chapter 2 of this volume). Most of the accounts of the 1989 revolutions refer to Gorbachev's role or "the Moscow factor," though disagreeing on the relative weight to attribute to it. Those who regard it as indispensable, perhaps even "decisive," include Ash, *We the People*, 140–41; Halliday, "The Ends of Cold War," 19; P. Grilli di Cortona, "From Communism to Democracy: Rethinking Regime Change in Hungary and Czechoslovakia," *International Social Science Journal* 128 (1991): 323–24; W. Osiatynski, "Revolutions in Eastern Europe," *University of Chicago Law Review* 58 (1991): 838, 843–44; Paul Hirst, "The State, Civil Society and the Collapse of Communism," *Economy and Society* 20 (1991): 229. For a dissent-

ing voice, see Tony Judt, in Tony Judt and others, "Post-Communist Eastern Europe: A Survey of Opinion," *Eastern European Politics and Societies* 4 (1990): 171.

28. Kuran, "Now Out of Never."

29. Geremek, "Between Hope and Despair," 99.

30. Ibid., 106.

31. See Ash, *We the People*, 141; Pye, "Political Science and the Crisis of Authoritarianism," 6; Kuran, "Now Out of Never," 24; Weitman, "Thinking the Revolutions of 1989," 14; Jowitt, *New World Disorder*, 291 n. 20.

32. Hence this cri de coeur of a Bulgarian student activist after the revolution: "We don't have the Hungarian 1956, the Czech 1968, the Polish 1980—nothing to show that the older generation have tried to change the system, nothing to wipe out the shame from their faces." Quoted in Sika Kovacheva, *The Student Movement in Post-Communist Bulgaria*, master's sociology thesis, Central European University, Prague, 1992.

33. Alexis de Tocqueville, *The European Revolution and Correspondence with Gobineau*, edited and translated by John Lukacs (New York: Doubleday Anchor, 1959).

34. The "East European tradition of revolt" is not, of course, restricted only to the anti-Soviet risings of the period after 1945. There is a history of revolt going back to the eighteenth century, which includes not just the revolutions in—and against—Russia, but the various revolts against Ottoman rule. There are also some important continuities between the older and newer kinds of revolt, especially regarding the role of intellectuals in them. For some brief remarks, see Hugh Seton-Watson, "Revolution in Eastern Europe," in J. P. Vatikiotis, ed., *Revolution in the Middle East, and Other Case Studies* (London: Allen and Unwin, 1972), 185–97; see also Zygmunt Bauman, "Intellectuals in East-Central Europe: Continuity and Change," *Eastern European Politics and Societies* 1 (1987): 162–86.

35. See Krishan Kumar, "The 1989 Revolutions and the Idea of Europe," *Political Studies* 40 (1992): 439–61 (see chapter 3 of this volume).

36. Quoted in Robert Darnton, "Runes of the New Revolutions," *Times Higher Education Supplement* (September 6, 1991), 17.

37. See, for example, Prins, ed., *Spring in Winter*.

38. There has, of course, always been an argument to the effect that the Russian Revolution was not really "European" at all, but reflected the peculiar, part-Asiatic, development of Russia. This despite the admitted fact that the revolution was carried out under the auspices of a clearly Western ideology, Marxism. For the view that the revolution of 1917 is better regarded as part of the Western inheritance, and Russia part of Europe, see Kumar, "The 1989 Revolutions and the Idea of Europe."

39. François Furet, "From 1789 to 1917 and 1989," *Encounter* (September 1990): 5.

40. East Europeans don't have much truck with those accounts that try to save Marxism by giving a Trotskyist account of both 1917 and 1989; see, for instance, Alex Callinicos, *The Revenge of History: Marxism and the East European Revolutions* (Cambridge, U.K.: Polity Press, 1991). On the irrelevance of the attempts by socialists to "save" socialism in this way, see Ander Gunder Frank, "Revolution in Eastern Europe: Lessons for Democratic Social Movements (and Socialists?)," *Third World Quarterly* 12 (1990): 36–52.

41. Habermas, "What Does Socialism Mean Today?" 26–27; see also Dahrendorf, *Reflections on the Revolution in Europe*, 23; Ash, *We the People*, 154; Robin Blackburn, "Fin de Siècle: Socialism after the Crash," in Blackburn, ed., *After the Fall*, 237; Hans-Magnus Enzensberger, "Ways of Walking: A Postscript to Utopia," in Blackburn, ed., *After the Fall*, 20.

42. Barrington Moore Jr., *Reflections on the Causes of Human Misery* (London: Allen Lane the Penguin Press, 1972), 168–69.

43. Hannah Arendt, *On Revolution* (London: Faber and Faber, 1963), 21–40. There is also, of course, restoration in a more obvious sense: According to Osyiatynski, "The revolution has also involved a restoration: in Poland, the Czech and Slovak Republics, and Hungary, property confiscated forty-five years ago is being returned to the heirs of the original owners." Osyiatynski, "Revolutions in Eastern Europe," 824.

44. See, for example, François Furet, *Interpreting the French Revolution,* translated by Elborg Forster (Cambridge, U.K.: Cambridge University Press, 1981), 79; François Furet, "From 1789 to 1917 to 1989," 5; Richard Sakwa, *Gorbachev and His Reforms 1985–1990* (Hemel Hempstead, U.K.: Philip Allan, 1990), 377.

45. Habermas, "What Does Socialism Mean Today?" 27, 29–30; see also Bozóki, "The Hungarian Transition in Comparative Perspective," 176.

46. See Kumar, "The Revolutions of 1989," 317–24 (and see chapter 2 of this book). In addition to the literature referred to there, in support of this view, see also, on the Czech case, M. Rady, "Rebels by Reputation," *Times Higher Education Supplement* (March 5, 1993), 30, and, on the Romanian case, the debate between Istvan Deak, Juan Linz, Marcia Krol, Gale Stokes, and others, "Survivors," *New York Review of Books* (March 5, 1992), 43–51, (May 28, 1992), 56–57, and (July 16, 1992), 53–54. The issue is debated in most of the contributions to Ivo Banac, ed., *Eastern Europe in Revolution* (Ithaca, N.Y.: Cornell University Press, 1992).

47. The classic statement of this view is J. L. Talmon, *The Origins of Totalitarian Democracy* (London: Mercury Books, 1961). And cf. Giuseppe di Palma: "Jacobinism Anticipated Communism's Cognitive Monopoly." Di Palma, "Legitimation from the Top to Civil Society," 77.

48. Isaiah Berlin, "The State of Europe: Christmas Eve 1989," *Granta* 30 (1990): 148; see also Hugh Trevor-Roper, "Europe's New Order," *The Independent Magazine* (December 30, 1989), 14; Michael Howard, "Impressions from a Journey in Central Europe," *London Review of Books* (October 25, 1990), 3; Ziolkowski, "The Roots, Branches and Blossoms of Solidarnosc," 41–42; Osyiatynski, "Revolutions in Eastern Europe," 823–24; Ash, *We the People,* 134–49.

49. Dahrendorf, *Reflections on the Revolution in Europe,* 26–27. Of course Burke's book on the French Revolution supplies the formal model for Dahrendorf's own reflections on the revolution of 1989.

50. Arato, "Revolution, Civil Society, and Democracy," 30.

51. Adam Seligman, *The Idea of Civil Society* (New York: The Free Press, 1992); see also John Keane, *Democracy and Civil Society* (London: Verso, 1988), 31–68.

52. Ash, *We the People,* 94.

53. Deidre Boden, "Reinventing the Global Village: Communication and the Revolutions of 1989," in A. Giddens, ed., *Human Societies: A Reader* (Cambridge, U.K.: Polity Press, 1992), 328–29; see also Sir John Eberle, "Understanding the Revolutions in Eastern Europe," in Prins, ed., *Spring in Winter,* 199; Dankwert A. Rustow, "Democracy: A Global Revolution?" *Foreign Affairs* 69 (1990): 79–80; Pye, "Political Science and the Crisis of Authoritarianism," 8–9; Cumings, "Illusion, Critique and Responsibility," 112–13.

54. Leo Panitch and Ralph Miliband, "The New World Order and the Socialist Agenda," in R. Miliband and L. Panitch, eds., *The Socialist Register 1992* (London: The Merlin Press, 1992), 2; see also Hill, "Revolutions Waiting to Happen?"; Lavigne, ed., *The Soviet Union and Eastern Europe in the Global Economy.*

55. See Rustow, "Democracy: A Global Revolution?"; Pye, "Political Science and the Crisis of Authoritarianism."

56. Bova, "Political Dynamics of the Post-Communist Transition," 113. The models for this kind of comparative politics are the studies of "transitions from authoritarian rule" in southern Europe and South America. See especially O'Donnell, Schmitter, and Whitehead, eds., *Transitions from Authoritarian Rule,* note 21. For applications to Eastern Europe, see Bova, "Political Dynamics of the Post-Communist Transition"; T. L. Karl and P. C. Schmitter, "Modes of Transition in Latin America, Southern and Eastern Europe," *International Social Science Journal* 128 (1991): 269–84; Bozóki, "The Hungarian Transition in Comparative Perspective"; J. J. Linz and A. Stephan, "Political Identities and Electoral Sequences: Spain, the Soviet Union, and Yugoslavia," *Daedalus* (spring 1992): 123–39. See also Adam Przeworski, "The 'East' Becomes the 'South'? The 'Autumn of the People' and the Future of Eastern Europe," *PS: Political Science and Politics* 24 (1990): 20–24; Barbara Misztal, "Must Eastern Europe Follow the Latin American Way?" *Archives Européennes de Sociologie* 33 (1992): 151–79.

57. On this see Niels Nielsen, *Revolutions in Eastern Europe: The Religious Roots* (Maryknoll, N.Y.: Orbis Books, 1991); George Weigel, *The Final Revolution: The Resistance Church and the Collapse of Communism* (Oxford: Oxford University Press, 1992).

58. In a skeptical note on what he calls the "facile concept" of the "transition to democracy," Ken Jowitt observes: "Economic and social development places democracy on a nation's political agenda; but *irreversible* breakthrough to democracy depends on quite different sociocultural and institutional factors." In his view, the "Leninist legacy" in Eastern Europe separates the region radically from "transitions to democracy" in other parts of the world. See Jowitt, *New World Disorder,* 274; see also 284–305.

It is clear that the main dividing line is between those who regard the communist regimes as essentially totalitarian and those who think that, particularly since the 1960s, they were closer to authoritarian regimes and therefore contained elements of pluralism. For the latter group, comparisons between Eastern Europe and other transitions from authoritarian rule in southern Europe, South America, and Southeast Asia, are not only legitimate, but illuminating; for the former group, they are not. For other examples of those who, like Jowitt, think that the comparisons are specious and misleading, see G. Ekiert, "Democratization Processes in East Central Europe," *British Journal of Political Science* 21 (1991): 287–89; Grilli di Cortona, "From Communism to Democracy," 324–25, 328.

59. Pye, "Political Science and the Crisis of Authoritarianism," 7.

60. For this approach, see Ekiert, "Democratization Processes in East Central Europe," 291–93; di Palma, "Legitimation from the Top to Civil Society," 52–53, 73–74; Andrew C. Janos, "Social Science, Communism, and the Dynamics of Political Change," *World Politics* 44 (1991): 81–112; Fukuyama, *The End of History and the Last Man,* 68–69; Eisenstadt, "The Breakdown of Communist Regimes"; K. Müller, "'Modernising' Eastern Europe: Theoretical Problems and Political Dilemmas," *Archives Européennes de Sociologie* 33 (1992): 109–50.

61. See Janos, "Social Science, Communism, and the Dynamics of Political Change," 88–93.

62. See, for example, Zygmunt Bauman, *Intimations of Postmodernity* (London: Routledge, 1992),169–70.

63. On this see Moshe Lewin, *The Gorbachev Phenomenon: An Historical Interpretation* (London: Hutchinson Radius, 1989).

64. Bauman, *Intimations of Postmodernity,* 179–80; see also 166–67.

65. Eisenstadt, "The Breakdown of Communist Regimes and the Vicissitudes of Modernity," 25–27.

66. Octavio Paz, "Poems from the End of History," *The Independent* (October 13, 1990), 29. And cf. the Slovak historian Ewa Kowalska's comment, in the light of her understanding of the 1989 revolutions as the culmination of the Western revolutionary tradition: "When I think about it, it seems to me that at last, after two hundred years, this revolution is drawing to a close." Quoted in Darnton, "Runes of the New Revolutions," 17. There is a more provocative rendering of this "sense of an ending" in Immanuel Wallerstein's view that the 1989 revolutions spell not just the end of communism but, more fundamentally, "the downfall of liberalism as an ideology." For Wallerstein, both capitalism and communism are variants of a basic liberal ideology stemming from the French Revolution of 1789. Liberalism was challenged—fatally, Wallerstein thinks—in 1968; communism was challenged and overthrown in 1989. See Immanuel Wallerstein, "The Collapse of Liberalism," in Miliband and Panitch, eds., *The Socialist Register 1992*, 96–110. This view certainly differs from most views of the meaning of 1989.

67. Habermas, "What Does Socialism Mean Today?" 29.

68. See, for example, Richard Rorty, *Contingency, Irony and Solidarity* (Cambridge: Cambridge University Press, 1989).

69. Bauman, *Intimations of Postmodernity,* 171; see also 222–25.

70. Czesław Miłosz "The State of Europe: Chrismas Eve 1989," *Granta* 30 (1990): 165.

71. See Arato, "Revolution, Civil Society and Democracy."

72. Gale Stokes, *The Walls Came Tumbling Down: The Collapse of Communism in Eastern Europe* (New York: Oxford University Press, 1993), 169.

73. Attila Ágh, *The Politics of Central Europe* (London: Sage Publications, 1998), 202; and, for the election results in the region to 1998 see 164–70, 192–94. On the elections, see also Keith Crawford, *East Central European Politics Today* (Manchester: Manchester University Press, 1996), 177–225; Richard Rose, Neil Munro, and Tom Mackie, *Elections in Central and Eastern Europe Since 1990* (Glasgow: Centre for the Study of Public Policy, University of Strathclyde, 1998).

74. Zygmunt Bauman, "After the Patronage State: A Model in Search of Class Interests," in Christopher G. A. Bryant and Edmund Mokrzyski, eds., *The New Great Transformation? Change and Continuity in East Central Europe* (New York: Routledge, 1994), 17.

75. For examples of this terminology in the more recent literature, see the works referred to in "A Further Note" to chapter 2 of this book.

76. Gale Stokes, "Modes of Opposition Leading to Revolution in Eastern Europe," in Stokes's *Three Eras of Political Change in Eastern Europe* (New York: Oxford University Press, 1997), 161–63.

77. László Bruszt, "1989: The Negotiated Revolution in Hungary," in András Bozóki, András Körösényi, and George Schöpflin, eds., *Post-Communist Transition: Emerging Pluralism in Hungary* (London: Pinter Publishers, 1992), 58–59. (Bruszt's essay was first published in *Social Research* 57, no. 2 [1990]: 365–87.) See also Rudolf Tökes, *Hungary's Negotiated Revolution: Economic Reform, Social Change and Political Succession* (Cambridge: Cambridge University Press, 1996); Michael D. Kennedy, "Contingencies and Alternatives of 1989: Toward a Theory and Practice of Negotiating Revolution," *East European Politics and Societies* 13, no. 2 (1999): 293–302.

78. See Bernard Wheaton and Zdenek Kavan, *The Velvet Revolution: Czechoslovakia, 1988–1991* (Boulder, Colo.: Westview Press, 1992). In some reflections published to mark the tenth anniversary of the 1989 revolutions, Timothy Garton Ash said he has

been prepared to see in this "nonrevolutionary revolution"—peaceful, self-limiting, and so on—a new model of revolution and the chief theoretical contribution of the 1989 revolutions: "The leaders of the popular movements deliberately set out to do something different from the classic revolutionary model, as it developed from 1789, through 1917, right up to the Hungarian revolution of 1956. . . . The fundamental insight underlying the actions of the opposition elites, born of their own Central European learning processes since 1945, but also of a deeper reflection on the history of revolution since 1789, was that you cannot separate ends from means. The methods you adopt determine the outcome you will achieve. You cannot lie your way through to the truth. As Adam Michnik memorably put it: those who start by storming Bastilles will end up building new Bastilles. The 1989 model combines an absolute insistence on nonviolence with the active, highly inventive use of mass civil disobedience, skillful appeals to Western media, public opinion, and governments, and a readiness to negotiate and compromise with the powerholders, while refusing to be co-opted by them. . . . If the symbol of 1789 was the guillotine, that of 1989 is the round table." Timothy Garton Ash, "Ten Years After," *New York Review of Books* (November 18, 1999), 18. This can stand so long as we remember that Edmund Burke and Lord Acton, in their different ways—not to mention a host of anarchist thinkers—had made a similar point about means and ends when talking about the fate of revolution. See the selections in Krishan Kumar, ed., *Revolution: The Theory and Practice of a European Idea* (London: Weidenfeld and Nicolson, 1971), especially 221–81.

79. Claus Offe, "Capitalism by Democratic Design? Democratic Theory Facing the Triple Transition in East Central Europe," *Social Research* 58, no. 4 (1991): 866–67. Similar objections to considering the 1989 events as revolutions in the classic sense have been advanced by Jan Pakulski: "Classic revolutions involve not only mass mobilisations but also organised activities of revolutionary groups and leaders who play the central role in political takeovers and direct the subsequent radical transformations. Such revolutions and revolutionaries were conspicuously absent in CEE [Central Eastern Europe]." Jan Pakulski, "Mass Movements and Plebiscitary Democracy: Political Change in Central Eastern Europe," *International Sociology* 10, no. 4 (1995): 413–14.

80. Sir Lewis Namier, "1848: Seed-Plot of History," in *Vanished Supremacies: Essays on European History 1812–1918* (Harmondsworth, U.K.: Penguin Books, 1962), 34.

81. Andrzej W. Tymowski, "Poland's Unwanted Social Revolution," *East European Politics and Societies* 7, no. 2 (1993): 175. And cf. Aleksander Smolar's corroborating statement that, in the eyes of many in Poland, "a revolution—twentieth-century experiences are invoked here—carries with it only destruction, divisions, and hatred which are . . . a negation of democratic culture." Aleksander Smolav, "Revolutionary Spectacle and Peaceful Transition," *Social Research* 63, no. 2 (1996): 441.

82. There can also be less positive meanings attached to "restoration." Smolar points out that for the ex-communist Left in Poland—the Left that took power in 1993 and 1995—what had happened between 1989 and 1995 amounted to an anachronistic reversion, "the return of demons from the past, Third World capitalism, dependence on the West and international financial institutions, clericalism, parochialism, and so forth." By contrast, the Left saw its return to power as a chance "for a reasonable, enlightened, and civilized development. . . . 'Poland is now coming back home to the West and to the tradition of the Enlightenment' [Jerzy Wiatr, minister of education in the Democratic Left Alliance government]." Smolar, "Revolutionary Spectacle and Peaceful Transition," 458–59.

83. Tymowski, "Poland's Unwanted Social Revolution," 200. For the argument that the workers (the bulk of Solidarity's support) were cheated of a revolution they made,

see also Tadeusz Kowalik, "The Polish Revolution," *Dissent* (spring 1997): 26–30. On the question of political revolution, Smolar observes, with respect to the negotiated character of the changes in Poland and Hungary in 1989: "If the severance of the principle of legitimacy constitutes a defining element of revolution, then—in contrast to Czechoslovakia, the former East Germany, Bulgaria, Romania, and Albania—Poland in this sense has not witnessed a revolution. Neither did Hungary." Smolar, "Revolutionary Spectacle and Peaceful Transition," 443.

84. András Bozóki, "The Hungarian Transition in a Comparative Perspective," in Bozóki, Körösényi, and Schöpflin, eds., *Post-Communist Transition*, 166–67. What happened in Hungary in 1956 is also considered a revolution.

85. See the discussion in my introduction to Krishan Kumar, ed., *Revolution: The Theory and Practice of a European Idea*, 1–90.

86. Piotr Sztompka, "Looking Back: The Year 1989 as a Cultural and Civilizational Break," *Communist and Post-Communist Studies* 2 (1996): 115–29. For Sztompka's earlier views, see the discussion in chapter 7 of this book.

87. Stokes, "Modes of Opposition Leading to Revolution in Eastern Europe," 163. And cf. Eugene Kamenka, who remarks that the "remarkable upheavals" in Central and Eastern Europe in 1989–91 not only constitute "what Marxists and Hegelians used to call a world-historical event," but "also constitute a revolution, or a series of revolutions, as decisive as those of 1848. . . . The years since 1989 have indeed achieved more spectacular successes than in 1848–49. The traditional power of an authoritarian and ubiquitous Communist party has been broken. The Soviet empire has collapsed, and so has its system of satellites. International military and political relations have undergone profound change. The future may be uncertain, but the past cannot be brought back to life." Eugene Kamenka, "Civil Society and Freedom in the Post-Communist World," in Margaret Latus Nugent, ed., *From Leninism to Freedom: The Challenges of Democratization* (Boulder, Colo.: Westview Press, 1992), 111.

88. Stokes, "Modes of Opposition Leading to Revolution in Eastern Europe," 163; see also 179.

89. Stokes, *The Walls Came Tumbling Down*, 23; see also 21–38 for a good account of the thinking and activities of the antipoliticians in Czechoslovakia and Poland. And cf. "Modes of Opposition Leading to Revolution in Eastern Europe," 170, where Stokes remarks that "the antipolitical project constituted an entirely new phase of opposition, and a devastating one." Stokes regards Solidarity in its opening phases as part of the antipolitical opposition. For a similar view that loss of moral legitimacy was the principal underlying cause of the 1989 revolutions, see also the account in Vladimir Tismaneanu, *Reinventing Politics: Eastern Europe from Stalin to Havel* (New York: The Free Press, 1992), especially chapter 6, "The Triumph of the Powerless."

For the view that "ideological exhaustion and 'utter moral rot'" was at the root of communism's demise in Eastern Europe, see also Christian Joppke, "Intellectuals, Nationalism, and the Exit from Communism: The Case of East Germany," *Comparative Studies in Society and History* 37, no. 2 (1995): 213–4. Joppke points out, however, that intellectuals in East Germany were peculiarly disabled from offering the moral critique developed by other East European intellectuals. This was owing partly to their strong anti-Westernism and anticapitalism and partly, because of Nazism, to the lack of a usable national tradition from the past to pit against communism. A "legitimation crisis" is also what Leslie Holmes sees as the main cause of the disintegration of the socialist system in *The End of Communist Power: Anti-Corruption Campaigns and Legitimation Crisis* (Cambridge, U.K.: Polity Press, 1993). Paul Hollander, focusing on the Soviet Union, also argues that an eroding sense of legitimacy, especially among the higher echelons of the party, was the principal cause of communism's collapse. See Paul Hollander, *Political Will and Personal Belief: The Decline and Fall of Soviet Communism* (New Haven: Yale University Press, 1999). For an interesting, though somewhat confused, discussion of the whole question of legitimacy in relation to the communist societies of Eastern Europe, see Fatos Tarifa, "The Quest for Legitimacy and the Withering Away of Utopia," *Social Forces* 76, no. 2 (1997): 437–74.

90. See Jeffrey Isaac, "The Meaning of 1989," *Social Research* 63, no. 2 (1996): 291–344. See also Neal Ascherson on "Forum politics," the politics of the opposition groups that took over in 1989, as a new species of democracy (which did not, alas, last): "1989 in Eastern Europe," in John Dunn, ed., *Democracy: The Unfinished Journey 508 BC to AD 1993* (New York: Oxford University Press, 1993), 221–37.

91. Stokes, *The Walls Came Tumbling Down,* 149–51.

92. Philip Longworth, *The Making of Eastern Europe: From Prehistory to Post-communism,* second edition (New York: St. Martin's Press, 1997), 9; and see generally 9–11, 64. For a similar view of the economic causes of the downfall of socialism in Eastern Europe, see Janusz Reykowski, "Why Did the Collectivist State Fail?" *Theory and Society* 23, no. 2 (1994): 233–52.

93. Cf. this recent general summary of the economic condition of communist societies in the decade preceding the 1989 revolutions: "From 1979 to 1983 . . . the East European economies were plunged into acute economic recessions from which they still had not fully recovered in 1989, when the 'iron curtain' finally lifted. Between 1979 and 1989, with the possible exception of the GDR and Bulgaria, the East European economies hardly grew at all in real per capita terms." Robert Bideleux and Ian Jeffries, *A History of Eastern Europe: Crisis and Change* (New York: Routledge, 1998), 572. See also David Mason: "By most measures, the centrally planned economies of Eastern Europe and the Soviet Union delivered hefty overall growth rates through the 1950s and most of the 1960s. However by the late 1960s and early 1970s, Eastern European growth rates began to decline. . . . The change became particularly evident in the 1970s. . . . By the 1980s, the economies of all the Eastern European states (and the Soviet Union) were in serious trouble." David Mason, *Revolution and Transition in East Central Europe,* second edition (Boulder, Colo.: Westview Press, 1996), 29, 32.

Ivan Szelenyi and Balazs Szelenyi concur with this picture. For them, economic explanations of the demise of socialism in Eastern Europe are wrong. The cause was not economic failure per se; that failure can be attributed to a more fundamental political weakness that was as much a cause as the consequence of economic failure: "The major problem with socialism was not that it did not work as an economic system, but that it was unable to establish itself as a democratic system and in the long run this undermined its legitimacy." Ivan Szelenyi and Balazs Szelenyi, "Why Socialism Failed: Toward a Theory of System Breakdown—Causes of Disintegration of East European State Socialism," *Theory and Society* 23, no. 2 (1994): 219.

Leszek Kolakowski also argues that the failure of socialism was due not fundamentally to economic, but to moral, causes—to the decline in belief in communist ideology—and he observes: "Perhaps the strongest case against Marx's immortal phrase that 'social being determines consciousness' is provided by the history of the states that have assimilated this very phrase as part of their ideology." Leszek Kolakowski, "Mind and Body: Ideology and Economy in the Collapse of Communism," in K. Z. Poznanski, ed., *Constructing Capitalism: The Re-emergence of Civil Society and Liberal Economy in the Post-Communist World* (Boulder, Colo.: Westview Press, 1992), 12.

94. For Gorbachev's own views on his thoughts and actions, see Mikhail Gorbachev, *Life and Reforms,* 2 volumes (Moscow: Novosti Publishers, 1996); Mikhail Gorbachev,

*Gorbachev: On His Country and the World,* translated by George Shriver (New York: Columbia University Press, 1999). See also Archie Brown, *The Gorbachev Factor* (Oxford: Oxford University Press, 1996). There is a view that, if not Gorbachev himself, at least a prominent group within the party elite deliberately worked toward the dismantling of the Soviet system and, by extension, its glacis in Eastern Europe. See David Kotz and Fred Weir, *Revolution from Above: The Demise of the Soviet System* (New York: Routledge, 1997); a somewhat similar line is taken by Robert English, *The Idea of the West: Gorbachev, Intellectuals, and the End of the Cold War* (New York: Columbia University Press, 2000).

The most general account of high Soviet strategy during these years is Jacques Lévesque, *The Enigma of 1989: The USSR and the Liberation of Eastern Europe* (Berkeley: University of California Press, 1997). On the "green light" to reformers in Hungary, Poland, and Bulgaria, see Stokes, *The Walls Came Tumbling Down,* 99, 129, 148; see also Bruszt, "Hungary's Negotiated Revolution," 55. And cf. Ferencz Miszlivetz: "The most direct meaning of 1989 was that the self-limiting revolutions of Central Europe cannot be treated as separate from the internal crisis of the Soviet Union." Ferencz Miszlivetz, "The Unfinished Revolutions of 1989: The Decline of the Nation-State?" *Social Research* 58, no. 4 (1991): 784. A similar argument is made by Barbara Misztal, "Understanding Political Change in Eastern Europe: A Sociological Perspective," *Sociology* 27, no. 3 (1993): 461–64. And cf. also Szelenyi and Szelenyi: "Gorbachev's decision to abandon Eastern Europe was decisive." Szelenyi and Szelenyi, "Why Socialism Failed," 226.

The importance of Soviet complacence in 1989 comes out strongly when comparison is made with the Polish crisis of 1980–81. General Victor Dubynin, commander of the Soviet troops stationed in Poland, has revealed that the Soviet Union was poised to invade Poland in December 1981 to crush the Solidarity movement, and would have done so had not General Jaruzelski declared martial law and put an end to Solidarity himself. See the report in *The Independent* (March 14, 1992); on this episode, see also Stokes, *The Walls Came Tumbling Down,* 42, 270.

95. Cf. Timothy Garton Ash: "The truth is that 1989 could have turned bloody at any point, as China did on the very same day as the historic Polish elections, June 4. . . . 'Tiananmen' was a word that I would hear muttered many times in Central and Eastern Europe capitals over the next few months." Garton Ash, "Ten Years After," 16. Anne Applebaum, who was present at the coming down of the Berlin Wall in November 1989, has a similar observation to make in her tenth anniversary reflections: "It is now known that only the timely persuasion of the West Germans prevented the Eastern border guards from firing on the huge crowds gathered at the Brandenburg Gate, right about the time we were sitting there. In Leipzig, the East German city where huge anti-communist demonstrations had been taking place a few weeks earlier, the hospitals were at one point cleared of non-emergency patients, and blood plasma was prepared for the crackdown that never came. . . . Nothing was inevitable, nothing had to happen the way it did—and nothing quite the way it later seemed on television." Anne Applebaum, "Blinded by What We Saw at the Wall," *The Washington Post* (November 7, 1999), B5.

Michael Kennedy makes a similar point about Poland, based on recent interviews. Observing that General Jaruzelski was only "very narrowly" (in fact, by one vote) elected president by a Solidarity-dominated Senate in June 1989, he comments: "Were he not, it is hard to predict whether the army and communist apparatus would have allowed the continued evolution of the system." For Kennedy, "contingency and negotiation shape the meaning of the 1989 transformations." He makes the important point that if we take contingency and negotiation seriously in our analyses of 1989, not only do we avoid reading it—with hindsight—as simply "a resumption of normality," but we can see the largely peaceful changes in Central Europe and the more violent nature of the changes in the Balkans within the same frame of reference: "If we see 1989 as a moment of violence averted, then we might recast the Wars of Yugoslav Succession as a case in the betrayal of negotiated and peaceful change." Michael Kennedy, "Contingencies and the Alternatives of 1989," 300, 302.

96. Stokes, *The Walls Came Tumbling Down*, 166–67. Cf. also Dean McSweeney and Clive Tempest: "People power was decisive in the transitions everywhere in Eastern Europe except Hungary." Dean McSweeney and Clive Tempest, "The Political Science of Democratic Transition in Eastern Europe," *Political Studies* 41, no. 3 (1993): 418; and András Bozóki, who stresses the symbolic importance of the mass demonstrations in Leipzig, Berlin, Prague, Sofia, and Budapest as a major contributing factor to the collapse of communism in 1989 in "The Hungarian Transition in a Comparative Perspective," 176. For Edward Tiryakian, too, factors such as internal decay, corruption, and Gorbachev's intervention were not enough to account for the revolutions of 1989: "What played an equally important part in this most unexpected social becoming was grass-roots social mobilisation, . . . the coming together of persons in public places." Edward Tiryakian, "Collective Effervescence, Social Change and Charisma: Durkheim, Weber and 1989," *International Sociology* 10, no. 3 (1995): 276.

97. Stokes, "Modes of Opposition Leading to Revolution in Eastern Europe," 174, 179.

98. On the lack of popular involvement in Poland in 1989, see Tymowski, "Poland's Unwanted Social Revolution," 193, 200; on a similar lack in Hungary, see Bruszt, "Hungary's Negotiated Revolution," 58. John Sislin attributes an important role to popular demonstrations in the Romanian case, though he also stresses the importance of the key role played by the army: "Revolution Betrayed? Romania and the National Salvation Front," *Studies in Comparative Communism* 24, no. 4 (1991): 398–400; but see also the later references to the Romanian revolution in chapter 2 of this book. As for East Germany, Christian Joppke attributes a considerable role to the people—not so much for acting as a force that directly opposed the government as for getting out of the country by the hundreds and thousands when given the chance in 1989. See "'Exit' and 'Voice' in the East German Revolution," *German Politics* 2, no. 3 (1993): 393–414. Czechoslovakia's opposition in 1989 was limited to a small circle of students and intellectuals; see Ladislav Holy, "The End of Socialism in Czechoslovakia," in C. M. Hann, ed., *Socialism: Ideals, Ideologies, and Local Practice* (London: Routledge, 1993), 204–5. Holy argues—unconvincingly, in my view—that the "symbolic critique" of communism offered by Havel and Charter 77 had the effect of mobilizing the masses in 1989 even though, as Havel had sorrowfully observed only the year before, "If there are millions of people behind Solidarity, only millions of ears stand behind Charter 77." Quoted in ibid., 205.

99. See Juan J. Linz and Alfred Stepan, *Problems of Democratic Transition and Consolidation: Southern Europe, South America, and Post-Communist Europe* (Baltimore: The Johns Hopkins University Press, 1996); see especially 3–15, and notes 21 and 55 to this chapter, for Linz and Stepan's earlier work and that of like-minded scholars. See in particular T. L. Karl and P. C. Schmitter, "Models of Transition in Latin America and Eastern Europe," *International Social Science Journal* 128 (1991): 269–85; Attila Ágh, "The 'Comparative Revolution' and the Transition in Central and Southern Europe," *Journal of Theoretical Politics* 5, no. 2 (1993): 231–52; Lisa Anderson, ed., *Transitions to Democracy* (New York: Columbia University Press, 1999). A comparison between Hungary and Spain, within the context of transition theory (or "transitology")

generally, is attempted by Bozóki, "The Hungarian Transition in a Comparative Perspective," 181–85.

See also Richard Rose, William Mishler, and Christian Haerpfer, *Democracy and Its Alternatives: Understanding Post-Communist Societies* (Cambridge, U.K.: Polity Press, 1998), which, although focusing mainly on the former communist bloc, draws much of its perspective from the comparative politics of democratization in general. Such is also the approach of most of the contributors to Geoffrey Pridham and Tatu Vanhanen, eds., *Democratization in Eastern Europe* (New York: Routledge, 1994). Some valuable general points on comparisons within the context of the 1989 revolutions are made by Jacques Coenen-Huther, "Transition As a Topic for Sociological Analysis," in Piotr Sztompka, ed., *Building Open Society and Perspectives of Sociology in East-Central Europe* (Krakow: Proceedings of the International Sociological Association Regional Conference, September 1996), 35–42; see also, in the same volume, Mira Marody, "Post-Transitology or Is There Any Life after Transition?" 43–51.

100. See Claus Offe, "Capitalism by Democratic Design? Facing the Triple Transition in East Central Europe," *Social Research* 58, no. 4 (1991): 865–92. And cf. John Hall: "Recent discussions of transitions to democracy [such as those of O'Donell et al.] have been based on the experience of authoritarian capitalism, and are of little use in understanding either state socialism or post-communism." John Hall, "After the Fall: The Analysis of Post-communism," *British Journal of Sociology* 45, no. 4 (1994): 527.

101. See McSweeney and Tempest, "The Political Science of Democratic Transition in Eastern Europe"; Barbara A. Misztal, "Postcommunist Ambivalence: Becoming a New Formation?" *Archives Européennes de Sociologie* 37, no. 1 (1996): 104–40; Ghia Nodia, "How Different Are Postcommunist Transitions?" *Journal of Democracy* 7, no. 4 (1996): 21–35; Valerie Bunce, "Can We Compare Democratization in the East versus the South?" *Journal of Democracy* 6, no. 3 (1995): 87–100. On the communist legacy and the difficulties it poses for transition in Eastern Europe as compared with transitions elsewhere, see János Mátyás Kovács, ed., *Transition to Capitalism? The Communist Legacy in Eastern Europe* (New York: Transaction Books, 1995); James R. Millar and Sharon L. Wolchik, eds., *Social Legacies of Communism* (Cambridge: Cambridge University Press, 1994); M. Mandelbaum, ed., *Postcommunism: Four Perspectives* (Washington: Council on Foreign Relations, 1996), especially the essay by Stephen Holmes, 21–76. See also William Miller, Stephen White, and Paul Heywood, *Values and Political Change in Postcommunist Europe* (London: Macmillan, 1998), which argues (62–66) that the different political and cultural legacies of Central and Eastern Europe from Western Europe, not to mention other parts of the world, make comparisons with "transitions to democracy" outside the region unhelpful and misleading.

102. Cf. J. F. Brown, who cautions against "transition" models drawn from different parts of the world and directs us instead to the history, recent and more distant, of the region itself: "As a guide to Eastern Europe today, better . . . turn not to Latin America but to historians like Joseph Rothschild, the late Hugh Seton-Watson, and others, to their histories of Eastern Europe between the two world wars, and to earlier histories of the empires to which the East European lands belonged." J. F. Brown, *Hopes and Shadows: Eastern Europe After Communism* (Durham: Duke University Press, 1994), 11–12. Chapter 1 of the present volume attempts such an approach.

103. In addition to those mentioned in the notes to this chapter, see Bruce Ackerman, *The Future of Liberal Revolution* (New Haven: Yale University Press, 1992), which includes an illuminating comparison between the 1989 revolutions and the American Revolution considered as inaugurating the liberal political project in the West. There are also some stimulating comparative reflections on the East European revolutions—both

communist and anti-communist—in François Furet, *The Passing of an Illusion: The Idea of Communism in the Twentieth Century,* translated by Deborah Furet (Chicago: University of Chicago Press, 1999). For comparisons between 1989 and 1968 (in France and elsewhere in the West), see G. M. Tamás, "A Disquisition on Civil Society," *Social Research* 61, no. 2 (1994): 205–22. Immanuel Wallerstein (see note 65 to the present chapter) has continued to see 1989 in the perspective of 1968; see *After Liberalism* (New York: The Free Press, 1995), and *Utopistics, or Historical Choices of the Twenty-first Century* (New York: The New Press, 1998), 28–33.

104. But see the interesting reflections in William McBride, *Philosophical Reflections on the Changes in Eastern Europe* (Lanham Md.: Rowman and Littlefield, 1999), especially 47–63, which considers the views of contemporary philosophers, East and West, on the events of 1989. Zygmunt Bauman, too, has in various works continued to reflect on the postmodern character of the changes heralded by 1989; see the references in the editors' essay on Bauman's work in Richard Kilminster and Ian Varcoe, eds., *Culture, Modernity and Revolution: Essays in Honor of Zygmunt Bauman* (New York: Routledge, 1996), 215–60. Particularly relevant is Z. Bauman, "A Post-Modern Revolution?" in J. Frentzel-Zagorska, ed., *From a One-Party State to Democracy: Transition in Eastern Europe* (Atlanta: Editions Rodopi, 1993), 3–20. On the role of information technology in the dissolution of the Soviet Union, see Scott Shane, *Dismantling Utopia: How Information Ended the Soviet Union* (Chicago: Ivan R. Dee, 1994).

105. See Stjepan G. Mestrovic, *The Balkanization of the West: The Confluence of Postmodernism and Postcommunism* (New York: Routledge, 1994), which considers the breakup of Yugoslavia as an instance of the same postmodern fragmentation that is afflicting the West.

106. McBride, *Philosophical Reflections on the Changes in Eastern Europe*, 8; see also Tiryakian, "Collective Effervescence," 269–81. For the reasons for the failure to predict the changes, together with the argument that a reasonable prediction could have been made and was indeed made by several persons (though not mostly social scientists), see Seymour Martin Lipset and Gyorgy Bunce, "Anticipations of the Failure of Communism," *Theory and Society* 23, no. 2 (1994): 169–210.

107. Jack A. Goldstone, "Why We Could (and Should) Have Foreseen the Revolutions of 1989–91 in the USSR and Eastern Europe," *Contention* 2, no. 2 (1993): 127–52 (quotation on 129). See also Nikki R. Keddie, "Can Revolutions Be Predicted; Can Their Causes Be Understood?" *Contention* 1, no. 1 (1992): 159–82.

108. Randall Collins, "Prediction in Macrosociology: The Case of the Soviet Collapse," *American Journal of Sociology* 100, no. 6 (1995): 1552–93. Collins's late 1970s prediction was published as "The Future Decline of the Russian Empire" in Randall Collins, *Weberian Sociological Theory* (New York: Cambridge University Press, 1986).

109. Timur Kuran, "The Inevitability of Future Revolutionary Surprises," *American Journal of Sociology* 100, no. 6 (1995): 1528–51.

## 5. Civil Society

1. John Keane, "Remembering the Dead," in *Democracy and Civil Society* (London: Verso, 1988), 33, 64.

2. See Jacques Rupnik, "Totalitarianism Revisited," in John Keane, ed., *Civil Society and the State: New European Perspectives* (London: Verso, 1988), 284–87.

3. For the following account I am largely indebted to the studies by Manfred Riedel, "'State' and 'Civil Society': Linguistic Context and Historical Origin," in Riedel's *Between Tradition and Revolution: The Hegelian Transformation of Political Philosophy,*

translated by Walter Wright (Cambridge: Cambridge University Press, 1984), 129–56; Norberto Bobbio, "Gramsci and the Concept of Civil Society," in Keane, ed., *Civil Society and the State,* 73–99; Keane, "Remembering the Dead"; John Keane, "Despotism and Democracy: The Origins and Development of the Distinction between Civil Society and the State 1750–1850," in Keane, ed., *Civil Society and the State,* 35–71. For a different approach, which considers civil society as an aspect of Habermas's concept of the "life-world" and its development, see Andrew Arato and Jean Cohen, "Civil Society and Social Theory," *Thesis Eleven,* 21, (1988): 40–64, and also their forthcoming book, *Civil Society and Democratic Theory* (Cambridge, Mass.: MIT Press, 1992). There is also much relevant material in Lucien Febvre, "*Civilisation:* Evolution of a Word and a Group of Ideas," in Peter Burke, ed., *A New Kind of History: From the Writings of Febvre,* translated by K. Folea (London: Routledge and Kegan Paul, 1973), 219–57.

4. A further contrast, important to some thinkers, was that between "civil" and "religious" society. This reflected the tumultuous role of religion in the wars, foreign and civil, of the seventeenth century, and the conviction of many eighteenth-century thinkers that society would not be orderly—"civilized"—until religion was removed from the public sphere. I owe this point to Quentin Skinner.

5. Keane, "Despotism and Democracy," 36–50. It is clear that this development is bound up with the whole discovery of "society," as an entity different from the state, which laid the foundations for the new science of sociology as well as political economy.

6. Keane, "Despotism and Democracy," 65. This allows Keane to fit Montesquieu's and Tocqueville's concepts of civil society into this tradition.

7. Karl Marx and Frederick Engels, *The German Ideology,* ed. R. Pascal (New York: International Publishers, 1963), 26–27. Pascal, in his note on the concept of civil society, said: "It arose and was used in the seventeenth and eighteenth centuries amongst bourgeois theoreticians as a theoretical attack on political forms which prevented the free accumulation of private property." Ibid., 203, n. 25. And cf. Ellen Meiksins Wood: "The full conceptual differentiation of 'civil society' required the emergence of an autonomous 'economy,' separated out from the unity of the 'political' and 'economic' which still characterized the absolutist state." Ellen Meiksins Wood, "The Uses and Abuses of 'Civil Society,'" in Ralph Miliband and Leo Panitch, eds., *The Socialist Register 1990* (London: The Merlin Press, 1990), 61. Riedel is probably right to say that the new meaning of civil society as primarily an economic sphere—thus reversing the classical meaning of civil society as something *opposed* to the 'economic' or domestic sphere—was owing to the dissolution of the household as the primary economic unit and its replacement by the more "social" organization of commercial and industrial enterprises at the end of the eighteenth century. Riedel, "'State' and 'Civil Society,'" 140.

8. Karl Marx, "Preface to A Contribution to the Critique of Political Economy," in Karl Marx and Frederick Engels, *Selected Works in Two Volumes* (Moscow: Foreign Languages Publishing House, 1962), vol. 1, 362.

9. This comes out in Riedel's account of Hegel's concept of civil society, despite his emphatic claim that "one might well say that before Hegel the concept of civil society in its modern sense did not exist." The term in its modern sense may well have originated with Hegel; the thing, however, seems clearly to predate him (as Marx, for instance, accepted). In any case, Riedel shows the persistence in Hegel's concept, right up to and including the *Philosophy of Right,* of strong elements of the older traditional political concept of civil society—elements that were derived largely from eighteenth-century ideas of "the policing of society." It is these that made Hegel's concept different from Marx's: Hegel's was informed by a *political* will and rationality in the way that Marx's was not. See Riedel, "'State' and 'Civil Society,'" 147, 148–56, and also his essay, "The

Hegelian Transformation of Modern Political Philosophy and the Significance of History," in *The Hegelian Transformation of Political Philosophy,* 159–88. For some interesting critical observations on Riedel that question the presumed identity of state and civil society in pre-Hegelian thought, and point to the importance of the "policing" concept as a way of consciously *making* an identification of state ("the police state") and society, see Arpad Szakolczai, "Were State and Civil Society Ever Identical?" paper presented to the 1991 Congress of the Hungarian Sociological Association, Budapest, June 1991; see also Febvre, "*Civilisation,*" 225–29.

10. Shlomo Avineri, *Hegel's Theory of the Modern State* (Cambridge: Cambridge University Press, 1972), 12. Elsewhere he remarks: "Hegel's definition of civil society follows the classical economists' model of the free market." Ibid., 142; for the elaboration of this idea, see 132–54.

11. *Hegel's Philosophy of Right,* translated and edited by T. M. Knox (Oxford: Clarendon Press, 1942), 110, para. 157; addendum to 266, para. 116; addendum to 267, para. 185. It should be said that the characterization of civil society under capitalism as the sphere of egoism, as "a system of perpetual warfare between man and man," as an "irrational" and "unnatural" system, was most vividly presented by the early French and English socialists. See Richard Adamiak, "State and Society in Early Socialist Thought," *Survey* 21, no. 1 (1982): 1–28.

12. T. M. Knox, editorial notes, *Philosophy of Right,* 353–54, 365. And cf. Riedel: "Society [for Hegel] would not be 'civil' if it were not ordered and maintained legally, morally, and politically." Riedel, "'State' and 'Civil Society,'" 151. This, as many have pointed out, amounts to a more or less complete statement of the principle of the modern liberal state, leaving very little apart from formal constitutional machinery to the sphere of the "universal state" in Hegel's schema.

13. Z. A. Pelczynski, "Solidarity and 'The Rebirth of Civil Society' in Poland, 1976–81," in Keane, ed., *Civil Society and the State,* 364. See also Pelczynski's introduction to Z. A. Pelczynski, ed., *The State and Civil Society: Studies in Hegel's Political Philosophy* (Cambridge: Cambridge University Press, 1984). This interpretation seems particularly well supported by the closing paragraph of the section on civil society in *Philosophy of Right,* 155, para. 256; see also 123, para. 183; 124–25, para. 187; 145, para. 229; and addendum to 278, para. 255, where Hegel refers to "the work of a public character" performed by the corporation as a qualification of the "private business" pursued by individuals. It is worth remarking that, somewhat contradicting his emphatic materialist pronouncement, Avineri's detailed account of civil society in Hegel brings out the pluralism of its character, though Avineri does not always distinguish very clearly between the institutions of civil society and those of the state. See, for example, Avineri, *Hegel's Theory of the Modern State,* 165, 167–68.

14. Shlomo Avineri, *The Social and Political Thought of Karl Marx* (Cambridge: Cambridge University Press, 1968), 155–56. Avineri bases his interpretation largely on a letter from Marx to Engels on July 23, 1854, where Marx spoke of "the conspiratorial and revolutionary character of the municipal movement in the twelfth century." Karl Marx and Frederick Engels, *Selected Correspondence* (Moscow: Foreign Languages Publishing House, n.d.), 105–08.

15. Alvin Gouldner, "Civil Society in Capitalism and Socialism," in *The Two Marxisms* (London: Macmillan, 1980), 356 (Gouldner's emphasis). A similar criticism was powerfully made earlier by Leszek Kolakowski, "The Myth of Human Self-Identity: Unity of Civil and Political Society in Socialist Thought," in Leszek Kolakowski and Stuart Hampshire, eds., *The Socialist Idea: A Reappraisal* (London: Quartet Books, 1977), 18–35. More recently Jean Cohen has repeated the charge: the "fundamental

flaw" in Marx was "the reduction of civil society to the capitalist mode of production." Jean Cohen, *Class and Civil Society: The Limits of Marxian Critical Theory* (Oxford: Martin Robertson, 1982), 48, and generally, 23–52.

16. Marx, "Preface to A Contribution to the Critique of Political Economy," 362. Cf. also his *Economic and Philosophical Manuscripts* (1844): "Society, as it appears to the economist, is civil society, in which each individual is a totality of needs and only exists for another person, as the other exists for him, in so far as each becomes a means for the other." In *Karl Marx: Early Writings*, translated and edited by T. B. Bottomore (London: C.A. Watts, 1963), 181.

17. F. Engels, "Ludwig Feuerbach and the End of German Classical Philosophy," in Marx and Engels, *Selected Works in Two Volumes*, vol. 2, 394–95.

18. Gouldner, "Civil Society in Capitalism and Socialism," 370. For a similar account of Marxism's failure to deal with the "germ-cells" of social organization, see Martin Buber, *Paths in Utopia,* translated by R. F. C. Hull (Boston: Beacon Press, 1958), 80–98.

19. Gouldner, "Civil Society in Capitalism and Socialism," 371 (Gouldner's emphasis).

20. For this interpretation of Tocqueville, see Jeff Weintraub, *Freedom and Community: The Republican Virtue Tradition and the Sociology of Liberty* (Berkeley: University of California Press, forthcoming). Weintraub points out that although Tocqueville himself used the term "political society" loosely, as more or less synonymous with *government* or *polity,* his account of politics makes it possible and indeed desirable to recognize a specific realm distinct both from the state and civil society. In neither Hegel nor Marx is there anything corresponding directly to Tocqueville's "political society," but—if my interpretation is correct—Hegel's concept of civil society certainly included elements of it.

21. Alexis de Tocqueville, *Democracy in America,* edited by J. P. Mayer, translated by George Lawrence (New York: Harper and Row, 1988), 244, 515, 517, 521–22.

22. Sociologist Jeff Weintraub, private communication, February 13, 1992.

23. Antonio Gramsci, *Selections from the Prison Notebooks of Antonio Gramsci,* edited and translated by Quintin Hoare and Geoffrey Nowell Smith (London: Lawrence and Wishart, 1971), 208. Norberto Bobbio uses this passage to argue that, "contrary to what is commonly believed, Gramsci does not derive his concept of civil society from Marx but is openly indebted to Hegel for it." Norberto Bobbio, "Gramsci and the Concept of Civil Society," 83.

24. *Selections from the Prison Notebooks,* 208–9.

25. Bobbio, "Gramsci and the Concept of Civil Society," 82.

26.Gramsci, *Selections from the Prison Notebooks,* 52, 57. And cf. Gramsci's warning against those who insist "on a distinction between political society and civil society, which is made into and presented as an organic one, whereas in fact it is merely methodological." Ibid., 160. Elsewhere he also says that "by 'State' should be understood not only the apparatus of government, but also the 'private' apparatus of 'hegemony' or civil society. . . . The general notion of State includes elements which need to be referred back to the notion of civil society (in the sense that one might say that State = political society + civil society, in other words, hegemony protected by the armour of coercion)." Ibid., 261, 263. For a good account of the evolution of Gramsci's thinking on the state-civil society relationship, see Perry Anderson, "The Antinomies of Antonio Gramsci," *New Left Review* 100 (November 1976–January 1977): 5–78, especially 12–34.

27. "What we can do, for the moment, is to fix two major superstructural 'levels': the one that can be called 'civil society,' that is the ensemble of organisms commonly called 'private,' and that of 'political society' or 'the state.' These two levels correspond on the one hand to the function of 'hegemony' which the dominant group exercises

throughout society and on the other hand to that of 'direct domination' or command exercised through the state and 'juridical' government." Gramsci, *Selections from the Prison Notebooks,* 12.

28. Ibid., 56. Bobbio suggests that this conception of civil society distinguishes Gramsci from both Marx and Lenin in "Gramsci and the Concept of Civil Society," 93. It is perhaps worth noting here that Gramsci tended to use "hegemony" in two rather different senses. In the first usage it was contrasted with "domination," and as such was bound up with the opposition "state (or political society)—civil society." In the other usage, "hegemonic" is opposed to "corporate" or "economic-corporate" and is employed "to designate an historical phase in which a given group moves beyond a position of corporate existence and defense of its economic position and aspires to a position of leadership in the political and social arena." Editors' note, *Selections from the Prison Notebooks,* xiv.

29. Gramsci, *Selections from the Prison Notebooks,* 170. Bobbio points out the dual corollary of this view of civil society, as neither base nor political society: "The confusion between civil society and base generates the error of trade unionism; the confusion between civil society and political society generates that of idolatry of the state." Bobbio, "Gramsci and the Concept of Civil Society," 90.

30. Anderson, "The Antinomies of Antonio Gramsci," 35.

31. For this general conception of civil society, see, for example, Andrew Arato, "Civil Society Against the State: Poland 1980–81," *Telos* 47, (1981): 23–47; John Keane, "Introduction," in Keane, ed., *Civil Society and the State,* 1; Janina Frentzel-Zagorska, "Civil Society in Poland and Hungary," *Soviet Studies* 42, no. 4 (1990): 759; see also the entry "Civil Society" in D. Miller, ed., *The Blackwell Encyclopaedia of Political Thought* (Oxford: Basil Blackwell, 1987), 77.

32. Pierre Rosanvallon, "The Decline of Social Visibility," in Keane, ed., *Civil Society and the State,* 206–7, 210–11.

33. Ibid., 204

34. Ibid., 205

35. Ibid., 217.

36. John Keane, "The Limits of State Action," in Keane's *Democracy and Civil Society,* 15. Keane agrees with Rosanvallon that "self-governing, publicly funded associations within civil society would need to be recognized as special legal subjects endowed with definite legal privileges independent of the state." Ibid., 20 n.

37. Ibid., 22–23. This conception of the relation of the "universal" state to "particularistic" civil society is evidently Hegelian.

38. John Keane, "Introduction," in Keane, ed. *Civil Society and the State,* 23.

39. See Christopher Pierson, "New Theories of State and Civil Society: Recent Developments in Post-Marxist Analysis of the State," *Sociology* 18, no. 4 (1984): 569. Pierson points out that in neoliberal theory such a sanction is provided in the form of private property—an uncomfortable observation for the mostly radical, neo-Marxist advocates of civil society.

40. See, for example, György Konrád, *Antipolitics: An Essay,* translated from the Hungarian by Richard E. Allen (London: Quartet Books, 1984); Adam Michnik, *Letters from Prison and Other Essays,* translated by Maya Latynski (Berkeley: University of California Press, 1985); Václav Havel, *Living in Truth,* edited by Jan Vladislav (London: Faber and Faber, 1989). The literature of the 1970s in Poland and elsewhere is well reviewed by Arato, "Civil Society Against the State"; see also Jacques Rupnik, "Dissent in Poland, 1968–78: The End of Revisionism and the Rebirth of the Civil Society," in Rudolf Tokes, ed., *Opposition in Eastern Europe* (Baltimore: Johns Hopkins University

Press, 1979), 60–112, and the references in Gail Kligman, "Reclaiming the Public: a Reflection on Creating Civil Society in Romania," *East European Politics and Societies* 4, no. 3 (fall 1990): 42L n. 45. There has been some questioning of this emphasis on civil society since the 1989 revolutions in East-Central Europe, but, as Arpad Szakolczai observes, "Civil society still seems to be the most popular concept, though with some shift in emphasis." Moreover, although it was previously not very important in the Soviet Union, "now it is taken up with a vengeance even there." Szakolczai, "Were State and Society Ever Identical?" 1–2. For the importance of the concept in recent Soviet debates, see Gail Lapidus, "State and Society: Toward the Emergence of Civil Society in the Soviet Union," in Seweryn Bialer, ed., *Gorbachev's Russia: Politics, Society and Nationality* (Boulder, Colo.: Westview, 1989); Richard Sakwa, *Gorbachev and His Reforms 1985–1990* (Hemel Hempstead, U.K.: Philip Allan, 1990), 198–230. In the popular resistance to the attempted coup against Gorbachev in August 1991, one eminent commentator discerned the coming of age of civil society in the Soviet Union. See Francis Fukuyama, "There's No Stopping Them Now," *The Independent on Sunday* (August 25, 1991), 11; see also Martin Malia, "The August Revolution," *New York Review of Books* (September 26, 1991), 22–28.

 41. Rupnik, "Dissent in Poland," 60.

 42. Arato, "Civil Society against the State," 24. See also Pelczynski, "Solidarity and 'The Rebirth of Civil Society' in Poland," 361–80; Frentzel-Zagorska, "Civil Society in Poland and Hungary," 768. On the "seminal" importance of the example of Solidarity, see Timothy Garton Ash, *We The People: The Revolution of '89* (Cambridge, U.K.: Granta Books, 1990), 134, and also Timothy Garton Ash, *The Polish Revolution: Solidarity* (London: Jonathan Cape, 1983); Konrád, *Antipolitics*, 136–45.

 43. For this conception of civil society, see especially Adam Michnik, "The New Evolutionism" (1976), in *Letters from Prison*, 135–48. This remained the dominant view of Solidarity's mission—inherited from Komitet Obrony Robotników (KOR)—up to the very last days before it was driven underground by the declaration of martial law in 1981. See Michnik, "What We Want and What We Can Do," *Telos* 47 (spring 1981): 66–77. The strategy was described by Michnik as "the crossing of the totalitarian structure of power with the democratic mechanism of corporate representation." For this strategy of "societal pluralism" (or "pluralism restricted to civil society"), see Arato, "Civil Society against the State," 36–43. And, on the parallel idea of the "second society" in Hungary as the positive counterpart to the official society, cf. Elemer Hankiss, "The 'Second Society': Is There an Alternative Social Model Emerging in Contemporary Hungary?" *Social Research* 55, nos. 1–2 (1988): 13–42.

 44. See Krishan Kumar, "The Revolutions of 1989: Capitalism, Socialism and Democracy," *Theory and Society* 21 (1992): 309–56 (reprinted as chapter 2 of this book).

 45. For the very real achievements of Solidarity, following this strategy, up to 1981, see Andrew Arato, "Empire vs. Civil Society: Poland 1981–82," *Telos* 50 (1981–82): 19–48. Writing before the events of 1989, Pelczynski argued that Solidarity had overreached itself in pitting itself directly against the state in 1981. Pelczynski, "Solidarity and 'The Rebirth of Civil Society' in Poland," 371–78. But it is not clear that in 1981 Solidarity had really changed its strategy. At any rate, the strategy proved remarkably successful even in Solidarity's underground period between 1981 and 1989. See Frentzel-Zagorska, "Civil Society in Poland and Hungary," 770–72.

 46. The problem, as Janina Frentzel-Zagorska has put it, is that "a leading part of 'the civil society against the state' became a leading part of the state"—and was ill prepared for it. Janina Frentzel-Zagorska, "Patterns of Transition from a One-Party State to Democracy in Poland and Hungary," in R. F. Miller, ed., *The Development of Civil*

*Society in Communist Systems* (London: Unwin Hyman, 1992). For this discussion of Solidarity I have also benefited from seeing a stimulating exchange of letters between Laszlo Bruszt and Jeff Weintraub.

47. See Arato, "Empire vs. Civil Society," 23. By the same token, however, this also limits the applicability of the Solidarity model to the West—despite Arato's claims on this score. Ibid., 23; see also Arato and Cohen, "Civil Society and Social Theory," 60. Arato has elsewhere indicated the contrary need, for East European theorists to learn from Western discussions of civil society. See Andrew Arato, "Revolution, Civil Society and Democracy," *Praxis International* 10 (April–July 1990): 40–55.

48. A tendency already remarked upon by Jerzy Szacki in "The Utopia of Civil Society in Poland Today," mimeographed paper, Warsaw, 1987. See also C. M. Hann, "Second Economy and Civil Society," in C. M. Hann, ed., *Market Economy and Civil Society in Hungary* (London: Frank Cass, 1990), 31. For an interesting defense of the concept of civil society as a "self-limiting utopia," linked to Habermas's idea of the democratization of the "life-world," see Arato and Cohen, "Civil Society and Social Theory," 52–53.

49. Quoted in Kligman, "Reclaiming the Public," 395–96. For Kligman this statement "succinctly encompasses the characteristic markers of 'civil society.' "

50. Gramsci, *Selections from the Prison Notebooks*, 238–39; on statolatry, see 268–69.

51. Anderson, "The Antinomies of Antonio Gramsci," 28–29. Anderson does not, however, want to follow Althusser and elide altogether the "state–civil society" distinction. Ibid., 34–36.

52. Wood, "The Uses and Abuses of 'Civil Society,' " 63. See also Hann, "Second Economy and Civil Society," 29–35. A similar position is forcibly stated by Frank Parkin in "Civil Society and the State in Classic Social Theory," paper presented to the 1991 Congress of the Hungarian Sociological Association, Budapest, June 1991.

53. See especially Keane, "The Limits of State Action," 1–6; Keane, "Introduction," in Keane, ed., *Civil Society and the State*. Wood has some incisive comments on this rediscovery of civil society by the left in "The Uses and Abuses of 'Civil Society,' " 60–80.

54. See, for example, Derek Heater, *Citizenship: The Civic Ideal in World History, Politics and Education* (London: Longman, 1990); J. M. Barbalet, *Citizenship* (Milton Keynes, U.K.: Open University Press, 1988); Geoff Andrews, ed. *Citizenship* (London: Lawrence and Wishart, 1991). We should note, too, that T. H. Marshall's discussion of citizenship does not rely on any concept of civil society. T. H. Marshall, "Citizenship and Social Class," in *Sociology at the Crossroads, and Other Essays* (London: Heinemann, 1963), 67–127. No more does Bryan Turner's restatement and defense of Marshall's position. Bryan Turner, *Citizenship and Capitalism: The Debate Over Reformism* (London: Allen and Unwin, 1986). For the view that, on the contrary, the concept of civil society is preferable to that of democracy, see Ernest Gellner, "Civil Society in Historical Context," *International Social Science Journal* 43, no. 3 (1991): 495–510.

Adam Seligman pointed out, at the 1991 Congress of the Hungarian Sociological Association, that the concept of civil society in most of its uses adds very little to the concept of democracy as expounded, for example, by Robert Dahl in *Polyarchy* (New Haven: Yale University Press, 1971).

55. See Sarah Benton, "Citizen Major," *Marxism Today* (July 1991), 9. For the need of a new constitutional settlement in Britain, see David Marquand, *The Unprincipled Society* (London: Jonathan Cape, 1988); see also the widely published Charter 88 Manifesto—for example, in *The Independent* (August 24, 1991), and Tony Benn's proposed Commonwealth of Britain Bill, published in The *Independent* (July 11, 1991).

56. Kligman, "Reclaiming the Public," 426.

57. Jeffrey C. Alexander, "Introduction. Civil Society I, II, III: Constructing an Empirical Concept from Normative Controversies and Historical Transformations," in Alexander, ed., *Real Civil Societies: Dilemmas of Institutionalization* (Thousand Oaks, Calif.: Sage Publications, 1998), 1.

58. For East European misgivings, see, for example, Jerzy Szacki, "Polish Democracy: Dreams and Reality," *Social Research* 58, no. 4 (1991): 711–22; Bronislaw Geremek, "Civil Society and the Present Age," in B. Geremek, György Varga, Czesław Miłosz, and Connor Cruise O'Brien, *The Idea of Civil Society* (Research Triangle Park, N.C.: The National Humanities Center, 1992), 11–18; G. M. Tamás, "The Legacy of Dissent," *Times Literary Supplement* (May 14, 1993): 14–19; G. M. Tamás, "A Disquisition on Civil Society," *Social Research* 61, no. 2 (summer 1994): 205–22. And, on the need for a "multiparty system and parliamentary democracy" as the necessary basis and precondition for the establishment or reestablishment of civil society in East Central Europe, cf. Ferenc Miszlivetz, "The Injuries of East Central Europe: Is the Auto-Therapy of Civil Society Possible?" in Vera Gathy and Jody Jensen, eds., *Citizenship in Europe?* (Budapest: Szombathely, 1992), 88. He warns, however, that this system should not allow itself to be *substituted* for civil society, as seems to be the danger in the transition period.

59. A very partial list would include the following useful collections, in addition to that of Alexander's mentioned above: Zbigniew Rau, ed., *The Reemergence of Civil Society in Eastern Europe and the Soviet Union* (Boulder, Colo.: Westview Press, 1991); C. Kukathas, D. W. Lovell, and W. Maley, eds., *The Transition from Socialism: State and Civil Society in the USSR* (Melbourne: Longman Cheshire, 1991); P. G. Lewis, ed., *Democracy and Civil Society in Eastern Europe* (London: Macmillan, 1992); Robert F. Miller, ed., *The Development of Civil Society in Communist Systems* (London: Unwin Hyman, 1992); John A. Hall, ed., *Civil Society: Theory, History, Comparison* (Cambridge, U.K.: Polity Press, 1995); Christopher G. A. Bryant and Edmund Mokrzycki, eds., *Democracy, Civil Society and Pluralism* (Warsaw: IFIS Publishers, 1995); Michael Walzer, ed., *Toward a Global Civil Society* (Providence, R.I.: Berghahn Books, 1995); Chris Hann and Elizabeth Dunn, eds., *Civil Society: Challenging Western Models* (New York: Routledge, 1996); Robert Fine and Shirin Rai, eds., *Civil Society: Democratic Perspectives* (London: Frank Cass, 1997); Sunil Khilnani, ed., *Civil Society* (Cambridge: Cambridge University Press, 1998); Robert K. Fullinwider, ed., *Civil Society, Democracy, and Civic Renewal* (Lanham, Md.: Rowman and Littlefield, 1999).

In addition, some important individual contributions have appeared since my article was written. Jean Cohen and Andrew Arato have published their long-awaited book, *Civil Society and Political Theory* (Cambridge, Mass.: MIT Press, 1992). The historical dimensions of the concept, and their implications for attempting to resurrect it today, are incisively explored in Adam B. Seligman, *The Idea of Civil Society* (New York: The Free Press, 1992). Ernest Gellner has drawn upon earlier work for a full-scale treatment, *Conditions of Liberty: Civil Society and Its Rivals* (London: Hamish Hamilton, 1994). And John Keane has returned to the subject he did so much to open up in the two volumes referred to in notes 1 and 2 of this chapter, in his new book of reflections, *Civil Society: Old Images, New Visions* (Cambridge, U.K.: Polity Press, 1998).

For valuable additional discussions of the history of the concept, see Neera Chandhoke, *State and Civil Society: Explorations in Political Theory* (London: Sage Publications, 1995); Dario Castiglione, "History and Theories of Civil Society: Outline of a Contested Paradigm," *Australian Journal of Politics and History* 40 (1994): 83–103; Charles Taylor, "Modes of Civil Society," *Public Culture* 3, no. 1 (1990): 95–118; Charles Taylor, "Civil Society in the Western Tradition," in Ethel Groffier and

Michael Paradis, eds., *The Notion of Tolerance and Human Rights: Essays in Honor of Raymond Klibansky* (Toronto: Carleton University Press, 1991), 117–34; Craig Calhoun, "Civil Society and the Public Sphere," *Public Culture* 5 (1993): 267–80; Melvin Richter, "Montesquieu and the Concept of Civil Society," *The European Legacy* 3 (1998): 33–41; John Ehrenberg, *Civil Society: The Critical History of an Idea* (New York: New York University Press, 1999).

Also relevant are two further historical contributions: Marvin B. Becker, *The Emergence of Civil Society in the Eighteenth Century* (Bloomington: Indiana University Press, 1994); Margaret C. Jacob, "The Enlightenment Redefined: The Formation of Civil Society," *Social Research* 58, no. 2 (summer 1991): 475–95. One might also add here some writing that, although it does not always explicitly use the language of civil society, clearly refers to the thing—for instance, Robert Putnam, *Making Democracy Work: Civic Traditions in Modern Italy* (Princeton: Princeton University Press, 1993); Robert Putnam, "Bowling Alone: America's Declining Social Capital," *Journal of Democracy* 6 (1995): 65–78.

60. Keane, *Civil Society*, 32; and see 12–31, with the literature referred to, for the "globalization" of the civil society idea.

61. The article was directly and vigorously combated by a member of the editorial board of the journal in which it appeared, and in the same issue. See Christopher G. A. Bryant, "Social Self-organisation, Civility and Sociology: A Comment on Kumar's 'Civil Society,'" *British Journal of Sociology* 44, no. 3 (1993): 397–401. I, in turn, replied to Bryant in "Civil Society Again: A Reply to Christopher Bryant's 'Social Self-organisation, Civility and Sociology,'" *British Journal of Sociology* 45, no. 1 (1994): 127–31, to which Bryant responded in "A Further Comment on Kumar's 'Civil Society,'" *British Journal of Sociology* 45, no. 3 (1994): 497–99. For references to the article in the literature, as an instance of dissent from the common approach and approbation, see, for example, John Hall, "In Search of Civil Society," in John Hall, ed., *Civil Society*, 27; Keane, *Civil Society*, 67; Philip Smith, "Barbarism and Civility in the Discourses of Fascism, Communism and Democracy," in Alexander, ed., *Real Civil Societies*, 133.

62. See especially the contributions in Hann and Dunn, eds., *Civil Society*; see also Chris Hann, "Civil Society at the Grassroots: A Reactionary View," in Lewis, ed., *Democracy and Civil Society in Eastern Europe*, 152–65; Chris Hann, "Zivilgesellschaft oder Bürgerschaft? Skeptische Überlegungen eines Ethnologen," in Manfred Hildermeier and Jürgen Kocka, eds., *Zivilgesellschaft in Ost und West: Begriff, Geschicte, Chancen* (Frankfurt: Campus Verlag, 2000).

63. Keane, *Civil Society*, 36. For a good example of the "muddle and delirium" that the term has given rise to, see Keith Tester, *Civil Society* (London and New York: Routledge, 1992). Tester sees "civil society" as the virtually utopian object of Western political speculation from Hobbes to Rousseau: "To talk of civil society has conventionally meant to distinguish the milieu of free humanity from the milieu of reification produced either by nature or the state. . . . Civil society meant to never again take the freedom of society and social relationships for granted." Ibid., 11. Here, as in so much of the literature on civil society, the celebratory and prescriptive purpose overwhelms historical accuracy and conceptual clarity.

It should be said that taking the broad or "long view" of civil society as more or less coterminous with modern Western liberal society is not necessarily inimical to productive uses. Ernest Gellner deploys such a conception with considerable force and ingenuity in his opposition of civil society to various forms of authoritarianism and totalitarianism, modern and premodern in *Conditions of Liberty*. But there are evident dangers here, as well, both in an overgenerous embrace that does not allow for important distinctions in

314 Notes to Chapter 5

the meaning of the term and in a certain complacency that regards Western liberal societies as basically unproblematic.

64. W. B. Gallie, "Essentially Contested Concepts," *Proceedings of the Aristotelian
Society,* New Series vol. 56 (1955–56): 172, 193.

65. Ibid., 194.

66. See note 16 to this chapter.

67. Víctor Pérez-Díaz, "The Public Sphere and A European Civil Society," in
Alexander, ed., *Real Civil Societies,* 211. See also Víctor Pérez-Díaz, *The Return of Civil
Society: The Emergence of Democratic Spain* (Cambridge, Mass.: Harvard University
Press, 1993); Víctor Pérez-Díaz, "The Possibility of Civil Society: Traditions, Character
and Challenges," in Hall, ed., *Civil Society,* 80–109. Pérez-Díaz characterizes his "gen-
eralist" concept of civil society as follows: "By 'civil society' I mean an ideal type referring to a set of political and social institutions, characterized by limited, responsible
government subject to the rule of law, free and open markets, a plurality of voluntary
associations and a sphere of free public debate." Pérez-Díaz, "The Public Sphere and a
European Civil Society," 220.

68. For a clear account of Habermas's conception, see William Outhwaite, *Habermas*
(Cambridge, U.K.: Polity Press, 1986).

69. See Jeffrey Alexander, "Introduction," in Alexander, ed., *Real Civil Societies,*
6–8; see also Jeffrey C. Alexander, "The Paradoxes of Civil Society," *International
Sociology* 12, no. 2 (1997): 115–33. In this latter piece Alexander mentions both
Gramsci and Habermas as influences on his conception. He also stresses the extent to
which civil society must not be understood as restricted to a separate societal sphere, but
operates rather as a universalizing discourse of solidarity and human rights crossing all
spheres and potentially encompassing the whole of humanity; see 122–23, 128–29.
Presumably the link is that the sphere of civil society has as its specific function the production and cultivation of this universalizing discourse that is available for mobilization
in other spheres. On this, see further Jeffrey C. Alexander and Philip Smith, "The Discourse of American Civil Society: A New Proposal for Cultural Studies," *Theory and
Society* 22 (1993): 151–207. This position has some similarities with Michael Walzer's
view of civil society as "a setting of settings"—that is, as a kind of liberal "anti-ideology"
that has no singularity of its own, but is a praxis wherein different versions of the good
life compete and are tested. See Michael Walzer, "The Civil Society Argument," in
Chantal Mouffe, ed., *Dimensions of Radical Democracy: Pluralism, Citizenship, Community* (New York: Verso, 1992), 97–98.

It is perhaps hardly necessary to say that the "minimalists" are not all of one mind,
any more than are the "generalists." Alexander, for instance, criticizes Cohen and Arato
for having an insufficiently differentiated concept. They distinguish civil society from
the state and economy, but not, in addition, religion, the family, and other spheres that
operate on principles different from those of civil society. Alexander, "Paradoxes,"
127–28; see also his review of Cohen and Arato's *Civil Society and Political Theory:*
Jeffrey Alexander, "The Return to Civil Society," *Contemporary Sociology* 22, no. 6
(1994): 797–803. It is possible that the highly differentiated view of civil society is derived, in part, from an American experience in which not only was religion made a voluntary activity, but the state, too, was radically demoted, conceptually and practically.
The distinguishing feature of the United States hitherto, says Daniel Bell, is that "it has
been the complete *civil society,* . . . perhaps the only one in history." Daniel Bell,
"'American Exceptionalism' Revisited: The Role of Civil Society," *The Public Interest*
95 (1989): 48.

70. Keane, *Civil Society,* 17–19; see also Pérez-Díaz, "The Public Sphere and a

European Civil Society," 213–15. And cf. Michael Walzer: "The market, when it is entangled in the networks of associations, when the forms of ownership are pluralized, is without doubt the economic formation most consistent with the civil society argument." Michael Walzer, "The Civil Society Argument," 98. A similar view is expressed by Edward Shils in "The Virtue of Civil Society," *Government and Society* 26, no. 1 (1991): 9.

Martin Malia has made the absence of market institutions the cardinal reason why civil society will be difficult to achieve in Eastern Europe in the near future: "The creation of a mature, diversified civil society in the East still lies many years in the future. What until now has been called 'civil society' has in fact been a moral civil society of dissidents, democrats, and ecclesiastics; it was not a material civil society, because there was almost no private property. Indeed the destruction of society was perhaps the greatest crime that the total Party-state committed against the populations it ruled." Martin Malia, "Leninist Endgame," *Daedalus* 121, no. 2 (spring 1992): 71–72.

71. Alexander, "Introduction," 8–9.

72. Warning against East European "anti-politics," with its rejection of the state, Walzer rightly says that the state "both frames civil society and occupies space within it. It fixes the boundary conditions and the basic rules of all associational activity. . . . Civil society requires political agency." Walzer, "The Civil Society Argument," 103–4. See also Shils, "The Virtue of Civil Society," 15. And, on the positive role of the state in enhancing the life of civil society, cf. Chris Hann, "Introduction: Political Society and Civil Anthropology," in Hann, ed., *Civil Society*, 7–9, 21–22. In a powerful piece, David Rieff warns against the "neo-medievalism" of uncontrolled private interests that may be the consequence of a victory of the civil society advocates: "In undermining the state, [these advocates] undermine the only remaining power that has at least the potential to stand in opposition to the privatization of the world, commonly known as globalization." David Rieff, "The False Dawn of Civil Society," *The Nation* (February 22, 1999), 12. A similar view, of the dangers of the antistatist concept of civil society now popular in both East and West, informs John Ehrenberg's study *Civil Society* (see note 3).

Two recent episodes are melancholy reminders of the dangers of advocating the strongly antistate, antipolitical version of civil society, as if civil society were some self-sufficient, self-sustaining entity. There is Rwanda, which before its descent into genocide was regarded by developmental experts as having one of the most developed civil societies in Africa; and there is Kosovo, where there was much support in the West for the strategy of the Albanian leader Ibrahim Rugova in taking a Solidarity-style, non-confrontational stance against the Serbian state in the early 1990s. With their organization of their own schools, hospitals, and even universities, as Charles King says, "Rugova's Democratic League of Kosovo was the closest thing to civil society that the southern Balkans had seen since the outbreak of [the Bosnian] war." Alas, it did little to save them against the Serbian troops. See Charles King, "Where the West Went Wrong," *Times Literary Supplement* (May 7, 1999), 3; for a similar view, see also Warren Zimmermann, "Milosevic's Final Solution," *New York Review of Books* (June 10, 1999): 41. On Rwanda, see Rieff, "The False Dawn of Civil Society," 15.

73. A point underlined by Keane's summary statement that "where there are no markets, civil societies find it impossible to survive. But the converse rule also applies: where there is no civil society, there can be no markets." Keane, *Civil Society*, 19.

74. It is clear in the case of Gellner, in *Conditions of Liberty*, that civil society is so equated with modern liberal society, and somewhat less clearly so in the writings of Pérez-Díaz. Neither of them fully explains why they need the concept of civil society. Shils, too, equates civil society with "liberal democratic society," in his case adding the

need for "civility" on the part of leaders and citizens. See Shils, "The Virtue of Civil Society," 16–18. Elsewhere he goes even further in arguing for the need for the idea of the nation as a precondition for the existence of civil society. See Shils, "Nation, Nationality, Nationalism and Civil Society," *Nations and Nationalism* 1, no. 1 (1995): 93–118.

75. One of the problems with Cohen and Arato's otherwise impressive *Civil Society and Political Theory* is their unwillingness to acknowledge that or to make use of the intellectual and historical material it offers. As Istvan Hont wrote in a review, they "choose to remain restricted within a modern German perspective," which means that they discuss civil society almost exclusively within the Hegelian and post-Hegelian tradition. The result is a considerable loss of scope and efficacy. Hont continued, "Arato and Cohen are so keen to get themselves and their friends out of the difficulties of *Kulturkritik* that they forget how much wider and historically deeper the debates between ancient and modern liberty, virtue and rights, direct democracy and constitutionalism, resistance and undivided sovereignty, mixed government and elective democracy, state and market, have all been. They refuse to learn from the theoretical traditions which predate the early 19th century and spurn their languages of politics." Istvan Hont, "Liberty, Equality, Prudence," *The Times Higher Educational Supplement* (October 9, 1992), 25. And cf. the similar point made by Alexander in "Paradoxes," 129, n. 3. The importance of the earlier tradition of use, specifically that associated with early English liberalism and the Scottish Enlightenment, is also urged by John Gray, who thinks it might help contemporary East Europeans to forget their obsession with "democracy" and concentrate more on the rule of law, the importance of contracts, and market institutions. See John Gray, "Post-Totalitarianism, Civil Society, and the Limits of the Western Model," in Rau, ed., *The Reemergence of Civil Society in Eastern Europe and the Soviet Union,* 145–60.

76. Hann, "Introduction," in Hann, ed., *Civil Society,* 1.

77. Ibid., 9–10, 17–21.

78. Seligman, *The Idea of Civil Society,* especially chapter 2.

79. A good start can be made with Margaret Somers's historical exploration of the concepts of "public culture" and the "public sphere," which she sees as linked to the Western—though mainly Anglo-Saxon—"metanarrative" of civil society, starting with John Locke. See Margaret Somers, "What's Political or Cultural about Political Culture and the Public Sphere? Toward an Historical Sociology of Concept Formation," *Sociological Theory* 13, no. 2 (1995): 113–44; Margaret Somers, "Narrating and Naturalizing Civil Society and Citizenship Theory: The Place of Political Culture and the Public Sphere," *Sociological Theory* 13, no. 3 (1995): 229–74. And cf. Eugene Kamenka: "The term *civil society,* like any other important social concept, needs not to be defined but to be understood in a multiplicity of often competing contexts." Eugene Kamenka, "Civil Society and Freedom in the Post-Communist World," in Margaret L Nugent, ed., *From Leninism to Freedom: The Challenges of Democratization* (Boulder, Colo: Westview Press, 1992), 117. A valuable aspect of John Ehrenberg's recent study, *Civil Society* (see note 3), is its historical span, moving from classical conceptions through medieval and early modern usages to its recent usages in Eastern Europe and its current usages in the West.

80. The introduction of the idea of "social capital," and its possible depletion, is clearly related to a similar concern. See the works by Putnam listed in note 3 to this chapter. "Political culture," popular in the 1960s, is also making something of a comeback—again, presumably, for the same reasons.

81. In what seems a rather desperate effort to save the concept of civil society in the

midst of the proliferation of uses and meanings, and in the face of criticism from anthropologists and others, Keane proposes a "post-foundationalist" understanding that "itself recognizes, and actively reinforces respect for, the multiplicity of and often incommensurable normative codes and forms of contemporary life." This new, postmodern, concept is meant to meet the objections that the idea of civil society is ethnocentric (that is, that it is too heavily reliant on liberal individualist Western thought), that it is unviable as a current project because it can no longer rely on its original moral and religious foundations (the Seligman argument), and, above all, that it is vacuous because of the multiple and contradictory meanings attached to it. See Keane, *Civil Society*, 53–56. No doubt a "post-foundationalist" concept is capable of meeting these and any other objections, but it seems to do so simply by becoming spongelike, taking in all and everything that comes its way. This hardly seems a solution; it is more a counsel of despair. For some stimulating remarks on the problem of universalism and relativism in conceptualizing civil society, see Hann, "Introduction," in Hann, ed., *Civil Society*, 17–21.

82. For the exuberance and exhilaration that still surrounded the concept in the early 1990s, see Vladimir Tismaneanu's encomium in *Reinventing Politics: Eastern Europe from Stalin to Havel* (New York: The Free Press, 1992), chapters 4 and 5. For the increasing doubts about the relevance of the concept, see the references in note 2 to this chapter. G. M. Tamás, a former Hungarian dissident, in particular has expressed increasing disillusionment (though now from a North American base). For him "the central myth of 1989 is civil society," and its legacy is an outburst of antinomian and anarchic sentiment—similar to that seen in 1968—that is making it almost impossible to construct stable and orderly democratic regimes in the region. Paradoxically, "like communism, the myth of civil society is a tale of a non-coercive political order." Tamás, "A Disquisition on Civil Society," 215–16.

83. For an often hilarious account of the attempt to "export" civil society to Eastern Europe, in the form of Western foundations and international agencies trying to set up or support "nongovernmental organizations" (NGOs) in the region, see Steven Sampson, "The Social Life of Projects: Importing Civil Society to Albania," in Hann, ed., *Civil Society*, 121–42. Sampson shows this to be a two-way affair, with East Europeans often exploiting these efforts for their own private, and occasionally public, agendas. For the view that these efforts are a substitute for the promised and more relevant material aid to the region, see Rieff, "The False Dawn of Civil Society," 12.

84. Cf. Bronislaw Geremek's melancholy observation, partly with the Church in mind: "In the light of the dangers that have appeared on the horizon for Poland in particular and for Central and Eastern Europe in general, we must ask whether the idea of civil society—however effective it was in helping to bring down communism—will turn out to be useless in the building of democracy." Bronislaw Geremek, "Civil Society and the Present Age," 18. At the same conference at which Geremek spoke, Connor Cruise O'Brien also expressed the view that "the threat to civil society comes not from the State alone, but from some of the components of civil society itself. Not least among these are the churches, almost all of which in the former Soviet Empire have strong authoritarian traditions and will now be working together with and not against other authoritarian traditions in the society." Connor Cruise O'Brien, "Religion, Nationalism, and Civil Society," in Geremek, Varga, Miłosz, and O'Brien, *The Idea of Civil Society*, 28.

For a more optimistic account of the Polish scene, but one recognizing that "civil society" might mean something very different now from what it did in the ebullient Solidarity era, see Michael Buchowski, "The Shifting Meanings of Civil and Civic Society in Poland," in Hann, ed., *Civil Society*, 79–98; and, for a similar perception of the switch of forms and meanings in the post-Solidarity period, with a guarded optimism about future developments, see Wlodzimierz Wesolowski, "The Nature of Social Ties and the Future of Postcommunist Society: Poland after Solidarity," in Hall, ed., *Civil Society,* 110–35. Piotr Sztompka has moved from a fundamentally pessimistic position to one where he sees more hope, particularly in the increase of the peculiarly important resource of trust. See Piotr Sztompka, "Mistrusting Civility: Predicament of a Post-Communist Society," in Alexander, ed., *Real Civil Societies,* 191–210; see especially the note on 206.

85. See the general survey of postcommunist societies in Larry Ray, *Social Theory and the Crisis of State Socialism* (Cheltenham, U.K.: Edward Elgar, 1996), 200–28.

86. The conference, convened by the Czech President Václav Havel, was entitled *Forum 2000.* It was held in Prague October 12–15, 1998.

## 6. The End of Socialism? The End of Utopia? The End of History?

1. For the millennial expectations at the end of the first millennium, see Henri Focillon, *The Year 1000,* translated by Fred D. Wieck (New York: F. Ungar Publishing Co., 1969). An early indication of those at the end of the second millennium was the channel 4 series on British television, *Fin de Siècle,* broadcast in February 1992 (summary booklet: London, Broadcasting Support Services, 1992). For other indications, see Martin Jay, "Apocalypse and the Inability to Mourn," in Jay's *Force Fields: Between Intellectual History and Cultural Criticism* (London: Routledge, 1992).

There is, of course, as Focillon himself admitted, no intrinsic or necessary relationship between the ordinary calendrical millennium and the millennial hopes and strivings born of the prophecies of the Book of Revelation (the Apocalypse of St. John of Patmos). The reason the year 1000 carried a millennial charge was that thinkers like St. Augustine identified the millennium of Revelation with the first thousand years of the Christian era. Thus, as the year 1000 approached, people were seized with the expectation that the vividly portrayed events of the Apocalypse were imminent. The disconfirmation of this characteristically did nothing to still millennial hopes in future centuries: indeed, the period from the eleventh century to the sixteenth was a time of the most intense millennialism in Europe. See Norman Cohn, *The Pursuit of the Millennium* (London: Mercury Books, 1962). On Joachim, see Marjorie Reeves, *Joachim of Fiore and the Prophetic Future* (London: SPCK, 1976). A compelling interpretation of the millennial impulse in literature is Frank Kermode, *The Sense of an Ending: Studies in the Theory of Fiction* (New York: Oxford University Press, 1968).

Calendrical endings, such as the end of a century, undoubtedly stimulate millennial-type prophecies of death and rebirth, of endings and new beginnings; see Hillel Schwartz, *Century's End: A Cultural History of the Fin de Siècle from the 990s to the 1990s* (New York: Collier-Macmillan, 1990). For the celebrated case of the last century, see Mikulas Teich and Roy Porter, eds., *Fin de Siècle and Its Legacy* (Cambridge: Cambridge University Press, 1991).

2. See especially Francis Fukuyama, *The End of History and the Last Man* (New York: The Free Press, 1922), 287–339. The sense of unease is particularly marked in the book, as compared to the more lighthearted treatment in Fukuyama's original article, "The End of History?" *The National Interest* (summer 1989): 3–18.

3. See chapter 2 of this book.

4. See my *Utopia and Anti-Utopia in Modern Times* (Oxford: Basil Blackwell, 1987), 380–88; see also my *Utopianism* (Milton Keynes: Open University Press, 1991), 90–95.

5. Anthony Sampson, "The Need for Utopias," *The Independent Magazine* 21 (September 1991): 14. And cf. Norberto Bobbio, reflecting on the collapse of communism in Central and Eastern Europe in 1989: "In a seemingly irreversible way, the great-

est political utopia in history . . . has been completely upturned into its exact opposite." Norberto Bobbio, "The Upturned Utopia," in Robin Blackburn, ed., *After the Fall: The Failure of Communism and the Future of Socialism* (London: Verso, 1991), 3.

6. For a good study of this way of thinking, see David Caute, *The Fellow-Travellers: Intellectual Friends of Communism,* revised and updated edition (New Haven: Yale University Press, 1988). For subsequent defections, see Richard Crossman, ed., *The God That Failed* (1950; reprint New York: Bantam Books, 1965).

7. On the utopian elements in fascism, see Zeev Sternhell, "Fascist Ideology," in Walter Lacquer, ed., *Fascism: A Reader's Guide* (Harmondsworth, U.K.: Penguin Books, 1979), esp. 354–64. For Soviet communism, see Jerome Gilison, *The Soviet Image of Utopia* (Baltimore: Johns Hopkins University Press, 1975). And cf. Joe Bailey: "The most dramatic test of socialist utopianism has been the experience of its actual practice in the Soviet Union or in China, where it is irredeemably tainted with, and condemned by, its totalitarian formation." Joe Bailey, *Pessimism* (London: Routledge, 1988), 69.

8. For the contemporary reception and interpretation of *Nineteen Eighty-Four,* see Bernard Crick's introduction to his edition of George Orwell, *Nineteen Eighty-Four* (Oxford: Clarendon Press, 1984); see also Kumar, *Utopia and Anti-Utopia in Modern Times,* 288–96.

9. *We,* written in Russia in 1920, was first published in English in New York in 1924, but for long remained a rarity. It was translated into various languages thereafter; Orwell reviewed a French edition in 1946. It was not published in the original Russian (again in New York) until 1952; and it was not available in Russia itself until the Khrushchev thaw of the 1960s. See Christopher Collins, *Evgenij Zamyatin: An Interpretive Study* (The Hague: Mouton, 1973).

10. On Koestler's "lost weekend in Utopia," see his contribution to *The God That Failed,* 11–66.

11. They belong to a whole "literature of disillusionment" that runs from Zamyatin to Pasternak and Solzhenitsyn, and includes both fictional and nonfictional works. For some of the former, see Alan Swingewood, *The Novel and Revolution* (London: Macmillan, 1975); Paul N. Siegel, *Revolution and the Twentieth-Century Novel* (New York: Monad Press, 1979).

12. K. R. Popper, *The Open Society and Its Enemies,* 2 volumes, 4th edition (London: Routledge and Kegan Paul, 1962), vol. 1, viii.

13. Ibid., vol. 1, 168; and generally, 157–68. This criticism is substantially repeated in Popper's essay, "Utopia and Violence" (1948), in Popper's *Conjectures and Refutations,* 2nd edition (London: Routledge and Kegan Paul, 1965), 355–63.

14. George Kateb called *The Open Society and Its Enemies* "the most inclusive book" of the antiutopian critique in *Utopia and Its Enemies* (New York: Schocken Books, 1972), 19. Kateb's study gives an excellent account of twentieth-century antiutopianism.

15. The inquiry was continued in two other books, *Political Messianism: The Romantic Phase* (London: Secker and Warburg, 1960), and *The Myth of the Nation and the Vision of Revolution* (London: Secker and Warburg, 1980). Talmon was born in Poland.

16. Cohn, *The Pursuit of the Millennium,* vi. Cohn's book was first published, in London, in 1957.

17. Isaiah Berlin, *The Crooked Timber of Humanity: Chapters in the History of Ideas* (London: Fontana Press, 1990), 68. For Berlin's other attacks on utopian forms of thinking, see his *Four Essays on Liberty* (London: Oxford University Press, 1969); see also "Philosophy and Life," an interview with Berlin by Ramin Jahanbegloo, *New York Review of Books* (May 28, 1992), 46–54.

18. Berlin's pessimism comes out in his comment that the "liberal sermon which recommends machinery designed to prevent people from doing each other too much harm, giving each human group sufficient room to realise its own idiosyncratic, unique particular ends without too much interference with the ends of others"—his own creed—"is not a passionate battle-cry to inspire men to sacrifice and martyrdom and heroic feats." Berlin, *The Crooked Timber of Humanity,* 47. This strikingly echoes Fukuyama's melancholy (see note 2 to this chapter).

19. Leszek Kolakowski, "The Death of Utopia Reconsidered," in Sterlin M. McMurrin, ed., *The Tanner Lectures on Human Values IV* (Cambridge: Cambridge University Press, 1983), 229, 237–38, 242. Kolakowski earlier took a more benevolent view of utopia, in "The Concept of the Left," in *Toward a Marxist Humanism,* translated from the Polish by J. Z. Peel (New York: Grove Press, 1969), 67–83. What he regarded as the most pernicious aspects of the Marxist utopia are discussed in volume 3 of his *Main Currents of Marxism,* 3 vols., translated from the Polish by P. S. Falla (Oxford: Oxford University Press, 1981). For Kolakowski's reflections—by no means entirely triumphalist—on the collapse of this utopia, in Poland and elsewhere, see Leszek Kolakowski, "Amidst Moving Ruins," *Daedalus* (spring 1992): 43–56.

20. Kolakowski, "The Death of Utopia Reconsidered," 229.

21. Popper, "Utopia and Violence," 360.

22. See my *Utopianism,* 86–99. I leave out here myths of Arcadia, Paradise, or the Golden Age, as well as fantasies of the Blessed Isles or the Land of Cockaygne. For these, see ibid., 3–19.

23. On this, see further my *Utopianism,* 64–73.

24. See Nicholas Berdyaev, "Democracy, Socialism and Theocracy," in *The End of Time,* translated by by D. Attwater (London: Sheed and Ward, 1935), 187–88. Utopia, for Berdyaev, largely meant the socialist utopia, and he warned: "Socialism is no longer an utopia or a dream: it is an objective threat." The threat consisted in the denial of "the right to imperfection," which is the cardinal requirement of freedom. Ibid., 188, 192. Kateb calls this objection to utopia "the essence of modern antiutopianism." Kateb, *Utopia and Its Enemies,* 13.

25. See Chad Walsh, *From Utopia to Nightmare* (London: Geoffrey Bles, 1962), 25; Elaine Hoffman Baruch, "Dystopia Now," *Alternative Futures* 2, no. 3 (1979): 56.

26. Gellner's remarks are in the report on the symposium on Fukuyama's *The End of History and the Last Man* in *The Times Higher Education Supplement* (March 20, 1992), 17. And cf. Peter Beilharz: "It can today be argued that the real ideological locus of the capitalist utopia is not market so much as *consumption.*" Peter Beilharz, *Labour's Utopias: Bolshevism, Fabianism, Social Democracy* (London: Routledge, 1992), 126. See also note 37 to this chapter.

27. Alexander Solzhenitsyn, *Rebuilding Russia,* translated by Alexis Klimoff (London: Harvill, 1991), 9. See also Vladimir Tismaneanu, *The Crisis of Marxist Ideology in Eastern Europe: The Poverty of Utopia* (New York: Routledge, 1988), esp. 91–107; Alex Kozinski, "The Dark Lessons of Utopia," *University of Chicago Law Review* 58, no. 2 (1991): 575–94.

For the antiutopianism and "antipolitics" of the East European dissidents, see my "The Revolutions of 1989"(chapter 2 of this book); see also Tony Judt, "The Dilemmas of Dissidence: The Politics of Opposition in East-Central Europe," *Eastern European Politics and Societies* 2, no. 2 (1988): 191–99; Timothy Garton Ash, "Does Central Europe Exist?" in *The Uses of Adversity* (Cambridge: Granta/Penguin Books, 1989), 161–91. Fredric Jameson noted the "canonical antiutopianism" of the East, and observed that "for Eastern intellectuals, the word 'utopia' has become as automatically stigmatized as the words 'totality' and 'totalization' are for us." Fredric Jameson, "Conversations on the New World Order," in Blackburn, ed., *After the Fall*, 261–62.

Those, incidentally, who think that Václav Havel gave up his "anti-political politics" when faced with the "realities" of presidential office are roundly rebutted by Havel himself. See his "Paradise Lost," *New York Review of Books* (April 9, 1992), 6–8.

28. Milan Simecka, "A World with Utopias or without Them?" in Peter Alexander and Roger Gill, eds., *Utopias* (London: Duckworth, 1984), 171. And cf. Milan Kundera: "The paradise of political utopia is based on the belief in man. That is why it ends in massacres." Milan Kundera, "An Interview with Milan Kundera," *Granta*, 11 (1984): 29.

29. Simecka, "A World with Utopias or without Them?" 173–74. For the popularity of Orwell in Eastern Europe, see Jacques Rupnik, "Totalitarianism Revisited," in John Keane, ed., *Civil Society and the State: New European Perspectives* (London: Verso, 1988), 263–89.

30. Hans Magnus Enzensberger, "Ways of Walking: A Postscript to Utopia," in Blackburn, ed., *After the Fall*, 20. By contrast, Enzensberger praises present-day Germans, both East and West, for their devotion to "ordinariness" and "everyday normality." Ibid., 24.

31. Jürgen Habermas, "The New Obscurity: The Crisis of the Welfare State and the Exhaustion of Utopian Energies," in *The New Conservatism*, edited and translated by Shierry Weber Nicholsen (Cambridge, Mass.: MIT Press, 1989), 48–69.

32. For a discussion of the nineteenth-century American communities, see my *Utopia and Anti-Utopia in Modern Times*, chapter 3; for some of the varieties of socialism, see Beilharz, *Labor's Utopias*.

33. André Gunder Frank, "Revolution in Eastern Europe: Lessons for Democratic Social Movements (and Socialists?)," *Third World Quarterly* 12, no. 2 (1990): 50. Frank equally dismissed the alternative of "world socialism" as unreal "for any foreseeable future." Moreover, he thought "it is difficult to imagine what this might ever mean. What could distinguish this world socialism from world capitalism, so long as competition reigns as a fact of life in the future as it has for millennia in the past?" He concluded gloomily that "things will, and will have to, get worse before they get better." Ibid.: 51–2. And cf. Robin Blackburn: "As we enter the last decade of the twentieth century the ruin of 'Marxist-Leninist' communism has been sufficiently comprehensive to eliminate it as an alternative to capitalism and to compromise the very idea of socialism." Robin Blackburn, "Fin de Siècle: Socialism After the Crash," in Blackburn, ed., *After the Fall*, 173.

34. André Gorz, *Critique of Economic Reason*, translated by by Gillian Handyside and Chris Turner (London: Verso, 1989), 183. See also the earlier essay, *Farewell to the Working Class: An Essay on Post-Industrial Socialism*, translated by Michael Sonenscher (London: Pluto Press, 1982). As Gorz said, "If one understands socialism as a form of society in which the demands deriving from [economic] rationality are subordinated to social and cultural goals, then socialism remains more relevant than ever." Gorz, "The New Agenda," in Blackburn, ed., *After the Fall*, 289.

35. For the ecosocialists, see Andrew Dobson, *Green Political Thought: An Introduction* (London: Unwin Hyman, 1990); for market socialism, see Robin Blackburn, "Fin de Siècle: Socialism after the Crash," in Blackburn, ed., *After the Fall*, 218–27; David Miller, *Market, State, and Community: Theoretical Foundations of Market Socialism* (Oxford: Clarendon Press, 1990). See also Jon Elster and Karl Ove Moene, eds., *Alternatives to Capitalism* (Cambridge: Cambridge University Press, 1989).

36. On socialism as the "counterculture" of capitalism, see Zygmunt Bauman, *Socialism: The Active Utopia* (London: Allen and Unwin, 1976); see also Beilharz, *Labor's*

*Utopias*, 15. For the persisting relevance of socialism, variously defined, see the essays in part 2 of Blackburn, ed., *After the Fall*, 173–325; see also Ralph Miliband and Leo Panitch, "The New World Order and the Socialist Agenda," in R. Miliband and L. Panitch, eds., *Socialist Register 1992: New World Order?* (London: Merlin Press, 1992); Lucio Magri, "The European Left between Crisis and Refoundation," *New Left Review* 189 (September/October 1991): 1–18; Christiane Lemke and Gary Marks, eds., *The Crisis of Socialism in Europe* (Durham, N.C.: Duke University Press, 1992); Paul Auerbach, "On Socialist Optimism," *New Left Review* 192 (March/April 1992): 5–35.

37. George Steiner, "The State of Europe: Christmas Eve 1989," *Granta* 30: *New Europe!* (Harmondsworth, U.K.: Granta/Penguin Books, 1990), 130. Steiner has developed this idea in his story "Proofs," a dialogue about Marxism and capitalism, in George Steiner, *Proofs and Three Parables* (London: Faber and Faber, 1992), 3–75. Cf. Erazim Kohák, a Czech philosopher who has lived in America for many years: "The unfortunate truth is that as the former subjects of the Soviet empire dream it, the American dream has very little to do with liberty and justice for all and a great deal to do with soap operas and the Sears catalogue." Erazim Kohák, "Ashes, Ashes . . . Central Europe after Forty Years," in a special issue of *Daedalus*, "The Exit from Communism," (spring 1992): 209. On consumerism as the cause of the 1989 revolutions, see also Noel Annan, "The State of Europe," *Granta* 30: 160; similarly Zygmunt Bauman, "Communism: A Post-Mortem," in *Intimations of Postmodernity* (London: Routledge, 1992), 171. For the contrary view, that the 1989 revolutions were driven by the nonmaterial demand for "recognition," see Fukuyama, *The End of History and the Last Man*, 177–80.

38. See, for example, John Kenneth Galbraith, "Revolt In Our Time: The Triumph of Simplistic Ideology," in Gwyn Prins, ed., *Spring in Winter: The 1989 Revolutions* (Manchester: Manchester University Press, 1990), 1–11; see also Eric Hobsbawm, "The Crisis of Today's Ideologies," *New Left Review* 192 (March/April 1992): 61. Hobsbawm also pointed to a different kind of misperception, a blindness to capitalism's deepening problems: "What confronts the ruins of the Eastern socialist economies today is not a triumphant capitalism but a global capitalist economy in trouble, and recognizing that it is in trouble." Ibid., 59.

39. See Ivan Szelenyi and Szonja Szelenyi, "The Vacuum in Hungarian Politics: Classes and Parties," *New Left Review* 187 (May/June 1991): 121–37. On "the recurrence of political apathy" in the region, see Mihaly Simai, "Hungarian Problems," *Government and Opposition* 27, no. 1 (1992): 55; see also Piotr Sztompka, "The Intangibles and the Imponderables of the Transition to Democracy," *Studies in Comparative Communism* 24, no. 3 (1991): 304.

40. It is undeniable, of course, that a revived socialism in East Central Europe could take on authoritarian forms. See Martin Malia, "Leninist Endgame," *Daedalus* (spring 1992): 73–75; Ken Jowitt, "The Leninist Legacy," in Ivo Banac, ed., *Eastern Europe in Revolution* (Ithaca, N.Y.: Cornell University Press, 1992), 207–24. And cf. Zygmunt Bauman: "East-Central European societies have victoriously accomplished their February revolution. The dangers of an October one are, as yet, far from being excluded." Bauman, "Communism: A Post-Mortem," 172.

41. Gorz, "The New Agenda," 293; see also Hobsbawm, "The Crisis of Today's Ideologies," 59.

42. R. W. Johnson, "Ahead Lies—What?" *London Review of Books* (March 12, 1992), 5. A similar point is made by Jürgen Habermas in "What Does Socialism Mean Today? The Revolutions of Recuperation and the Need for New Thinking," in Blackburn, ed., *After the Fall*, 45. The general point holds, I think, despite the poor perfor-

mance of the French socialists in the regional elections of March 1992 and the British Labor Party in the general election of April 1992. For the view that these elections are further evidence of the "terminal decline" of socialism in Europe, see Peter Jenkins, "Goodbye to All That," *New York Review of Books* (May 14, 1992), 16–17; Stanley Hoffman, "France Self-Destructs," *New York Review of Books* (May 28, 1992), 25–30.

It has been fascinating, incidentally, to see the growing acclaim on the contemporary Left for the social democratic legacy of Bernstein and Kautsky, as critics of Bolshevism and advocates of socialist democracy. See, for example, Blackburn, "Fin de Siècle," 175–89; Beilharz, *Labor's Utopias*, xi, 93–124.

43. Frank Manuel, "A Requiem for Karl Marx," *Daedalus* (spring 1992): 18. Manuel was too readily dismissive of Marxism as a theory. For, whatever the fate of so-called Marxist societies, Marxism as a theory should surely have no difficulty in explaining the predicament of communists following 1987. As Fredric Jameson says: "It does not seem to make much sense to talk about the bankruptcy of Marxism, when Marxism is very precisely the science and study of just that capitalism whose global triumph is affirmed in talk of Marxism's demise." Jameson, "Conversations on the New World Order," 255. See also Immanuel Wallerstein, "Marx, Marxism-Leninism, and Socialist Experiences in the Modern World-System," in Wallerstein's *Geopolitics and Geoculture: Essays on the Changing World-System* (Cambridge: Cambridge University Press, 1991), 85, 96–97.

44. Kohak, "Ashes, Ashes . . . Central Europe after Forty Years," 203–4.

45. Simecka, "A World with Utopias or without Them?" 175–6. A similar claim, that we cannot do without a "concrete utopia," a coherent vision to oppose to the "irrational forces" current in the world today, is made by a veteran Trotskyist reflecting on the fall of "real socialism." See Yvan Craipeau, "L'implosion du 'Socialisme Réel': Une Nouvelle Période de l'histoire," *Les Temps Modernes* 544 (November 1991) 80.

46. For the ecological and the feminist utopia, see Kumar, *Utopianism*, 101–6.

47. See Richard Rorty, *Contingency, Irony, and Solidarity* (Cambridge: Cambridge University Press, 1989). The consequences of this conception of utopia, Rorty pointed out, is that "it would regard the realization of utopias, and the envisaging of still further utopias, as an endless process—an endless, proliferating realization of Freedom, rather than a convergence toward an already existing Truth." Ibid., xvi. For a somewhat similar conception of utopia as "metautopia," a "framework" for the further realization of diverse utopias, see Robert Nozick, *Anarchy, State and Utopia* (New York: Basic Books, 1974), 297–334.

48. It is idle to pretend that there is any agreement on the meaning of postmodernism. For a helpful guide, see Margaret A. Rose, *The Post-Modern and the Post-Industrial: A Critical Analysis* (Cambridge: Cambridge University Press, 1991). Postmodernism's rejection of utopia has some similarities to its rejection by Popper et al.—but they get there by very different routes; and postmodernists would have no truck with Popperian "social engineering" as the solution.

49. Scott Lash and Jonathan Friedman, "Introduction: Subjectivity and Modernity," in S. Lash and J. Friedman, eds., *Modernity and Identity* (Oxford: Basil Blackwell, 1992), 1. Cf. Robert Venturi, the postmodernist American architect and author of *Learning from Las Vegas* (1972): "Disney World is nearer to what people want than what architects have ever given them." Disneyland is "the symbolic American utopia." Quoted in David Harvey, *The Condition of Postmodernity* (Oxford: Basil Blackwell, 1989), 60.

50. Fredric Jameson, *Postmodernism or, The Cultural Logic of Late Capitalism* (London: Verso, 1991), 160, 180.

51. Berlin, *The Crooked Timber of Humanity,* 24.

52. Fukuyama, *The End of History and the Last Man*, 42. For more on the "world-wide democratic revolution," see Dankwart A. Rustow, "Democracy: A Global Revolution?" *Foreign Affairs* 69, no. 4 (1990): 75–91.

53. Piotr Sztompka, *Society in Action: The Theory of Social Becoming* (Cambridge: Polity Press, 1991), 20. Cf. also Zygmunt Bauman, "Living without an Alternative," in *Intimations of Postmodernity*, 183. Fukuyama himself commented: "One of the most striking facts about the original debate on 'The End of History?' was that not one single critic put forward the vision of a society fundamentally different from contemporary liberal democracy and at the same time better." Francis Fukuyama, "The End of History is Still Nigh," *The Independent* (March 3, 1992). For some typically bad-tempered reviews of Fukuyama's book that, nevertheless, often making some telling points, see Alan Ryan, "Professor Hegel Goes to Washington," *New York Review of Books* (March 26, 1992), 7–13; John Dunn, "In the Glare of Recognition," *Times Literary Supplement* (April 24, 1992), 6. A more balanced review is Steven Lukes, "Hegel's Recurrence," *New Statesman and Society* (March 6, 1992), 44. There is no room to consider here the striking view of Immanuel Wallerstein that the 1989 revolutions mark the end of *liberalism* as much as socialism—his argument being that the two were but varieties of the same thing, and both had been steadily undermined since the "1968 revolution" against the state and bureaucracy. See Immanuel Wallerstein, "The Collapse of Liberalism," in Miliband and Panitch, eds., *The Socialist Register 1992*; see also "The Lessons of the 1980s" and "1968, Revolution in the World-System," in Wallerstein, *Geopolitics and Geoculture*, 1–15, 65–83.

54. Ryan, "Professor Hegel Goes to Washington," 12; see also Hobsbawm, "The Crisis of Today's Ideologies," 60–61.

55. The victory of capitalism is seen as the result of the worldwide recognition that the free market is the best institution for realizing the full potential of modern science and technology. The victory of liberal democracy is attributed to the growing force of the "thymotic" factor in human history—the desire and struggle for recognition of our innate worth and dignity as equal human beings. See Fukuyama, *The End of History and the Last Man*, xiii–xix.

56. See the debate on this in Dietrich Rueschmeyer, Evelyne Huber Stephens, and John D. Stephens, *Capitalist Development and Democracy* (Cambridge: Polity Press, 1992); and see also Samuel Bowles and Herbert Gintis, *Democracy and Capitalism: Property, Community and the Contradictions of Modern Social Thought* (New York: Basic Books, 1987).

57. Fukuyama, *The End of History and the Last Man*, 46 (his emphasis).

58. Fukuyama, "The End of History Is Still Nigh."

59. Fukuyama, *The End of History and the Last Man*, 288–89, 326–39.

60. On the destructive consequences of McDonald's and other global fast-food chains, see Peter Singer, "Bandit and Friends," *New York Review of Books* (April 9, 1992), 9–13; Joseph K. Skinner, "Big Mac and the Tropical Forests," *Monthly Review* (December 1985), 25–32.

61. Many of these points were powerfully made some years ago by Fred Hirsch, *Social Limits to Growth* (London: Routledge and Kegan Paul, 1977). See also Adrian Ellis and Krishan Kumar, eds., *Dilemmas of Liberal Democracies: Studies in Fred Hirsch's* Social Limits to Growth (London: Tavistock, 1983). And cf. Paul Auerbach, "On Socialist Optimism," 20, 33–34. Ecological movements have already, of course, in most cases adopted religious language and religious concepts, often from Eastern religions. For this and other elements of the "Green utopia," see Dobson, *Green Political Thought*; Adrian Atkinson, *Principles of Political Ecology* (London: Belhaven Press,

1991), esp. 169–219. On the need for a religious—"theistic"—dimension to our thinking about our predicament, see also Charles Taylor, *Sources of the Self: The Making of the Modern Identity* (Cambridge: Cambridge University Press, 1989); a robust rebuttal of this is Quentin Skinner, "Who Are 'We'? Ambiguities of the Modern Self," *Inquiry* 34 (1991): 145–50.

62. See, for example, R. E. Pahl, "The Search for Social Cohesion: From Durkheim to the European Commission," *European Journal of Sociology* 32 (1991): 345–60.

63. See, for example, Kohak, "Ashes, Ashes . . . Central Europe after Forty Years," 208.

64. A point forcibly put by Sztompka in "The Intangibles and Imponderables of the Transition to Democracy"; see also Jowitt, "The Leninist Legacy"; Edmund Mokrzycki, "The Legacy of Real Socialism and Western Democracy," *Studies in Comparative Communism* 24, no. 2 (1991): 211–17. A contrary view, that communism has left virtually no legacy in Eastern Europe, has engagingly been argued by Stephen Howe, "Hiccup In the Long March of History," *New Statesman and Society* (March 6, 1992), 12–14. (See also chapter 7 of this book.)

65. Quoted in the *New York Times* (September 28, 1998), A10. Gerhard Schröder's Social Democratic Party won in Germany in 1998, Lionel Jospin's Socialist Party in France and Tony Blair's Labor Party in Britain both won in 1997. Social democratic governments also came to power in Greece, Spain, and Austria, leading commentators to speak of a "wave of Social Democracy" sweeping over Europe. For the return of former communists in East Central Europe, see "A Further Note" in chapter 4 of this book.

François Furet was one of the many who saw no need to change the general verdict on socialism and communism despite the return to power of socialists and former communists in Western and Eastern Europe; he also accepts the "end of history" corollary that it implies: "The ex-communist countries all tried to base their rebirth on the very 'bourgeois' principles that they once had claimed to have abolished and surpassed. As a result, the presence or return to power of former members of communist parties did nothing to change the fact that communism had come to an end along with the regime that had taken it as its banner; communism died with the Soviet Union. The proof is that the European of the present fin de siècle finds himself bereft of a vision of the future. If bourgeois democracy is no longer what comes before socialism, but rather what comes after it, then those living in bourgeois democracy can no longer imagine anything beyond the horizon within which they now dwell." François Furet, "Democracy and Utopia," *Journal of Democracy* 9, no. 1 (1998): 74.

Former socialists and other leftists concur that what died in 1989 was not just socialism, but the whole radical tradition: "In 1989, not only Leninism, but national liberation movements, social-democracy, and all the other heirs of post-1789 revolutionary 'liberalism' collapsed ideologically, that is, as strategies for efficacious action in the transformation of the world." Giovanni Arrighi, Terence Hopkins, and Immanuel Wallerstein, "1989, the Continuation of 1968," *Review* 15, no. 2 (1992): 239. For further reflections, see Peter Beilharz, "Socialism in Europe: After the Fall," *International Journal of Politics, Culture and Society* 11, no. 1 (1997): 49–72. Beilharz's lament is not so much about the failure to achieve socialism as about the loss of a vital part of capitalism's life: "The point is not that socialism has failed to conquer capitalism so much as it is that socialism has failed to keep its role as the alter ego of capitalism. Not Victory, but the struggle is what matters. . . . What we have lost, today, is the painful yet creative tension between the forces and ideologies which we used to call 'capitalism' and 'socialism.'" Ibid., 71. See also Michael Cox, "Rebels Without a Cause? Radical Theorists and the World System after the Cold War," *New Political Economy* 3, no. 3 (1998):

445–60; James E. Cronin, *The World the Cold War Made: Order, Chaos, and the Return of History* (New York: Routledge, 1996), especially 237–42. One attempt to re-suscitate the radical project in the West, albeit in a highly attenuated and for the most part ridiculed form, has been the advocacy of the "Third Way." For a statement, see Anthony Giddens, *The Third Way: The Renewal of Social Democracy* (Cambridge: Polity Press, 1998); for a riposte, see Steven Lukes, "Left Down the Middle," *Times Literary Supplement* (September 25, 1998), 3–4.

66. See, for instance, the reflections of a disillusioned conservative in John Gray, *False Dawn: The Delusions of Global Capitalism* (Cambridge, U.K.: Granta Books, 1998). Gray denounces the "utopia" of the single global market. Also intriguing are the warnings of the global capitalist George Soros in "The Capitalist Threat," *The Atlantic Monthly* (February 1997), 45–58; and also George Soros, *The Crisis of Global Capitalism* (Boston: Little, Brown, 1999). See also Francis Fukuyama, "The Great Disruption: Human Nature and the Reconstitution of the Social Order," *The Atlantic Monthly* (May 1999), 55–80; Paul Kennedy, "Forecast: Global Gales Ahead," *New Statesman and Society* (May 31, 1996), 28–29. For East European reflections on the impact of free market capitalism on postcommunist societies, see the essays by Andrezej Rychard, Jirina Siklova, and Rumyana Kolarova in the special issue of *Social Research,* "Gains and Losses of the Transition to Democracy," *Social Research* 63, no. 2 (1996). See also the special issue of *East European Politics and Societies,* "Transforming the Economies of East-Central Europe," *East European Politics and Societies* 6, no. 1 (1992); Christopher G. A. Bryant, "Economic Utopianism and Sociological Realism: Strategies for Transformation in East-Central Europe," in Christopher G. A. Bryant and Edmund Mokrzycki, eds., *The New Great Transformation? Change and Continuity in East-Central Europe* (New York: Routledge, 1994), 58–77. Maurice Glasman, in *Unnecessary Suffering: Managing Market Utopia* (New York: Verso, 1996), argues that East Europeans lost a golden opportunity to follow the path to a "social market economy" laid out by West Germany after 1945—an economy based on a national consensus and involving such institutions as works councils in a policy of "co-determination" or joint management by workers and employers.

Socialism's historic function of "civilizing" capitalism, and the importance of something like it maintaining a healthy existence, is traced and argued in masterly fashion by Donald Sassoon in *One Hundred Years of Socialism: The West European Left in the Twentieth Century* (New York: The New Press, 1996). See also Donald Sassoon, ed., *Looking Left: Socialism in Europe after the Cold War* (New York: The New Press, 1997).

67. Ironically, says Timothy Garton Ash, "the end of Marxist regimes in Europe has contributed to a revival of Marxist analysis. It is not just old Marxists who have pointed out that the raw, early capitalism of the postcommunist world recalls that described by Karl Marx. . . . As importantly, the relentless globalization of the world capitalist economy—to which the end of the cold war certainly contributed—has made some of Marx's analytical insights (although not his solutions) seem more rather than less relevant." Timothy Garton Ash, "Ten Years After," *New York Review of Books* (November 18, 1999), 16. And see Manuel Castells's basically Marxist understanding of the new world order in his *The Information Age: Economy, Society and Culture,* 3 volumes (Cambridge, Mass.: Blackwell Publishers, 1996–98). Immanuel Wallerstein also continues to use a Marxist framework for his analysis of the capitalist "world-system" in its current and future forms; in his case, the collapse of the capitalist system remains on the agenda. See, for example, *After Liberalism* (New York: The Free Press, 1995). For a Marxist approach to the globalization of culture, see Frederick Jameson and Masao

Miyoshi, eds., *The Cultures of Globalization* (Durham, N.C.: Duke University Press, 1999). A robust defense of socialism as a theory and as a continuing necessity is Michael Harrington, *Socialism: Past and Future* (London: Pluto Press, 1993). See also, for the renewed relevance of Marx in the postcommunist era, Jacques Derrida, *Specters of Marx* (New York: Routledge, 1994); and, for the continuing relevance of the Left-Right distinction, see Norberto Bobbio, *Left and Right: The Significance of a Political Distinction* (Cambridge, U.K.: Polity Press, 1996).

The 150th anniversary of the *Communist Manifesto* (1848) in 1998 provoked an outpouring of writing on the continuing relevance (or otherwise) of Marx. For an example of those who urge that he is more relevant now than ever, see Colin Leys and Leo Panitch, eds., *The Communist Manifesto Now: The Socialist Register 1998* (New York: Monthly Review Press, 1998). There is useful review and commentary on the relevant publications of the anniversary year by Paul Lewis in "Marx's Stock Resurges on a 150-Year Tip," *New York Times* (June 27, 1998), A17–19. An earlier work in which the European Left contemplates its future role is David S. Bell, ed., *Western European Communists and the Collapse of Communism* (Oxford: Berg Publishers, 1993).

68. Among the newer contributions to this well-known argument are Andrzej Walicki, *Marxism and the Leap to the Kingdom of Freedom: The Rise and Fall of the Communist Utopia* (Cambridge: Cambridge University Press, 1995); and François Furet, *The Passing of an Illusion: The Idea of Communism in the Twentieth Century*, translated by Deborah Furet (Chicago: University of Chicago Press, 1999). One might mention here a number of other autopsies on the socialist ideal, though not all conclude that it was an unrealizable utopia. See Irwin Silber, *Socialism: What Went Wrong?* (London: Pluto Press, 1994); Carl Boggs, *The Socialist Tradition: From Crisis to Decline* (New York: Routledge, 1995); David Lane, *The Rise and Fall of State Socialism: Industrial Society and the Socialist State* (Cambridge, U.K.: Polity Press, 1996); Minxin Pei, *From Reform to Revolution: The Demise of Communism in China and the Soviet Union* (Cambridge: Harvard University Press, 1998). Moreover, even those hostile to the socialist utopia recognize that its demise—if such it is—leaves modern society in something of a predicament, since it seems to remove utopian thought altogether and thus impoverishes modern life. As François Furet put it in a lecture given just before his death in July 1997: "Communism never conceived of any tribunal other than history's, and it has now been condemned by history to disappear, lock, stock, and barrel. Its defeat, therefore, is beyond appeal. But must we conclude from this that it is necessary categorically to banish utopia from the public life of our societies? That might perhaps be going too far, because it would also mean destroying one of the great props of civic activity. For if the social order cannot be other than what it is, why should we trouble ourselves about it? The end of the communist idea has closed before our eyes the greatest path offered to the imagination of modern man in the matter of collective happiness. But it has by the same token deepened the political deficit that has always characterized modern liberalism. . . . The democratic individual finds himself poised before a closed future, incapable of defining even vaguely the horizon of a *different* society from the one in which we live, since this horizon has become almost impossible to conceive." Furet, "Democracy and Utopia," 79.

69. For some current responses to this opportunity, see my "Utopia and Anti-Utopia in the Twentieth Century," in Gregory Claes and Lyman Tower Sargent, eds., *Utopian Essays* (Paris: Bibliothèque Nationale, 2000). A powerful antiutopian critique, though not in the fictional mode, is James C. Scott, *Seeing Like a State: How Certain Schemes to Improve the Human Condition Have Failed* (New Haven: Yale University Press, 1998).

70. A notable exception was the sociologist Edward Tiryakian: "Sociologists should

begin treating Francis Fukuyama's *The End of History and the Last Man* as seriously as they did yesterday's inspirational secular eschatology, Marx's *Communist Manifesto,* to which it is 180 degrees opposed." Edward Tiryakian, "The New Worlds and Sociology," *International Sociology* 9, no. 2 (1994): 134.

71. Cf. Gale Stokes, in a direct echo of Fukuyama: "Fascism and Communism will never be able to generate the same kind of enthusiastic hopefulness among broad strata of society that was their hallmark at the peak of their twentieth century success. The great message of the twentieth century is not positive but negative: we have not learned what works so much as what does not work." Gale Stokes, *The Walls Came Tumbling Down: The Collapse of Communism in Eastern Europe* (New York: Oxford University Press, 1993): 6.

72. The most sustained and celebrated disagreement with Fukuyama has come in Samuel P. Huntington, *The Clash of Civilizations and the Remaking of the World Order* (New York: Touchstone Books, 1997). For a discussion of that work, as well as further thoughts on Fukuyama and the "end of history," see my "Post-History: Living at the End," in Gary Browning, Abigail Halchi, and Frank Webster, eds., *Understanding Contemporary Society, Understanding the Present* (London: Sage Publications, 2000). See also Perry Anderson's updated thoughts on Fukuyama in *The Ends of History* (New York: Verso, 1994), and Paul G. Lewis, "History, Europe and the Politics of the East," in Stephen White, Judy Batt, and Paul G. Lewis, eds., *Developments in East European Politics* (London: Macmillan, 1993): 262–79.

73. For some additional thoughts on this, see my "Apocalypse, Millennium and Utopia Today," in Malcolm Bull, ed., *Apocalypse Theory and the Ends of the World* (Cambridge, Mass.: Blackwell, 1995), 200–24. For the apocalyptic tradition generally, and its impact on current thought and feeling about the end of the millennium, see also Nicholas Campion, *The Great Year: Astrology, Millenarianism and History in the Western Tradition* (London: Penguin Books, 1994); Damian Thompson, *The End of Time: Faith and Fear in the Shadow of the Millennium* (Hanover, N.H.: University Press of New England, 1997); Stephen Jay Gould, *Questioning the Millennium: A Rationalist's Guide to a Precisely Arbitrary Countdown* (New York: Harmony Books, 1998).

## 7. History and Identity in the Revolutions of 1989

1. Jacques Rupnik, *The Other Europe: The Rise and Fall of Communism in East-Central Europe* (New York: Pantheon Books, 1989), 36.

2. A good example is the treatment of the potentially disruptive case of World War II. See Tony Judt, "The Past is Another Country: Myth and Memory in Postwar Europe," *Daedalus* 121, no. 4 (1992): 83–118. The contrast between Western and Eastern European views of history, at least as perceived by the West, is nicely caught in a remark by Richard Holbrooke, U.S. assistant secretary of state for European and Canadian affairs: "The people of Central and Eastern Europe now have a real opportunity to create a lasting peace. But to do so they must be prepared for one final act of liberation, this time from the unresolved legacies of their own tragic, violent and angry past. . . . History as our guide and teacher, history as a cautionary tale that informs us, is indispensable to our self-awareness. But can this region free itself from history's ghosts and myths?" Richard Holbrooke, address to the spring session of the North Atlantic Assembly, Budapest, May 1995, quoted in Jonathan Sunley, "Post-Communism: An Infantile Disorder," *The National Interest* 44 (1996): 4.

3. See Renata Saleci, "National Identity and Socialist Moral Majority," *New Formations* 12 (1990): 28; Veljko Vujacic, "Serbian Nationalism, Slobodan Milosevic and the

Origins of the Yugoslav War," *The Harriman Review* (December 1995): 31. For the long-lasting significance of Kosovo in Serbian national life, see also Thomas Emmert, *Serbian Golgotha: Kosovo, 1389* (New York: Columbia University Press, 1990); Wayne S. Vucinich and Thomas A. Emmert, eds., *Kosovo: Legacy of a Medieval Battle* (Minneapolis: University of Minnesota Press, 1991); Adrian Hastings, *The Construction of Nationhood: Ethnicity, Religion and Nationalism* (Cambridge: Cambridge University Press, 1997), 130–33, 146–47. Since these lines were first written (in 1997), Kosovo has of course become the occasion of a major international war. Its symbolic significance to Serbia has been demonstrated in the most brutal possible way, by the expulsion of more than half a million Albanians from the province of Kosovo. With Serbia's defeat in the war, the Serbs are now, in their turn, refugees from Kosovo, making it all but certain that Kosovo will continue to be a central point of reference for Serbia. For a helpful review of recent literature on Kosovo and its place in the current conflicts in the Balkans, see Eric Alterman, "Untangling Balkan Knots of Myth and Countermyth," *New York Times* (July 31, 1999): A15–17.

4. In response to which President Árpád Göncz of Hungary applauded the pope's choice of model and declared, "St. Adalbert's spirit is the reality of the new Central Europe." See the *New York Times* (June 4, 1997), A4. Later on the same visit the pope invoked the memory of the fourteenth-century Polish Queen Jadwiga as an example of how best to balance the often conflicting claims of religion and politics: a clear message to Poland's current political rulers. *New York Times* (June 9, 1997), A9. For the other examples, see the *New York Times* (March 28, 1997), A10; (May 31, 1997), A6.

5. On the symbolic importance of the 1956 rising for the Hungarians, see Gale Stokes, *The Walls Came Tumbling Down: The Collapse of Communism in Eastern Europe* (New York: Oxford University Press, 1993), 100–01. Moreover, it could be linked as a marker in a "massive morality play" touching on other memorable moments in Hungarian history, in this case especially the liberal revolution of 1848. In the big demonstration of March 15, 1989, the opposition made sure that marchers stopped at six locations in central Budapest that had significant links to both revolutions, those of 1848 and 1956. As Stokes said, "By touching on as many interlinked markers of Hungarian history as possible, [the opposition] hoped to rekindle memories of a liberal and democratic past interrupted by war and communism." Ibid., 101. The public reinterment on June 16, 1989, of the body of Imre Nagy, the executed leader of the 1956 reform government, served the same purpose. Nor was 1956 buried in 1989. In September 1999, ten years after this second revolution, four men were put on trial, accused of firing on unarmed demonstrators during the 1956 uprising. See the *New York Times* (September 19, 1999), A5.

6. Judt, "The Past Is Another Country," 100. A particularly good, detailed study of this phenomenon is Catherine Wanner, *Burden of Dreams: History and Identity in Post-Soviet Ukraine* (University Park, Pa.: Penn State University Press, 1998).

7. Andrew C. Janos, "Continuity and Change in Eastern Europe: Strategies of Post-communist Politics," *East European Politics and Societies* 8, no. 1 (1994): 8.

8. Michnik is quoted in Rupnik, *The Other Europe*, 28.

9. See Eric Hobsbawm, *Echoes of the Marseillaise: Two Centuries Look Back on the French Revolution* (London: Verso, 1990), xi; François Furet, "From 1789 to 1917 to 1989," *Encounter* (September 1990): 3–7. And on this see further chapter 4 of this book.

10. See Steven Lukes, "Marxism and Morality: Reflections on the Revolutions of 1989," in Lyman H. Letgers, ed., *Eastern Europe: Transformation and Revolution, 1945–1991* (Lexington, Mass.: D. C. Heath, 1992), 612–21.

11. See, for example, Ralf Dahrendorf, *Reflections on the Revolution in Europe*

(London: Chatto and Windus, 1990); Timothy Garton Ash, *We the People: The Revolution of '89 Witnessed in Warsaw, Budapest, Berlin and Prague* (London: Granta Books, 1990); Robert H. Dix, "Eastern Europe's Implications for Revolutionary Theory," *Polity* 24, no, 2 (1991): 227–42; George Schöpflin, *Politics in Eastern Europe 1945–1992* (Oxford: Blackwell, 1993), 254. And see further chapter 4 of this book.

12. See, for example, Eric Hobsbawm, *The Age of Extremes: The Short Twentieth Century, 1914–1991* (London: Abacus, 1995), 487.

13. Andrew Arato, "Revolution and Restoration: On the Origins of Right-wing Ideology in Hungary," in Christopher G. A. Bryant and Edmund Mokrzycki, eds., *The New Great Transformation? Change and Continuity in East-Central Europe* (London: Routledge, 1994), 103. Interestingly, there seems to have been no such inhibition about 1956, for which the Hungarian word for revolution, *forradalom*, is regularly used.

14. Hannah Arendt, *On Revolution* (London: Faber and Faber, 1963), 27.

15. György Varga, "Economics and Human Values," in Bronislaw Geremek, György Varga, Czesław Miłosz, and Connor O'Brien, *The Idea of Civil Society* (Research Triangle Park, N.C.: National Humanities Center, 1992), 19.

16. G. M. Tamás, "The Legacy of Dissent," *The Times Literary Supplement* (May 14, 1993), 15.

17. See Hobsbawm, *The Age of Extremes*, 490; Ash, *We the People*, 139–49.

18. See chapters 2 and 4 of this book.

19. Piotr Sztompka, *Theoretical Implications of an A-Theoretical Revolution* (Uppsala: The Swedish Collegium for Advanced Studies in the Social Sciences, 1992), 1. Cf. also S. N. Eisenstadt, "The Breakdown of Communist Regimes and the Vicissitudes of Modernity," *Daedalus* 121, no. 2 (1992): 25–27; Zygmunt Bauman, "After the Patronage State: A Model in Search of Class Interests," in Bryant and Mokrzycki, eds., *The New Great Transformation?* 14–15. The need to distinguish their revolution from the classic Western model was very strong in the minds of many dissidents in the early months of the 1989 revolutions. For some this meant denying the very term *revolution* in relation to their hopes and strivings. Cf. Jacek Kuroń: "The problem is that the world has already seen dozens of revolutions. It is an old story: people invest all their hopes in a revolution which cannot fulfil them. And they are always followed by a crisis, hatred. . . . There have been no other revolutions. . . . Today it would be much worse because the country has been ruined and a revolution would not rebuild it but destroy it further. . . . It is our duty to try out a course of action which would enable the whole of society to organise itself and the existing order to change gradually." Jacek Kurón, "Instead of Revolution," *Eastern European Reporter* (spring–summer 1989): 13.

20. See, for example, Theda Skocpol, *States and Social Revolutions* (New York: Cambridge University Press, 1979).

21. G. A. Bryant and Edmund Mokrzycki, "Introduction: Theorizing the Changes in East Central Europe," in Bryant and Mokrzycki, eds., *The New Great Transformation?* 1.

22. See Vernon Snow, "The Concept of Revolution in Seventeenth-Century England," *Historical Journal* 5, no. 2 (1962): 167–90; and, more generally, J. C. D. Clark, *Revolution and Rebellion: State and Society in England in the Seventeenth and Eighteenth Centuries* (Cambridge: Cambridge University Press, 1986).

23. Arendt, *On Revolution*, 40–49.

24. Tony Judt, "Nineteen Eighty-Nine: The End of *Which* European Era?" *Daedalus* 123, no. 3 (1994): 10.

25. For one kind of "postmodern" interpretation of the 1989 revolutions, as the rejection of modernity, see Zygmunt Bauman, *Intimations of Postmodernity* (London: Routledge, 1992), 156–74, 179–80. See also Larry Ray, "Post-Communism: Post-modernity

or Modernity Revisited?" *British Journal of Sociology* 48, no. 2 (1997): 112–30. And see also chapter 4 of this book.

26. See Eva Hoffman, *Exit into History: A Journey through the New Eastern Europe* (London: William Heinemann, 1993); Tina Rosenberg, *The Haunted Land: Facing Europe's Ghosts after Communism* (New York: Vintage, 1995).

27. Misha Glenny, *The Rebirth of History: Eastern Europe in the Age of Democracy*, new edition (London: Penguin Books, 1993), 183.

28. Giuseppe di Palma, "Legitimation from the Top to Civil Society: Politico-Cultural Change in Eastern Europe," *World Politics* 44, no. 1 (1991): 77.

29. Milan Kundera, "The Tragedy of Central Europe," *New York Review of Books* (April 26, 1984), 33–38.

30. On these schemes, see Nicholas Stargardt, "Origins of the Constructivist Theory of the Nation," in Sukumar Periwal, ed., *Notions of Nationalism* (Budapest: Central European University Press, 1995), 83–105. And see also Rupnik, *The Other Europe*, 193–223; István Rév, "The Postmorten Victory of Communism," *Daedalus* 123, no. 3 (1994): 165–66. See also chapter 3 of this book.

31. Marcin Król, "Postcommunist Eastern Europe: A Survey of Opinion," *East European Politics and Societies* 4, no. 2 (1990): 193.

32. Geoff Eley, "Culture, Britain and Europe," *Journal of British Studies* 31, no. 4 (1992): 408. See also Ivan Szelenyi, "Social and Political Landscape, Central Europe, Fall 1990," in Ivo Banac, ed., *Eastern Europe in Revolution* (Ithaca, N.Y.: Cornell University Press, 1992), 234–41.

33. Robin Okey, "Central Europe/Eastern Europe: Behind the Definitions," *Past and Present* 137 (1992): 129.

34. Hobsbawm, *Age of Extremes,* 420.

35. See Melvin Croan, "1989: Ten Years On," *East European Politics and Societies* 13, no. 2 (1999): 253–55.

36. Glenny, *Rebirth of History,* 183–86; Joseph Rothschild, *Return to Diversity: A Political History of East-Central Europe Since World War II,* second edition (New York: Oxford University Press, 1993); Jens Hohensee, "The Return to Diversity in Eastern Europe," *Contemporary European History* 2, no. 1 (1993): 87–100; Rév, "The Postmortem Victory of Communism," 166.

37. See, for example, Okey, "Central Europe/Eastern Europe," 130.

38. Glenny, *Rebirth of History,* 204.

39. Quoted in *The Independent* (September 24, 1991), 10.

40. Though this prevents repeated statements of Czechoslovakia's unique heritage in this respect. Cf. Erazim Kohák: "Under Masaryk's presidency, Czechoslovakia between the wars was genuinely a bulwark of freedom and a refuge for the persecuted in a troubled Europe." Erazim Kohák, "Consolidating Freedom in Central Europe," *Dissent* (spring 1997): 23; and see also Václav Havel's response to a letter by Joseph Brodsky, *New York Review of Books* (May 27, 1993), 30.

41. See Sika Kovacheva, *Education and National Identity in Postcommunist Bulgaria,* sociology M.A. thesis, Central European University, Prague, 1994.

42. On the difficulties faced by Poland—and most East Central European countries—in attempting to resurrect its past, see Jerzy Jedlicki, "The Revolution of 1989: The Unbearable Burden of History," *Problems of Communism* 39 (July–August 1990): 39–45, and Roman Szporluk's comment, "The Burden of History—Made Lighter by Geography?" in the same issue, 45–48.

43. Cf. Vladimir Tismaneanu, *Fantasies of Salvation: Democracy, Nationalism, and Myth in Postcommunist Europe* (Princeton: Princeton University Press, 1998). Tismaneanu

argues that Eastern Europe has shallow liberal roots, owing to the long dominance of extreme nationalistic and authoritarian traditions, and that the prospects for liberal democracy in the region are consequently not very good. The history of the region, in other words, cannot be a guide or an inspiration to its current strivings to achieve liberal democracy. On this general question, see further chapter 1 of this book.

44. On this see Michael G. Roskin, *The Rebirth of Eastern Europe* (Englewood Cliffs, N.J.: Prentice-Hall, 1991).

45. Rupnik, *The Other Europe*, 96.

46. See Rothschild, *Return to Diversity*, 76–123; Geoffrey Swain and Nigel Swain, *Eastern Europe Since 1945* (London: Macmillan, 1993), 12–55; Hohensee, "The Return to Diversity in Eastern Europe," 92; Richard Crampton, *Eastern Europe in the Twentieth Century—and After*, second edition (New York: Routledge, 1997), 211–39; Fatos Tarifa, "The Quest for Legitimacy and the Withering Away of Utopia," *Social Forces* 76, no. 2 (1997): 444–46.

47. Judt, "The Past Is Another Country," 102. Cf. Rupnik, *The Other Europe*, 14; C. Hann, "Introduction" to C. Hann, ed., *Socialism: Ideals, Ideologies, and Local Practice* (New York: Routledge, 1993), 12; Rév, "The Postmortem Victory of Communism," 168; Tarifa, "The Quest for Legitimacy," 449.

48. See Schöpflin, *Politics in Eastern Europe*, 5–37; C. M. Hann, *The Skeleton at the Feast: Contributions to East European Anthropology* (Canterbury, U.K.: Centre for Anthropology and Computing, University of Kent, 1995); Janos, "Continuity and Change in Eastern Europe"; Philip Longworth, *The Making of Eastern Europe: From Prehistory to Postcommunism*, second edition (New York: St. Martin's Press, 1997), 5–6; Ekaterina Makarova, *Paradoxes of Development in Soviet and Post-Soviet Central Asia: With Special Reference to the Role of the Mahalla in Uzbek Cities* (Ph.D. dissertation, Department of Sociology, University of Manchester, 1999). Contributions by anthropologists best bring out the "fit" between communist rule and many traditional institutions and practices in Eastern Europe, especially at the local level. See, for example, Hann, ed., *Socialism*. For the continuing pattern of negotiation between traditional (including socialist) ways and the emerging requirements of the market, see Michael Burawoy and Katherine Verdery, eds., *Uncertain Transition: Ethnographies of Change in the Postsocialist World* (Lanham, Md.: Rowman and Littlefield, 1999).

49. Cf. Judt, "The Past Is Another Country," 102; Judt, "Nineteen Eighty-Nine," 8; Rév, "The Postmortem Victory of Communism," 169.

A similar skepticism needs to be shown toward those many accounts that regard the revival of nationalist and ethnic conflicts in the region as the "revenge of history"—or, if one sees it positively, the "rebirth of history"—following a period in which historic enmities were forcibly suspended and put into cold storage by the communist leadership. See, for instance, George F. Kennan, "The Balkan Crisis 1913 and 1993," *New York Review of Books* (July 15, 1993), 3–8; Mark Juergensmeyer, *The New Cold War? Religious Nationalism Confronts the Secular State* (Berkeley: University of California Press, 1993), 111; Jacques Rupnik, "Europe's New Frontiers," *Daedalus* 123, no. 3 (1994): 95; Manuel Castells, *The Power of Identity* (Malden, Mass.: Blackwell Publishers, 1997): 41. The communist period was not simply a blank period during which old sentiments slumbered, to be awakened like the sleeping beauty by the kiss of 1989. It was itself a material shaping force of the ethnic and nationalist rivalries that emerged after 1989, many of which were new or expressed in new forms. See Velijko Vujacic and Victor Zaslavsky, "The Causes of Disintegration of the USSR and Yugoslavia," *Telos* 88 (1991): 120–40; Michael Ignatieff, "The Balkan Tragedy," *New York Review of Books* (May 13, 1993), 3–5; Christian Joppke, "Revisionism, Dissidence, Nationalism: Opposition in Leninist Regimes," *British Journal of Sociology* 45, no. 4 (1994): 557–58; Yuri Slezkine, "The USSR As a Communal Apartment, or How a Socialist State Promoted Ethnic Particularism," in Geoff Eley and Ronald Grigor Suny, eds., *Becoming National: A Reader* (New York: Oxford University Press, 1996), 203–38; Rogers Brubaker, *Nationalism Reframed: Nationhood and the National Question in the New Europe* (Cambridge: Cambridge University Press, 1996), 23–54.

50. Václav Havel, "The Power of the Powerless," in Václav Havel, *Václav Havel: Living in Truth,* edited by Jan Vladislav (London: Faber and Faber, 1989), 53.

51. A good start can be made with the following: Piotr Sztompka, "The Intangibles and the Imponderables of the Transition to Democracy," *Studies in Comparative Communism* 24, no. 3 (1991): 295–311; Edmund Mokrzycki, "The Legacy of Real Socialism and Western Democracy," *Studies in Comparative Communism* 24, no. 2 (1991): 211–17; Hanna Swida-Ziemba, "Psychological Heritage of Totalitarianism," in Zdzislaw Sadowski, ed., *Post-Totalitarian Society: The Course of Change* (Warsaw: Polish Association for the Club of Rome, 1993), 37–49; Petr Mares, Libor Musil, and Ladislav Rabusic, "Values and the Welfare State in Czechoslovakia," in Bryant and Mokrzycki, eds., *The New Great Transformation?* 78–98; Ákos Róna-Tas, "Postcommunist Transition and the Absent Middle Class in East-Central Europe," in Victoria E. Bonnell, ed., *Identities in Transition: Eastern Europe and Russia after the Collapse of Communism* (University of California at Berkeley: Center for Slavic and East European Studies, 1996), 29–44; Wendy Hollis, *Democratic Consolidation in Eastern Europe: The Influence of the Communist Legacy in Hungary, the Czech Republic, and Romania* (New York: Columbia University Press, 1999).

52. Havel has explained the reasons for which, as president, he gave his reluctant acquiescence to the lustration bill. See "Paradise Lost," *New York Review of Books* (April 9, 1992), 8.

53. See, for example, Rosenberg, *The Haunted Land.*

54. On the Polish "thick line," and the continuing controversy it has caused within Poland itself, see Aleksander Smolar, "Revolutionary Spectacle and Peaceful Transition," *Social Research* 63, no. 2 (1996): 444–47; see also Irena Grudzinska Gross, "Postcommunist Resentment or the Re-writing of Polish History," *East European Politics and Societies* 6, no. 2 (1993): 141–51. The Polish "thick line" seems to have been influenced by what was seen as the success of the Spanish *pacto del olvido,* "a tacit agreement to engage in collective amnesia" and so avoid dangerous recriminations, at the time of Spain's transition to democracy in the mid-1970s. See William Miller, Stephen White, and Paul Heywood, *Values and Political Change in Postcommunist Europe* (London: Macmillan, 1998), 64–65.

55. The tragicomic aspect of the long-running trial of Todor Zhivkov, the former communist leader of Bulgaria, is sparklingly brought out in Julian Barnes's novel *The Porcupine* (1992).

56. Timothy Garton Ash, "Central Europe: The Present Past," *New York Review of Books* (July 13, 1995), 21; cf. Sunley, "Post-Communism: An Infantile Disorder," 5–6. In some later speculations Garton Ash has been more definite: "I believe, with the benefit of hindsight, that all the countries of Central Europe could and should have tried the expedient of a truth commission. . . . A truth commission, before which the political leaders of the former regime and those accused of crime under it have to testify, brings both greater public knowledge of the misdeeds of the past and a formal, almost ceremonial acknowledgement to the victims. It symbolically draws a line between the new era and the old, without calling for forgetting or even, necessarily, forgiving. It is probably the closest a nonrevolutionary revolution can come to revolutionary catharsis." Timothy

Garton Ash, "Ten Years After," *New York Review of Books* (November 18, 1999), 18. Cf. also Jan Gross on the need to come to terms with the past, in East Central Europe and other areas making the transition to democracy: "A spiritual imperative seems to be at work here: a need to give public accounting of past misdeeds as an indispensable minimum of mutual-confidence-building, without which the body politic cannot function." Jan Gross, "The Burden of History," *East European Politics and Societies* 13, no. 2 (1999): 286.

57. See Vic Duke and Keith Grime, "Privatization in East Central Europe: Similarities and Contrasts in Its Application," in Bryant and Mokrzycki, eds., *The New Great Transformation?* 144–70.

58. Róna-Tas, "Post-communist Transition," 41. Tony Judt suggests another, "utterly unresolvable," dilemma associated with the restoration of property in postcommunist Eastern Europe: "What good does it do to restore property when you cannot return to tens of millions of people the loss of opportunity and liberty they suffered after 1948? Is there not something wrong in an outcome whereby the Schwarzenberg family gets back its palaces, and long-departed emigrés are paid for a loss which their descendants have turned to advantage, while those who had nothing get nothing and watch bitterly as their own and their children's lost chances go for nought? It may or may not be just but it certainly does not look very fair and it is politically most imprudent." Judt, "The Past Is Another Country," 104.

59. See Larry J. Ray, *Social Theory and the Crisis of State Socialism* (Cheltenham, U.K.: Edward Elgar, 1996), 190–92. For the general history of privatization in the region after 1989, and the various outcomes, see David Stark and Lásló Bruszt, *Postsocialist Pathways: Transforming Politics and Property in East Central Europe* (New York: Cambridge University Press, 1998).

60. See Michael Safir, "The Revival of the Political Right in Postcommunist Romania," in Joseph Held, ed., *Democracy and Right-Wing Politics in Eastern Europe in the 1990s* (Boulder, Colo.: Westview Press, 1993), 153–74. For the rehabilitation of Tiso and Pavelic, see the *New York Times* (June 16, 1997), A10.

61. See the observations in Eric Hobsbawm, "The New Threat to History," *New York Review of Books* (December 16, 1993), 62–64; and cf. Rév, "The Postmortem Victory of Communism," 169.

62. Hugh Seton-Watson, *The East European Revolution,* 3rd edition (London: Methuen, 1956).

63. See George Schöpflin, "The Pattern of Political Takeovers: How Eastern Europe Fell," *Encounter* 64, no. 2 (1985): 65–69; see also Schöpflin, *Politics in Eastern Europe 1945–1992,* 58–63; Rupnik, *The Other Europe,* 76–77; Z. A. B. Zeman, *The Making and Breaking of Communist Europe* (Oxford: Blackwell, 1991), 206–20; Judt, "The Past Is Another Country," 100; Longworth, *The Making of Eastern Europe,* 39–44; Crampton, *Eastern Europe in the Twentieth Century—and After,* 214–15; Jan Gross, "War and Revolution," in Norman Naimark and Leonid Gibianskii, eds., *The Establishment of Communist Regimes in Eastern Europe, 1944–1949* (Boulder, Colo.: Westview Press, 1998), 5–39.

64. Schöpflin, *Politics in Eastern Europe,* 60.

65. On the eve of 1989, the proportion of the work force employed in agriculture ranged from 10 percent in the German Democratic Republic to 30 percent in Romania. Before World War II the range was from 34 percent in Czechoslovakia to 60 percent in Poland and around 75–80 percent in the Balkan countries. See Robin Okey, *Eastern Europe 1740–1985,* 2nd edition (London: Hutchinson, 1985), 218; Piotr S. Wandycz, *The Price of Freedom: A History of East Central Europe from the Middle Ages to the*

*Present* (New York: Routledge, 1992), 206; Tarifa, "The Quest for Legitimacy and the Withering Away of Utopia," 456. And cf. Norman Naimark: "The war and the history of communism in these countries changed society in ways that would have been unrecognizable to earlier generations. The postcommunist populations of East Central and Southeastern Europe were far more literate and urban, nationally much more homogeneous, and socially and economically much more egalitarian than the societies that produced the political formations of the interwar period. Moreover, communism had a profound, even irreversible, effect on the cultures—political, economic, and national—of these societies." Norman Naimark, "Ten Years After: Perspectives on 1989," *East European Politics and Societies* 13, no. 2 (1999): 325.

66. See Jürgen Habermas, "What Does Socialism Mean Today? The Revolutions of Recuperation and the Need for New Thinking," in Robin Blackburn, ed., *After the Fall: The Failure of Communism and the Future of Socialism* (New York: Verso, 1991), 25–46.

## 8. The Revolutionary Idea in the Twentieth-Century World

1. On the distinctly cool French response to the bicentenary, see Eric Hobsbawm, *Echoes of the Marseillaise* (London: Verso, 1990), ix–x, 96–113. Hobsbawm quoted Michel Rocard, the French (socialist) prime minister at the time, who welcomed the bicentenary "because it convinced a lot of people that revolution is dangerous and that if one can do without it, so much the better." Ibid., x. The changing attitude of French intellectuals toward the French Revolution, and revolution in general, is well chronicled in Sunil Khilnani, *Arguing Revolution: The Intellectual Left in Postwar France* (New Haven: Yale University Press, 1993); see also Tony Judt, *Marxism and the French Left* (Oxford: Oxford University Press, 1986).

On the lively debates among French historians and others about the meaning of 1989 and the revolutionary legacy for France and the world, see Steven Laurence Kaplan, *Farewell, Revolution: The Historians' Feud, France 1789/1989* and *Farewell, Revolution: Disputed Legacies, France 1789/1989* (Ithaca, N.Y.: Cornell University Press, 1995).

On the general "derogation of revolution" today, see Fred Halliday, "Revolution in the Third World: 1945 and After," in E. E. Rice, ed., *Revolution and Counter-Revolution* (Oxford: Basil Blackwell, 1991), 130; see also Fred Halliday, *Revolution and World Politics: The Rise and Fall of the Sixth Great Power* (Durham, N.C.: Duke University Press, 1999), especially 1–23. The decline of the revolutionary idea in the West is also traced by Theodor Hamerow, *From the Finland Station: The Graying of Revolution in the Twentieth Century* (New York: Basic Books, 1990).

2. Richard Cobb's remark, from a talk given on July 21, 1981, was quoted in the *Times Literary Supplement* (August 7, 1981), 919. For some examples of the revisionist historiography of the French Revolution, see my review essay, "Revolution: History's Cheshire Cat," *History Workshop Journal* 27 (spring 1989): 186, n. 3; see also Kaplan's volumes cited in note 1 to this chapter. A brilliant popularization of the revisionist approach, and a best-seller at the time of the bicentenary, is Simon Schama, *Citizens: A Chronicle of the French Revolution* (London: Viking, 1989).

3. Richard Lowenthal, "The 'Missing Revolution' of Our Times: Reflections on New Post-Marxist Fundamentals of Social Change," *Encounter* (June 1981): 18. The same issue of *Encounter* contained Seymour Martin Lipset's requiem for the (putatively) revolutionary working class, "Whatever Happened to the Proletariat? An Unhistoric Mission Unfulfilled?" *Encounter* (June 1981): 18–34. For Lipset's further reflections on

what he saw as the continuing retreat of the Left, both revolutionary and reformist, see "No Third Way: A Comparative Perspective on the Left," in Daniel Chirot, ed., *The Crisis of Leninism and the Decline of the Left: The Revolutions of 1989* (Seattle: University of Washington Press, 1991), 183–232.

4. And not just in Eastern Europe, but even further east. The Chinese students who constructed the "Goddess of Democracy" in Tiananmen Square in May 1989 paid explicit homage to the French Revolution in their struggle to achieve democratic rights. On the importance of the revolution's bicentenary to the Democracy Movement in China, see Tu Wei-Ming, "Intellectual Effervescence in China," *Daedalus* 121 (1992): 282; for the longer historical view, see Zhang Zhillian, ed., *China and the French Revolution* (Oxford: Pergamon Press, 1989). And cf. Hosbawm: "It is a satisfactory irony of history that at the very moment when French liberals, anxious to distance themselves from a Jacobin past, were declaring that the Revolution had nothing further to say to the present, the immediate relevance of 1789 to 1989 was being observed by students in Beijing and newly elected members of the Congress [of People's Deputies] in Moscow." Hobsbawm, *Echoes of the Marseillaise*, xi; on the French Revolution's "centrality and relevance" today, see also ibid., 110–13. The continuing relevance of the French Revolution, to the world if not to the French themselves, is the theme of most of the contributions to Geoffrey Best, ed., *The Permanent Revolution: The French Revolution and its Legacy 1789–1989* (London: Fontana Press, 1988); see also the special issue of *Social Research*, "The French Revolution and the Birth of Modernity," *Social Research* 56, no. 1 (1989).

The ironies of history were observable a number of times in 1989, during the host of conferences and symposia that were occasioned by the bicentenary of the French Revolution. Wolfson College, Oxford, ran a series of commemorative lectures in February and March on the theme of "Revolution and Counter-Revolution." Editing the lectures for publication the following year, E. E. Rice commented: "No one in the audience can have had any thought that 1989 would itself prove to be a year of European revolutions so widespread, unforeseen and devastating that their impact cannot yet be assessed. . . . 1989 may prove to be one of the great Years of Revolution in history." E. E. Rice, "Preface," E. E.Rice, ed., *Revolution and Counter-Revolution*, vii, x.

I, too, was at an Oxford conference on revolution, at Exeter College in April 1989. In the (unpublished) paper I wrote for the conference I concluded: "History is full of surprises. 1789, it is true, may no longer be a model; but it remains a spectacular example of historical creativity. No one can say that this cannot or will not happen again." I, too, had no inkling—despite the opening of Round Table talks between Solidarity and the Polish government in early spring of that year—of the events that were to erupt in Eastern Europe later in the year; but I am glad to see that my assessment of the prospects for revolution—generally unhopeful—at least left the door open.

5. Albert Camus, "Neither Victim nor Executioner" (1946), in Krishan Kumar, ed., *Revolution: The Theory and Practice of a European Idea* (London: Weidenfeld and Nicolson, 1971), 302–3.

6. Quincy Wright, quoted in Sigmund Neumann, "The International Civil War," *World Politics*, 1 (1949), 334, n. 2.

7. Neumann, ibid. This approach has also been applied specifically to Europe. See Ernst Nolte, *Der Europaische Burgerkrieg 1917–1945: Nationalsozialismus und Bolschewismus* (Berlin: Propylaen Verlag, 1987). See also Baruch Knei-Paz, "The National Revolution As an International Event," *Jerusalem Journal of International Relations* 3 (1977): 1–27; Jonathan R. Adelman, ed., *Superpowers and Revolution* (New York: Praeger, 1986). On the international dimension of the French Revolution,

see Theda Skocpol, *States and Social Revolutions* (Cambridge: Cambridge University Press, 1979), chapter 2; more comprehensive is Bailey Stone, *The Genesis of the French Revolution: A Global-Historical Interpretation* (Cambridge: Cambridge University Press, 1994). See also Joseph Klaits and Michael Haltzel, *The Global Ramifications of the French Revolution* (Cambridge: Cambridge University Press, 1994).

Alfred Cobban was one of the many who drew the parallels between the revolutionary wars of 1789–1815 and those of our century. See Alfred Cobban, "An Age of Revolutionary Wars: An Historical Parallel" (1951), in *France Since the Revolution, and Other Aspects of Modern History* (London: Jonathan Cape, 1970), 142–54. And cf. Reinhart Koselleck: "All modern expressions of 'Revolution' spatially imply a *world revolution* and temporally imply that they be *permanent* until their objective is reached." Reinhart Koselleck, "Historical Criteria of the Modern Concept of Revolution," in *Futures Past: On the Semantics of Historical Time,* translated by Keith Tribe (Cambridge, Mass.: MIT Press, 1985), 49.

8. On the Russian Revolution of 1917 as the model for Third World revolutions, see Theodore H. Von Laue, *Why Lenin? Why Stalin? A Reappraisal of the Russian Revolution, 1900–1930,* 2nd ed. (Philadelphia: J. B. Lippincott Company, 1971). For E. H. Carr it was the very "backwardness of the Russian economy and society" that marked it as the type of twentieth-century revolution. The Russian revolution was the "first stage" of "the world revolution . . . which will complete the downfall of capitalism, and [which] will prove to be the revolt of the colonial peoples against capitalism in the guise of imperialism rather than a revolt of the proletariat of the advanced capitalist countries." E. H. Carr, "The Russian Revolution and the West," *New Left Review* 111 (1978): 35.

On the significance of the Mexican revolution of 1910 in the pattern of twentieth-century revolutions, see John Dunn, *Modern Revolutions,* 2nd ed. (Cambridge: Cambridge University Press, 1989), chapter 2, and Eric R. Wolf, *Peasant Wars of the Twentieth Century* (New York: Harper and Row, 1969), chapter 1. However, Wolf also noted how far Mexico diverged from the general pattern, and Dunn elsewhere observed that "The Mexican revolution eludes the pattern by having commenced before the pattern was set." John Dunn, "The Success and Failure of Modern Revolutions," in *Political Obligation and Its Historical Context: Essays in Political Theory* (Cambridge: Cambridge University Press, 1980), 228.

Fred Halliday rightly pointed out that it is anachronistic to apply the term "Third World revolution" to revolutions that occurred before 1945, as the "Third World" is essentially a concept created by the post-1945 Cold War and the bipolar world system that went with it. See Halliday, "Revolution in the Third World," 141. But it seems reasonable to follow common practice and refer to earlier twentieth-century revolutions as "Third World" revolutions where they seem to fit the general pattern of revolutions in underdeveloped societies (that is, they are peasant based, occur in conditions of colonial or semicolonial dependence, and so on).

9. Thus John Dunn, in seeking to explain the relatively high number of revolutions in the twentieth century, put this down to "the dramatic intensification in the economic relations between human populations across the globe," leading to an "increasingly direct and hectic interaction of state powers across the globe." Dunn, *Modern Revolutions,* xix. See also Dunn, "The Success and Failure of Modern Revolutions," 228–33; "Revolution," in Terence Ball, James Farr, and Russell L. Hanson, eds., *Political Innovation and Conceptual Change* (Cambridge: Cambridge University Press, 1989), 350.

10. On the play of international forces, specifically Portugal's NATO allies, in the Portuguese revolution of 1974, see Martin Kayman, *Revolution and Counter-Revolution*

*in Portugal* (London: Merlin Press, 1987); and cf. Samuel Huntington: "The Western intervention led by the Germans [against the Portuguese communists] was crucial to Portuguese democratization." Samuel Huntington, *The Third Wave: Democratization in the Late Twentieth Century* (Norman: University of Oklahoma Press, 1993), 89.

11. Friedrich Engels, "Introduction" (1895) to Karl Marx, "The Class Struggles in France 1848–50," in Karl Marx and Friedrich Engels, *Selected Works in Two Volumes* (Moscow: Foreign Languages Publishing House, 1962), vol. 1, 118–38. On "the end of the barricades and the romantic revolution," see also Neumann, "The International Civil War," 342, n. 2; Camus, "Neither Victim nor Executioner," 302. On the growing obsolescence of the barricade in the country of its birth, see Mark Traugott, "Barricades As Repertoire: Continuities and Discontinuities in the History of French Contention," in Mark Traugott, ed., *Repertoires and Cycles of Collective Action* (Durham, N.C.: Duke University Press, 1995), 43–56. There is a good brief survey of the military factor in revolution in John M. Gates, "Toward a History of Revolution," *Comparative Studies in Society and History* 28 (1986): 535–44; see also E. J. Hobsbawm, "Cities and Insurrections," in *Revolutionaries: Contemporary Essays* (London: Weidenfeld and Nicolson, 1973), 220–33. The pioneering and still indispensable study is Katharine Chorley, *Armies and the Art of Revolution* (London: Faber and Faber, 1943; reprint Boston: Beacon Press, 1973).

12. Though the ingenious use of laptop computers and the Internet by some contemporary insurgents, such as the restyled Zapatistas of southern Mexico and the Shining Path guerrillas of Peru, should be noted. On this see Manuel Castells, *The Power of Identity* (Malden, Mass.: Blackwell Publishers, 1997), 68–83. Castells calls the Zapatistas "the first informational guerrilla movement." Publishing can also be a cheap computer-based cottage industry today, allowing for the promotion of a wide range of dissident causes. But it is typical of contemporary radicals to exaggerate the revolutionary potential of such technological developments. See, for example, Geoff Mulgan, *Politics in an Unpolitical Age* (Cambridge: Polity Press, 1994), 197.

For Castro's remark, see Régis Debray, *Revolution in the Revolution?* translated by Bobbye Ortiz (Harmondsworth, U.K.: Penguin Books, 1968), 67.

13. Debray, *Revolution in the Revolution?* 24. On the "militarization of action" on the part of revolutionary theorists (as well as social scientists), see Sheldon S. Wolin, "The Politics of the Study of Revolution," *Comparative Politics* 5 (1973): 343–58.

14. For an example of Comintern thinking of the 1920s, see *Armed Insurrection,* published in 1928 and attributed to the pseudonymous "A. Neuberg" (London: New Left Books, 1970). The danger of the kind of thinking represented by Debray was stressed by a number of contributors to Leo Huberman and Paul M. Sweezy, eds., *Régis Debray and the Latin American Revolution* (New York: Monthly Review Press, 1968). On the limitations of guerrilla warfare, see also E. J. Hobsbawm, "Vietnam and the Dynamics of Guerrilla War," in Hobsbawm, *Revolutionaries,* 163–76.

15. See, for example, Elbaki Hermassi, "Toward a Comparative Study of Revolution," *Comparative Studies in Society and History* 18 (1976): 211–35. On "the misleading model" of the French Revolution for the understanding of later nineteenth- and twentieth-century revolutions, see also Bruce Mazlish, "The French Revolution in Comparative Perspective," *Political Science Quarterly* 85 (1970): 240–58.

16. On this see further my "Twentieth Century Revolutions in Historical Perspective," in Krishan Kumar, *The Rise of Modern Society: Aspects of the Social and Political Development of the West* (Oxford: Basil Blackwell, 1988), 177–83. There I considered certain episodes, such as the German revolution of 1918–20, and May 1968 in France, which may be considered instances of attempts at revolution.

17. See James H. Billington, *Fire in the Minds of Men: Origins of the Revolutionary Faith* (London: Temple Smith, 1980); also Melvin Lasky, *Utopia and Revolution,* part 1 (Chicago: University of Chicago Press, 1976). Both Billington and Lasky, like Talmon before them, exaggerated the messianic quality of nineteenth-century revolutionism.

18. Karl Marx, "Contribution to the Critique of Hegel's Philosophy of Right," in T. B. Bottomore, trans. and ed., *Karl Marx: Early Writings* (London: C. A. Watts and Co., 1963), 55.

19. Lenin was quoted by C. B. A. Behrens, "The Spirit of the Terror," *New York Review of Books* (February 27, 1969), 19. For the influence of the French Revolution on nineteenth-century European socialists, and especially Russian Marxists, see Hobsbawm, *Echoes of the Marseillaise,* 33–66.

20. See especially Leon Trotsky, *The Revolution Betrayed* (1936) (London: New Park Publications, 1967), 86–114. For an illuminating comparison of the French and Russian revolutions, drawing upon Trotsky but also upon Sorel, see Isaac Deutscher, "Two Revolutions," in Deutscher's *Marxism, Wars and Revolution: Essays from Four Decades* (London: Verso, 1984), 34–45. A more critical view of Trotsky's handling of the comparison is Jay Bergman, "The Perils of Historical Analogy: Leon Trotsky and the French Revolution," *Journal of the History of Ideas* 48 (1989): 73–98. Comparisons can work the other way around as well, of course. It is undoubtedly the case that much of the recent "revisionist" approach to the French Revolution has been inspired by seeing it through the prism of the Russian revolution.

21. The debates on these issues among Russian intellectuals in the early years of the revolution are discussed in Jane Burbank, *Intelligentsia and Revolution: Russian Views of Bolshevism, 1917–22* (New York: Oxford University Press, 1986).

22. For these developments, see the characteristically incisive discussion in Perry Anderson, *Considerations on Western Marxism* (London: New Left Books, 1976). See also two books by Richard Gombin, *The Origins of Modern Leftism,* translated from the French by M. K. Perl (Harmondsworth, U.K.: Penguin Books, 1975), and *The Radical Tradition: A Study in Modern Revolutionary Thought,* translated from the French by Rupert Swyer (London: Methuen, 1978).

23. For Mao's attempt to "transform a whole culture" through the "Great Proletarian Cultural Revolution," and the relevance of this attempt to Western radicals, see the sympathetic account by Richard M. Pfeffer, "The Pursuit of Purity: Mao's Cultural Revolution," in Bruce Mazlish, Arthur D. Kaledin, and David B. Ralston, eds., *Revolution: A Reader* (New York: The Macmillan Company, 1971), 338–57. For Isaac Deutscher, on the contrary, the cultural revolution represented a disastrous step backward in the Chinese revolution. See "The Meaning of the Cultural Revolution," in Deutscher's *Marxism, Wars and Revolutions,* 212–17.

24. Aldous Huxley, "Foreword" (1946) to *Brave New World* (Harmondsworth, U.K.: Penguin books, 1964), 10.

25. Herbert Marcuse's most important work in this respect is *Eros and Civilization: A Philosophical Inquiry into Freud* (New York: Vintage Books, 1962). For the general approach of the Freudo-Marxists, see Bruce Brown, *Marx, Freud and the Critique of Everyday Life: Toward a Permanent Cultural Revolution* (New York: Monthly Review Press, 1973).

26. See Herbert Marcuse, *An Essay on Liberation* (London: Allen Lane, The Penguin Press, 1969). For the underlying critique of traditional concepts of revolution, see Henri Lefebvre, *Everyday Life in the Modern World,* translated from the French by Sacha Rabinovitch (London: Allen Lane, The Penguin Press, 1971).

27. Raoul Vaneigem, *The Revolution of Everyday Life,* translated by John Fullerton

and Paul Sieveking (London: Practical Paradise Publications, 1973), 11. See also the work of another leading Situationist theoretician, Guy Debord, *Society of the Spectacle* (Detroit: Black and Red Publications, 1970). There is a good study of the Situationists by Sadie Plant, *The Most Radical Gesture: The Situationist International in a Postmodern Age* (London: Routledge, 1992).

28. The best account of the thinking behind the May events is Alfred Willener, *The Action-Image of Society: On Cultural Politicization,* translated from the French by A. M. Sheridan Smith (London: Tavistock Publications, 1970). The most balanced account of the events themselves is Bernard E. Brown, *Protest in Paris: Anatomy of a Revolt* (Morristown, N.J.: General Learning Press, 1974).

29. See my "Twentieth Century Revolutions in Historical Perspective," 190–99.

30. Leszek Kolakowski, "The Palace of Alienation," *New Statesman* (July 27, 1973): 119.

31. It is probably true to say that *all* serious conceptions of revolution have been "totalistic," in the general sense that—at least since the French Revolution of 1789—they have aimed at the creation of a new species of humanity in a totally transformed social environment. For the intellectual sources of such a conception of revolution, see Bernard Yack, *The Longing for Total Revolution: Philosophic Sources of Social Discontent from Rousseau to Marx and Nietzsche* (Berkeley: University of California Press, 1992). There is a famous portrait of such a "new man," created by the socialist revolution, at the conclusion of Leon Trotsky, *Literature and Revolution* (1923), translated from the Russian by Rose Strunsky (Ann Arbor: University of Michigan Press, 1960), 252–56.

But up to the Russian Revolution, it was possible to some extent to separate "the revolution"—the taking of state power on some more or less realistic model—from the creation of the "new man" at some fairly unspecified date after the revolution. This was still, for instance, Trotsky's view in the 1920s. What has changed in the West in the period since then is the fusion of these two phases or episodes. The revolution *is,* and must be, the making of the new man. These are virtually synonymous concepts and occur within a simultaneous process. The recoil in particular from the Russian revolution has made it appear dangerous to separate the two.

32. See T. J. Clark, *The Absolute Bourgeois: Artists and Politics in France 1848–51* (Princeton: Princeton University Press, 1982), 9–30. For the symbolism of the French Revolution of 1789, see Lynn Hunt, *Politics, Culture and Class in the French Revolution,* part 1 (London: Methuen, 1986); see also Ronald Paulson, *Representations of Revolution (1789–1820)* (New Haven: Yale University Press, 1983).

33. See John Berger, *Art and Revolution: Ernst Neizvestny and the Role of the Artist in the USSR* (Harmondsworth, U.K.: Penguin Books, 1967), 31–48; Stephen White, *The Bolshevik Poster* (New Haven: Yale University Press, 1988).

34. Halliday, "Revolution in the Third World," 136. To the examples in the text we might want to add Turkey in 1919, Yugoslavia in 1945, Egypt in 1952, Mozambique and Angola in 1975, perhaps Afghanistan in 1978—and even Russia in 1917, which has good claim to be considered, among other things, a Third World revolution. For good studies of Third World revolutions, see, in addition to Halliday's essay, Wolf, *Peasant Wars of the Twentieth Century*; Dunn, *Modern Revolutions*; Jack A. Goldstone, ed., *Revolutions: Theoretical, Comparative, and Historical Studies,* part 2 (San Diego: Harcourt Brace Jovanovich, 1986); Theda Skocpol, "What Makes Peasants Revolutionary?" and Theda Skocpol and Jeff Goodwin, "Explaining Revolutions in the Contemporary Third World," in Theda Skocpol, *Social Revolutions in the Modern World* (Cambridge: Cambridge University Press, 1994), 213–39, 259–78. For an unfashionably Marxist

view of these revolutions, see James Petras, "Socialist Revolutions and Their Class Components," *New Left Review* 111, (1978): 37–64.

35. As was admirably brought out by Halliday, *Revolution and World Politics*, especially 293–338.

36. See Elie Kedourie, "The Third World: The Idea of Revolution," in Rice, ed., *Revolution and Counter-Revolution*, 196. And see also Mike Mason, *Development and Disorder: A History of the Third World Since 1945* (Hanover, N.H.: University Press of New England, 1997), 1–41.

37. Fidel Castro, *History Will Absolve Me* (London: Jonathan Cape, 1968), 95 ff.

38. Jean-Paul Sartre, "Preface" to Frantz Fanon, *The Wretched of the Earth*, translated from the French by Constance Farrington (Harmondsworth, U.K.: Penguin Books, 1967), 18–19. For Fanon's influence among Third World liberation theorists, see Edward W. Said, *Culture and Imperialism* (London: Vintage, 1994), 322–36.

39. See David Caute, *Fanon* (London: Fontana, 1970), 94.

40. On the role of the middle stratum of the peasantry in Third World revolutions, see especially Wolf, *Peasant Wars of the Twentieth Century*, 276–302.

41. Fanon, *The Wretched of the Earth*, 254.

42. The conclusion also of Caute, *Fanon*, 97.

43. For some examples, see Henry Munson, Jr., *Islam and Revolution in the Middle East* (New Haven: Yale University Press, 1988).

44. Marquis de Condorcet, "Sur le Sens du Mot Révolutionnaire" (1793), in Kumar, ed., *Revolution*, 93 (my translation). In my introduction to this volume I tried to defend such a concept of revolution; today I would do so still, but differently.

45. For interesting discussions of some of these examples, see E. Weber, "Revolution? Counter-Revolution? What Revolution?" in W. Laqueur, ed., *Fascism: A Reader's Guide* (Harmondsworth, U.K.: Penguin Books, 1979), 488–531; R. H. Dix, "The Varieties of Revolution," *Comparative Politics* 15 (1983): 281–93; E. K. Trimberger, *Revolution from Above: Military Bureaucrats and Development in Japan, Turkey, Egypt and Peru* (New Brunswick, N.J.: Transaction Books, 1978).

46. See especially Halliday, "Revolution in the Third World," 148–50; Halliday, *Revolution and World Politics*, 188–90; see also Theda Skocpol, "Rentier State and Shi'a Islam in the Iranian Revolution," in *Social Revolutions in the Modern World*, 240–58; Val Moghadam, "One Revolution or Two? The Iranian Revolution and the Islamic Republic," in Ralph Miliband, Leo Panitch, and John Saville, eds., *Revolution Today: Aspirations and Realities (The Socialist Register 1989)* (London: The Merlin Press, 1989), 74–101.

47. Peter Kropotkin, *The Great French Revolution 1789–1793*, translated by N. F. Dryhurst (London: William Heinemann, 1909), 582.

48. Fred Halliday, "The Ends of Cold War," *New Left Review* 180 (1990): 5.

49. Jürgen Habermas, "What Does Socialism Mean Today? The Revolutions of Recuperation and the Need for New Thinking," in Robin Blackburn, ed., *After the Fall: The Failure of Communism and the Future of Socialism* (London: Verso, 1991), 27.

50. François Furet, "From 1789 to 1917 to 1989: Looking Backward at Revolutionary Traditions," *Encounter* (September 1990): 5.

51. See Gale Stokes, *The Walls Came Tumbling Down: The Collapse of Communism in Eastern Europe* (New York: Oxford University Press, 1993), 140.

52. Quoted in Robert Darnton, "Runes of the New Revolutions," *The Times Higher Education Supplement* (September 6, 1991), 17.

53. Bronislaw Geremek, "Between Hope and Despair," *Daedalus* (winter 1990): 99.

54. See chapter 3 of this book. The desire to link up with the Western, not "Eastern,"

that is, Russian, revolutionary inheritance is evident in the views of many of the leading participants in the 1989 revolutions. For examples, see Gwyn Prins, ed., *Spring in Winter: The 1989 Revolutions* (Manchester: Manchester University Press, 1990).

55. Habermas, "What Does Socialism Mean Today?" 26. See also Ralf Dahrendorf, *Reflections on the Revolution in Europe* (London: Chatto and Windus, 1990), 23; Timothy Garton Ash, *We the People: The Revolution of '89* (Cambridge: Granta/Penguin Books, 1990), 154.

56. See Hannah Arendt, *On Revolution* (London: Faber and Faber, 1963), 21–40.

57. On this see further chapters 2 and 4 of this book.

58. See, for example, Ash, *We the People,* 14. On the question of whether the 1989 events can be called "revolutions" in anything like the classic sense of the term, see S. N. Eisenstadt, "The Breakdown of Communist Regimes and the Vicissitudes of Modernity," *Daedalus* (spring 1992): 21–41; Charles Tilly, *European Revolutions, 1492–1992* (Cambridge, Mass.: Blackwell, 1993), 233–48. The question is extensively discussed in chapter 4 of this book.

59. Lenin, "Lecture on the 1905 Revolution" (January 1917), in *Selected Works in Three Volumes,* vol. 1 (Moscow: Foreign Languages Publishing House, n. d.), 842.

60. For the changes that have made revolution less likely in twentieth-century industrial societies, see my "Twentieth Century Revolutions in Historical Perspective," esp. 183–90.

61. See, for example, Octavio Paz, "Twilight of Revolution," in I. Howe, ed., *Twenty-Five Years of Dissent* (New York: Methuen, 1979), 314–25. For pronouncements of "the end of revolution" in the 1930s, see E. Rosenstock-Huessy, *Out of Revolution: The Autobiography of Western Man* (London: Jarrolds, 1938), 708–39.

62. Albert Camus, *The Rebel,* translated by A. Bower (Harmondsworth, U.K.: Penguin Books, 1962), 29.

# 9. The Return of the Repressed

1. The financier-philanthropist George Soros, who has been active in launching cultural and educational initiatives, such as the Central European University, in Central and Eastern Europe, has called his principal foundations in the region "Open Society" foundations, in homage to his erstwhile mentor Karl Popper. He now wishes to turn his money, and similar "open society" initiatives, homeward, toward the West. See the article on Soros by William Shawcross, "Turning Dollars Into Change," *Time* (September 1, 1997), 48–57. For advocacy of the term "open society"—"in the tradition illustrated by Raymond Aron, Ralf Dahrendorf, Ernest Gellner, Claude Lefort, and Karl Popper"—to describe the direction of change in Eastern Europe, see also Vladimir Tismaneanu, "Introduction" to a special issue of *East European Politics and Societies,* "The Revolutions of 1989: Lessons of the First Postcommunist Decade," *East European Politics and Societies* 13, no. 2 (1999): 232.

2. G. M. Tamás has seen them in this postmodern light, largely in terms of what he considers their (willful and childlike) antinomianism and anarchism. The 1989 revolutions were a revolt against the "rational utopia" of communism. Their patron saints were "not F. A. Hayek and Michael Oakeshott, but Thomas Münzer and Yemelyan Pugachev." In this sense they shared much with a similar outburst of anarchic "irrationality" in the May events in Paris in 1968: "1968 and 1989 are not so different. Both were outbursts of sentiment, irrational celebrations of caprice. . . ." G. M. Tamás, "A Disquisition on Civil Society," *Social Research* 61, no. 2 (1994): 214–15. For the parallel between 1968 and 1989, see also Tiryakian, "The New World and Sociology: An

Overview," 139; Edward Tiryakian, "Collective Effervescence, Social Change and Charisma: Durkheim, Weber and 1989," *International Sociology* 10, no. 3 (1995): 269–81; and, somewhat differently, G. Arrighi, T. Hopkins, and I. Wallerstein, "1989, the Continuation of 1968," *Review* 15, no. 2, (1992): 221–42. Stjepan Mestrovic sees a "confluence" between a "Balkanized," amoral, Western postmodernism and a violent, Eastern postcommunism. Stjepan Mestrovic, *The Balkanization of the West: The Confluence of Postmodernism and Postcommunism* (New York: Routledge, 1994). And cf. Larry Ray's comment on Habermas's view that the 1989 revolutions were "rectifying revolutions" of modernity: "A defining characteristic of the recuperating revolutions was that they offered no utopian vision of the future, but signalled the end of 'redemptive politics.'. . . In this sense they might have more in common than Habermas and others acknowledge, with postmodernism's deep aversion to projects of universal human emancipation." Larry Ray, "Post-Communism: Postmodernity or Modernity Revisited?" *British Journal of Sociology* 48, no. 2 (1997): 131. For Zygmunt Bauman's view of 1989 as postmodern, see chapter 4 of this book. On the postmodern character of the 1989 revolutions, see also Göran Therborn, note 40 to this chapter.

3. See chapters 2 and 4 of this book.

4. See Jeffrey Alexander, "Modern, Anti, Post, and Neo: How Intellectuals Have Coded, Narrated, and Explained the 'New World of Our Time,'" in his *Fin de Siècle Social Theory: Relativism, Reduction, and the Problem of Reason* (New York: Verso. 1995), 6–64. And cf. Slavoj Žižek, "Eastern Europe's Republics of Gilead," *New Left Review* 183 (1990): 50–62. Of course, Soviet-style communism was also a species of modernity—the very climax of it, according to Zygmunt Bauman in making his case for 1989 as a postmodern revolt against modernity. It is modernity Western-style—capitalist and liberal—that, according to Alexander and others, is regenerated by the anticommunist revolt. For communism and modernity, see Larry J. Ray, *Social Theory and the Crisis of State Socialism* (Cheltenham, U.K.: Edward Elgar, 1996), 1–3; Ray, "Postcommunism: Postmodernity or Modernity Revisited?"

5. See Francis Fukuyama, *The End of History and the Last Man* (London: Penguin Books, 1992), 68–69, 133; Edward A. Tiryakian, "Modernisation: Exhumetur in Pace (Rethinking Macrosociology in the 1990s)," *International Sociology* 6, no. 2 (1991): 165–80; and, for the fullest discussion, see Alexander, "Modern, Anti, Post and Neo." On the relevance of modernization theory to 1989, see Ilja Srubar, "Variants of the Transformation Process in Central Europe: A Comparative Assessment," *Zeitschrift für Soziologie* 23, no. 3 (1994): 198–221; Piotr Sztompka, "The Lessons of 1989 for Sociological Theory," in Piotr Sztompka, ed., *Building Open Society and Perspectives of Sociology in East Central Europe* (Krakow: International Sociological Association, 1998), 14–19.

6. A full-blooded application is Rossen Vassilev, "Modernization Theory Revisited: The Case of Bulgaria," *East European Politics and Societies* 13, no. 3 (1999): 566–99. It also demonstrates, incidentally, how easily Marxist categories can be adapted to deck out the well-known bourgeois thesis that "there is a causal relationship between socioeconomic development and political democratization," Vassilev's explanation of the "democratic revolution of 1989–90" in Bulgaria. As he says, "The case of Bulgarian democratization adds yet another instance supportive of the historically optimistic modernization hypothesis." Ibid., 566, 598.

7. A good résumé and audit is Mike Mason, *Development and Disorder: A History of the Third World since 1945* (Hanover, N.H.: University Press of New England, 1997); on the rise of the "fourth world" of underprivileged nations and peoples, including several pockets in the "advanced" industrial world, see also Manuel Castells, *End of Millennium* (Malden, Mass.: Blackwell, 1998), 71–165.

8. See the essays in Immanuel Wallerstein, *The Capitalist World-Economy* (Cambridge: Cambridge University Press, 1979).

9. As spectacularly revealed, for instance, by the economic crisis that began in East Asia in early 1997 and then, over the next twelve months, spread to many other areas of the world, including Eastern Europe and Latin America. Russia, in particular, has every reason to be aware of its new dependence on the capitalist world economy, especially its financial markets.

10. A good example of the way the Cold War structured social theory is the well-regarded sociology text by Richard Scase and Howard Davis, *Western Capitalism and State Socialism* (Oxford: Basil Blackwell, 1987). For the consequences for social theory of the loss of this convenient opposition, see Alexander, "Modern, Anti, Post and Neo," 8. For the impact of the Cold War on Western culture generally, see Fred Inglis, *The Cruel Peace: Everyday Life and the Cold War* (New York: Basic Books, 1991); and, for its impact—not necessarily always baleful—on Western societies, see James E. Cronin, *The World the Cold War Made: Order, Chaos, and the Return of History* (New York: Routledge, 1996).

11. See Jürgen Habermas, *The Past as Future*, translated and edited by Max Pensky (Cambridge, U.K.: Polity Press, 1994), 11–12. On the other hand, in the Kosovo conflict of 1999 NATO took unilateral action against Serbia, thus demonstrating the ambiguity of what "international cooperation" might mean.

12. See Anthony D. Smith, "Nationalism and Classical Social Theory," *British Journal of Sociology* 34, no. 1 (1983): 19–38. Anthony Giddens has also frequently made the point; see, for example, *The Nation-State and Violence* (Berkeley: University of California Press, 1985). For similar unquestioned assumptions among political theorists, see Margaret Canovan, *Nationhood and Political Theory* (Aldershot: Edward Elgar, 1996). For a questioning of the "boundedness" of social forms such as the nation-state, see Michael Mann, *The Sources of Social Power*, vol. 1 (Cambridge: Cambridge University Press, 1986); see also Richard Handler, *Nationalism and the Politics of Culture in Quebec* (Madison: University of Wisconsin Press, 1988). For an all-out assault on the whole concept of the Westphalian state, with its assumptions of unity, autonomy, sovereignty, and, more latterly, nationality, see Yale H. Ferguson and Richard W. Mansbach, *Polities: Authority, Identities and Change* (Columbia: University of South Carolina Press, 1996). See also Jean-Marie Guéhenno, *The End of the Nation-State*, translated by Victoria Elliott (Minneapolis and London: University of Minnesota Press, 1995); and the essays in Pheng Cheah and Bruce Robbins, eds., *Cosmopolitics: Thinking and Feeling Beyond the Nation* (Minneapolis: University of Minnesota Press, 1998).

13. See my *Prophecy and Progress: The Sociology of Industrial and Post-Industrial Society* (Harmondsworth, U.K.: Penguin Books, 1978), chapter 3.

14. A courageous and compelling start has been made by Manuel Castells in his trilogy *The Information Age: Economy, Society and Culture* (Malden, Mass.: Blackwell Publishers, 1996–1998). The individual titles are *The Rise of the Network Society* (1996), *The Power of Identity* (1997), and *End of Millennium* (1998).

15. Perhaps the major dissenter from this position is Samuel P. Huntington, *The Clash of Civilizations and the Remaking of the World Order* (New York: Touchstone Books, 1997). See also Ken Jowitt, *New World Disorder: The Leninist Extinction* (Berkeley: University of California Press, 1992), especially chapters 7–9. Both are resolutely opposed to Fukuyama's "end of history."

16. See Dankwart A. Rustow, "Democracy: A Global Revolution?" *Foreign Affairs* 69, no. 4 (1990): 75–91; Samuel P. Huntington, *The Third Wave: Democratization in the Late Twentieth Century* (Norman: University of Oklahoma Press, 1993). One has,

of course, to be careful of taking current trends as a guide to the future. In late 1999 Pakistan went back to a military dictatorship, and several of the states of the former Soviet Union show distinctly authoritarian tendencies.

17. One can do no more here than list a handful of the recent works by some of the leading contemporary theorists and students of democracy: Dietrich Rueschemeyer, Evelyne Huber Stephens, and John D. Stephens, *Capitalist Development and Democracy* (Cambridge, U.K.: Polity Press, 1992); Robert D. Putnam, *Making Democracy Work: Civic Traditions in Modern Italy* (Princeton: Princeton University Press, 1993); Thomas L. Pangle, *The Ennobling of Democracy: The Challenge of the Postmodern Age* (Baltimore: The Johns Hopkins University Press, 1993); David Held, *Democracy and the Global Order: From the Modern State to Cosmopolitan Governance* (Cambridge, U.K.: Polity Press, 1995); Daniele Archibugi and David Held, eds., *Cosmopolitan Democracy: An Agenda for a New World Order* (Cambridge: Polity Press, 1995); Adam Przeworski, *Sustainable Democracy* (Cambridge, U.K.: Cambridge University Press, 1995); Michael J. Sandel, *Democracy's Discontent: America in Search of a Public Philosophy* (Cambridge: Harvard University Press, 1996); Sanford Lakoff, *Democracy: History, Theory, Practice* (Boulder, Colo.: Westview Press, 1996); Amy Gutmann and Dennis Thompson, *Democracy and Disagreement* (Cambridge: Harvard University Press, 1996); Seyla Benhabib, ed., *Democracy and Difference* (Princeton: Princeton University Press, 1996); Alain Touraine, *What is Democracy?* (Boulder, Colo.: Westview Press, 1997); Robert A. Dahl, *On Democracy* (New Haven: Yale University Press, 1998); Arend Lijphart, *Patterns of Democracy* (New Haven: Yale University Press, 1999). For the Left-Radical view, see Paul Hirst, *Associative Democracy: New Forms of Economic and Social Governance* (Cambridge, U.K.: Polity Press, 1994); Chantal Mouffe, ed., *Dimensions of Radical Democracy* (New York: Verso, 1992). In celebration, and explanation, of democracy's "overwhelmingly dominant and well-nigh exclusive" claim to "set the standard for legitimate political authority" today, there is John Dunn, ed., *Democracy: The Unfinished Journey 508 BC to AD 1993* (Oxford: Oxford University Press, 1993). A good selection of articles from the *Journal of Democracy* is Larry Diamond and Marc F. Plattner, eds., *The Global Resurgence of Democracy,* 2nd edition (Baltimore: The Johns Hopkins University Press, 1996). For those who want still more, there is Seymour Martin Lipset, ed., *The Encyclopedia of Democracy,* four volumes (New York: Routledge, 1996). See also my review article, "Democracy Again," *Review of International Political Economy* 5, no. 2 (1997): 124–34.

18. Marshall's essay, "Citizenship and Social Class" (1950), is in T. H. Marshall, *Sociology at the Crossroads, and Other Essays* (London: Heinemann, 1963), 67–127. For recent sociological work, see Bryan Turner, *Citizenship and Capitalism* (London: Allen and Unwin, 1986); Geoff Andrews, ed., *Citizenship* (London: Lawrence and Wishart, 1991). For approaches from political theory and philosophy, see Ronald Beiner, ed., *Theorizing Citizenship* (Albany: State University of New York Press, 1995); see also J. M. Barbalet, *Citizenship* (Milton Keynes: Open University Press, 1988). A wide-ranging collection is Gershon Shafir, ed., *The Citizenship Debates* (Minneapolis: University of Minnesota Press, 1998). On trust, see Diego Gambetta, ed., *Trust: Making and Breaking Cooperative Relations* (Oxford: Blackwell, 1988); Francis Fukuyama, *Trust: The Social Virtues and the Creation of Prosperity* (New York: The Free Press, 1995); Adam B. Seligman, *The Problem of Trust* (Princeton: Princeton University Press, 1997); and, with a special emphasis on Eastern Europe, Piotr Sztompka, "Trust and Emerging Democracy," *International Sociology* 11, no. 1 (1996): 37–62. See also John A. Hall's advocacy of Tocqueville as a guide to the predicament of postcommunist societies, with their absence of trust and a tendency to fragmentation and atomization in "After the

Fall: An Analysis of Post-Communism," *British Journal of Sociology* 45, no. 4 (1994): 525–42; Tocqueville is also recommended, because of his emphasis on "habits of the heart," by Sztompka, "The Lessons of 1989 for Sociological Theory," 17.

19. See, for example, Rogers Brubaker, ed., *Immigration and the Politics of Citizenship in Europe and America* (Lanham, Md.: University Press of America, 1989); Rogers Brubaker, *Citizenship and Nationhood in France and Germany* (Cambridge: Harvard University Press, 1992); Adrian Favell, *Philosophies of Integration: Immigration and the Idea of Citizenship in France and Britain* (London: Macmillan, 1998); Christian Joppke, *Immigration and the Nation-State: The United States, Germany and Great Britain* (New York: Oxford University Press, 1999). Eastern Europe receives some attention in Tariq Modood and Pnina Werbner, eds., *The Politics of Multiculturalism in the New Europe* (New York: Zed Books, 1997).

20. See, for example, Yasemin Nuhoglu Soysal, *Limits of Citizenship: Migrants and Postnational Membership in Europe* (Chicago: University of Chicago Press, 1994); Rainer Bauböck, *Transnational Citizenship: Membership and Rights in International Migration* (Cheltenham, U.K.: Edward Elgar, 1994); David Jacobson, *Rights Across Borders: Immigration and the Decline of Citizenship* (Baltimore: Johns Hopkins University Press, 1996); Thomas Faist, "International Migration and Transnational Social Spaces," *Archives Européennes de Sociologie* 39, no. 2 (1998): 213–47.

21. Samuel Pisar, quoted in *The Washington Post* (October 25, 1998): A21. See also Caroll Bogert, "The Pinochet Precedent," *New York Times* (December 2, 1998): A31. In the summer of 1999 the British House of Lords upheld a lower court decision to extradite the general from Britain to Spain.

22. Michael Ignatieff, "Human Rights: The Midlife Crisis," *New York Review of Books* (May 20, 1999), 58.

23. For some recent work on human rights, see Louis Henkin, *The Age of Rights* (New York: Columbia University Press, 1996); Paul Gordon Lauren, *The Evolution of International Human Rights: Visions Seen* (Philadelphia: University of Pennsylvania Press, 1999); see also Johannes Morsink, *The Universal Declaration of Human Rights: Origins, Drafting and Intent* (Philadelphia: University of Pennsylvania Press, 1999). The dilemmas and debates are well explored in Joanne R. Bauer and Daniel A. Bell, eds., *The East Asian Challenge for Human Rights* (Cambridge: Cambridge University Press, 1999); William Theodore de Bary and Tu Weiming, eds., *Confucianism and Human Rights* (New York: Columbia University Press, 1999); Irene Bloom, J. Paul Martin, and Wayne L. Proudfoot, eds., *Religious Diversity and Human Rights* (New York: Columbia University Press, 1996). See also Bhikhu Parekh, "Towards the Just World Order: The Aims and Limits of Humanitarian Intervention," *Times Literary Supplement* (September 26, 1997), 14–15. The journal *Human Rights*, edited by Thomas Cushman, is one of the many that have sprung up to reflect the new interest. It maintains good coverage of postcommunist societies. For the clash between (individual) human rights and the collective rights of cultures in those societies, see Sabrina P. Ramet, *Whose Democracy? Nationalism, Religion, and the Doctrine of Collective Rights in Post-1989 Eastern Europe* (Lanham, Md.: Rowman and Littlefield, 1997); Sabrina Ramet, "Eastern Europe's Unfinished Business," *East European Politics and Societies* 13, no. 2 (1999): 345–52.

24. See Yuri Slezkine, "The USSR As a Communal Apartment, or How a Socialist State Promoted Ethnic Particularism," in Geoff Eley and Ronald Grigor Suny, eds., *Becoming National: A Reader* (New York: Oxford University Press, 1996), 203–38; Velijko Vujacic and Victor Zaslavsky, "The Causes of Disintegration of the USSR and Yugoslavia," *Telos* 88 (1991): 120–40; Rogers Brubaker, *Nationalism Reframed: Nation-*

*hood and the National Question in the New Europe* (Cambridge: Cambridge University Press, 1996), 23–54.

25. For a rehabilitation of List, see Roman Szporluk, *Communism and Nationalism: Karl Marx and Friedrich List* (New York: Oxford University Press, 1991).

26. As always, statements such as this demand qualification. In retrospect it can be seen that some important works on nationalism appeared during this period, such as Karl W. Deutsch, *Nationalism and Social Communication* (Cambridge, Mass.: MIT Press, 1953, revised 1966); Elie Kedourie, *Nationalism* (London: Hutchinson, 1961); and an early statement of Ernest Gellner's theory of nationalism in his *Thought and Change* (London: Weidenfeld and Nicolson, 1965). But the main point stands, which is that these works were isolated contributions that did not lead to any sustained scholarly study of nationalism at the time. As David McCrone says: "By the middle of the twentieth century much of social and political science had confined it to the dustbin of history. Nationalism was 'over.' It had ushered in the modern state in the nineteenth century, and had reached its deformed apotheosis in fascism in the twentieth. Its final purpose seemed to be to break up empires thereafter, as post-colonial regimes used it as a vehicle for state-building." David McCrone, *The Sociology of Nationalism: Tomorrow's Ancestors* (New York: Routledge, 1998), 1.

27. Once more, all that one can do here is list some of the works that, by general agreement, have marked the field of nationalism studies: Ernest Gellner, *Nations and Nationalism* (Oxford: Basil Blackwell, 1983); Benedict Anderson, *Imagined Communities: Reflections on the Origin and Spread of Nationalism,* revised edition (New York: Verso, 1991); Anthony D. Smith, *The Ethnic Origins of Nations* (Cambridge, Mass.: Blackwell, 1986); E. J. Hobsbawm, *Nations and Nationalism Since 1780,* 2nd edition (Cambridge: Cambridge University Press, 1992); John Breuilly, *Nationalism and the State,* 2nd edition (Chicago: University of Chicago Press, 1994); Liah Greenfeld, *Nationalism: Five Roads to Modernity* (Cambridge: Harvard University Press, 1992); Partha Chatterjee, *Nationalist Thought and the Colonial World* (Minneapolis: University of Minnesota Press, 1993). A good guide to the recent literature is Anthony D. Smith, *Nationalism and Modernism* (New York: Routledge, 1998); McCrone, *The Sociology of Nationalism.*

An important meeting place for East-West interchange on nationalism was the Centre for the Study of Nationalism, directed by Ernest Gellner at the Central European University, Prague, until his death in 1995. Some of the centre's work can be sampled in Sukumar Periwal, ed., *Notions of Nationalism* (Budapest: Central European University Press, 1995); for a good study of East Central European nationalism, see also Aleksandar Pavkovic, *The Fragmentation of Yugoslavia: Nationalism in a Multinational State* (London: Macmillan, 1997), and, more generally, Aleksander Pavkovic, Halyna Koscharsky, and Adam Czarnota, eds., *Nationalism and Postcommunism* (Brookfield, Vt.: Dartmouth, 1995); see also Peter Sugar, ed., *Eastern European Nationalism in the Twentieth Century* (Washington: American University Press, 1995); Klaus von Beyme, "A New Movement in an Ideological Vacuum: Nationalism in Eastern Europe," in Gregory Andrusz, Michael Harloe, and Ivan Selenyi, eds., *Cities after Socialism* (Oxford: Blackwell Publishers, 1996), 268–25. A special issue of *Social Research,* "Nationalism in Central and Eastern Europe," contains essays by leading scholars from East Central Europe. *Social Research* 58, no. 4 (1991).

28. On the secularization debate, see Peter Berger, "Secularism in Retreat," *The National Interest* 46 (winter 1996/97): 3–12; see also Steve Bruce, ed., *Religion and Modernization: Sociologists and Historians Debate the Secularization Thesis* (Oxford: Clarendon Press, 1992).

29. For the worldwide religious revival, see Mark Juergensmeyer, *The New Cold*

*War? Religious Nationalism Confronts the Secular State* (Berkeley: University of California Press, 1993). A massive treasury of source material is Martin E. Marty and R. Scott Appleby, eds., *The Fundamentalism Project*, five volumes (Chicago: University of Chicago Press, 1991–95); see also Lionel Caplan, ed., *Studies in Religious Fundamentalism* (London: Macmillan, 1987); Jeffrey Hadden and Anson Shupe, eds., *Secularization and Fundamentalism Reconsidered* (New York: Paragon House, 1993); Jacques Derrida and Gianni Vattimo, eds., *Religion: Cultural Memory in the Present* (Stanford: Stanford University Press, 1996).

One needs, of course, to use the term *fundamentalism* with caution. See Bikhu Parekh, "The Concept of Fundamentalism," in Alexandras Shtromas, ed., *The End of "Isms"? Reflections on the Fate of Ideological Politics after Communism's Collapse* (Cambridge, Mass.: Blackwell Publishers, 1994), 105–26. Wolf Lepenies has seen the return of religion as just one species of "fundamentalism," which also includes "a rebirth of nationalism, a revival of ethnic cleansings, a retreat to civil wars, and a refuge into antisemitic thought and action." This is "the return of the particular," but because it is a response to conditions in all contemporary modern societies "it returns in universal disguise," especially in the form of religious fundamentalism. See Wolf Lepenies, "God's Timely Revenge," *The Times Higher Education Supplement* (June 23, 1995): 16.

30. The most judicious discussion is in José Casanova, *Public Religions in the Modern World* (Chicago: University of Chicago Press, 1994).

31. See Benjamin R. Barber, *Jihad vs. McWorld* (New York: Ballantine Books, 1996); also Manuel Castells, *The Power of Identity* (Malden, Mass.: Blackwell Publishers, 1997), esp. 5–67.

32. See the discussion in Stjepan G. Mestrovic, *The Coming Fin de Siècle: An Application of Durkheim's Sociology to Modernity and Postmodernism* (New York: Routledge, 1991). For the encounter between religion and modernity, see, for example, James Davison Hunter, *American Evangelicalism: Conservative Religion and the Quandary of Modernity* (New Brunswick: Rutgers University Press, 1983); and, more generally, James Davison Hunter, *Culture Wars: The Struggle to Define America* (New York: Basic Books, 1991).

33. Parekh, "The Concept of Fundamentalism," 116; cf. Berger, "Secularism in Retreat," 6.

34. See George Weigel, *The Final Revolution: The Resistance Church and the Collapse of Communism* (New York: Oxford University Press, 1992); Niels Nielsen, *Revolutions in Eastern Europe: The Religious Roots* (Maryknoll, N.Y.: Orbis Books, 1991). For past and present developments, see also Patrick Michel, *Politics and Religion in Eastern Europe: Catholicism in Hungary, Poland and Czechoslovakia*, translated by Alan Braley (Cambridge, U.K.: Polity Press, 1991); Adam Michnik, *The Church and the Left* (Chicago: University of Chicago Press, 1993); William H. Swatos, Jr., ed., *Politics and Religion in Central and Eastern Europe: Traditions and Transitions* (New York: Praeger Publishers, 1994); Mirella W. Eberts, "The Roman Catholic Church and Democracy in Poland," *Europe-Asia Studies* 50, no. 5 (1998): 167–83; Sabrina P. Ramet, *Nihil Obstat: Religion, Politics, and Social Change in East-Central Europe and Russia* (Durham, N.C.: Duke University Press, 1998).

35. As argued especially by Huntington in *The Clash of Civilizations and the Remaking of World Order*. A sharp critique of this work is Jacinta O'Hagan, "Civilizational Conflict? Looking for Cultural Enemies," *Third World Quarterly* 16, no. 1 (1995): 19–38. For the revival of cultural theories of international relations, see Stephanie Lawson, "Dogmas of Difference: Culture and Nationalism in Theories of International

Politics," *Critical Review of International Social and Political Philosophy* 1, no. 4 (1998): 62–92.

36. Fred Halliday, *Revolution and World Politics: The Rise and Fall of the Sixth Great Power* (Durham, N.C.: Duke University Press, 1999), 28. The author, nevertheless, demonstrates its great power for most of this century in the non-Western world.

37. See especially chapter 4 of this book.

38. See chapter 8 of this book.

39. Halliday, *Revolution and World Politics,* 338.

40. Sztompka, "The Lessons of 1989 for Sociological Theory," 15, 18.

41. Göran Therborn, "1989 and After: Meanings, Explanations, Lessons," in Sztompka, ed., *Building Open Society and Perspectives of Sociology in East-Central Europe,* 28–29.

42. On all this, see S. N. Eisenstadt, *Japan and the Multiplicity of Cultural Progammes of Modernity* (Hong Kong: Social Sciences Research Centre, University of Hong Kong, 1994); Eisenstadt, *Japanese Civilization: A Comparative View* (Chicago: University of Chicago Press, 1996); Manuel Castells, *End of Millennium* (Malden, Mass.: Blackwell Publishers, 1998), 206–309; Ray, "Post-Communism: Post-modernity or Modernity Revisited?" And cf. G. M. Tamás: "1989 was a shift within modernity, not a detour." G. M. Tamás, "Paradoxes of 1989," *East European Politics and Societies* 13, no. 2 (1999): 354. For the distinction between the Enlightenment program of modernity and other possible conceptions, see Scott Lash, *Another Modernity, A Different Rationality* (Malden, Mass.: Blackwell Publishers, 1999); see also Robert Wokler, "The Enlightenment and the French Revolutionary Birth Pangs of Modernity," in Johan Heilbron and others, eds., *The Rise of the Social Sciences and the Formation of Modernity* (Dordrecht, Netherlands: Kluwer Academic, 1998), 35–76.

43. See Cronin, *The World the Cold War Made,* 237–42; see also John Lukacs, *The End of the Twentieth Century and the End of the Modern Age* (New York: Ticknor and Fields, 1993).

# Bibliography

This is a select bibliography of some of the works that I have found most useful or interesting in considering the topics in this book. All have a bearing in one way or another on the revolutions of 1989. For fuller references on each topic, consult the relevant chapters.

## Atlases of East and Central Europe

Crampton, Richard, and Ben Crampton. *Atlas of Eastern Europe in the Twentieth Century.* New York: Routledge, 1996.
A valuable supplement to the following work. Especially useful for social and demographic data, but strong also on political changes. Extensive treatment of post-1989 developments.

Magocsi, Paul Robert. *Historical Atlas of East Central Europe.* Seattle: University of Washington Press, 1995.
Unique and indispensable. Covers the whole of East Central Europe from the early fifth century to 1992. Splendid maps and lucid commentaries.

## Historical, Political, and Cultural Background

Barraclough, Geoffrey, ed. *Eastern and Western Europe in the Middle Ages.* London: Thames and Hudson, 1970.
A pioneering work of comparative history, alive to commonalities as well as differences. Wide-ranging essays by leading historians from both Eastern and Western Europe.

Berend, Ivan T. *Central and Eastern Europe 1944–1993: Detour from the Periphery to the Periphery.* Cambridge: Cambridge University Press, 1996.
A magisterial survey by an established expert on the economic history of the region.

Places the period within the context of the *longue durée* of the region's history. Pinpoints the interaction of politics and economics throughout.

———. *Decades of Crisis: Central and Eastern Europe before World War II*. Berkeley: University of California Press, 1998.
Vivid studies of the chief political, ideological, and cultural developments in the first half of the century. Important, in particular, for understanding the legacy of the interwar period.

Bideleux, Robert, and Ian Jeffries. *A History of Eastern Europe: Crisis and Change*. New York: Routledge, 1998.
Covers the history of the whole region from medieval times to the revolutions of 1989 and beyond. A remarkable work of synthesis, packed with information. Reliable and up-to-date.

Chirot, Daniel, ed. *The Origins of Backwardness in Eastern Europe: Economics and Politics from the Middle Ages until the Early Twentieth Century*. Berkeley: University of California Press, 1989.
A valuable set of essays interrogating the well-known thesis of "backwardness" in explaining the region.

Crampton, R. J. *Eastern Europe in the Twentieth Century—and After*. Second edition. New York: Routledge, 1997.
The best one-volume account of the region's history in this century. Sterling narrative qualities, crisp analytical judgments, excellent bibliography. Second edition includes a good section on post-1989 developments.

Hann, C. M. *The Skeleton at the Feast: Contributions to East European Anthropology*. Canterbury, U.K.: University of Kent Centre for Social Anthropology and Computing, 1995.
Papers on the economic, political, and cultural condition of the region by one of the foremost specialists in the field. Brings the perspective of the anthropologist to bear on a host of important questions. Vivid studies, full of insights.

Held, Joseph, ed. *The Columbia History of Eastern Europe in the Twentieth Century*. New York: Columbia University Press, 1992.
Reliable contributions by well-established scholars.

Hupchick, Dennis P. *Culture and History in Eastern Europe*. New York: St. Martin's Press, 1994.
Wide-ranging reflections by a well-known student of the region. Especially good on religious divisions and their long-term consequences.

———. *Conflict and Chaos in Eastern Europe*. New York: St. Martin's Press, 1994.
Applies the conceptual framework developed in the preceding work to a series of case studies that show the persistence of long-term historical and cultural factors in the current situation.

Janos, Andrew C. *The Politics of Backwardness in Hungary, 1825–1945*. Princeton: Princeton University Press, 1982.
The most influential statement of the "backwardness" thesis applied to the region, with implications that extend well beyond the case of Hungary. Original and provocative

Johnson, Lonnie R. *Central Europe: Enemies, Neighbours, Friends*. New York: Oxford University Press, 1996.
A readable and reliable work of historical synthesis written for the nonspecialist. Ranges over the whole history of the region. Sympathetic and engaging.

Lewis, Paul G. *Central Europe since 1945*. London: Longman, 1994.

Solid and clearly written. Especially strong on politics and on the region's relation to the Soviet Union.

Longworth, Philip. *The Making of Eastern Europe: From Prehistory to Postcommunism.* Second edition. New York: St. Martin's Press, 1997.
A lively and stimulating survey. Has the unusual feature of telling the history of the region backward, starting with the collapse of communism, and seeking to explain the region's current problems in terms of its sometimes distant past.

Lovenduski, Joni, and Jean Woodall. *Politics and Society in Eastern Europe.* Bloomington: Indiana University Press, 1988.
An advanced textbook that ranges widely over the region's history and its social and political institutions. Still very useful for an account of the region on the eve of the 1989 revolutions.

Maczak, Antoni, Henryk Samsonowicz, and Peter Burke, eds. *East Central Europe in Transition from the Fourteenth to the Seventeenth Century.* Cambridge: Cambridge University Press, 1985.
Specialists from East and West consider a crucial period in the divergence of Eastern and Western development. Discusses feudalism, capitalism, the growth of towns, and related matters.

Okey, Robin. *Eastern Europe 1740–1985: Feudalism to Communism.* Second edition. London: Hutchinson, 1986.
Still a valuable account of the major lines of historical development. Concise but comprehensive, sure-footed and judicious. Good annotated bibliography.

Palmer, Alan. *The Lands Between: A History of East-Central Europe Since the Congress of Vienna.* London: Weidenfeld and Nicolson, 1970.
Remains one of the best histories of the region. Perceptive and informative.

Ramet, Sabrina, ed. *Eastern Europe: Politics, Culture and Society Since 1939.* Bloomington: Indiana University Press, 1998.
A useful collection of articles by specialists.

Rothschild, Joseph. *Return to Diversity: A Political History of East Central Europe Since World War II.* Second edition. New York: Oxford University Press, 1993.
The most useful single source for the region's postwar history. Strong narrative drive, peppered with provocative observations but solidly based. Sets the breakup of communist regimes in long-term perspective.

Rupnik, Jacques. *The Other Europe.* New York: Pantheon Books, 1989.
A remarkable portrait of communist society on the eve of its demise. Remains invaluable for its breadth as well as its perceptiveness. Especially strong on intellectual and cultural themes.

Schöpflin, George. *Politics in Eastern Europe 1945–1992.* Cambridge, Mass.: 1993.
Wide-ranging essays by a seasoned commentator. Deftly picks out and analyzes the main lines of development, from World War II to the 1989 revolutions and postcommunist society.

Swain, Geoffrey, and Nigel Swain. *Eastern Europe Since 1945.* London: Macmillan, 1993.
Concise and thoughtful, written from a left-wing perspective. Takes the communist experiment seriously, arguing that it was more its economic than its political deficiencies that undermined it.

Szücs, Jenö. "The Three Historical Regions of Europe." *Acta Historica Academiae Scientiarum Hungaricae* 29, nos. 2–4 (1983): 131–84.
An influential account of the political and economic differences between Western, Central, and Eastern Europe. Powerful and penetrating.

Wandycz, Piotr S. *The Price of Freedom: A History of East Central Europe from the Middle Ages to the Present*. New York: Routledge, 1992.
A first-rate account for nonspecialists by an established scholar of the region. Lucid and readable. Firmly within the "backwardness" school of Central European historians, but gives one the material to judge for oneself.

Zeman, Z. A. B. *The Making and Breaking of Communist Europe*. Cambridge, Mass.: Blackwell Publishers, 1991.
A comprehensive overview, in the form of a historical narrative, of the rise and fall of communism in the region. Agreeable and engaging in style, with some unusual details.

## The Revolutions of 1989: Events, Causes, Contexts, Theories

Ackerman, Bruce. *The Future of Liberal Revolution*. New Haven: Yale University Press, 1993.
An incisive essay on the worldwide implications of the 1989 revolutions, seen as "liberal" revolutions akin to those of Britain and America.

Ash, Timothy Garton. *We the People: The Revolution of '89 Witnessed in Warsaw, Budapest, Berlin and Prague*. Second edition with a new preface. London: Granta Books/Penguin, 1999. Published in the United States as *The Magic Lantern*. New York: Random House, 1999.
Probably the most celebrated account of these events, by a scholar who was present at many of the key moments. Eyewitness descriptions mixed with insightful reflections. Vivid, personal, moving. Conveys the excitement of the times as does no other account.

Banac, Ivo, ed. *Eastern Europe in Revolution*. Ithaca, N.Y.: Cornell University Press, 1992.
Specialists in their fields consider the revolutions in individual countries. Thoughtful and illuminating case studies that throw up many helpful general reflections.

Blackburn, Robin, ed. *After the Fall: The Failure of Communism and the Future of Socialism*. New York: Verso, 1991.
Essays, mostly reprinted from the British journal *New Left Review*, by leading left-wing theorists. Includes the famous essay by Habermas on the "rectifying revolutions" of 1989.

Brown, J. F. *Surge to Freedom: The End of Communist Rule in Eastern Europe*. Durham N.C.: Duke University Press, 1991.
A country-by-country account by a knowledgeable commentator. Clear, forceful, analytically astute. Includes a detailed chronology of the main events of 1989.

Bunce, Valerie. *Subversive Institutions: The Design and Destruction of Socialism and the State*. New York: Cambridge University Press, 1999.
A subtle, theoretically driven account of why and when the different socialist regimes collapsed. Emphasizes the differences of timing and outcome. Elegant and persuasive.

Chirot, Daniel, ed. *The Crisis of Leninism and the Decline of the Left: The Revolutions of 1989*. Seattle: University of Washington Press, 1991.
Nine scholars discuss the events of 1989 and their implications for socialism and communism in the world at large. Strong on the international dimension. Unusual for including comparisons with China and North Korea.

*Daedalus*. Special issue, "The Exit from Communism." *Daedalus* 121, no. 2, 1992.
Wide-ranging essays by noted scholars, such as Kolakowski, Eisenstadt, and Malia, on the significance and nature of the breakdown of communist regimes.

Dahrendorf, Ralf. *Reflections on the Revolution in Europe*. London: Chatto and Windus, 1990.

Time has not diminished the value of these powerful and stimulating reflections, among the first to appear after—virtually in the midst of—the events of 1989. Couched in the form of a letter à la Edmund Burke, they raise practically all the questions that have preoccupied commentators since.

———. *After 1989: Morals, Revolution, and Civil Society.* London: Macmillan, 1997. Occasional essays and lectures that instructively add to the reflections in the preceding work.

*East European Politics and Societies.* Symposium, "Post-Communist Eastern Europe: A Survey of Opinion." *East European Politics and Societies* 4, no. 2, 1990: 153–207. Scholars of Eastern Europe reflect on the revolutions of 1989 in their immediate aftermath. Vivid sense of the time. Many of the assessments hold up remarkably well.

———. Special issue, "The Revolutions of 1989: Lessons of the First Post-Communist Decade." *East European Politics and Societies* 13, no. 2, 1999. Brief, but often telling, observations by well-known scholars reflecting on the revolutions on their tenth anniversary.

Frankland, Mark. *The Patriots' Revolution: How Eastern Europe Toppled Communism and Won Its Freedom.* Chicago: Ivan R. Dee, 1993. A splendidly robust account by the East European correspondent of the London *Observer.* Full of illuminating details and observations based on a thorough, first-hand knowledge of the region.

Glenny, Misha. *The Rebirth of History: Eastern Europe in the Age of Democracy.* Second edition. London: Penguin Books, 1993. One of the best accounts of the revolutions, by the BBC's longtime Central European correspondent. First-class reporting mixed with perceptive historical commentary. Especially strong on the Balkans.

Holmes, Leslie. *The End of Communist Power: Anti-Corruption Campaigns and Legitimation Crisis.* Cambridge, U.K.: Polity Press, 1993. A theoretically inflected account of the collapse of communism, in terms of a gathering legitimation crisis. Interesting material on corruption as a symptom of the crisis.

Jowitt, Ken. *New World Disorder: The Leninist Extinction.* Berkeley: University of California Press, 1992. Masterly studies of communist rule, and the reasons for its end. Not an account of the revolutions themselves, but full of interesting material for considering their nature and significance.

Kriesberg, Louis, ed. *Research in Social Movements, Conflict and Change.* Volume 14: Special issue, "The Revolutions of 1989." Greenwich, Conn.: JAI Press, 1992. A useful collection that discusses theories predicting the anticommunist revolutions, as well as social movements leading to them.

Mason, David S. *Revolution and Transition in East-Central Europe.* Second edition. Boulder, Colo.: Westview Press, 1996. Though primarily intended as a text for undergraduates, this is a skillfully organized, clearly written, and well-informed account of the causes and consequences of the 1989 revolutions. Contains a useful chronology of events to 1996.

Prins, Gwyn, ed. *Spring in Winter: The 1989 Revolutions.* Manchester: Manchester University Press, 1990. One of the earliest, and still one of the best, collections to appear on the events of 1989. Particularly interesting for the reflections of East European participants. Contains an outstanding comparative chronology of the revolutions from 1988–90.

Ray, Larry. *Social Theory and the Crisis of State Socialism.* Cheltenham, U.K.: Edward Elgar, 1996.

Approaches the collapse of communism from the approach of theoretical sociology, focusing especially on issues of legitimation, social integration, and crisis management. Contains interesting discussion of communism and modernity.

Stokes, Gale. *The Walls Came Tumbling Down: The Collapse of Communism in Eastern Europe.* New York: Oxford University Press, 1993.
Widely regarded as the best single account of the revolutions. A vivid narrative that is strong on the importance of history and political ideas. Makes good use of contemporary interview material.

Sword, Keith, ed. *The Times Guide to Eastern Europe.* Second edition. London: Times Books, 1991.
A compilation by regional experts, this is a handy guide to the 1989 revolutions, full of hard-to-find information and containing deft historical summaries. Excellent maps and statistical material.

*Theory and Society.* Special issue, "Theoretical Implications of the Demise of State Socialism." *Theory and Society* 23, no. 2, 1994.
A number of the contributors consider the causes of the 1989 revolutions and the breakdown of state socialism generally.

Tismaneanu, Vladimir. *Reinventing Politics: Eastern Europe from Stalin to Havel.* New York: The Free Press, 1992.
An exuberant account of the collapse of communism, from a scholar who sees no need to hide his satisfaction at the event. Vivid and colorful. Especially good on political developments and ideas.

———, ed. *The Revolutions of 1989.* New York: Routledge, 1999.
A collection of articles, some old and some new, on the meaning of 1989 on the occasion of its tenth anniversary.

Waller, Michael. *The Ends of the Communist Power Monopoly.* New York: Manchester University Press, 1993.
A thoughtful, theoretically informed account of the mechanisms of power that slowly, but inevitably, corroded the ability of communist parties to control their societies.

Weigel, George. *The Final Revolution: The Resistance Church and the Collapse of Communism.* New York: Oxford University Press, 1992.
One of the few works to consider the role of religion and the churches in the downfall of communism. Rightly emphasizes the importance of the election of a Polish pope, though perhaps exaggerates the role of the Catholic Church.

Weiner, Robert. *Change in Eastern Europe.* New York: Praeger Publishers, 1994.
A deft account of the revolutions, emphasizing legitimation problems and the construction of an alternative political culture in civil society.

## Central Europe: Concept and Reality

Ash, Timothy Garton. *The Uses of Adversity: Essays on the Fate of Central Europe.* London: Granta Books/Penguin Books, 1989.
Characteristically lively and pungent essays on various aspects of Central European thought and politics in the 1980s. Includes the excellent "Does Central Europe Exist?"

Burgess, Adam. *Divided Europe: The New Domination of the East.* London: Pluto Press, 1997.
A spirited argument that a new "orientalism" informs Western attitudes toward contemporary East Central Europe.

Croan, Melvin. "Lands In-Between: The Politics of Cultural Identity in Contemporary Eastern Europe." *East European Politics and Societies* 3, no. 2 (1989): 176–97.
An incisive essay that critically discusses past and present concepts.

*Daedalus.* Special issue, "Eastern Europe . . . Central Europe . . . Europe." *Daedalus* 119, no. 1 (winter 1990). Also published as *Eastern Europe . . . Central Europe . . . Europe.* Edited by Stephen R. Graubard. Boulder, Colo.: Westview Press, 1991.
An outstanding collection, with wide-ranging reflections on Central Europe by such scholars as Hankiss, Judt, Rupnik, and Schöpflin.

Fehér, Ferenc. "Eastern Europe's Long Revolution Against Yalta." *East European Politics and Societies* 2, no. 1 (1988): 1–34.
Traces the unraveling of the postwar "Yalta system" on the eve of its final breakup.

———. "On Making Central Europe." *East European Politics and Societies* 3, no. 3 (1989): 412–47
Splendidly wide-ranging account, delving deep into history and political ideas.

Judt, Tony. "The Dilemmas of Dissidence: The Politics of Opposition in East-Central Europe." *East European Politics and Societies* 2, no. 2 (1988): 185–240.
Far wider than the title suggests, a comprehensive look at Central European politics and culture.

Kundera, Milan. "The Tragedy of Central Europe." *New York Review of Books* (April 26, 1984), 33–38. Also published as "A Kidnapped West, or Culture Bows Out." *Granta* 11 (1984): 93–123.
The key contribution of the 1980s, the piece that reopened the debate on Central Europe.

Neumann, Iver B. "Russia as Central Europe's Constituting Other." *East European Politics and Societies* 7, no. 2 (1993): 349–69.
Takes issue with Kundera on Russia, and generally traces the perceptions of Russia held by Central European intellectuals.

———. *Uses of the Other: "The East" in European Identity Formation.* Minneapolis: University of Minnesota Press, 1998.
Builds on the preceding article to develop a comprehensive analysis of European identity through the hypostasizing of the East.

*Paradigms: The Kent Journal of International Relations.* Special issue, "Building the New Europe." *Paradigms* 5, nos. 1–2, 1991.
Scholars from East and West debate "the common European home," Russia's relation to Europe, and other aspects of Central and East European identity.

Schöpflin, George, and Nancy Wood, eds. *In Search of Central Europe.* Cambridge, U.K.: Polity Press, 1989.
Largely conceived as a symposium on Kundera's essay, this collection is the most valuable single source of discussion on the idea of Central Europe. Contributions from distinguished scholars from both East and West.

*Social Research.* Special issue on Central and Eastern Europe. *Social Research* 55, nos. 1–2 (spring–summer 1988).
Scholars from East and West take stock of Central Europe in the 1980s. Interesting *samizdat* contributions.

Stokes, Gale. *Three Eras of Political Change in Eastern Europe.* New York: Oxford University Press, 1997.
Essays dealing with broad aspects of East Central European history, politics, and culture. Includes "Eastern Europe's Defining Fault Lines" and "The Social Origins of East European Politics."

Todorova, Maria. *Imagining the Balkans.* New York: Oxford University Press, 1997.
Traces Western conceptions and preconceptions of Balkan societies from the eighteenth century to the present time, and argues that stereotypes still prevail in current Western thinking and practice.

Wolff, Larry. *Inventing Eastern Europe: The Map of Civilization and the Mind of the Enlightenment*. Stanford: Stanford University Press, 1994.
How Enlightenment thinkers constructed an image of a barbarous "Eastern" Europe as a way of defining and celebrating their own civilized "West." A valuable and stimulating piece of intellectual history with great contemporary relevance.

## Civil Society

Alexander, Jeffery C., ed. *Real Civil Societies: Dilemmas of Institutionalization*. Thousand Oaks, Calif.: Sage Publications, 1998.
A valuable collection of essays critically interrogating the relationship between the concept and reality of civil society.
Bryant, Christopher G. A., and Edmund Mokrzycki, eds. *Democracy, Civil Society and Pluralism*. Warsaw: IFIS Publishers, 1995.
Studies, by scholars from both East and West, of the concept in comparative perspective, with a focus on Poland, Great Britain, and the Netherlands.
Cohen, Jean, and Andrew Arato. *Civil Society and Political Theory*. Cambridge, Mass.: MIT Press, 1992.
A full-scale critical examination of the concept, from its Hegelian roots to contemporary usage. Searching and sophisticated inquiry by two of the concept's pioneering students, and leading advocates.
Gellner, Ernest. *Conditions of Liberty: Civil Society and Its Enemies*. London: Hamish Hamilton, 1994.
A passionate advocacy, by a leading social theorist. Interprets the concept in the broadest possible way.
Hall, John A. *Civil Society: Theory, History, Comparison*. Cambridge, U.K.: Polity Press, 1995.
A satisfying collection of studies, by senior scholars from a wide range of disciplines.
Hann, Chris, and Elizabeth Dunn, eds. *Civil Society: Challenging Western Models*. New York: Routledge, 1996.
A valuable collection that critically examines the concept, especially from the point of its ethnocentrism. Important contribution by anthropologists.
Keane, John. *Democracy and Civil Society*. New York: Verso, 1988.
Essays on democracy and socialism by one of the foremost exponents of the civil society idea. Includes a valuable historical essay on the concept of civil society.
————. *Civil Society: Old Images, New Visions*. Cambridge, U.K.: Polity Press, 1998.
Further reflections by the thinker who did so much to popularize the idea.
————, ed. *Civil Society and the State: New European Perspectives*. New York: Verso, 1988.
One of the best collections of such essays, with a particularly important section on Eastern Europe.
Kukathas, Chandran, David W. Lovell, and William Maley, eds. *The Transition from Socialism: State and Civil Society in the USSR*. Melbourne: Longman Cheshire, 1991.
An excellent collection, ranging far wider than the focus on the USSR might suggest.
Pérez-Díaz, Víctor. *The Return of Civil Society: The Emergence of Democratic Spain*. Cambridge: Harvard University Press, 1993.
A powerful and illuminating application of the concept to a particular case, with far-reaching theoretical implications.
Seligman, Adam B. *The Idea of Civil Society*. New York: The Free Press, 1992.

An incisive exploration of the historical roots of the concept, and the extent to which it can be applied in contemporary conditions.

## Intellectuals and Ideas in East Central Europe

Ash, Timothy Garton. "Prague: Intellectuals and Politics." *New York Review of Books* (January 12, 1995): 34–41.
A vibrant report on intellectuals in Central Europe, and their political role yesterday and today.

Bauman, Zygmunt. "Intellectuals in East-Central Europe: Continuity and Change." *East European Politics and Societies* 1, no. 2 (1987): 162–86.
A penetrating account of intellectual life in the region, before and during communism. Emphasizes the key role played by intellectuals in politics.

Bozóki, András, ed. *Intellectuals and Politics in Central Europe.* Budapest: Central European University Press, 1998.
Contributors from eight countries in the region discuss the role of intellectuals in the political transitions of the late 1980s and early 1990s, and their involvement in current politics. A rich source of information and insights.

Goldfarb, Jeffrey C. *Beyond Glasnost: The Post Totalitarian Mind.* Chicago: Chicago University Press, 1989.
A valuable account of the thinking of "opposition intellectuals"—Michnik, Havel, Konrád, and others—of the 1980s. A strong emphasis on the "civil society" idea.

———. *After the Fall: The Pursuit of Democracy in Central Europe.* New York: Basic Books, 1992.
Continues the inquiry of the preceding study, after the 1989 revolutions. A wide-ranging exploration of the ideas of Central European intellectuals and activists, many of them now in power.

Havel, Václav. *Living in Truth.* Edited by Jan Vladislav. London: Faber and Faber, 1989.
Some of Havel's most important essays of the 1970s and 1980s, including the seminal "The Power of the Powerless."

———. *Summer Meditations: On Politics, Morality and Civility in a Time of Transition.* Edited and translated by Paul Wilson. London: Faber and Faber, 1992.
Essays, lectures, and addresses from the time of Havel's assumption of the presidency of Czechoslovakia in 1990.

———. *Toward a Civil Society: Selected Speeches and Writings 1990–1994.* Edited and translated by Paul Wilson (Prague: Lidové Noviny, 1994).
Some overlap with the preceding, but also contains later presidential speeches.

Isaac, Jeffrey C. "The Meanings of 1989." *Social Research* 63, no. 2 (1996): 291–344.
A positive evaluation of the "antipolitics" of Havel, Konrád, and others, linking it to the thought of Hannah Arendt and a new conception of radical politics.

Konrád, György. *Antipolitics: An Essay.* Translated from the Hungarian by Richard E. Allen. London: Quartet Books, 1984.
The most influential statement of a major philosophy among dissident intellectuals of the 1980s.

———. *The Melancholy of Rebirth: Essays from Post-Communist Central Europe, 1989–1994.* Selected and translated by Michael Henry Heim. San Diego: Harcourt Brace & Company, 1995.
Meditations on Hungary and other Central European societies in postcommunist times. In turn exhilarating and sobering.

McBride, William L. *Philosophical Reflections on the Changes in Eastern Europe.*
Lanham, Md.: Rowman and Littlefield, 1999.
Engaging and thought-provoking general reflections, partly a response to Central
European ideas, partly the application of Western ideas.

Michael, John. "The Intellectual in Uncivil Society: Michnik, Poland, and Community."
*Telos* 88 (summer 1991): 141–54.
An interesting critical study of Michnik's thought and role in Poland before and
after the 1989 revolution.

Michnik, Adam. *Letters from Prison and Other Essays.* Edited by Irena Grudzinska
Gross. Translated by Maya Latynski. Berkeley: University of California Press, 1985.
Some of Michnik's best-known writing from the 1970s and 1980s, including the in-
fluential "The New Evolutionism."

———. *Letters from Freedom: Post-Cold War Realities and Perspectives.* Edited by
Irena Grudzinska Gross. Translated by Jane Cave. Berkeley: University of California
Press, 1998.
Essays, articles, and interviews (with Havel, Miłosz, and Jaruzelski, among others)
by Poland's foremost intellectual ambassador. Bracing and stimulating.

*New York Times Magazine.* Special report, "The Dissidents: A Decade Later." November 7, 1999, 71–81.
Interviews with leading Central European dissidents, such as Michnik, Rajk, Kiss,
and Reich, discussing their past and present thoughts and activities.

Pithart, Pitr. "Intellectuals in Politics: Double Dissent in the Past, Double
Disappointment Today." *Social Research* 60, no. 4 (1993): 642–61.
A leading theoretician of the Czech Civic Forum and a former Czech prime minis-
ter's reflections, from an invaluable vantage point.

Skilling, H. Gordon. *Samizdat and an Independent Society in Central and Eastern
Europe.* Basingstoke, U.K.: Macmillan, 1989.
A unique portrait of intellectual life in the 1970s and 1980s, as revealed by *samizdat*
publications. An invaluable resource.

Tökés, Rudolf, ed. *Opposition in Eastern Europe.* London: Macmillan, 1979.
A valuable collection of studies of the birth of new opposition thinking in the
1970s, including the idea of civil society.

Tucker, Aviezer. "Václav Havel's Heideggerianism." *Telos* 85 (1990): 63–78.
Discusses the influence of the Czech philosopher Jan Patocka on Havel's thinking.

Whipple, Tim D., ed. *After the Velvet Revolution: Václav Havel and the New Leaders
of Czechoslovakia Speak Out.* New York: Freedom House, 1991.
Former intellectuals, many now the new leaders of their country, assess their past and
consider their future. An excellent collection, containing a wide range of opinions.

## Postcommunism and Transition in Central and Eastern Europe

Since my volume is not principally concerned with developments in postcommunist societies, I note merely those works that contain useful material on 1989.

Agh, Atilla. *The Politics of Central Europe.* Thousand Oaks, Calif.: Sage Publications,
1998.
A concise, informative, and perceptive portrait of the postcommunist political
scene, with strong general chapters on the 1989 transformations.

Anderson, Lisa, ed. *Transitions to Democracy.* New York: Columbia University Press,
1999.

A critical discussion of Dankwart Rustow's classic "transition" model. A valuable discussion of Eastern Europe in a comparative context.

Bonnell, Victoria E., ed. *Identities in Transition: Eastern Europe and Russia after the Collapse of Communism.* Berkeley: University of Berkeley Center for Slavic and East European Studies, 1996.
Studies that range over class, gender, ethnicity, and nationalism in assessing the forces that brought down communism and the directions of change since.

Brown, J. F. *Hopes and Shadows: Eastern Europe after Communism.* Durham, N.C.: Duke University Press, 1994.
A seasoned scholar and commentator takes stock of the East European landscape in the light of the goals of the 1989 revolutions and the legacy of the region's past.

Bryant, G. A., and Edmund Mokrzycki, eds. *The New Great Transformation? Change and Continuity in East-Central Europe.* New York: Routledge, 1994.
Valuable essays by scholars from East and West on what happened in 1989 and how far the hopes of that time have been borne out.

Cohen, Shari J. *Politics without a Past: The Absence of History in Postcommunist Nationalism.* Durham, N.C.: Duke University Press, 1999.
A closely argued account, using Slovakia as a case study, of the unprecedented nature of the postcommunist predicament, largely owing to the "ideological vacuum" created by communism's collapse and the absence of a usable national past.

*Contemporary Sociology.* Symposium, "The Great Transformation? Social Change in Eastern Europe." *Contemporary Sociology* 21 (May 1992): 299–312.
Valuable review articles by such scholars as David Stark and Claus Offe, considering the nature of the changes in and future prospects for the region.

Feffer, John. *Shock Waves: Eastern Europe after the Revolutions.* Boston: South End Press, 1992.
The aftermath of revolution. An informative and perceptive account based on travels and interviews.

Hollis, Wendy. *Democratic Consolidation in Eastern Europe: The Influence of the Communist Legacy in Hungary, the Czech Republic, and Romania.* New York: Columbia University Press, 1999.
A massive inquiry that aims to show the importance of the communist legacy in East Central Europe. Detailed, informative, suggestive.

Holmes, Leslie. *Post-Communism: An Introduction.* Durham, N.C.: Duke University Press, 1997.
A textbook with much useful information. Chapters on the 1989 revolutions, before and after. Good bibliographies.

Janos, Andrew C. "Change and Continuity in Eastern Europe: Strategies of Post-Communist Politics." *East European Politics and Societies* 8, no. 1 (1994): 1–31.
An authoritative exponent of the "backwardness" thesis applies this perspective to contemporary conditions, emphasizing the legacy of a troubled past.

Linz, Juan J., and Alfred Stepan. *Problems of Democratic Transition and Consolidation: Southern Europe, South America, and Post-Communist Europe.* Baltimore: Johns Hopkins University Press, 1996.
A sober and scholarly example of the "transition" literature, by two of its most eminent practitioners. Contains an excellent section on Eastern Europe.

Miliband, Ralph, and Leo Panitch, eds. *Socialist Register 1991. Communist Regimes: The Aftermath.* London: The Merlin Press, 1991.
Western socialists reflect on the revolutions and the future prospects of post-communist societies.

Miller, William L., Stephen White and Paul Heywood. *Values and Political Change in Postcommunist Europe*. Basingstoke, U.K.: Macmillan, 1998.
A study of values and value change based on public opinion surveys in five former communist countries. Skillfully put into historical and theoretical context. Casts an interesting backward light on 1989.

Rose, Richard, William Mishler and Christian Haerpfer. *Democracy and Its Alternatives: Understanding Post-Communist Societies*. Cambridge, U.K.: Polity Press, 1998.
A survey-based account of attitudes and beliefs. Densely informative. Enlivened by theoretical reflections on democracy in the context of the 1989 revolutions.

Rosenberg, Tina. *The Haunted Land: Facing Europe's Ghosts after Communism*. New York: Vintage Books, 1996.
A compelling, vividly written inquiry into guilt and complicity by a first-rate reporter. Sheds much light on the collapse of communism.

Sakwa, Richard. *Postcommunism*. Buckingham, U.K.: Open University Press, 1999.
A rigorous analysis of the concept that includes a valuable discussion of the nature of the communist society it claims to supersede.

*Social Research*. Special issue, "Gains and Losses of the Transition to Democracy." *Social Research* 63, no. 2 (summer 1996).
A splendid stocktaking, with contributions from Eastern and Western scholars. Much material bears directly on 1989.

Stark, David, and László Bruszt. *Postsocialist Pathways: Transforming Politics and Property in East Central Europe*. Cambridge: Cambridge University Press, 1998.
A sophisticated and scholarly study that casts much interesting light back on the conditions of socialist societies and the manner of their transformation.

Tismaneanu, Vladimir. *Fantasies of Salvation: Democracy, Nationalism, and Myth in Post-Communist Europe*. Princeton: Princeton University Press, 1998.
Points to the antiliberal, authoritarian leanings of the region's leaders, born of a long history. A pessimistic view of the future. A sobering account, vivid and passionate.

Verderey, Katherine. *What Was Socialism, and What Comes Next?* Princeton: Princeton University Press, 1996.
Insightful essays by an anthropologist with intimate knowledge of Eastern Europe. A persuasive account of the fall of socialism and the possible forms of capitalism in the region.

White, Stephen, Judy Batt, and Paul G. Lewis, eds. *Developments in East European Politics*. Basingstoke, U.K.: Macmillan, 1993.
The starting point for all contributors are the 1989 revolutions. Detailed, country-by-country account of the changes. Compendious and reliable.

## The "End of History," the Future of Socialism, and the New World Order

Alexander, Jeffrey C. *Fin de Siècle Social Theory: Relativism, Reduction, and the Problem of Reason*. New York: Verso, 1995.
Contains a magisterial essay on the intellectual consequences of the fall of communism.

Anderson, Perry. *The Ends of History*. New York: Verso, 1994.
The most sustained and stimulating discussion of Fukuyama and other announcements of the end of history, or of Marxism.

Blackburn, Robin, ed. *After the Fall: The Failure of Communism and the Future of Socialism*. New York: Verso, 1991.

Prominent left-wing thinkers, including Habermas, Hobsbawm, and Edward Thompson, consider the predicament of socialism in the wake of the 1989 revolutions.

Bobbio, Norberto. *Left and Right: The Significance of a Political Distinction.* Translated by Allan Cameron. Cambridge, U.K.: Polity Press, 1996.
A brilliant polemical essay by a noted theorist, arguing for the persisting relevance of the Left-Right distinction despite the fall of communism.

Cronin, James E. *The World the Cold War Made: Order, Chaos, and the Return of History.* New York: Routledge, 1996.
A fascinating argument about the effects of the Cold War on Western and Eastern societies. Concludes with observations on the world after the end of the Cold War.

*Daedalus.* Special issue, "After Communism—What?" *Daedalus* 123, no. 3 (summer 1994).
Wide-ranging reflections, by distinguished scholars such as Hankiss, Judt, Rupnik, Schöpflin, and Szporluk, on the significance of the fall of communism.

Derrida, Jacques. *Specters of Marx: The State of the Debt, the Work of Mourning, and the New International.* New York: Routledge, 1994.
The master's characteristically oblique but original contribution to the debate on Marx in the wake of the 1989 revolutions. Invigorating and provocative.

Fukuyama, Francis. *The End of History and the Last Man.* London: Penguin Books, 1992.
The book version of the article that launched the celebrated debate. As challenging as ever.

Habermas, Jürgen. *The Past As Future.* Translated by Max Pensky. Cambridge, U.K.: Polity Press, 1994.
An extended interview in which Habermas offers his thoughts on the fall of communism, the new world order, German unification, and much else. Clear, forceful, stimulating.

Halliday, Fred. *Revolution and World Politics: The Rise and Fall of the Sixth Great Power.* Durham, N.C.: Duke University Press, 1999.
The 1989 revolutions seen within the context of the theory and practice of revolution on a world scale, with reflections on the future role of revolution in the international order. A masterly treatment.

Hann, C. M., ed. *Socialism: Ideals, Ideologies, and Local Practice.* London and New York: Routledge, 1993.
Several of the studies deal with socialist practice in Eastern Europe, considering the implications for postsocialist societies. Detailed local studies by anthropologists provide an unusual and fresh perspective on socialism as a system.

Huntington, Samuel P. *The Clash of Civilizations and the Remaking of the World Order.* New York: Touchstone Books, 1997.
The most influential riposte to Fukuyama, and a powerful statement of an alternative—less reassuring—future.

Krzeminski, Adam, Adam Michnik, and Jürgen Habermas. "More Humility, Fewer Illusions." *New York Review of Books* (March 24, 1994): 24–29.
An illuminating three-sided conversation that, beginning with the events of 1989, ranges around socialism, postcommunism, nationalism, and Europe. Brimming with bons mots.

Miliband, Ralph, and Leo Panitch, eds. *Socialist Register 1992: New World Order?* London: The Merlin Press, 1992.
The so-called new world order, as seen by mainly skeptical and alarmed leftists.

Ryan, Alan. "Twenty-First Century Limited." *New York Review of Books* (November 19, 1992), 20–24.
Opposed to "the end of history," the view of an unsettling and unpredictable era that has succeeded the relative stability of the Cold War. Characteristically trenchant and unorthodox.

Shtromas, Alexsandras, ed. *The End of "Isms"? Reflections on the Fate of Ideological Politics after Communism's Collapse.* Cambridge, Mass.: Blackwell Publishers, 1994.
Political theorists consider ideology after the fall of communism. Thought-provoking contributions from the likes of Minogue, Parekh, and Kamenka.

Steiner, George. *Proofs and Three Parables.* Boston: Faber and Faber, 1992.
The title story is a fictional examination of the effects of the apparent demise of Marxism on a devoted believer. A subtle and ironic essay by a master of the genre.

Woo-Cumings, Meredith, and Michael Loriaux, eds. *Past as Prelude: History in the Making of a New World Order.* Boulder, Colo.: Westview Press, 1993.
Exemplary essays by distinguished political scientists on the consequences of the fall of communism for the future of world politics.

It may be helpful, finally, to list some of the journals that have provided much of the material for this volume, and which may profitably be consulted by the reader.

*Cross Currents: A Yearbook of Central European Culture*
*Daedalus*
*Dissent*
*East European Politics and Societies*
*East European Quarterly*
*East European Reporter*
*Foreign Affairs*
*New Left Review*
*New York Review of Books*
*Praxis International*
*Social Research*
*Studies in Comparative Communism*
*Telos*
*Theory and Society*

# Permissions

The University of Minnesota Press gratefully acknowledges permission to reprint the following essays in this book.

An earlier version of chapter 2 appeared as "The Revolutions of 1989: Socialism, Capitalism, and Democracy," *Theory and Society* 21 (1992): 309–56; reprinted with kind permission of Kluwer Academic Publishers.

An earlier version of chapter 3 originally appeared as "The 1989 Revolutions and the Idea of Europe," *Political Studies* 40 (1992): 439–61; reprinted with permission of Blackwell Publishers.

An earlier version of chapter 4 originally appeared in *Culture, Modernity, and Revolution: Essays in Honor of Zygmunt Bauman,* Richard Kilminster and Ian Varcoe, eds. (London: Routledge, 1996), 127–53; reprinted with permission of Taylor & Francis.

An earlier version of chapter 5 originally appeared as "Civil Society: An Inquiry into the Usefulness of an Historical Term," *British Journal of Sociology* 44, no. 3 (1993): 375–95; copyright 1993, Routledge, Taylor & Francis, Ltd., on behalf of the London School of Economics; reprinted with permission of Taylor & Francis, P.O. Box 25, Abingdon, Oxfordshire, OX14 3UE.

An earlier version of chapter 6 appeared as "The End of Socialism? The End of Utopia? The End of History?" in *Utopias and the Millennium,* Krishan Kumar and Stephen Bann, eds. (London: Reaktion Books), 63–80; copyright 1993 Reaktion Books, London; reprinted with permission of Reaktion Books, Ltd.

An earlier version of chapter 8 appeared as "The Revolutionary Idea in the Twentieth-Century World" in *Twentieth-Century Revolutions,* Moira Donald and Tim Rees, eds. (London: Macmillan Press, 2000); copyright 2000 by Macmillan Press; reprinted with permission of Macmillan Press Ltd.

# Index

Created by Eileen Quam

KRISHAN KUMAR is professor of sociology at the University of Virginia. He is the author of *Prophecy and Progress: The Sociology of Industrial and Post-Industrial Society*; *Utopia and Anti-Utopia in Modern Times*; *The Rise of Modern Society*; *Utopianism*; and *From Post-Industrial to Post-Modern Society.*

## DATE DUE

| | | |
|---|---|---|
| MAY 24 '02 S | | |
| MAY 0 6 2002 | | |
| | | |
| | | |
| | | |
| | | |
| | | |
| | | |
| | | |
| | | |
| | | |
| | | |
| | | |
| | | |
| | | |
| | | |
| | | |
| GAYLORD | | PRINTED IN U.S.A. |